DCRV
01408

Hayek and the
Keynesian Avalanche

Hayek and the Keynesian Avalanche

B.J. McCormick
School of Management, The University of Sheffield

HARVESTER
WHEATSHEAF

New York   London   Toronto   Sydney   Tokyo   Singapore

First published 1992 by
Harvester Wheatsheaf,
Campus 400, Maylands Avenue, Hemel Hempstead,
Hertfordshire, HP2 7EZ
A division of
Simon & Schuster International Group

© 1992 B.J. McCormick

All rights reserved. No part of this publication may be
reproduced, stored in a retrieval system, or transmitted,
in any form, or by any means, electronic, mechanical,
photocopying, recording or otherwise, without the prior
permission, in writing, from the publisher.

Typeset in 10/12 pt Times by
Mathematical Composition Setters Ltd, Salisbury, Wiltshire

Printed in Great Britain by BPCC Wheatons Ltd, Exeter

British Library Cataloguing in Publication Data

McCormick, B.J.
  Hayek and the Keynesian avalanche.
  I. Title
  330.15

ISBN 0-7450-1080-6

1 2 3 4 5 96 95 94 93 92

For
J.C. Gilbert

Contents

Preface		xi
Acknowledgements		xiii
Chapter 1	Introduction	1
Chapter 2	**From Cannan to Robbins**	11
	Introduction	11
	Edwin Cannan	14
	Allyn Young	23
	Lionel Robbins	24
	The seminars and lectures: personalities and organization	29
	Summary and conclusions	35
	Notes	
Chapter 3	**Prices and production**	37
	Introduction	37
	The London School of Economics	44
	Cambridge	50
	The public debate	61
	The Cambridge criticisms	64
	Opinions within the LSE	69
	Summary and conclusions	75
	Notes	
Chapter 4	**Beiträge zur Geldtheorie**	79
	Introduction	79
	From Wicksell to Myrdal	79

	Lindahl and studies in the theory of money and capital	81
	The demand for money: portfolio analysis	85
	Simplifying the theory of money	91
	Economists who wrote above their times?	92
	Neutral money	94
	Summary and conclusions	95
	Notes	
Chapter 5	**The capital controversy**	99
	Introduction	99
	The time structure of production	101
	Knight's critique of Austrian capital theory	105
	The pure theory of capital	122
	Capital and its structure	126
	The maintenance of capital	129
	Summary and conclusions	131
	Notes	
Chapter 6	**The socialist debate**	135
	Introduction	135
	Collectivist economic planning	136
	The nature of the firm	145
	Eastern Europe	147
	Summary and conclusions	151
	Notes	
Chapter 7	**The open economy**	153
	Introduction	153
	The transfer problem	156
	Tariffs	157
	Fluctuating exchange rates	159
	Fixed exchange rates	160
	Summary and conclusions	164
	Notes	
Chapter 8	**The nature of the Keynesian avalanche**	167
	Introduction	167
	Scholarship	172
	Methodology	176
	Vision	182
	Summary and conclusions	184
	Notes	

Chapter 9	**The neoclassical synthesis: Hicks and Lerner**	187
	Early impressions	187
	The ISLM diagram	190
	Value and capital	191
	The economics of control	197
	The marginal efficiency of investment	199
	Shackle's elaboration	201
	Functional finance and the debt burden	203
	Summary and conclusions	205
	Notes	
Chapter 10	**The thaw**	207
	Introduction	207
	The demand for money	207
	Expectations, uncertainty and causality	209
	Loanable funds v. liquidity preference	210
	Productivity and the price level	217
	Capital, growth and the traverse	220
	Growth and distribution	224
	Hicks and Gilbert on the trade cycle and growth	225
	Hicks on the traverse	226
	Summary and conclusions	232
	Notes	
Chapter 11	**The road from serfdom**	235
	Introduction	235
	The Chicago programme	235
	The brain cannot know itself	238
	The re-emergence of Hayek	244
	Constitutional politics and the limitations of Hayek's research programme	252
	Summary and conclusions	256
	Notes	
Chapter 12	**A summing up**	259
Bibliography		263
Index		279

Preface

What are the factors responsible for the business cycle? Are they the result of monetary disturbances or do they arise out of variations in the real forces of technology, productivity and thrift? If monetary disturbances create perturbations in the real economy how should such changes in the real structure be analyzed? Is it meaningful to talk about changes in the capital structure of an economy? If the business cycle is due to monetary disturbances then what conditions must be satisfied in order that money be neutral in its effects? And if it is necessary for the state to intervene in the workings of the economy should that degree of intervention lead to the abolition of markets and their replacement by central planning?

These questions have a modern ring to them. They have, in various guises and at various times throughout the postwar period, been raised and addressed. But they were first prompted by the events of the interwar years and in a series of debates between Friedrich Hayek and John Maynard Keynes. The debates enveloped their respective institutions – the London School of Economics and Cambridge – and they determined the research programmes of their colleagues. Hayek attributed the business cycle to monetary disturbances which disrupted the capital structures of production and he criticized Keynes's *Treatise on Money* (1930) for its lack of a theory of capital. Keynes conceded that he had not provided such a theory and went on to write *The General Theory of Employment, Interest and Money* (1936). But Keynes's setback and his subsequent triumph was at the expense of failings by Hayek who, in his *Prices and Production* (1931c), also neglected to provide an adequate theory of capital and, more to the point, did not deal adequately with the slump of the 1930s. He attempted to remedy his deficiencies by writing *The Pure Theory of Capital* (1941). Unfortunately, it was swept aside by the Keynesian avalanche.

In the aftermath of the *General Theory* there were attempts to assimilate many of the ideas discussed in the London School of Economics (LSE) to the New Economics. But as the postwar Keynesian policies seemed to become increasingly ineffective in the 1970s and as the planned economies of Eastern Europe disintegrated in the 1980s, Hayek's ideas underwent a revival and reappraisal and his answers to the questions set out in the first paragraph of this Preface gained an audience among politicians as well as academics. He became a guru of political leaders in Britain and the United States. In this book I have attempted to consider the relationship between the ideas of Hayek and Keynes and how they influenced subsequent generations of economists and politicians.

Acknowledgements

At an early stage in the development of this book I greatly benefited from discussions with Tom Duffy, John Diffley, Anthony Kivell, Anne Nicholson, Joan Marshall, Patricia Maher, Neville Pakeman and Derek Lees. Abbott Bryning, who was my constant companion in undergraduate days as well as my lifelong friend, supplied me with his copy of J.C. Gilbert's lecture notes. Simon Vicary dispelled my confusion over Durbin and Gilbert. Trevor Brooks, a good footballer, an indifferent swimmer and now an honest golfer, improved my knowledge of the LSE. In 1989 I presented a paper on Hayek at the History of Economics Conference at Richmond, Virginia, and the results were that Lawrence Moss turned me round intellectually and Harald Hagemann sent me off to UCLA. At the same conference I also had useful discussions with Jeremy Shearmur and John Pheby. Later Dudley and Louise Dillard provided splendid hospitality in Maryland. My secretary, Wendy Rodgerson, did a wonderful job of sorting out the manuscript. The dedication reflects a lifelong friendship with a gentleman and an economic theorist whose unfailing kindness has been a great help to me throughout my career. However, the greatest debt is, as always, to Monica who has had to put up with an untidy house and a husband whose mind has persistently strayed to other things.

I am indebted to the Department of Official Publications of the London School of Economics and Political Science, for permission to reproduce syllabuses from the 1930s *Calendars* of the School. I am also indebted to Dr Nadim Shehadi, Director of the Centre for Lebanese Studies, Oxford, for permission to consult his transcripts of interviews he conducted with former members of the London School of Economics.

1
Introduction

In his book, *On Keynesian Economics and the Economics of Keynes*, Axel Leijonhufvud (1968) referred to the Keynesian avalanche which descended on pre-Keynesian theory and in a *Festschrift* for Hicks he noted that: 'what went on at the London School in the early thirties appears in retrospect almost as important as what was going on at Cambridge. At LSE the world of Anglo-American economics was being won over from the tradition of Ricardo and Marshall to modern neoclassical economics'.[1] Now the metaphor of an avalanche lends itself to varying interpretations. On the one hand, it can signify the obliteration of the intellectual landscape. On the other hand, it can suggest that frozen in the ice are interesting items which have been perfectly preserved and could be retrieved by diligent explorers. Furthermore, 'almost as important' is a qualification which suggests that even when the items have been recovered, they may still only serve as museum pieces which have no importance for contemporary theorizing – despite the preoccupation of many economists with a programme of neoclassical economics. And history would also reveal that Frank Knight had a major role in weaning American economics and LSE economics from Ricardo and Marshall. Knight had been in Vienna in the 1920s and his PhD thesis had been supervised by Allyn Young who was later, and but briefly, to be Professor of Economics at the LSE. Moreover, Knight's thesis, *Risk, Uncertainty and Profit* (1921) was to become a standard text at the LSE.

So what then are the interesting items to which Leijonhufvud drew our attention? He picked out the controversy over capital theory but conceded that there must have been a state of widespread exasperation with a debate which was at the same time so technically difficult and so inconclusive that it became a major reason for the fact that Keynes's work was made the excuse for dismissing the problem. He also drew attention to Hayek's work on the price mechanism and Hicks's work on portfolio theory. But do these items constitute the case for a rescue operation? The role of the price mechanism as a means of aggregating and disseminating information would have been familiar to any Cambridge economist brought up on Marshallian economics. Moreover, Marshall had noted that the Walrasian auctioneer was *a* way but not *the* way to general equilibrium and Lavington had expounded portfolio theory.

What then are we to make of these interesting experiments? The aims of this book are as follows.

1. To explore the research programme laid down by Hayek and Robbins.
2. To examine the response from the younger economists at the LSE to Hayek's ideas and to Keynes's ideas.
3. To trace out the subsequent development of Hayek's ideas and their relationship to economic policies pursued in the 1980s.

The LSE research programme was contained in Robbins's *Nature and Significance of Economic Science* (1932) and in Hayek's *Prices and Production* (1931c) as well as Hayek's inaugural lecture, 'The trend of economic thinking' (1933a) and in his earlier book, *Monetary Theory and the Trade Cycle* (1929). The programme was an encouragement to come to terms with the European economic literature and to reject the older LSE approach as well as that pursued at Cambridge. Economics was to be a study of how choices are made between scarce means and competing ends, which implied a rejection of Cannan's emphasis upon a material definition of economics. The new approach led to a change in the LSE's journal, *Economica*, which went into a new series and in its first year contained Hicks and Allen on ordinal utility and indifference curves. It rejected Marshall's emphasis upon the study of men in the ordinary business of life and it was opposed to Keynes's view that economics was a moral science which used introspection and value judgements. In propounding this programme Robbins and Hayek acted as complements. Despite a foray into macroeconomics in his book, *The Great Depression* (1934a), Robbins's research was mainly confined to value theory and to statics whereas Hayek was preoccupied with money and dynamic economics.

To this programme the younger LSE economists responded and in doing so, with the exception of Lachmann, they became rebels in opposition to the 'Austrians', Hayek, Robbins, Gregory and Benham. The most notable casualty of the response was Hayek. Indeed, a conclusion of this book is that Hayek's theories were undermined by the young rebels – in contrast to the support that Keynes received from the younger economists at Cambridge and the critical stance adopted by Robertson and Pigou. But while criticizing Hayek's ideas, many of the LSE economists adopted Keynesian positions imbued with Paretian/ Walrasian notions. Which brings us to an examination of the Keynesian avalanche.

It is customary to distinguish between Keynes's intellectual revolutions and LSE scholarship. But in truth, the Keynesian avalanche contained three elements namely scholarship, orthodoxy, and vision and originality. Scholarship was displayed in Keynes's critiques of Fisher, Knapp, Helfferich, Mises and Lindahl as well as his substantial appraisals of the English economists: Malthus, Jevons and Marshall. Indeed, Keynes's awareness of the ideas of earlier and contemporary economists matched those of Hayek and Robbins – it could not be otherwise given that he was the editor of the *Economic Journal* for such a long period. There is, therefore, an element of irony in Robbins's verdict that Keynes would probably be remembered in the long run for his *Essays in Persuasion* (1931) and his *Essays in Biography* (1933). There were, of course, some misinterpretations; but such misinterpretations might be forgiven in someone who had received no formal training in economics – error was, however, not the prerogative of Keynes.

Orthodoxy was displayed in *Indian Currency and Finance* (1913), his appendix to the *Indian Currency Report*, and which was acknowledged by Marshall to be 'a prodigy of constructive work'[2] and by Foxwell in his review of the sequel, *Indian Currency and Finance* (1913), as 'likely to remain the standard work on its subject'.[3] Orthodoxy was continued in *A Tract on Monetary Reform* (1923) which in its treatment of the demand for money relied heavily upon Marshall and Pigou. There was, of course, some originality in the treatment of the monetary theory of the balance of payments, but originality is usually confined to the *Treatise on Money* (1930) and the *General Theory* (1936). However, this view tends to diminish the true extent of the avalanche for the rumblings begin with the *Treatise on Probability* (1921) – with its critique of Hume and its heavy emphasis upon a logical theory of probability. In short, there was an alternative research programme laid down by Keynes. Finally, originality emerged out of a vision of the workings of the British and American economies in the interwar years from Keynes's ability to adapt Marshallian economics to current problems.

Hayek was, therefore, subjected to two lines of criticism; from within the LSE and from Cambridge. How then should we assess his reputation? The exercise might seem futile; a verdict – a Nobel prize – has been awarded. But the prize was awarded for scholarly achievements which included, but which also went beyond, economics. What we are interested in is a verdict in terms of his work at the LSE and the effects of the Keynesian avalanche. Confronted by so complex a scholar it is tempting to isolate aspects. First, there is the dispassionate scholar encouraging his colleagues and students to read widely and immerse themselves in the European literature. Second, there is the economist advancing his own theories and grappling with the problems of describing a dynamic economy subject to disturbances without resorting to the comparative statics approach of Keynes. In the process he may have become confused. Hence, the research programme he set himself, his colleagues and his students, may have led to his downfall. But might not self-destruction be the possible fate of a scholar? However, there is another picture – that of an economist who asked the wrong questions and therefore put the wrong answers to the problems confronting the British economy in the 1930s. Coming from Austria and the European inflations of the 1920s, he propounded the thesis that the trade cycle was a monetary phenomenon which gave rise to real disturbances, and which littered the landscape with half-completed projects, known as 'Hayeks'. For some of the booms of the early nineteenth century the thesis seemed to provide a plausible explanation. Rising prices and increased imports would lead to a capital outflow which, in turn, would lead to a credit contraction and the end of the boom. But for the weak booms of the late nineteenth century and for the depressed conditions of the interwar years an alternative explanation seemed to be required. When full employment was not attained then it suggested an explanation in terms of the weakness of real forces. For these conditions Hayek's theory seemed to provide an inadequate explanation. In the 1930s it no longer seemed possible for the British economy to unwind still further. There was a deficiency of aggregate money demand. It was therefore confusing to litter the blackboard with triangles purporting to explain capital intensity.

These then are the themes which are the subject of development in succeeding chapters and which offer a study of the interaction of ideas, actors (whose brief biographical details are set out in Table 1.1) and organizations. Thus Chapter 2 deals with four issues. First, there is the economic outlook of Edwin Cannan. Second, there is the Robbins research programme. Taken together these two topics serve to define the distinction between old and new LSE. Third, there are Cannan's monetary theories which provide a backcloth against which to judge the new theories introduced by Hayek. Fourth, there is the contrast between Robbins's methodology and that prevailing at Cambridge as well as the later intrusion of positivism into the LSE and into economics in general.

Chapter 3 presents Hayek's *Prices and Production* (1931c) which arose out of a series of lectures given at the LSE. It traces his monetary overinvestment theory of the trade cycle to earlier discussions by

Table 1.1 Dramatis Personnae, 1920–45.

Edwin Cannan	Professor of Political Economy; retired 1928
Theodore Gregory	Reader in Commerce; 1926 Professor of Banking and Currency; 1934 Professor of Economics
Hugh Dalton	1922 Reader in Commerce; 1926 Reader in Economics
Frederic Benham	1929–30 Assistant in Imperial Economic Relations; 1930–1 Lecturer in Commerce; 1931–42 Reader in Commerce; 1945 Professor of Commerce
Lionel Robbins	1926 Lecturer in Economics; 1929 Professor of Economics
Phillip Barratt Whale	1926 Lecturer in Commerce; 1931 Reader
J.R. Hicks	1926–9 Assistant; 1932–5 Lecturer in Economics
W.F. Crick	1920–4 Sir Ernest Cassell Travelling Scholar
Dennis H. Robertson	Fellow of Trinity College, Cambridge; 1930–1 Visiting Lecturer at the School; 1938 Professor of Economics at the School
E.F.M. Durbin	1929 Assistant; 1934 Lecturer in Economics
J.C. Gilbert	1929–31 Assistant
Friedrich August von Hayek	1931 Professor of Economics and Statistics
Nicholas Kaldor	1932 Assistant; 1938 Lecturer
Brinley Thomas	1932 Assistant; 1938 Lecturer
R.F. Fowler	1933 Assistant
Frank Paish	1935 Lecturer in Commerce
Ronald Coase	1935 Assistant; 1938 Lecturer in Commerce
Abba P. Lerner	1935 Assistant
Victor Edelberg	1931–5 Research Fellow
S. Paul Chambers	1932–4 Research Student
Vera C. Smith	1932–6 Research Student
Ludwig Lachmann	1933–8 Research Student
Harold Barger	1934–7 Research Student
George L.S. Shackle	1934–7 Research Student
Helen Makower	1934–7 Research Student
T. Scitovsky	1935–9 Research Student
Thomas A. Wilson	1936–40 Research Student
S.C. Tsiang	1941–5 Research Student

Sources: LSE Archives; LSE Calendars.

Wicksell, Mises, Schumpeter. It goes on to examine the Cambridge critique of Hayek and in doing so sets out the various Cambridge theories which were in circulation in the 1930s. The chapter concludes with an examination of the early criticisms within the LSE.

In Chapter 4, *Beiträge zur Geldtheorie*, edited by Hayek (1933c), serves as a useful peg upon which to hang a discussion of expectations, monetary equilibrium and neutral money. It was reviewed by Hicks and Gilbert. Hicks's early work on money is then considered in the light of the Robbins research programme. It is noted that a side-effect of Hicks's work was to undermine Hayek's ideas by drawing attention to risk and real forces. The writings of Chambers are then considered and two questions are raised. First, were Hicks and Chambers the true progenitors of modern portfolio theory? Second, was their work engulfed by the

Keynesian avalanche from which it had to be retrieved by the editors of the American Economics Association's *Readings in Monetary Theory*, and by William Baumol and James Tobin? Attention is then directed to the neglected work of Lavington and Schlesinger and a further question arises: why was Hicks's work retrieved and that of Lavington and Schlesinger ignored? The next theme of the chapter is Gilbert's review of Koopman's essay on neutral money and the discussions of neutral money within the LSE by Gilbert, Durbin and Barger. The chapter concludes with Hayek's response to Myrdal and Lachmann's verdict on the Austrian approach to expectations and the theoretical work of Lindahl.

'God knows what the Austrians mean by "period of production". Nothing in my opinion. *Vide* Knight's forthcoming article in the March *EJ*' wrote Keynes to Robertson on 20 February 1935. The comment reflected Keynes's preoccupation with Hayek's criticism of the *Treatise on Money* for its lack of a theory of capital. But his reference to Knight also serves as an introduction to the capital controversy conducted by Knight and Kaldor in which Kaldor began by being sympathetic to Hayek's ideas and then ended up rejecting them and producing his own theory of the trade cycle. Hayek attempted to respond to Kaldor and in doing so produced a major treatise on capital. The chapter also examines Lerner's contribution to the capital controversy.

Intertwined with Hayek's interest in the trade cycle was his involvement with the economics of socialism. In the late 1930s he came under attack from Lange and, despite the fact that Mises had anticipated some of the criticisms, Hayek conceded that Lange had produced a plausible economic theory of socialism. The economics of socialism is the substance of Chapter 6.

Chapter 7 begins with Cannan's observations on international and interregional trade and moves on to consider Hayek's proposals for creating a framework for international monetary stability. This is followed by an examination of the reactions of Barratt Whale, Gilbert and Paish and the analysis of optimal currency areas.

Chapter 8 explains the nature of the Keynesian avalanche in terms of its scholarship, orthodoxy and originality. It concludes that the avalanche was more destructive of the LSE research programme than had previously been acknowledged.

Chapter 9 draws attention to the differing responses to the *General Theory* by economists in Cambridge and in the LSE. At the LSE there was a striking absence of criticism from the senior members of the School. Explanations of the lack of response of Hayek, Robbins and Gregory are then put forward. In contrast, there were trenchant criticisms from Cambridge by Pigou and Robertson. Pigou accepted for the purposes of the debate Keynes's use of a comparative statics framework and then pointed to the failure to incorporate the effects of falling prices upon the real value of money balances. Robertson rejected a static framework and emphasized the dynamic factors ignored by Keynes. Among the younger LSE economists there was a more receptive response. Hicks and Lerner both wrote reviews of the book and both went on to provide neoclassical syntheses which reconciled neoclassical and Keynesian ideas. There were, however, Hayekian elements in the synthesis.

Chapter 9 returns to the question of how money is introduced into an economy. Gilbert sought a reconciliation of Austrian and Keynesian approaches, emphasizing the importance of both time and uncertainty. Gilbert's stress upon time also served to record Robertson's influence and removed the apparent absence of time from the comparative statics treatment by Keynes. It is a theme which also appears in Tsiang's analysis and, despite being a fundamentalist Keynesian, Shackle has also accepted the importance of time as well as uncertainty. In contrast, Hicks tended to take a different approach and treated the transactions demand not as a true demand with elements of volition in the amount held, but as the amount of money needed to drive a given amount of goods around an economy. The insertion of money into an economy does, of course, require the analysis of the simultaneous determination of the money rate of interest and the price level. In the aftermath of the *General Theory*, a dispute arose as to the correctness of the liquidity preference and loanable funds theories of the rate of interest. Hicks assumed that it was a sham dispute since real and monetary influences were involved in the determination of the rate of interest; he suggested that in a general equilibrium framework the choice of the theory was determined by which equation was dropped. If the equation for liquidity preference was dropped then a loanable funds theory emerged. If a loanable funds equation was dropped then a liquidity preference theory was left. To which Lerner quipped: 'What happened if the equation for peanuts was dropped?'.[4] Tsiang attempted to resolve the dispute in favour of Robertson's loanable funds theory although Hicks could still find Keynes's theory both useful and relevant for the 1930s.

Chapter 10 also treats the subject of neutral money in the context of changing productivity and price levels. Gilbert's conclusion that any behaviour of the price level was compatible with equilibrium served as the basis for resolving many of the interwar years' disputes. But given the price level and the rate of interest what determines the trade cycle? While recognizing that a difference of opinion existed between Keynes (deficient demand leading to a weak boom) and Hayek (excess demand leading to a strong boom), Gilbert thought that the difference of opinion over the upper turning point could be resolved through empirical work and he sought to provide an explanation of the lower turning point which was compatible with Hayek's assumptions. In contrast Hicks sought to produce a Keynesian explanation of the strong boom in terms of the interaction of the multiplier and accelerator and the presence of a full employment ceiling. His model was a growth and trade cycle model in which growth was provided by a floor of autonomous investment. Subsequently, Hicks attempted to explain the shifts from one growth path to another in terms of vertical displacements stemming from changes in the amount of autonomous investment brought about by technological change — which he called impulses. And he continued to believe that real forces were more important than monetary forces.

This brings us to the philosophical and political basis of Hayek's writings and their contrast with the ideas of Keynes, to their contribution to the attempted revival of liberalism and to their relevance to the shifting political and social issues of the 1980s and 1990s. From the 1980s onwards there has been a movement towards the deregulation of markets and to the control of the money supply. The movement began in the United States, emerged in Britain under Margaret Thatcher and was then transmitted to Eastern Europe. It was a product of the inflation of the 1960s and 1970s. Increasing the importance of markets does, however, draw attention to the nature of the political and social framework within which markets operate.

In 'The end of laisser — faire' Keynes (1931)[5] drew attention to the confluence of several rivulets of opinion which converged to form the broad stream of liberal thinking which dominated the eighteenth and nineteenth centuries. One stream was individualism which emerged out of the seventeenth-century political convulsions and the speculations of Locke and Hume. Individualism emphasized liberty, toleration and property rights. However, there was another rivulet which carried forward the idea of equality. Utility, derived from Hume and his predecessors, was then enlarged into social utility and the social contract of Locke was fashioned into the general will of Rousseau and Bentham with the emphasis upon the happiness of the greatest number. Individualism and equality were reconciled through the workings of markets, through the operations of the invisible hand. Individuals pursuing their self-interest were presumed to promote the general good. Furthermore, the pursuit of self-interest was deemed to be efficient.

In Britain this social thought was not embedded in a written constitution. Britain had an unwritten constitution which was in marked contrast to those countries in which equality was given greater emphasis. Instead a primitive constitution with its conferment of sovereignty to the monarch was buttressed by an unwritten constitution in which intimations were preferred to rationalist principles, in which Burke was preferred to Descartes. The guardian of this unwritten constitution was a propertied class which imbibed Hume and Locke, Smith and Marshall with their port and claret. The social structure filled the vacuum left by parliament, although it would be apposite to say that parliament was dominated by a propertied class which diffused power by checking the onslaughts of the executive and keeping local affairs firmly in their hands.

By and large this unwritten constitution, and this propertied class, survived most of the industrial and social changes of the eighteenth and nineteenth centuries. It survived the repeal of the Corn Laws and it provided much of the finance for industry. It also survived the extension of the vote to the working class. Indeed the most striking feature of the socialist revolution of the 1940s was the acceptance of the unwritten constitution and the success with which the propertied class adapted to nationalization. It was as if Attlee socialists imbibed liberal principles through their tea.

The Thatcher revolution of the 1980s transformed this social and economic and political landscape by promoting a bourgeoise revolution which swept away paternalism and aristocratic mores. The informal constraints of the older political culture and liberal values were no longer effective. What replaced the old patricians was a larger, potentially more powerful, but politically uneducated propertied class which was bent on making money and inclined to leaving public affairs to others. Thatcherism seemed to provide an economic solution to the economic ills of the 1960s and 1970s. Keynesian demand–management policies had appeared to leave a vacuum in the marketplace which was replaced by the Thatcherite return to efficiency through the market. But a problem then emerged. Within the context of a strong state it was assumed that a free market could operate. But what determined the nature of the strong state when the traditional countervailing powers had been swept away?

Hayek seemed to provide an answer to the question. In political and social theorizing he has drawn upon one strand of liberalism – that which is associated with the Scottish Enlightenment of Smith, Hume and Ferguson to which he has added Kant. He has sought to overcome the tyranny of the majority in voting systems and he has grounded his proposals in an intensive study of the human psyche. According to Hayek there are limits to reason stemming from the fact that the brain cannot know itself. Given the limits to human reason it follows that the rationalist proposals for planning are fraught with dangers and decision making based upon majority votes must be suspect because the accumulation of a majority requires concessions to various interest groups. Therefore, Hayek has sought to restrict the coercion of the majority by the introduction of general and non-discriminatory rules. He has proposed a complete separation of powers between a legislative assembly which would determine rules of conduct and parliament which would make laws within the rules laid down by the legislature. The legislature would be elected from a group of well established members of society and it is intended that they would be free from the pressures of interest groups. Thus Hayek offers the attractions of a strong state, but not a tyrannical state, within which markets would operate. Hayek's political and social theory receives a critical appraisal in Chapter 11.

Notes

1. Leijonhufvud, A. (1984). 'Hicks on time and money', in Collard *et al.* (1984) *Economic Theory and Hicksian Themes*, Oxford: Oxford University Press.
2. Marshall, A. (1971), in *The Collected Writings of John Maynard Keynes*, Vol. XV, *Activities: India and Cambridge, 1906–14*, London: Macmillan, p. 268.
3. Foxwell, H.A. (1913), 'Review of Keynes's *Indian Currency and Finance*', *Economic Journal*, XXIII: 57.
4. Quoted in Patinkin, D. (1958), 'Liquidity preference and loanable funds: stock flow analysis', *Economica*, NS25: 287–301.
5. Keynes, J.M. (1931, 1972), 'The end of laisser faire', in *The Collected Writings of John Maynard Keynes*, Vol. IX, *Essays in Persuasion*, London: Macmillan, pp. 272–94.

2
From Cannan to Robbins

Introduction

The LSE was established in 1895 by Sydney Webb to act as a counterweight to Marshall's monopoly of economics. In the same year Edwin Cannan was appointed to a lectureship in the School and in 1905 he was promoted to a chair. Webb was assisted in the founding of the School by the sudden availability of a will whose terms allowed some latitude in the use of the monies, and also by the emergence in the 1880s and 1890s of pressures to separate economic history from traditional historical studies and by the existence of a group of dissatisfied and disaffected young Oxford economists from whose ranks Webb was able to draw a director (Hewins) and a lecturer (Cannan). Finally, there were factors peculiar to the location of a social science institute in London.[1]

On Thursday 24 November 1932, Sydney Webb visited the School to talk about the early days. He said that:

> 'he and his friends wanted to create a centre of Economics teaching which was not dominated by individualists'. And in the teaching of economics, Mr. Webb wanted to see the subject treated from different angles. He said: 'I was in revolt against one Professor of Economics. I wanted a lot of Professors'. He it was also, who wanted to see Public Administration taught at the School and from the very beginning the School was called the School of Economics and Political Science to indicate the scope of teaching. And of the first director (Hewins) he said: 'He was not a theoretic economic historian, he was not a Cambridge orthodox person'.[2]

Hewins was, in fact, a supporter of Joseph Chamberlain in the campaign for tariff reform – a position from which later School economists such as Cannan and Robbins were to depart when in the 1920s and 1930s they advocated free trade.

Why were the Webbs so critical of Cambridge economists? The answer is not obvious, nor is it simple. In *Industrial Democracy* the Webbs (1902a) deferred to Marshall. The core of the book was an analytical framework based upon a distinction between closed and open unions which, in turn owed much to the Marshallian determinants of derived demand and the later Hicksian qualification concerning the importance of labour's contribution to total costs. In their *History of Trade Unionism* they suggested that the apparent alternation between closed and open unions was due to the accidental prominence of one or other form of union in particular periods (Webb and Webb, 1902b). In *My Apprenticeship* Beatrice Webb (1926) dismissed the idea that sweating was synonymous with exploitation because there was no lack of competition between employers. Low wages, she observed, were due to the low value productivity of workers who had no supply price above the subsistence level. The Webbs were, in fact, very orthodox in their economics.

And even Hewins felt obliged to have his ideas approved by Marshall. It could not be otherwise given the position that Marshall occupied in economics. In 1900 Hewins submitted for appraisal an MA scheme. Marshall replied: 'In the hands of second-rate examiners it will I think foster socialism as regards facts and frivolity as regards reasoning'.[3]

In 1902 Marshall wrote once more to Hewins:

> I have heard rumours that led me to think there was some danger that the economics department of the London University might be 'captured' by people more or less in accord with some Fabian opinions and aims than are many academic economists but I could not contemplate such a danger without grave anxiety. I have spoken without reserve to Miss Brook and to Bowley and I think you may have heard something of my views on it. So I write at once to say that Acworth has convinced me that my fears were based on a misapprehension.[4]

Of course, there was no orthodoxy at Cambridge. As Coase has noted there was no happy band of brothers.[5] Marshall was critical of J.N. Keynes's discussion of methodology in his book *The Scope and Method of Political Economy* (J.N. Keynes, 1891). He thought the distinction between deduction and induction was too sharply drawn. There were also differences of opinion between Marshall and Cunningham. And Marshall was concerned with the fact that, despite an apparent monopoly of economics, Cambridge had produced very few good economists. Hence, his desire that Pigou became his successor. But in so far as there were differences between Marshall and Sydney Webb then, perhaps, it was a difference of emphasis. Perhaps Webb could not have accepted

Marshall's *obiter dictum*, 'the Many in the One, the One in the Many'.[6] Perhaps there was a feeling that after Marshall had published his great organon of truth there would be no significant breakthrough in economics for a long time. After all, even Lavington and Shove believed that it was all in Marshall. There was, of course, a difference in emphasis in the undergraduate courses at Cambridge and the LSE. At Cambridge Marshall had shifted the emphasis to theory; at the LSE equal weight was given to both theory and economic history. But the distinction can be misconstrued. Marshall spent the greater part of his life in theorizing and in curbing the excesses of the Historical School. But he thought that his work was a prelude to the study of economic history. It was therefore ironic that Pigou chose to emphasize the static aspects of the Marshallian thought – most notably in his treatment of the representative firm.

But years later Sydney Webb did offer the Directorship of the School to John Maynard Keynes and it was only when Keynes declined did he offer it to William Beveridge. Even then Sydney Webb was not put off. He invited Keynes to stand as the Labour Party candidate for the Cambridge University seat. Furthermore, Keynes lectured at the School in the early decades of the twentieth century and throughout the interwar years the Webbs dined and corresponded with Keynes. But perhaps Keynes was not a Cambridge orthodox person! The truth, however, may be, as Lionel Robbins observed in his *Autobiography* (1971) that the Webbs were as much interested in the pursuit of truth as they were in the promulgation of socialism. The first generation of academics at the School contained Graham Wallis who had broken with the Fabians, Bowley who was a conservative and who had prescribed a meagre meal for Ernest Bevin's dockers during a pay dispute, Foxwell who was a Tory social reformer and who had been beaten for Marshall's chair by Pigou, and Hobhouse who was a Liberal. Moreover, Cannan, who could be critical of Marshall, insisted upon his students reading the *Principles of Economics* (Marshall, 1920). In so far as there was a bias then it was to Oxford, rather than to Cambridge, that the School went for its first generation of academics. But later, Dalton, a pupil of Pigou, was recruited to the School and he was to have a decisive influence in the appointment of Robbins as the first full-time professor of economics.

Historical studies suited the Webbs who thought that the study of history might reveal an evolution of political and social organizations towards socialism. And within Oxford there were a group of young economists who belonged to the historicist camp in that faint echo of the German *Methodenstreit* which infected England in the 1880s and 1890s. However, the historicist strand should not be emphasized unduly. At Cambridge Marshall displayed an interest in economic history and in the evolution of social organizations. 'The Mecca of Economics', he wrote, 'was biology'.[7] But there was also within Oxford and among the younger economists a lack of sympathy for the analytics of Edgeworth. To these influences must be added the distinctive catchment area for students provided by London. The School attracted a large number of mature students. Abba P. Lerner, for example, started life as a tailor and then switched to printing. When his print shop went bankrupt he enrolled at the School as an evening student.

The combination of part-time and mature students gave rise to an intellectual atmosphere which was distinct from that obtaining within the Oxbridge colleges, although, perhaps, not noticeably different from that prevailing in the provincial universities. And the Webbs' aims and the students' desires led to an emphasis upon practical subjects. When Lionel Robbins took over the headship of the economics department he noted that:

> There was adequate coverage of the specialisms: Banking and Currency, Commerce, Transport, and Accounting including Business Administration. But Economics, Analytical and Descriptive, including Public Finance, was understaffed at the junior level and the Chair itself in Cannan's time had been on a part-time basis. This was clearly unsatisfactory especially at an institution where economics was part of the title.[8]

Edwin Cannan

Into this intellectual atmosphere Cannan fitted easily. Throughout his career he emphasized simple economics. At the 1933 annual meeting of the Royal Economics Society he 'deplored the fact that the almost complete absorption of the younger teachers in what they rightly or wrongly believe to be important advances in the higher branches of learning is leaving the public at the mercy of quacks'.[9] And he concluded that they should not 'hold their noses and avert their eyes from the disgusting mess and turn back to find peace and contentment in neat equations and elegant equilibria'.[10] He was critical of Marshall. Of the concept of consumer surplus he wrote that it is:

> a method which involves not a single hypothesis, but an infinite number of different hypotheses, each of which is inconsistent with all the others as well as with the actual facts . . . inconsistent hypotheses which no one would have thought of if it had not been for the 'space' which happens to be under the curve of a demand schedule.[11]

Cannan's reputation has tended to rest upon his edition of Adam Smith's *Wealth of Nations* (1904) which, until the appearance of the Glasgow edition, was regarded as definitive. But he also edited the *Paper*

Pound of 1797–1821 (1919a) which contained a reprint of the *Bullion Report* of 1810 as well as a lengthy commentary drawing attention to its relevance to the the postwar discussion of convertibility. There was a preoccupation with the history of economic thought with the publication of *A History of Theories of Production and Distribution* (1919b) and his *Review of Economic Theory* (1929) both of which contained an implicit rejection of Marshall's attempt to establish a continuity between classical and neoclassical economics. There was also a *History of Local Rates in England and Wales* (1912). But our main interests are in his outlook upon economics as a discipline and his views upon monetary economics.

The demand for money

Cannan took the view that: 'marginal utility plays the same part with regard to gold (both for ordinary purposes and for currency) as it does with other commodities'.[12] But he then went on to suggest that the elasticity of demand for money was less than unity. Thus, confronted with a rise in prices, and anticipating further increases in prices, an individual would cut down his or her money balances with the result that the demand for money would fall to zero before the supply of money increased to infinity. The notion that the demand for money was less than unity contrasted with the Cambridge view, as espoused by Pigou. Many years later, under the influence of Patinkin, Robertson adopted Cannan's assumption.[13] However, he did not consider the implications of his conversion for his own doctrine of forced saving (induced lacking). In the 1920s Robertson had, in his book *Banking Policy and the Price Level*, explored various concepts of forced saving while assuming a unit elastic demand curve. But a less than elastic demand curve would place severe limits upon the inflationary process (Robertson, 1949).

In contrast, Keynes, in *A Tract on Monetary Reform*, gave a qualified approval to Cannan's thesis on the elasticity of demand for money and quoted Lehfeldt's evidence that 'between July 1920 and April 1922, the elasticity of demand for money fell to an average of about 0.73 in Austria, 0.67 in Poland, and 0.5 in Germany'. But he went on to observe that: 'the conveniences of using money in daily life are so great that the public are prepared rather, than forgo them, to pay the inflation tax, provided that it is not raised to a prohibitive level'.[14]

The supply of money

On the supply side Cannan defined money as notes and coins and did not include bank deposits. Banks, he said, were merely cloakrooms; they could only lend what was lent to them. His thesis received support from the bankers, although there were a few dissenting voices, such as Hartley Withers who maintained that on the basis of a given amount of cash, banks could expand loans ten-fold.

The first major criticism of Cannan's thesis came in 1927 when Crick suggested that the power of a bank in a multi-banking system to create deposits would be limited by leakages to other banks. Unfortunately, his analysis was incomplete because he had concentrated upon the relationship (N) of cash in the banks and at the Bank of England to deposits and ignored the relationship (L) of cash in circulation to deposits. These inter-relationships were later clarified by Robertson, in his unpublished lectures on the 'Principles of currency' delivered at the School in the session 1930–1 (Table 2.1) by means of a simple algebraic formula:

$$B = C/(L + N)$$

where B stood for bank deposits, C represented cash and L and N took on the definitions set out above.

Now knowledge of the credit multiplier can be traced back at least to Pennington (1829, 1838) and Torrens (1837). Why then did it take so long for it to be adopted at the School? Two reasons may be adduced. First, there was the empirical problem; it was difficult to disentangle the relationships from the data. As the Committee on Finance and Industry

Table 2.1 Session 1930–1. Principles of Currency. Mr. Robertson.

Twenty lectures, Michaelmas and Lent Terms. Thursdays, 10.00–11.00, beginning M.T. 9 October, L.T. 15 January.
or (e) Wednesdays, 6.00–7.00, beginning M.T. 8 October, L.T. 14 January.
For B.Sc. (Econ) Final and B.Com. Final Part I.
Fees: Day: For the course, £3; Terminal, £1 16s
      Evening: For the course, £2; Terminal, £1 4s.

SYLLABUS: The nature of money. The meaning of the value of money. The theory of the value of money as a special case of the general theory of value. The kinds of money and the classification of monetary systems. The value of money as affected by the relations between saving and investment. Cyclical fluctuation in the value of money.

BOOKS RECOMMENDED: **Elementary**: Witless, *The Meaning of Money*; Cannan, *Money*; Robertson, *Money*; Layton, *Introduction to the Study of Prices*; *Treatises*: Hawtrey, *Currency and Credit*; Fisher, *Purchasing Power of Money*; Keynes, *A Treatise on Money*; L. von Mises, *Theories des Geldes und der Umlaufsmittel*; Cassel, *Money and Exchange since 1914*; Nogaro, *La Monnaie et les Phenomenes monetaires contemporains*.

Note: Robertson includes Mises's *Theories des Geldes und der Umlaufsmittel* in his reading list before Hayek appeared at the School. Witless may have been a misprint for (Hartley) Withers.

Source: LSE *Calendar* 1930–1.

noted:

> The monthly figures published by the clearing banks are not true daily averages but averages of one day selected in each week of the month. It seems that in order to present a better appearance, most of the banks concerned are at pains to manipulate their balances with the Bank of England on the selected day of the week so that they stand at a higher figure than usual. Moreover, each of the four biggest institutions pursuing these practices selects a different day of the week for the purpose, calling in loans from the money market on its selected day, but returning them next morning in time for the next big bank to call them for its making-up day. Thus, a certain part of the published reserves of the clearing banks in the shape of deposits with the Bank of England is like a stage army, the same liquid resources doing duty four times over in the course of each week. At the end of each half-year the same practice, euphemistically known as 'window dressing' is followed on a grander scale. On these occasions other banks which only publish figures on these dates also make a brave show in their balance sheets with deposits at the Bank of England which they temporarily acquire for the purpose. The net result is that the average Bank of England balances at the Bank of England of the clearing banks are less than 3.5 per cent of their deposits (perhaps not more than 3 per cent) and those of the country as a whole less than 3 per cent.[15]

Window dressing was discontinued in 1946 when the banks agreed to draw up their accounts on a common day of the month which were synchronized with the weekly return of the Bank of England and they also agreed to maintain a weekly cash ratio of 8 per cent.

Cannan's consolation was that when the empirical relationships were established the actual multiplier was $3\frac{1}{3}$ which was nearer to Cannan's 1 than Hartley Wither's 10. However the window dressing argument cannot obscure the fact that there was an exercise in logic involved in analysing the credit multiplier. Both Gregory (1927) and Robbins (1935) attempted to provide another reason for Cannan's cloakroom banking theory which rested upon the effect of credit expansion upon the distribution of wealth. In effect, Cannan was trying to prevent forced saving.

Robertson's intervention in the controversy (and there were other later interventions, such as the lecture on 'Theories of banking policy' delivered at the School in 1928 and his appointment to a chair in 1938) does draw attention to the Cambridge theory of bank deposits and to Keynes's observations upon Cannan. It also serves to draw attention to the work of the American economist, C.A. Phillips. In the margin of his copy of Giffen's *Stock Exchange Securities* (1887) Marshall had set out the algebra of the credit multiplier and in his evidence before the Gold and Silver Commission (1886) he had elaborated upon the note. In 1922 Phillips set out a rigorous treatment of the deposit multiplier in his book

Table 2.2 Session 1930–1. Theory of Banking and the Money Market. Professor Gregory.

Six lectures, Summer Term. Mondays, 5.00–6.00, beginning S.T. 27 April.
For B.Sc. (Econ) Final – Special subject of Banking, Currency and the Finance of International Trade; and B.Com. Group A.
Fee: 18s.

SYLLABUS: The functions and economic significance of banking. The general structure and methods of banking. The cheque system and the nature of deposits. Banking in relation to the price level. The functions of central banks. The regulation of note-issues and the Bank Acts. Comparison with foreign systems. Recent developments in banking.

BOOKS RECOMMENDED: Cannan, 'Bank Deposits' (*Economica* No. 1); Lavington, *The English Capital Market*; Robertson, *Banking Policy and the Price Level*; Hahn, *Volkwirtschaftliche Theorie des Bank Kredits*; Wicksell, *Vorlesungen uber National Œkonomie*, Part II; Phillips, *Bank Credit*; Bellerby, *Monetary Stability*.

Source: LSE *Calendar* 1930–1.

Bank Credit. However, the book did not appear on Gregory's reading list (Table 2.2) until Cannan had retired and Robertson was lecturing at the School.

The quantity theory of money

In the interwar years it is possible to distinguish several phases of monetary discussion at the School. The first was in the 1920s and coincided with the revival of monetary economics in Britain. Reviewing Irving Fisher's *The Purchasing Power of Money* (1911), Keynes observed the absence of acute monetary problems in the closing decades of nineteenth century Britain which meant that 'economists had to rely upon an oral tradition distilled from Marshall's teaching'.[16] Keynes set out what he thought were Marshall's original contributions in a biographical essay. Eshag has disputed the originality of the contributions but has conceded that:

> The significance of a writer's work measured by reference to its impact on the progress of theory and of policy, does not depend solely on the degree of originality of the ideas embodied in such work; no less important are the methods of presentation of such ideas, and especially the social and economic context within which they are presented.[17]

Later Hicks was to observe that: 'You cannot get brilliant answers to a dull question paper and the question paper that was set to Marshall by his monetary facts really was a bit dull.'[18] The revival of interest therefore coincided with Pigou's 1917 article in which, by way of a criticism of Fisher, he concluded that the Cambridge approach conferred a 'real advantage because it brings us at once into relation with volition – the ultimate cause of demand'.[19] And the revival was sustained by three great Cambridge treatises: Hawtrey's *Currency and Credit*, (1919), Keynes's *A Tract on Monetary Reform* (1923) and Robertson's *Banking Policy and the Price Level* (1926).

The interaction of the new theory and policy received its first airing in Keynes's *A Tract on Monetary Reform* which was published in 1923. It was originally written as thirteen articles in the *Reconstruction of Europe* which he edited for the *Manchester Guardian Commercial* in 1922. The core of the book consisted of the following propositions:

1. Stabilization of the domestic price level should be the object of monetary policy.
2. Stability would be achieved by watching credit creation rather than currency creation.
3. The trade cycle can be controlled through credit control (even though the cycle may be caused by real forces) and not by credit manipulation.
4. The most effective instruments for controlling credit are bank rate and open market operations.

The context of the propositions was a situation in which the British economy was not on the gold standard but had an inconvertible paper currency, had come through a period of intense inflation and deflation and entered a period when there was considerable discussion as to the appropriateness of returning to the gold standard at the prewar parity. In the early postwar period there had been a sharp rise in prices and widespread reductions in hours of work which had not been accompanied by a reduction in the weekly wage nor by an improvement in productivity. And although there was a sharp fall in price after 1920 the increase in labour costs aggravated the performance of the economy even before the return to the gold standard in 1925.

In analyzing the postwar inflation and deflation Keynes took the quantity theory of money for granted. 'This theory', he wrote, 'is fundamental. Its correspondence with fact is not open to question.' But, he went on:

> My exposition follows the general lines of Professor Pigou (*Quarterly Journal of Economics*, November 1917) and of Dr Marshall (*Money, Credit and Commerce*, 1, iv) rather than the perhaps more familiar analysis of Professor Irving Fisher. Instead of starting with the amount of cash held by the public, Professor Fisher begins with the volume of business transacted by means of money and the frequency with which each unit of money changes hands. It comes to the same thing in the end and it

is easy to pass from the above formula to Professor Fisher's; but the above method of approach seems less artificial than Professor Fisher's and nearer to the observed facts.[20]

Keynes took the supply of money to be controlled by the central bank and he wrote his market clearing equation as:

$$n = p\,(k + rk')$$

where n is the number of units of currency in circulation, p is the retail price index, k is the number of consumption units of purchasing power the public wishes to hold as cash, k' is the number of units of purchasing the public wishes to hold as bank deposits against cash and r is the proportion of deposit liabilities that the banks choose to hold as cash reserves.

In his 1917 article Pigou had linked the demand for money to the volume of transactions and income on the assumption that there was a constant ratio of total transactions to total resources and he ignored the question of whether wealth rather than income might be a better proxy for total resources. What Keynes did was to relate both k and k' to real income and the cost of money and linked the demand for money to the inflation rate rather than to the nominal interest rate because the inflation rate measured the opportunity cost of holding money rather than bonds. Thus an increase in the money supply was seen as increasing the velocity of circulation and reducing the real quantity of money:

> During the collapse of the German mark beginning with December 1920, the rate of depreciation proceeded for some time roughly twice as fast as that of inflation, and eventually by June 1923, when the volume of the note issue had increased 200-fold compared with December 1920, the value of a paper mark had fallen 2,500 fold.[21]

Keynes's emphasis upon price stability started from the observation that in the nineteenth century prices were remarkably stable. He then went on to analyze the effects of inflation and deflation upon investors, businessmen and wage earners. He noted that inflation and deflation affected the distribution of wealth as well as its production:

> inflation redistributes wealth in a manner very injurious to the investor, very beneficial to the businessman, and probably, in modern industrial conditions, beneficial on the whole to the wage earner . . . On the other hand deflation . . . is liable in these days of huge national debts expressed in legal-tender money, to overturn the balance so far the other way in the interests of the *rentier*, that the burden of taxation becomes intolerable on the productive classes of the community . . . Thus inflation is unjust and deflation is inexpedient.[22]

In the chapter entitled 'Public finance and the value of money', Keynes analyzed the means by which governments could obtain command over resources by means of currency creation and inflation. Confronted by increases in public debt exceeding possible postwar capacity for taxation, governments would resort to hyperinflation because 'It is the form of taxation which the public finds it hardest to evade and even the weakest government can enforce, when it can enforce nothing else.'[23] The tax, the inflation tax, arose because the rise in prices caused by the increase in the money supply would cause people to increase their real money balances by spending less on goods and services.

Given the incentive for governments to increase the money supply, Keynes went on to consider the effect of inflation on the exchange rate. With national price levels and inconvertible paper currencies the exchange rate was explained in terms of the purchasing power doctrine which had been popularized by Cassell, although Keynes noted that 'the theory as distinct from the name is essentially Ricardo's'.[24] And with the rate of exchange depreciation established as the difference between national inflation rates, he set out a theory of forward exchanges:

> ... forward quotations for the purchase of a currency tend to be cheaper than spot quotations by a percentage per month equal to the excess of the interest which can be earned in a month in the dearer market over what can be earned in the cheaper. It must be noticed that the governing factor is the rate of interest obtainable for short periods, so that a country where owing to the absence or ill-development of an organized money market, it is difficult to lend money satisfactorily at call or for very short periods, may for the purposes of this calculation, reckon as a low-interest earning market, even though the prevailing rate of interest for longer periods is not low at all. This consideration tends to make London and New York more attractive markets for short money than any Continental centres.[25]

He also went on to consider other possible reasons for the deviation of the forward rate from the short-term interest rate differential, for example, risk default.

In his conclusions Keynes proposed that price stability should be preferred to exchange rate stability. If Britain were on a fixed exchange rate then gold inflows and outflows would lead to movements in the domestic price level with attendant repercussions on production and the distribution of wealth even when price movements were anticipated:

> When prices are falling between 30 to 40 per cent between the average of one year and that of the next, as they were in Great Britain and the United States during 1921, even a bank rate of 1 per cent would have been oppressive to business, since it would have corresponded to a very high real rate of interest. Anyone who could have foreseen the movement

even partially would have done well for himself by selling out his assets and staying out of business.[26]

Keynes's policy recommendations were therefore that domestic stability should be achieved by stabilizing the domestic price level and external stability should be achieved by varying the exchange rate.

A Tract on Monetary Reform was reviewed by two members of the LSE: Cannan and Gregory. Cannan's ideas were shaped by the Bullionist Controversy and by what he thought were the parallels which could be drawn between events after the Napoleonic Wars and the events after the First World War. They were also influenced by his views on the creation of credit. Cannan thought that the authorities should attempt to control the amount of cash and not the amount of credit which in terms of his theory of banking was merely a substitute for cash. He therefore laid great stress upon the creation of cash during the First World War and wanted a limitation on the supply of currency which he thought could be achieved by a return to the gold standard at the prewar parity.

Replying to Cannan, Keynes wrote:

> I criticized the old-fashioned policy of looking at the volume of legal tender in circulation as the regulator of the standard of value on two grounds: (1) that by concentrating too much on one factor in the quantity equation to the exclusion of others, it was theoretically unsound; and (2) that used as a *criterion* for compensatory action through the bank-rate or otherwise, it gave the signal too late and was therefore practically inefficient.[27]

He concluded:

> Professor Cannan is unsympathetic with nearly everything worth reading – as it seems to me – which has been written on monetary theory in the last ten years . . . The ideas are new. They are only just beginning to be capable of complete or clear expression. But it is not natural that Professor Cannan should write as though none of this existed, as though his own subject were incapable of development and progress, and as though the last word has been said long ago in elementary textbooks.[28]

The new ideas were that: bank deposits were the main form of money and were loosely linked to the supply of cash; inflation was a tax on money balances and there was a revenue maximizing rate of inflation; and the nominal interest rate differential was the forward premium in the foreign exchange market. In his more appreciative review, Gregory began by saying that 'The temptation to label this article the "Currency Theory of the Cambridge School of Economists" was very great.'[29] In

1926 Robertson in his *Banking Policy and the Price Level* adopted the credit economy as the model for his analysis. And in 1932 Frederic Benham, who was later to become famous in the 1940s and 1950s for his introductory textbook on economics, reviewed *Economic Essays and Addresses* by Pigou and Robertson (1931), and said 'At Cambridge it seems to be thought that wage rates must remain eternally the same, resources forever immobile; at any rate much of this book consists of ingenious discussions of how best to make capitalism work under these conditions.'[30] Unfortunately, wage rates were becoming eternally the same and labour was becoming immobile.

Allyn Young

When Cannan retired he was succeeded by an American, Allyn Young, whose recruitment was assisted by a generous grant from the Rockefeller Foundation. Young had been a member of Woodrow Wilson's delegation to the Peace Conference. He had been sympathetic to the substance of Keynes's *The Economic Consequences of the Peace* (1919) but disliked his portrayal of Wilson. He was not a prolific writer and is chiefly remembered for his critique of Pigou's *Wealth and Welfare* (1912) (Young, 1913) and for his article on 'Increasing returns and economic progress' which was published in the *Economic Journal* in 1928. In *Wealth and Welfare* Pigou had suggested that increasing cost industries should be taxed and the proceeds should be used to subsidize decreasing cost industries with the taxes falling on the rents of the resources in the increasing cost industries. However, Young argued that the rents were a necessary element in the allocation of resources and were determined by the cost of transferring resources at the margin. This point was elaborated by Knight (1924) and by Robbins (1934b). In his article on 'Increasing returns and economic progress' Young developed Adam Smith's thesis that the division of labour was limited by the extent of the market and the ability of entrepreneurs to exploit external economies might give rise to cumulative forces of expansion. Kaldor was later to admit to being strongly influenced by Young in his own theorizing about economic growth and there was a more pervasive influence exerted by the fact that Kaldor attended Young's lectures on value theory and they were to guide him in his initial steps in research.

Unfortunately, Young's tenure at the School was terminated abruptly in 1927 when he died as a result of contracting influenza. In the search for a successor Hugh Dalton, then a reader in economics, was successful in getting Lionel Charles Robbins appointed to the chair.

Lionel Robbins

Robbins's appointment raised a few eyebrows. He was young – a mere 31 years of age. He had published only a few articles. He had been an undergraduate at the School; he had specialized in government and his finals mark in economics was not outstanding. But he had been taught by Cannan and Dalton and after graduation he had been employed by the School's Director, William Beveridge, to update some of the material in Beveridge's book, *Unemployment: a problem of industry*. While devilling for Beveridge he was able to read and absorb much of the existing literature on the causes of unemployment and the trade cycle. In 1926 he was awarded a Fellowship at New College, Oxford and this had the effect of broadening his horizons and bringing him into contact with the historian H.A.L. Fisher, the mathematician G.H. Hardy, the biologist Julian Huxley, and the philosopher H.W.B. Joseph. Yet even while at Oxford Robbins retained his LSE connections and gave a set of lectures on economic thought in the School. Hindsight therefore suggests that Robbins was well placed to succeed to the chair. He was not an obvious theoretical economist – although later in the 1930s he and Beveridge were to clash over the renewal of Hicks's tenure with Robbins being the loser and Hicks having to leave for Cambridge.

The nature and significance of economic science

In his early years Robbins produced some fine theoretical papers and in his later years he devoted his energies to the history of economic thought. But writing before Hicks and Allen had drawn attention to the distinction between income and substitution effects, he suggested that the effect of a wage change upon the supply of labour was ambiguous unless the elasticity of demand for income in terms of effort was known. He produced an interesting article on the effects of changes in hours of work which had a revival in the 1970s when there were suggestions that reductions in hours of work might be a solution to the problem of unemployment. There was also an article on Marshall's concept of the representative firm which argued that it was not necessary for the derivation of supply price. And in the 1920s and 1930s he went on holiday to Vienna, fell in love with the city and was strongly influenced by Mises. And the Austrian influence is noticeable in his monograph *An essay on the Nature and Significance of Economic Science* (1932a).

The essence of *The Nature and Significance of Economic Science* lay in four propositions. First, Robbins argued against the definitions adopted by Cannan, Marshall and the Marxists which ran, respectively, in terms of material wealth, the study of men in the ordinary business of life and the interaction of the social classes. Instead, Robbins proposed scarcity as the organizing principle of economics. 'Economics', he wrote, 'is the science which studies human behaviour as a relationship between ends and scarce means which have alternative uses.'[31] Second, a distinction was drawn between positive and normative propositions, between what is and what ought to be. Economics was considered to be neutral as to desired ends and the concept of economic welfare was thought to be ambiguous because it rested upon interpersonal comparisons of utility. Third, scarcity was defined in relation to demand; economic quantities did not depend upon some absolute scale but upon the quality of scarcity inherent in demand. Valuation was therefore not so much a problem in measurement as a relationship between ends and means; it was an approach designed to get rid of psychological hedonism. Fourth, verification or falsification of economic laws was rejected in favour of apriorism. Significant non-empty economic laws could be based upon postulates (such as scarcity) which were beyond dispute and in no need of testing:

> The propositions of economic theory, like all scientific theory, are obviously deductions from a series of postulates. And the chief of these postulates are assumptions involving in some way simple and indisputable facts of experience relating to the way in which scarcity of goods which is the subject matter of our science actually shows itself in the world of reality. The main postulate of the theory of value is the fact that individuals can arrange their preferences in an order, and in fact, do so. The main postulate of the theory of production is the fact that there is more than one factor of production. The main postulate of the theory of dynamics is the fact that we are not certain regarding future scarcities. These are not the postulates the existence of whose counterpart in reality admits of extensive dispute once their nature is fully realized. We do not need controlled experiments to establish their validity; they are so much the stuff of our everyday experience that they have only to be stated to be recognized as obvious.

To the indisputable facts of experience were added subsidiary postulates such as the state of markets. These marked a concession to the Historical School although Robbins was reluctant to make economics an historical subject. Thus, he cited the example of a price control set below the free market price and leading to excess demand but he also argued that:

> it should not be necessary to spend much time showing that it cannot rest upon an appeal to 'History'. The frequent concommitance of certain phenomena in time may suggest a problem to be solved. It cannot by itself be taken to imply a definite causal relationship.[33]

The Nature and Significance of Economic Science owed something to Hume's distinction between *is* and *ought* and his views on causality, to Weber's views on the notion of *Wertfreiheit*, to Mill's observations on economic generalizations and to the writings of Wickstead and Mises. Indeed its paternity served to underline Robbins's conclusion that his definition did not exclude the views of earlier and contemporary economists but provided a more adequate perspective. Thus the classical economists were interested in economic development and the growth and the causes of the wealth of nations but nature was niggardly and there were constraints upon the ability of men to move resources out of agriculture. Nor could the classical economists' distinction between productive and unproductive labour alter the fact that wages were paid to both sewer men and members of an orchestra. Similarly, the choice between work and leisure was a problem in the allocation of scarce resources irrespective of whether the needs were considered to be economic or non-economic. Economics was therefore concerned with the relationship between ends and limited means irrespective of whether the ends were economic or non-economic. It was a relationship which was not defined by technology except to the extent that techniques of production influenced scarcity. And in making choices individuals were guided by the concept of opportunity cost which was defined as the validation placed upon the highest ranked alternative.

But in presenting his ideas as a synthesis of the views of earlier and contemporary economists, Robbins blurred the distinction between two strands of thought in neoclassical economics. On the one hand, there was the approach, favoured by Jevons, Walras, Pareto, Edgeworth and Marshall, which stressed the attempt to measure economic phenomena; marginal utility may be measured with a measuring rod of money; factors of production are paid according to their marginal products. It is an approach which stresses the subjective nature of economics but it is a passive subjectivity in which human beings are not active, purposive agents but who, once their preference functions are given are led to equilibrium by the calculus. On the other hand, the Austrian tradition, associated with Menger, Böhm-Bawerk and Wieser, emphasized the active subjectivism of people pursuing their own advantage. This blurring of traditions was to have fatal consequences during the socialist debate because it permitted Lange and Lerner to treat the economic problem as one of mere computation – such was the later contention of Hayek.

These two approaches became blurred in Robbins's *The Nature and Significance of Economic Science* because he drew heavily upon Mayer's emphasis upon ends and means with individuals tending to have a clear knowledge of the rank ordering of ends and the means to satisfy those ends. Economics then became a problem of computation. It was this shift in emphasis which may have led Lange and Lerner to view the problem of a socialist economy as essentially the same as that of a capitalist economy; that is to say, both were engaged in problems of computation in which the sets of equations detailing preferences, production possibilities and the prices to be determined were the same. And it was this blurring of the distinctions which Hayek unwittingly accepted when he acquiesced in the Lange–Lerner market model of socialism. It was not until 1937 that Hayek decisively rejected the notion that the 'data' of the economic problem could be taken as given. Furthermore, Robbins's blurring of the distinctions may have also been responsible for the subsequent acceptance in the School of Hutchison's approach which was based upon positivism, and which stressed the testing of theories, even though Robbins seemed to reject many of the ideas advanced by Hutchison. Indeed, the paradox is that, later, Robbins came to admit that he had failed to allow for the possibilities of testing (refutation) along the lines suggested by Popper.

Robbins's approach did, however, mark a significant shift away from the customary stances adopted at the LSE and Cambridge, especially with regard to value judgements. As Cannan observed:

> Benefactors endow chairs of economics, audiences listen to economics lectures, purchasers buy economics books, because they think that understanding economics will make them better off. Is it really necessary for professors of economics to destroy the demand for economics teaching by alleging that they do not know what 'better off' means?[34]

But Robbins did not attempt to deny economists to make value judgements but only that they should not derive such pronouncements from economics. Cannan, in contrast, thought the public assumed that economists were able to make better judgements than laymen. Part of the difficulty lay in the fact that Robbins blurred over the distinction between value judgements and interpersonal comparisons. Robbins assumed that it was not possible to make interpersonal comparisons that were statements of fact. But people do make such comparisons and do regard them as matters of fact.

Robbins's monograph dominated the approach to economics at the LSE until the appearance of Hutchison's *The Significance and Basic Postulates of Economic Theory* which was published in 1938. Hutchison had been an undergraduate at Cambridge and then served as a lecturer at the University of Bonn from 1935 to 1938 where he came under the influence of members of the Vienna Circle and their ideas of positivism. Hutchison therefore took the view that if economics was a science then it must appeal to the facts; it must be tested. But the trouble with most theories was that they were hedged around with *ceteris paribus* clauses which obscured what was to be tested and turned all propositions into tautologies. Later, Robbins was to concede that he had paid insufficient attention to testing and to the ideas of Karl Popper who was to arrive in the School in the 1940s. Hutchison also argued that it was not enough to point to the existence of scarcity. It was necessary to assume that all economic agents attempted to maximize even though they might make mistakes. However, Hutchison's book came too late to exert any influence in the 1930s.

Robbins's views must therefore be contrasted with those prevailing at Cambridge. Marshall and Keynes had accepted the distinction between positive and normative economics. Indeed Marshall had been responsible for making economics a science. But at the beginning of the twentieth century there emerged a preoccupation with poverty, unemployment and the distribution of income. This found its greatest expression in Pigou's *Wealth and Welfare* (1912) which in its second edition was rewritten as *The Economics of Welfare* (1928). Following Marshall, economics became the study of those activities which could be brought under the measuring rod of money with each individual attempting to maximize utility and being guided by a law of diminishing marginal utility whereby successive increments of a good consumed would yield successively diminishing units of utility. At the margin the utility derived from the last unit was measured by the price paid and by subjecting an individual to a process of extortion the total utility from each purchase could be derived. There were, of course, problems and qualifications, such as the utility derived from the first glass of water but given the qualifications it was possible to measure national income and to assume that taking a pound from a rich man and giving it to a poor man would increase economic welfare. It was this conclusion which Robbins denied and which led to a search for rules which would enable economists to pronounce on economic policies which might have distributional implications. The Robbins programme therefore led to the birth of new welfare economics by Kaldor (1939a), Hicks (1939b) and Scitovsky (1941).

Alongside the clash over welfare economics there was another source of conflict between LSE and Cambridge. Robbins's approach to economics assumed that there might be a scarcity of supply but not of demand. In 1932, when *The Nature and Significance of Economic Science* was published the assumption of no scarcity of demand seemed a little difficult to swallow. Hence it was necessary for Robbins and the LSE to deny that there could be a deficiency of aggregate demand, that there could be oversaving or its obverse underconsumption. This particular theme was to lead to the recruitment of Hayek to the LSE by Robbins because Hayek did publish an article on the 'Paradox of saving' – first in German and then in English when it was published in *Economica* (Hayek, 1931a, 1931b). This clash of opinions runs through bitter disputes between Keynes and Robbins in the Macmillan Committee where Keynes was taking the view that protectionist policies might be wanted to eliminate unemployment. Robbins had to reject this argument and also the arguments for an increase in public spending because they would have suggested that his monograph represented an incomplete view of the nature and significance of economics. In the *General Theory* Keynes did accept that there might on occasions, be a scarcity of supply, but in the context of the 1930s he chose to stress that there could be deficiencies of demand which might not be due to monetary mismanagement (as Hayek and Robbins and the Old Guard of the LSE were to stress) but to problems associated with the workings of real forces.

The seminars and lectures: personalities and organization

Robbins's influence extended beyond the confines of his own research. His view of economics exerted a strong influence through his conduct of his staff seminar, lectures on economic principles and the 'tea parties' for members of staff. We have accounts of the seminars from Hayek, Robbins, Coase and Lachmann. There were, in fact, five separate seminars operating in the School in the 1930s. First, there was Robbins's seminar. Second, Hayek ran a separate seminar for his own students which coincided with the fact that many of his lectures and classes were held in the evenings whereas the Robbins seminar was held on a Tuesday afternoon and sometimes on a Thursday afternoon. Third, there was the London Economic Club which included any economists working in London; for example, Hawtrey. Fourth, there was Lerner's seminar which tended to be run in conjunction with the meetings of the executive board of the *Review of Economic Studies*. Finally, there were the seminars which arose out of the meetings of the members of the London and Cambridge bulletin.

We have no copies of the papers given at the Robbins seminar although there is evidence that Robbins did keep copies of the papers which were delivered. When Samuelson published his articles on the factor price equilization theorem in the 1940s, Robbins recalled that a paper on the subject had been presented at his seminar by Lerner. He retrieved a copy from his files and it was published in *Economica* in 1952 (Lerner, 1952). Lerner did not possess a copy and Scitovsky later hazarded a guess that Lerner had lost the copy which he was correcting for publication and was too embarrassed to ask Robbins for his copy.[35] How else can we explain the failure of Lerner to publish the article in *Economica* or in the *Review of Economic Studies* of which he was an editor? However, the Robbins files seemed to have been destroyed after his death and we are left with fragments and anecdotes.

The Robbins seminar was a large one and comprised some thirty or forty people. In addition to the staff there were visitors from University College, such as Gaitskell and Rosenstein Rhodan. There were also foreign visitors: Mises, Haberler and Machlup from Vienna; Viner, Marget and Knight from the United States and Bresciani-Turroni from Italy. A topic might be chosen for a session and sometimes discussions of particular points might extend over several weeks. In his autobiography Robbins recalled with pride some of the advances in knowledge that emanated from the seminars: 'Chapters from Hayek's *Pure Theory of Capital*; Hicks and Allen's *Reconsideration of the Theory of Value*; Plant's *Economics of Patents*; Lerner's *Factor Prices in International Trade*; Kaldor's *Classificatory Note on Equilibrium*; Victor Edelberg's *Ricardian Theory of Profits*.'[36] The seminars were organized by Robbins. In the early years Hayek was a dominant influence; later Kaldor and Lerner became the stars.

There were weekly seminars at Cambridge but the numbers in attendance were much smaller than at the LSE and their importance has tended to be overshadowed (distorted?) by the emphasis placed upon the 'Circus' and the fact that we possess a considerable amount of Keynes's correspondence. But the Circus was not a long-lived affair. It was formed after the publication of the *Treatise on Money* and it was confined to the younger members of the Cambridge School. But because Keynes enjoyed an active life in London many of the discussions of the *Treatise* and the *General Theory*, as well as Robertson's *Banking Policy and the Price Level*, tended to be undertaken through the exchange of letters in which the main participants were Hawtrey, Robertson and Keynes.

Differences in the methods of advancing research depend upon the ideas to be expounded or unravelled, the nature of the individuals engaged in research and the types of organizations which are evolved to expound and propagate ideas. At Cambridge three streams emerged in the Marshallian tradition. First, there was welfare economics as presented by Pigou. Second, there was the theory of the firm as expounded by Joan Robinson. Third, there was the problem of unemployment which was explored by Hawtrey, Robertson and Keynes. Increasingly through the later 1920s and the 1930s the focus of attention became the problem of unemployment and the construction of a short run theory of the economy. The theory did not seem to be capable of setting out in articles but required book-length treatment. Of course, there were articles on particular topics, such as Kahn's treatment of the multiplier, but the problem of unemployment was seen as one requiring book-length treatment — along the lines which Marshall had used in his writings.

There was no Marshallian tradition at the LSE and the *Economic Journal*, the organ of the Royal Economics Society, was under the editorship of Keynes. Robbins had to create a tradition, to differentiate his product and revitalize the School's journal *Economica*. The same problem had been present in Cannan's time but Cannan had been a part-time professor whereas Robbins was a full-time professor with a need to defend his appointment. Now Beveridge had been preoccupied with unemployment but Beveridge was opposed to economic theorists. And because there was no tradition out of which a theoretical interest in unemployment could emerge and because the staff were recruited from diverse sources there was a greater temptation to write articles. After 1931 there was a dominant theorist appointed in Hayek but he became the focus of intense criticism from Cambridge and lacked sufficient support from within the School. Hicks might have been expected to provide such support but he was developing his own ideas within a Paretian–Walrasian framework which was alien to Hayek's Austrian ideas.

Teaching at the LSE was research-led. Hayek regarded Robbins as a brilliant teacher who should have written the textbook of economic principles of his generation because he was aware of the developments in Austria, the United States, Sweden and Cambridge. He tried twice but circumstances caused postponements — at the beginning of the Second

Table 2.3 Session 1934–5. General Principles of Economic Analysis. Professor Robbins.

Twenty-eight lectures. Sessional. Michaelmas and Lent Terms. Wednesdays, 10.00–11.00; Summer Term, Wednesdays, 12.00–1.00, beginning M.T. 10 October, L.T. 16 January, S.T. 1 May.
or (e) Mondays, 7.00–8.00, beginning M.T. 8 October, L.T. 14 January, S.T. 29 April.
For B.Sc. (Econ) and B.Com. 1st year Final, and Academic Diploma in Public Administration. Recommended also for postgraduate students.
Fees: Day: £4 4s; Terminal, M.T. or L.T. £1 16s; S.T. £1 10s.
     Evening: £2 16s; Terminal, M.T. £1 4s; S.T. £1.

SYLLABUS: A. **Introduction**: The nature of economic phenomena. Economic goods and their classification. Types of economic analysis.
B. **General outline of equilibrium analysis**:
1. *Exchange equilibrium*: The utility theory of value and the theory of choice. Simple exchange. Multiple exchange.
2. *Equilibrium of production*: Simple production. The labour theory of value and the fundamental law of cost. Joint production. The idea of marginal productivity and its place in the general conception of price equilibrium. Supply of labourers and the iron law of wages. Supply of labour from given labourers and the concept of elasticity of effort demand. The nature of capital. Direct and indirect production. Interest theories. The relationship between rent and interest. The 'time–structure' of production.

(*continued*)

Table 2.3 (Continued)

3. *General view of economic equilibrium*: Inter-spatial and Inter-temporal price relationships.
C. **Analysis of variations**: Costs and variations. Hours of labour. Population. Taxation. Invention. Money and interest.
   The treatment will be non-mathematical in character. Students who wish to witness the same problems treated mathematically should attend course No. 66 (Introduction to Mathematical Economics).
   BOOKS RECOMMENDED: A. **Historical classics**: Quesnay, *Works*, ed. Oncken; *Tableau Economique*; Turgot, *Reflections sur la Formation et Distribution de la Richesse*; Hume, *Essays Moral Political and Literary*; *Adam Smith, *Wealth of Nations*; *Malthus, *An Essay on Population*; *Ricardo, *Influence of a Low Price of Corn on the Profits of Stock*; *Principles of Political Economy*; Bailey, *A Critical Dissertation on Value*; Senior, *Political Economy*; *Three Lectures on the Cost of Obtaining Money*; Longfield, *Lectures on Political Economy*; J.S. Mill, *Principles of Political Economy*; Jevons, *Theory of Political Economy*; Menger, *Grundsätze der Volkwirtschaftslehre*; Walras, *Elements d'Économie Politique Pure*.
   B. **Modern works in general theory**: Marshall, **Principles of Economics*; **Pigou, *Economics of Welfare*; *Industrial Fluctuations*; Cannan, *A Review of Economic Theory*; **Wicksteed, *The Commonsense of Political Economy*; Böhm-Bawerk, *Kapital und Kapitalismus* (Vierte Auflage) *English Translation of the First Edition by Smart; Gesammeite Schriften (especially *Mecht oder okonomisches Gesetz*); Schumpeter, *Theorie der wirtschaftlichen Entwicklung*; Mises, *Theory of Money and Credit*; *Die Gemeinwirtschaft*; J.B. Clark, *Distribution of Wealth*; Taussig, *Wages and Capital*; Davenport, *Economics of Enterprise*; Fetter, *Economic Principles*; Carver, *The Distribution of Wealth*; Fisher, *The Nature of Capital and Income*; *The Theory of Interest*; **Knight, *Risk, Uncertainty and Profit*; Pareto, *Manuel d'Economie Politique*; Pantaleoni, *Pure Economics*; Barone, *Grundzuge der theoretischen Nationalokonomie*; **Wicksell, *Lectures on Political Economy*; Cassell, *Theory of Social Economy*; Robbins, *An Essay on the Nature and Significance of Economic Science*; *Robinson, *Economics of Imperfect Competition*.
   C. SPECIAL STUDIES: Cuhel, *Zur Lehre der Bedurfnissen*; Schonfeld, *Grensnutzen und Wirtshafts-rechnung*; Rosenstein-Rodan, *Grensnutzen* (art. in *Handworterbuch fur Staatswissenschaft*, 4th Auflage); Mayer, *Untersuchungen zu dem Grundgesetz der Wirtschaftlichen Wertrechnung* (Zeitschrift fur Volkswirtschaft und Sozialpolitik, N.F.Bde. I and II); 'Produktion' (article in *Handworterbuch fur Staatswissenschaft*); Schultz, *The Statistical Laws of Supply and Demand*; J.M. Clark, *Economics of Overhead Costs*; Young, 'Increasing returns and economic progress' (*Economic Journal*, 1928); Sraffa, 'The laws of returns under competitive conditions' (*Economic Journal*, 1926); Robbins, 'The representative firm' (*Economic Journal*, 1928); The conception of stationary equilibrium' (*Economic Journal*, 1930); 'Remarks on the theory of costs' (*Economic Journal*, 1934); Robertson, Sraffa and Shove, 'Increasing returns and the representative firm' (*Economic Journal*, 1930); Viner, *Cost Curves and Supply Curves* (Zeitschrift fur Nationalokonomie Bd. III. p. 23 et seq.); Schumpeter, 'Das Grundprinzip der Vertezlungtheorie' (*Archiv fur Sozialwissenschaft*, 1916); Robertson, *Wage Grumbles* (Essay in Economic Fragments); Valk, *Theory of Wages*; Landry, A., *L'Interet du Capital*; Fetter, *Relation between Rent and Interest*; Opie, 'Die Lehre von Quasi-Rent' (*Archiv fur Sozialwissenschaft*, 1929); O'Brien, 'Notes on the theory of profit' (*Economica*, 1931); Hicks, 'The theory of profit', (*Economica*, 1931); *The Theory of Wages*; Hicks and Allen, *A Reconsideration of the* 'Theory of value' (*Economica*, February 1934); Hutt, *The Theory of Collective Bargaining*; Robertson, *Banking Policy and the Price Level*; *Money*; Schumpeter, 'Das Sozialprodukt und die Rechenpfennige' (*Archiv fur Sozialwissenschaft*, vol. 44); Mises, *Theorie des Geldes*; *Geldwetstabilisierung und Konjunkturpolitik*; Hayek, *Prices and Production*; *Monetary Theory and the Trade Cycle*; *Das intertemporale Gleichgewichtsystem der Preise und die Bewung der 'Geldwetes'* (Weltwirtschaftliches Archiv, 1929); Edgeworth, *Papers Relating to Political Economy*.
   Books marked with an asterisk (*) may be regarded as having the first claim on students not taking Economics as a special honours subject. Those marked with a double asterisk (**) are indispensable to the attainment of the minimum standard in the final examinations.

Source: LSE *Calendar* 1934–5.

The seminars and lectures 33

World War and at the time of the Robbins Enquiry into Higher Education. Unfortunately there appear to be no extant copies of his lecture notes. But we do have some insights. First, there are the synopses of his lectures and reading lists printed in the School's calendars which reveal a wide sweep of the literature (Tables 2.3, 2.4 and 2.5). He would begin with Chapter 1 of Knight's *Risk, Uncertainty and Profit* and then move on to consider partial and general equilibrium analysis. From his review

Table 2.4 Session 1934–5. Disputed Problems in the Methodology of Economics. Professor Robbins.

Four lectures, Summer Term. Wednesdays, 5.00–6.00, beginning S.T. 22 May.
Fee: 10s.
For postgraduate students and optional for B.Sc. (Econ) Final – Special subject of Economics.

SYLLABUS: This course will assume a knowledge of the generally accepted principles of economic methodology and will be confined to a discussion of outstanding points of controversy. Among the subjects to be discussed will be: the relation between Economics and Sociology; the meaning of the term 'rational' in relation to behaviour with an economic aspect; the alleged deficiencies of a 'wertfrei' analysis; the methodological discussions aroused by the publication of Sombart's *Drei Nationalökonomien*.

BOOKS RECOMMENDED: Menger, *Untersuchungen über die Methode*; Lifschitz, *Die historishe Schule der Wirtschaftwissenschaft*; Knies, *Politische Okonomie*; Cliff Leslie, *Essays*; Mises, *Grundproblem der Nationalokonomie*; Knight, 'Ethics and the economic interpretation' (*Quarterly Journal of Economics*, 1922); 'Fact and metaphysics in economic psychology' (*American Economic Review*, 1925); Kaufmann, 'Was kann die mathematische Methode in der nationalokonomie liesten' (*Zeitschrift fur Nationalokonomie*, 1931); Morganstern, *Wirtschaftsprognose Bemerkungen uber die Problematik der Amerikanischen Institutionalisten*; Haberler, *Der Sinn des Indexzalen*; Keynes, *A Treatise on Money* (Vol. I, Bk. II); Martha Stephanie Braun, *Theorie der staatlichen Wirtschaftpolitik*; Max Weber, *Gesammeite Aufsatze zue Wissenschaftslehre*; Strigl, *Die Ökonomischen Kategorien*; Rickert, *Kulturwissenschaft und Naturwissenschaft*; Robbins, *An Essay on the Nature and Significance of Economic Science*.

Source: LSE *Calendar* 1934–5.

Table 2.5 Session 1938–9. General principles of Economic Analysis. Professor Robbins.

Thirty-five lectures. Sessional, Wednesdays, 10.00–11.00; and Michaelmas Term, Tuesdays, 10.00–11.00 beginning M.T. 4 October, L.T. 11 January, S.T. 26 April.
or (e) Sessional, Mondays, 7.00–8.00; and Michaelmas Term, Thursdays, 7–8, beginning M.T. 3 October, L.T. 9 January, S.T. 24 April.
or B.Sc. (Econ) B.Com. 1st year Final and B.A. General and Academic Diploma in Public Administration. Recommended also for postgraduate students.
Fees: Day: £5 5s; Terminal, M.T., £3 12s; L.T., £1 16s; S.T., 18s.
 Evening: £3 10s; Terminal, M.T., £2 8s; L.T., £1 4s; S.T., 12s.

SYLLABUS: The course will cover the main principles of economic analysis. As a rule the different branches of theory will be treated positively. But where the history of earlier developments has

(*continued*)

Table 2.5 (*Continued*)

significance for the understanding of modern thought a comparative method will be adopted. The following synopsis indicates roughly the ground which the course is intended to cover. The treatment, however, will be designed to supplement the gaps in the more easily accessible literature rather than to provide a complete systematic whole; and it is improbable that all parts of the syllabus will be treated in equal detail. The synopsis, therefore, should be regarded rather as some indication of the main parts of the subject with which students should be familiar rather than as an exact outline of the content of the lectures.

BOOKS RECOMMENDED: (It is assumed that students will have read Benham's *Economics* and Wicksteed's *Commonsense of Political Economy* (Vol. I) before taking the intermediate examination or immediately after.)

The ground covered by the source is roughly the same as that covered in Knight's *Risk, Uncertainty and Profit*. But to understand this work much preliminary reading is necessary, and there are many matters on which its treatment needs supplementing. All students preparing for the final examination should read Marshall's *Principles*, Wicksell's *Lectures on Political Economy*, Vol. I, and Pigou's *Economics of Welfare*. The following works will also be found useful in connection with this and the closely related courses obligatory for non-specialist students: Hicks, *The Theory of Wages*; Robinson, *The Economics of Imperfect Competition* (omitting the sections marked as especially technical); Mises, *The Theory of Money and Credit*; Haberler, *The Theory of International Trade*; Robbins, *The Nature of Significance of Economic Science* (2nd edn); Schumpeter, *Epochen der Dogmnen und Methodengesechicte*.

Students who have mastered these works and who wish to proceed to more intensive study of special subjects treated in the lectures may consult some of the following:

A. **Introduction**: Cairnes, *The Character and Logical Method of Political Economy*; Mises, *Grundproblem der Nationalökonomie*; Menger, *Grundsätze der Volkwirtschaftslehre, Untersuchungen u. d. Methode*.

B. **Statics**: 1. *The Theory of Valuation and Exchange*: Bailey, *A Critical Dissertation on Value*; Hicks and Allen, 'A reconsideration of the theory of value' (*Economica*, N.S. 1); Edgeworth, *Mathematical Psychics*; Pareto, *Manuel d'Économie Politique* (chapters III–VII); Marshall, *The Pure Theory of Foreign and Domestic Values*.

2. *Theory of Production and Distribution*:

(a) *Acapitalistic Production*: Ricardo, *Principles of Political Economy*; Böhm-Bawerk, *Karl Marx and the Close of his System*; Senior, *On the Cost of Obtaining Money*; Taussig, 'Wages and prices in international trade' (*Quarterly Journal of Economics*, 1906); Lerner, 'The diagrammatic representation of cost conditions in international trade (*Economica*, 1932); 'The diagrammatic representation of demand conditions in international trade' (*Economica*, 1934); Schneider, *Theorie der Produktion*; Williams, 'Suggestions for constructing a model of a production function' (*Review of Economic Studies*, Vol. I); Jacob Viner, *Costs Curves and Supply Curves* (Zeitschrift fur Nationalokonomie, Bd. III); Chamberlin, *The Theory of Monopolistic Competition*; Hicks, 'The theory of monopoly' (*Econometrica*, Vol. III).

(b) *Capitalistic production*: Fisher, *The Theory of Interest*; Taussig, *Wages and Capital*; Böhm-Bawerk, *Kapital und Kapitalzins*; Hayek, *Prices and Production*; 'The relationship between investment and output' (*Economic Journal*, 1934); Fetter, *The Relation between Rent and Interest*.

C. **Comparative statics**: Ricardo, *Principles of Political Economy*; (especially the chapters on taxation); Robinson, *Economics of Imperfect*; Robbins, 'On the economic effects of variations of hours of labour' (*Economic Journal*, 1929); Lerner, 'The elasticity of substitution' (*Review of Economic Studies*, Vol. I); Benham, 'Taxation and the relative prices of the factors of production' (*Economica*, Vol. II, N.S.); Hicks, 'Distribution and economic progress' (*Review of Economic Studies*, 1936).

D. **Dynamics**: Hicks, 'The theory of uncertainty and profit' (*Economica*, 1931); Rosenstein Rodan, 'The role of time in economic theory' (*Economica*, Vol. I, N.S.); Kaldor, 'A classificatory note on the determinateness of equilibrium' (*Review of Economic Studies*, Vol. I); Lavington, *The English Capital Market*; Hayek, *Monetary Theory and the Trade Cycle*; Pigou, *Industrial Fluctuations*; Haberler, *Prosperity and Depression*; Hicks, 'Gleichgewicht und Konjunktur' (Zeitschrift fur Nationalokonomie, Bd.IV); '*Mr Keynes and the "Classics"*: a suggested interpretation' (*Econometrica*, Vol. 3).

Source: LSE *Calendar* 1938–9.

of Schumpeter's *A History of Economic Analysis* (Schumpeter, 1954) we know that he would have placed Marshall higher than Walras. We also have his analyses of the Classical economists. He would not, perhaps, have matched Schumpeter's grasp of preclassical thought, nor his grasp of European and American literature, but it would have been a book worth possessing.

Summary and conclusions

Economics at the LSE was dominated in the 1920s by Cannan and in the 1930s by Robbins. Cannan adopted a commonsense approach to economics and was a vigorous advocate of the quantity theory. However, he did put forward a distinct and wrong view of banking which led him into difficulties in the debates about monetary theory and policy in the 1920s. He also favoured a return to the gold standard at the prewar parity. In contrast, Robbins was less insular and created a distinct research programme at the LSE out of which came the classics, such as *Value and Capital* (Hicks, 1939a). There was also a much more noticeable break with Cambridge which was dictated by his view of the nature and significance of economics.

Notes

1. The early history of the LSE is dealt with in Harris (1977) and Hayek (1946). Ralf Dahrendorf is producing a history of the School to mark its centenary in 1995. There is a symposium dealing with the economics departments in the interwar years in *The Atlantic Economic Review* (1983). The interactions of economics and economic history are traced out in Koot (1987), Collini (1983) and Kadish (1989).
2. Webb, S. (1932), *Documents relating to the early history of the LSE*, LSE archives.
3. Hewins, W.S. (1900), *Correspondence and papers of W.S. Hewins*, Sheffield University.
4. op. cit. (1902).
5. Coase, R.H. (1976). 'Marshall on method', *Journal of Law and Economics*, XVII: 25–32.
6. Marshall, A. (1924), *Principles of Economics* (8th edn), London: Macmillan, p. 641.
7. op. cit., p. 772.
8. Robbins, L.C. (1971), *Autobiography of an Economist*, London: Macmillan, p. 78.
9. Cannan, E. (1933), 'The need for simpler economics', *Economic Journal*, 43: 367.
10. op. cit., p. 378.

11. Cannan, E. (1924a), '"Total utility" and "consumer surplus"', *Economica*, 4: 22.
12. Quoted by Gregory in Gregory, T. and Dalton H. (1927), *London Essays in Economics*, London: Routledge.
13. Robertson, D.H. (1957), *Lectures on Economic Principles*, London: Fontana.
14. Keynes, J.M. (1923, 1971), *The Collected Writings of John Maynard Keynes*, Vol. IV, *A Tract on Monetary Reform*, London: Macmillan, pp. 42–3.
15. *Report of the Committee on Finance and Industry*, Cmnd 3897, London: HMSO, pp. 155–6.
16. Keynes, J.M. (1911), 'Review of Irving Fisher *Purchasing Power of Money*', *Economic Journal*, XXI: 393.
17. Eshag, E. (1963), *From Marshall to Keynes*, Oxford: Blackwell, p. xiii.
18. Hicks, J.R. (1967b), *Critical Essays in Monetary Theory*, Oxford, Clarendon p. 157.
19. Pigou, A.C. (1917), 'Value of money', *Quarterly Journal of Economics*, 32: 54.
20. Keynes, J.M. (1923, 1971), *A Tract on Monetary Reform*, p. 24.
21. op. cit., p. 30.
22. op. cit., p. 36.
23. op. cit., p. 37.
24. op. cit., p. 71 fnl.
25. op. cit., pp. 103–04.
26. op. cit., p. 23.
27. Keynes, J.M. (1925), 'Comment on Professor Cannan's article', *Economic Journal*, 34: 68. Reprinted in Vol. XI of *Collected Writings*, pp. 372–5.
28. op. cit., p. 67.
29. Gregory, T.E. (1924), 'Recent theories of currency reform', *Economica*, 4: 163.
30. Benham, F.C. (1932), 'Review of Pigou and Robertson, *Economic Essays and Addresses*', *Economica*, 12: 229.
31. Robbins, L.C. (1932), *An Essay on the Nature and Significance of Economic Science*, London: Macmillan, p. 16.
32. op. cit., pp. 78–9.
33. op. cit., p. 73.
34. Cannan, E. (1932a), 'Review of Robbins *The Nature and Significance of Economic Science*', *Economic Journal*, 42: 426.
35. Scitovsky, T. (1980s), in *Conversations with LSE Economists in the early 1980s*, conducted by N. Shehadi, London: LSE archives.
36. Robbins, L.C. (1971), *Autobiography of an Economist*, pp. 131–2.

3
Prices and production

Introduction

Friedrich August von Hayek was born in Vienna on 8 May 1899 and into a family which seemed to exude the importance of the heredity principle. His paternal grandfather was a zoologist and a Darwinian who taught at the University of Vienna. His maternal grandfather taught law at the University of Innsbruck and was a colleague and climbing companion of the distinguished economist, Böhm-Bawerk. His father was by profession a doctor but, by inclination, a botanist. Although he became a visiting or representative professor, he always had a hankering to be a full-time professor. Years later Hayek recalled that he grew up in a household in which to become a professor was the sum of achievement and he assumed that his determination to become a university professor stemmed from his father's unsatisfied ambition. Hayek also had one brother who became a professor of anatomy at Vienna and another who taught chemistry at Innsbruck. Later he was to have a son who became a doctor and a daughter who became an entomologist.

Hayek was brought up as a Catholic and, although he had one grandmother who was interested in the ritual, it was a relaxed Catholicism which surmounted the problems posed by nineteenth-century science. Later he was to marry, divorce and remarry but he has always considered himself to be a Catholic – a Catholic non-pratiquant. Despite growing up in Vienna, Hayek rejected Freud's ideas. To Hayek repressions are a civilizing influence and are not to be abandoned lightly. He has always accepted the great truths expressed by the major religions and has not cast them into the class of myths which are to be contrasted with refutable scientific propositions. Religions are complex phenomena which do not admit of simple analysis. However, he has in his later years expressed a distaste for the Western monotheistic religions, with their sharp distinctions between orthodox and heterodox, and has looked with favour upon the Japanese way of life which permits a person to be born and married a Shintoist but to be buried a Buddhist.

At the age of 10 or 11 Hayek's father gave him a book on genetics and until the age of 15 he was immersed in biology, especially evolution but not taxonomy. Later he became interested in psychology and psychiatry. However, preferences became constrained by opportunities. Jobs in psychology were scarce and even a full-time academic career was not possible. During the First World War he served on the Italian front and managed to further his education by attending army classes on philosophy. He also managed to obtain his gymnasium degree while on active service. And on the basis of his educational qualifications and his veteran's privileges he enrolled for a law degree at Vienna. Because he entered as a veteran his course was foreshortened and he did the second part in a rush. Consequently, he acquired a considerable knowledge of legal history but little knowledge of modern law. However, this uneven exposure to law did serve to awaken an interest in the evolution of rules and institutions and it was strengthened by reading Dicey, Vinogradoff and Maitland. Years later, in the 1940s, he contemplated becoming a barrister. But studying law was a sideline – a passport to a meal ticket – and he spent most of his time reading psychology and economics. His interest in economics seems to have been sparked off by the social turbulence around the turn of the century. He became a social democrat, an Austrian Fabian Socialist. He was influenced by Walter Rathenau, an industrialist and a minister, who sought to reorganize industry by an admixture of planning and markets. Studying economics, however, brought him into contact with the Austrian School of Economics which had at its core marginal utility analysis. At Vienna he was exposed to that strand of Austrian economics which descended from Menger through Wieser to Mayer and Spann.

Friedrich Wieser was an immediate pupil of Menger and a brother-in-law of Böhm-Bawerk. He had been a minister but had returned to academic life and, according to Hayek, acted as his godfather. From Wieser he got a grounding in marginal utility analysis and the theory of imputation. Hayek was also taught by Hans Mayer whom he was later to describe as a bad neurotic, but Mayer also expounded marginal utility analysis and had an influence upon Robbins. Finally, there was Othmar Spann who held a chair of economics and psychology. Hayek concluded that he had a curious mind. Spann's *History of Economics* (1912) attempted to distinguish two strands in the development of economic thought: one was romantic and organic and was to be found in the writings of Müller, Fichte, List, Thunen, Carlyle, Ruskin and Carey, and the other which stressed individualism was to be found in the works of Smith, Ricardo, Say, Menger and Jevons. But for Hayek, Spann's importance lay in the fact that he recommended him to read Menger's *Grundsätze* (1923) which was the first book to give him the idea of a theoretical approach to economic problems. Menger's writings may also have insulated him from the general equilibrium analysis of Walras and Pareto. Menger's examples of markets tend not to be purely competitive but abound in problems of bilateral monopoly and imperfect competition. As such the approach emphasized the approach to equilibrium rather than its attainment. From Menger Hayek also got the idea of spontaneous co-ordination.

The University of Vienna gave Hayek a grounding in law, economics and psychology. It also gave him access to some of the most brilliant minds in Europe. There was no obligation to attend lectures nor were there any written assignments. Examinations were oral and conducted at the end of the session. Consequently the relaxed atmosphere meant that it was possible to attend a lecture in law followed by one in history and then go on to one on literature. Discussions groups abounded. They met in the coffee houses and when economic conditions worsened they would meet in houses and in the offices of bankers and industrialists. In 1921 Hayek founded a discussion group called the *Geistkreisse*. It contained the economists Haberler, Machlup and Rosenstein Rhodan, the mathematician Karl Menger, the industrialist Furth as well as Kaufmann, Voegelin, Schutz and Overhoff. Hayek read a paper on psychology which contained ideas that he later developed in his book *The Sensory Order* (1952b). He also read a paper on rent control. Kaufmann, who had been brought in from Schlick's Vienna Circle, read papers on entropy and topology. Voegelin read a paper on Rembrandt and Schutz read one on phenomenology. And there were other discussion groups to which Hayek had an entrée. The Wittgensteins, to whom Hayek was related, had a grand musical salon. But the most famous group was the Vienna Circle of Mach, Schlick and Neurath which espoused positivism and to which Hayek was initially attracted by its attacks on the Marxists and Freudians. He met Schrödinger the physicist, and he was introduced to Popper by Haberler. He was also present when Popper launched his attack on positivism.

The intellectual bonds which Hayek forged in that period were retained in later years and served to colour his outlook. He left Vienna in 1931 and many other intellectuals left in the late 1930s. Subsequently, they were to meet either in England or in the United States. Rosenstein Rhodan went to University College, London, Haberler, Machlup and Morganstern went to the United States but they all wrote articles in

Economica. Schumpeter was an early migrant; first to Switzerland and then to the United States. Jacob Marschak was at the Oxford University Institute of Statistics before going to America. Schrödinger went to Dublin. Namier went to Manchester. At LSE there were Kaldor, Scitovsky and Lachmann.

In 1921 Hayek obtained his degree in law, *dr Juris*, and decided to stay on and read for a doctorate in political science which he obtained in 1923. After graduating he got a job in the reparations office which sought to resolve private debts which had been frozen during the First World War and had subsequently had their values affected by exchange rate fluctuations. While at the reparations office he chanced to meet Jeremiah Jenks, the President of the Alexander Hamilton Institute, New York. Jenks had written a book on trusts and was proposing to write one on Central Europe. Hayek convinced him of his desire to go to America in order to further his understanding of economics. Jenks made him a tentative offer of a research assistantship. In 1932 Hayek left Vienna for the United States with twenty-five dollars in his pocket and letters of introduction from Schumpeter. Unfortunately, when he landed in New York he discovered that Jenks had gone on his vacation and had left strict instructions that he was not to be contacted. The twenty-five dollars were quickly spent and the letters of introduction did not get him a job although they did get him some free lunches. He was just on the point of accepting a job as a dishwasher in a New York restaurant when Jenks returned. Jenks then set him to work in the New York Public Library.

Hayek was fortunate to find a seat at the same table as Frederick Macauley, Willard Thorp and Baggott Beckhart who were all members of the National Bureau of Economic Research. From them he learned about time series analysis and his studies were amplified by attendance at Wesley Clair Mitchell's lectures at Columbia University. He also read a paper at J.B. Clark's last seminar. For Hayek it was an exciting period. It coincided with an intense discussion of monetary policy and the trade cycle. There was a belief that the Federal Reserve Board had managed to eliminate the cycle and Beckhart was writing a book on the Board's discount policy and Hayek registered for a Ph.D. at New York University on the subject 'Is the stabilization of the value of money compatible with the functions of money?' It was never completed. But he did note that US monetary policy seemed to lead to an expansion of the capital goods industries and this was to be the germ of his monetary overinvestment theory. And at the same time he was preparing a volume on money for the *Grundrisse der Sozialökonomie* (Encyclopedia of Social Sciences) and writing the sections on Germany and Austria for Thorp's business annals.

On his return to Vienna he received from Wieser a letter of introduction to Mises. In the letter Wieser stated that Hayek was a promising student. Mises's retort was that he had never observed him at his seminars. Thus, did Hayek encounter the second strand of the Austrian School of Economics which descended from Menger via Böhm-Bawerk to Mises. At Mises's seminar, which was a private seminar, sat the shade of Böhm-Bawerk. But to understand fully the effect of Mises upon Hayek it is essential to consider the economic, political and social history of the Austro-Hungarian Empire and its disintegration after the First World War.

In the 1860s a liberal constitutional order emerged in the Austro-Hungarian Empire based upon a rising commercial class of bankers, merchants and manufacturers whose social and ethnic origins were located among the urban middle-class Germans and Jews. This group challenged the upper class but in the last quarter of the nineteenth century it was challenged, in turn, by a coalition of the upper and lower classes. According to Schorske, in his brilliant study of *fin de siècle* Vienna:

> The Catholics routed from the school and courthouse as the handmaiden of aristocratic oppression, returned as the ideology of the peasant and artisan for whom liberalism meant capitalism, and capitalism meant Jew. *Laisser faire* addressed to free the economy from the fetters of the past called forth the Marxist revolutionaries of the future.[1]

Despite the efforts of the Emperor Franz Joseph and the Catholic hierarchy, Karl Leguger, the anti-capitalist leader of the Christian Social party, was elected Mayor of Vienna. Leguger sought to represent the interests of the petty bourgeoisie and he was opposed to the free thinking, well educated middle-class Jewish capitalists and the doctrine of Manchesterismus. At the centre of the Empire Vienna attracted a large number of Jews. In 1860 there were 6,000; by 1918 there were 200,000. They were loyal members of the Empire. Finally, there was the Austrian Social Democratic Party which was founded in 1898 and which had its power base in the urban working class and its ideological base in Marx and Lasalle.

In 1907 the Social Democratic Party organized a massive demonstration which resulted in the granting of universal suffrage. The event impressed itself on Mises. 'Vienna was completely paralysed', he wrote in his memoirs, 'and 250,000 workers marched on the Ringstrasse, past Parliament in military fashion in rows of eight, under the leadership of the Party officials.'[2] The outcome of the first election under universal suffrage was that the Social Democrats won 83 out of 516 seats. However, the socialist threat was deemed to be less severe than the nationalist stirrings among the Czechs and the Slovenes, whose demands could not be met by universal suffrage.

In 1918 the First World War ended and the Austro-Hungarian Empire disintegrated. Trieste, Istria and the Tyrol up to the Brenner Pass were ceded to Italy. Bohemia, Moravia and Austrian Silesia as well as parts of lower Austria were handed over to Czechoslovakia. Bukovina was granted to Romania. Bosnia, Herzogovina and Dalmatia were transferred to a newly formed Yugoslavia. Some three million Magyars found themselves under Romanian rule and everywhere there were sizeable ethnic minority groups. *Anschluss* (union) with Germany was forbidden. The result was a highly unstable economy shorn of its industrial resources which now lay in other countries. Vienna became the enlarged capital of this tiny country and it was swollen by an influx of army officers and civil servants from the former provinces. The oversized capital became the power base of the Social Democrats while the Alpine provinces were mainly Catholic and regarded the capital as communist and infected by Jews. Influenced by the success of the Russian Revolution, the Hungarians, under Bela Kuhn, attempted to establish a red republic but it was short lived and put down with outside assistance. In Austria the Social Democrats, with 48 per cent of the vote, were forced to form a coalition with the Christian Socials but this did not prevent the introduction of a nationalization programme which had the qualified support of Schumpeter who was, for a brief period, the minister of finance. However, Schumpeter lost the battle for a capital levy and resigned.

The War had been financed, as in most of the belligerents, by printing money. In the immediate postwar period the increased money supply met a greatly diminished flow of goods and services and this latter was reduced to a trickle by the magnitude of the reparations bill. Inflation was rampant (Table 3.1) and poverty endemic. In his *A Revision of the Treaty* (1922), Keynes wrote:

> Austria's problems are well known and attract a general sympathy. The Viennese were not made for tragedy; the world feels that and there is none so bitter as to wish ill to the city of Mozart. Vienna has been the capital of degenerate greatness but, released from imperial temptations, she is now free to fulfil her true role of providing for a quarter-part of Europe the capital of commerce and arts. Somehow she has laughed and cried her way through the last two years; and now, I think, though on the surface her plight is more desperate than before, a very little help will be enough. She has no army, and by virtue of the depreciation of her money a trifling internal debt. Too much help may make her a lifelong beggar; but a little will raise her from despondency and render her financial problem no longer beyond solution.[3]

Table 3.1 Austria: Economic indicators.

GNP at constant (1937) prices: 1913 and 1920–9			
1913	10.80		
1920	7.17	1925	10.21
1921	7.94	1926	10.35
1922	8.66	1927	10.70
1923	8.56	1928	11.19
1924	9.57	1929	11.36
Cost of living indices, 1914–29			
1914	90	1922	237,568
1915	142	1923	68
1916	303	1924	77
1917	605	1925	87
1918	1,047	1926	93
1919	2,243	1927	95
1920	4,604	1928	97
1921	8.984	1929	100

Source: B.R. Mitchell (1957) *European Historical Statistics*.

In 1922 the coalition broke down, the nationalization programme was abated and the currency was stabilized with the aid of a League of Nations conditional aid programme which required severe monetary and fiscal restraint. This then was the context in which Mises conducted his seminar. He railed against government, against socialism, against inflation, against trade unions and he introduced into the thought of the Austrian School a greater emphasis upon individualism.

Had Hayek not been a graduate of some experience, he might have succumbed too readily to Mises's ideas. Certainly, he was influenced by an article on economic calculation which Mises had written in 1919 and his democratic idealism was questioned by Mises's book on socialism. But his initial reactions were hostile. He was convinced that the book was an exaggerated polemic. And although he could accept some of his conclusions, he could not accept his underlying reasoning. The difference in approaches stemmed from the fact that Mises relied heavily upon a priori arguments – a procedure which he communicated to Robbins. In contrast, Hayek accepted an a priori logical approach for the individual but insisted on empirical evidence on the workings of markets because it was necessary to study the interactions of individuals. In effect, Mises followed Bentham. Bentham assumed that because institutions were found to be useful they must have been deliberately designed. But Hayek took the view that institutions were the product of an evolutionary process whose outcome could not be predicted. Yet despite the differences of opinion, Hayek considered that they got on well together. Mises helped Hayek found the Austrian Institute of Business Cycle Research and became one of its vice-presidents. And among the articles which Hayek wrote when he was the director was one which predicted the American crash of 1929.

In addition to his work at the Institute, Hayek gave lectures at the University and his lecture fees were used to pay his taxi fares from the Institute. In 1929 he presented his 'Habilitation' lecture which was entitled '*Geldtheorie und Konjunkturtheorie*' and it was later translated by Nicholas Kaldor and Honor Croome as *Monetary Theory and Trade Cycle Theory* (1933). In order to obtain his licence to lecture (*Privatdozent*) he was required to give a test lecture and he chose as his title 'the paradox of savings'. The substance of this lecture was a critique of underconsumptionist theories and it was this lecture that attracted the attention of Robbins. Robbins invited him to lecture at the LSE. Years later Hayek recalled that as an undergraduate he had dreamt of becoming a professor of economics at the LSE which he considered to be the centre of economics. In 1931 he left Vienna and was appointed to a chair at the LSE. A casualty of his move was the projected book on money. The publisher asked to be released from the contract because he had gone to England. But the time and effort involved in the research were not wasted because they provided him with the intimate knowledge of nineteenth-century monetary theory which formed the substance of his first lecture on 'Prices and production' that he delivered in the LSE in January, 1931.

The London School of Economics

With the arrival of Hayek the LSE took on a more cosmopolitan air and the economics syllabuses, as printed in the School's calendars were replete with articles in German, French and Italian (Tables 3.2, 3.3 and 3.4). There were however elements of continuity. In the late 1920s Gregory had taken students to Vienna in order to allow them to listen to Mises. Robbins was a former student of Cannan's and both Robbins and Hayek shared Cannan's interest in the history of economic thought. In an extremely appreciative obituary notice on Cannan, Hayek drew attention to the affinities between passages in Cannan's *Money* and the writings of Mises, presumably because both writers adopted a marginal utility approach to money. Hayek was however critical of the lack of references to the writings of European economists.[4] In 1930 Barratt Whale published his first book, *Joint Stock Banking in Germany*, which was a product of numerous visits to Germany and which drew attention

Table 3.2 Session 1933–34. Theory of Value. Professor Hayek

Fifteen lectures to be given in the Session 1933–34. For postgraduate students and B.Sc. (Econ) Final. Special subject of Economics

SYLLABUS: The development of marginal utility analysis, the theory of imputation, utility and costs. The system of wants and their complementary character. The problem of measurability and 'quantification'. Value and time.

BOOKS RECOMMENDED: It is assumed that students will be familiar at the beginning of the course with such elementary introductions as F. W. Taylor *Principles of Economics*. M. Pantaleoni, *Pure Economics*; W. Smart, *Introduction to the Theory of Value*, and H. Oswait, *Vorträge uber wirtschaftliche Grundbegriffe*. In the following list of the more important works which deal with the problems discussed in the lectures, the chief are marked with an asterisk. F. Wieser, *Natural Value*; H. J. Davenport, *Value and Distribution*; P. Wicksteed **The Commonsense of Political Economy*; J. Viner, 'The utility concept in value theory' (*Journal of Political Economy*, vol. 33); F. H. Knight, **Risk Uncertainty and Profit* (chapters 3 and 4); A suggestion for simplifying the statement of the general theory of price' (*Journal of Political Economy* vol. 30); C. Menger, **Grundsatze der Volkwirtschaftslehre*, t. Aurf. 1871; E. von Böhm-Bawerk *Grundzuge der Theorie des wirtschaftlichen Güterwertes*; F. V. Wieser, *Theorie der gesellschaftlichen Wirtschaft*; G. Sulzer, *Die Wirtschaftlichen Grundgesetz*; L. Schönfeld, *Grenznutzen und Wirtschaftsrechnnung*; H. Mayer, **'Unterschung sum Grundgesetz der wirtschaftlichen Wertrechnung'* (*Zeitschrift fur Volkwirtschaft*, 1921 and 1922) and articles on *Bedurfuis* and *Zurechnung* in *Handworterbuch der Staatswissenschaften*, fourth edition; F. A. Hayek, *Bermerkungen sum Zurechnungsproblem*; *Jahrbuch fur Nationalok*, 1926) *P. N. Rosenstein, article on *Grenznutzen* in *Handworterbuch der Staatswissenschaften*, **Die Wirtschaftstheorie der Gegenwart*, vol. II; *Beiträge zur Wertheorie, Schriften der Verein fur Sozialpolitik*, vol. 183 (articles by Mises, Morganstern, etc.); J. Moret, *Emploi des mathématiques en économie politique*; V. Pareto, *Manuel d'economise politique*

Note: So far as I am aware there are no published references to Hayek lecturing on what is now known as microeconomics. The reading list contains no reference to Marshall, although it does contain Marshall's critic, Davenport. There is also a reference to Moret's book on mathematics in economics.

Source: LSE *Calendar* 1933–4.

to the importance of the banking system for the financing of industry. Finally, there was the strong influence of Austrian theorizing on Robbins' *The Nature and Significance of Economic Science*. Robbins and Hayek ran a joint seminar which was also attended by other senior staff, such as Gregory and Arnold Plant who was the Professor of Commerce. It was usually attended by some thirty or forty members of staff and postgraduate students as well as by visiting Europeans (such as Lange) and Americans. Robbins would organize the general topics for the seminar and Hayek would tend to monopolize the discussions in the early 1930s. In his University of California interview (1978) Hayek paid generous tribute to Robbins both as organizer and scholar. He was, said Hayek, a brilliant teacher who really knew the world literature of economics and he regretted that Robbins had not produced a textbook of economic theory, a synthesis of diverse schools, which might have changed the development of economics. Indeed, there appears to have been only one issue upon which Robbins and Hayek disagreed. When a vacant lectureship arose, Robbins opted for Kaldor whereas Hayek

Table 3.3 Session 1930–1. Principles of Currency. Dr. Hayek.

Twenty lectures. Michaelmas and Lent Terms. Thursdays 10.00–11.00 beginning M.T. 8 October, L.T. 14 January.
or (e) Wednesdays, 6.00–7.00, beginning M.T. 7 October, L.T. 13 January.
For B.Sc. (Econ) Final and B.Com. Final. Part I.
Fees: Day: For the course, £3; Terminal, £1 16s.
   Evening: For the course, £2; Terminal, £1 4s.

SYLLABUS: The place of monetary theory in economic analysis and functions of money. Metallic money and its early history. Development of monetary institutions and monetary theory in modern times.

Types of modern money. Effects of changes in its quantity on the price-system and the price-level. 'Velocity of circulation' and the 'demand for money'. The problem of deferred payments. Money, credit and capital. The money market. International problems.

BOOKS RECOMMENDED: A. **Historical**: Burns, *Money and Monetary Policy in Early Times*; Monroe, *Monetary Theory before Adam Smith*; Harsin, *Les doctrines monetaires et financieres en France*; Andreades, *History of the Bank of England*; McLeod, *Theory and Practice of Banking*; Gregory, *Introduction to Tooke and Newmarch's History of Prices*; *British Banking Statutes and Reports*; Kemmerer, *Modern Currency Reforms*; and the historical chapters in the works of Beckhart, Hawtrey and Helfferich mentioned below. B. **Theoretical**: Hume, *Essays, On Money, Of Interest, On the Balance of Trade*; Thornton, *Paper Credit of Great Britain*; Ricardo, *High Price of Bullion*; *Proposals for an Economical and Secure Currency*; *Bullion Report*, ed. Cannan; Senior *Lectures on the Value of Money*; *Lectures on the Cost of Obtaining Money*; Bagehot, *Lombard Street*; Goschen, *Theory of the Foreign Exchanges*; Marshall, *Official Papers*; Wicksell, *Geldzins und Guterpriese*; *Vorlesungen* II*; Helfferich, *Das Geldes* (one of the prewar editions); Johnson, *Money and Currency*; Fisher, *The Purchasing Power of Money*; Mises, *Theorie des Geldes und der Umlaufmittel*, *Geldwertstabilisierung und Konjunkturpolitik*; Fanno, *La Banche e il Mercato Monetario*; Schumpeter, *Das Sozialprodukt und die Rechenpfennige Archiv*, f Sozialw. Vol. 44; Hawtrey, *Currency and Credit**; *Monetary Reconstruction*; Cannan, *Money**; Robertson, *Money*, *(3rd edition); *Banking Policy and the Price Level**; Beckhart, *The Discount Policy of the Federal Reserve System*; Halm, *Das Zinsproblem und Geld- und Kapitalmarket*; *Jahrbucher fur Nationalökonomie*, 1926. Haberler, *Der, Sinn der Indexzahlen*; Hayek, *Geldtheorie und Konjunturtheorie*; *Prices and Production*; Keynes, *Treatise on Money**; *Committee on Finance and Industry*, Report, Cmd. 3897; Machlup, *Goldkernwahrung*; *Borsenkredit*; *Industriekredit und Kapitalbildung*; *De Omloopssneldheid van het Gelt*; Neisser, *Tauschwert des Geldes*.

Books marked with an asterisk have the first claims on the attention of those students taking the final examination who are not specialising in Banking and Currency.

Source: LSE *Calendar* 1930–1.

preferred Lerner. Kaldor was appointed and Lerner left for the United States.

Hayek was interested in the intertemporal allocation of resources. In one direction this led him to consider the relative merits of central planning and the market mechanism. It was a theme which was to emerge early in his writings, as for example in his inaugural lecture. 'The trend of economic thinking' and in his latter works, such as *The Fatal Conceit* (1989). He concluded (in 'The use of knowledge in society', 1945: 520) that central planners could not possess 'the knowledge of particular circumstances and place'. But since a decentralized economy used money his second line of enquiry led him to consider the operations of a

Table 3.4 Session 1936–7. Industrial Fluctuations. Professor Hayek.

Ten Lectures. Michaelmas Term. Tuesdays, 12.00–1.00, beginning M.T. 6 October.
or (e) Mondays, 6.00–7.00, beginning M.T. 5 October.
For B.Sc. (Econ) and B.Com. and Year Final.
Fees: Day: £1 10s.
   Evening: £1.

SYLLABUS: A survey of the history of industrial fluctuations. The typical movements and the concept of the trade cycle. Main types of early explanations. Modern theories. Underconsumption and changes in the structure of production. Monetary causes of the fluctuations in investment.

BOOKS RECOMMENDED: Mitchell, Business Cycles; Tougan-Baranowski, *Les Crises Industrielles en Angleterre*; Cassel, *Social Economy* (Part IV); Robertson, *Study of Industrial Fluctuations*; Pigou, *Industrial Fluctuations*; Haberler, *Systematic Analysis of the Theories of the Business Cycle* (League of Nations); Spiethoff, *Krisen*, in *Handwörterbuch der Staatswissenschaften*; Macfie, *Theories of the Trade Cycle*; Hayek, *Monetary Theory and the Trade Cycle* and *Prices and Production* and *Preiserwartungen*, *Monetare Störungen und Fehlinvestitione*; National Okonomisk Tidskrift, 1935, (French translation in *Revue de science Economiques*, October 1935); Durbin, *Purchasing Power and the Trade depression*; J.M. Clark, *Strategic Factors in Business Cycles*; Bergamann, *Geschicte der nationalökonomischen Krisentheoreten*; Ropke, *Crisis and Cycles*.

Source: LSE *Calendar* 1936–7.

monetary economy and the effects of monetary disturbances. And, thirdly, the intertemporal allocation of resources involved the possibilities of current resources being used to produce durable instruments of production which might yield enhanced future benefits and so the role of capital in an economy had to be explored. None of these themes were peculiar to Hayek but were central problems of Austrian economists from Menger onwards. Thus, Menger had stressed that an important feature of decentralized economies was how order was produced out of apparent chaos and Menger had also drawn attention to the importance of money. Böhm-Bawerk had criticized the Marxian system and had produced a major treatise on capital theory. Mises had analyzed the factors leading to business fluctuations. What was distinctive about Hayek's research programme was that he brought these strands together and presented them to an English audience.

Before going to the LSE Hayek had written the important article, 'Das intertemporale Gleichgewichtssystem der Preise und die Bewungen des Geldwertes' (1928a) in which he set out in quasi-mathematical form the intertemporal equilibrium in terms of the ratios of marginal utilities to prices in successive periods. Unfortunately, he assumed that a barter system would be in equilibrium and would not be subject to disturbances from real forces. He also assumed that prices would be established in the first period with the result that there would be no need for money. He had created a perfect foresight model.

Prices and production

The framework of the 1928 article was carried over into the 1931 lectures at the LSE (which were subsequently published as *Prices and Production*, 1931c). In the lectures Hayek drew upon several strands in the European tradition (see Table 3.5). First, there was his own book, *Geldtheorie und Konjunkturtheorie*, published in 1929 but not translated into English until 1934 as *Monetary Theory and the Trade Cycle*. Behind both books lay Mises's *Theories des Geldes und der Umlaufsmittel* (1912) which was not translated into English until 1934 as *The Theory of Money and Credit*. Second, there was Wicksell's theory of cumulative processes arising from differences between real and money rates of interest. Third, there was Böhm-Bawerk's theory of capital which assumed that capital could be measured in terms of its period of production.

Wicksell assumed that monetary equilibrium could be defined in

Table 3.5 Theory of Value. Professor Hayek.

Fifteen lectures to be given in the Session 1934–5.
For postgraduate students and B.Sc. (Econ) Final. Special subject of Economics.

SYLLABUS: The development of marginal utility analysis, the theory of imputation, utility and costs. The system of wants and their complementary character. The problem of measurability, and 'quantification'. Value and time.

BOOKS RECOMMENDED: It is assumed that students will be familiar, at the beginning of the course, with such elementary introductions as F.W. Taylor *Principles of Economics*; M. Pantaleoni, *Pure Economics*; W. Smart, *Introduction to the Theory of Value*, and H. Oswalt, *Vorträge uber wirtschaftliche Grundbegriffe*. In the following list of the more important works which deal with the problems discussed in the lectures, the chief are marked with an asterisk. F. Wieser, *Natural Value*; H.J. Davenport, *Value and Distribution*; P. Wicksteed, **The Commonsense of Political Economy*; J. Viner, 'The Utility Concept in Value Theory' (*Journal of Political Economy*, Vol. 33); F.H. Knight, **Risk, Uncertainty and Profit* (Chapters 3 and 4); 'A suggestion for simplifying the statement of the general theory of price' (*Journal of Political Economy*, Vol. 36); C. Menger, **Grundsätze der Volkwirtschaftslehre*, 1 Aufl. 1871; E. von Böhm-Bawerk, *Grundzüge der Theorie des wirtschaftlichen Guterwertes*; F.V. Wieser, *Theorie der gesellschaftlichen Wirtschaft*; G. Sulzer, *Die wirtschaftlichen Grundgesetz*; L. Schonfeld, *Grenznuten und Wirtschaftsrechnung*; H. Mayer, ***'Untersuchung zum Grundgesetz der wirtschaftslichen Wertrechnung' (*Zeitschrift fur Volkwirtschaft*, 1921 and 1922 and articles on *Bedürfnis* and *Zurechnung* in *Handwörterbuch der Staatswissenschaften*, fourth edition; F.A. Hayek, 'Bemerkungen zum Zurechnungsproblem' (*Jahrbuch fur Nationalök*, 1926); **P.N. Rosenstein, article on *Grenznuten* in *Handwörterbuch der Wissenschaften*, **Die Wirtschaftheorie der Gegenwart*, Vol. II; **Beiträge zur Werttheorie*; *Schriften des Verein für Sozialpolitik*, Vol. 183/1 (articles by Mises, Morganstern, etc.); J. Moret, *L'emploi des mathematiques en économie politique*; V. Pareto, *Manuel d'economie politique*.

Note: This is, as far as I am aware, the only indication of Hayek's interest in what was then regarded as value theory and which is now considered to be microeconomics. Some of the themes, such as imputation, were dealt with in articles that have been published in the McCloughery collection of Hayek's early writings.

Source: LSE *Calendar* 1933–4.

terms of equality of savings and investment, equality of real and money rates of interest rates, and stability of the price level. The criterion of price stability had become the subject of controversy between Wicksell and Davidson. Wicksell had suggested that in a progressive economy the price level should be held constant and wages should be allowed to increase in line with productivity whereas Davidson argued that wages should be held constant and prices should fall as productivity increased. The debate was not resolved. But setting aside the controversy we should note that if the banking system expanded the money supply then there would be a cumulative process leading to a general rise in prices and it was this idea that Mises adopted in propounding his monetary theory of the trade cycle. What Hayek then did was to combine this theory with Böhm-Bawerk's theory of capital. Starting from a position of full employment an increase in the money supply would lead to a shift of resources into the capital goods industries and to a lengthening of the period of production. The end of the expansion would occur if the banks ceased to increase the money supply. There would then be a reallocation of resources to the consumer goods sector.

Hayek's theory carried a great many implications – not all of which were spelled out in 1931. First, money entered an economy at a particular point and altered relative prices. In Hayek's model changes in the rate of interest are equivalent to changes in the price margins obtained by different producers in different sectors. Thus, the margin between the factors of production and the prices of consumer goods is treated as if it were the interest paid on the lapse of time between the input of factors and the price of consumer goods with the result that the margin will fall when the structure of production is lengthened and rise when it is shortened. In other words, a fall in the rate of interest will be equivalent to a reduction in the margin and lead to a lengthening of the production process. Second, the change in relative prices could occur without a rise in the general level of prices (of which the experience of the United States in the 1920s was thought by Hayek to be an example). Third, the task of monetary economics was not to determine the value of money but to discover how changes in the money supply altered relative prices. Fourth, the stability of the price level and the equality of savings and investment might be incompatible in a growing economy because the interest rate that stabilizes the price level, by permitting a monetary expansion corresponding to the increase in output, must be below the rate that keeps the money supply equal to the volume of voluntary savings. Fifth, the cause of the crisis is not underconsumption but overinvestment. Sixth, the authorities must not intervene during a slump but must allow prices to unwind and find their equilibrium values. If they attempted to check the downswing by reducing interest rates then they would prevent the desired shortening of the structure of production. If they introduced consumer credits then they might intensify the shortening of the production structure and cause an overshoot of the desired balance between the consumption goods and capital goods sectors.

Cambridge

Although published after Keynes's *Treatise on Money*, Hayek used the substance of his theory to criticize the *Treatise* and in the process he provoked a sharp reaction from all the Cambridge economists. To understand that reaction it is necessary to consider the fact that in the 1920s Cambridge was the centre of an intense discussion of monetary theory which began with the work of Hawtrey.

Ralph Hawtrey

Ralph Hawtrey was a Cambridge graduate and, like Keynes, a Kingsman and a member of the Apostles. But he did not graduate in economics nor did he hold an academic post and his knowledge of economics was not derived directly from Marshall. Hawtrey graduated in mathematics and then stayed on to read for the Civil Service examinations. In 1903 he entered the Admiralty but transferred to the Treasury in 1904 where he remained until his retirement in 1947. During his period at the Treasury he 'picked up' his economics and wrote a number of books and numerous articles. Despite not being an academic he was in close contact with the Cambridge economists. Reviewing his *Currency and Credit* (1919), Keynes said:

> This is one of the most original and profound treatises on the theory of money which has appeared for many years . . . it is a book with some fundamental thought in it, and likely, in my judgement to exercise a significant influence on future expositions of monetary theory, at any rate in England.[5]

In the 1920s *Currency and Credit* was a set book at Cambridge. Keynes's *Treatise on Money* was a reaction to *Currency and Credit* and it was only with the publication of the *General Theory* that Keynes broke away from the influence of Hawtrey – although it has to be recognized that it was Hawtrey who drew Keynes's attention to the importance of output movements. There are also close similarities between Hawtrey's work and that of Robertson.

Hawtrey has been presented as a proponent of a monetary theory of the trade cycle but it is an epithet which needs qualification. First, Hawtrey did not accept a simple quantity theory approach: 'Scientific treatment of the subject of currency is impossible without some form of the quantity theory',[6] he acknowledged, 'but the quantity theory by itself is inadequate, and it leads up to the method of treatment based on what I have called the consumers' income and consumers' outlay . . . that is to say simply the aggregates of individual incomes and individual expenditures.'[7] Second, Hawtrey emphasized the instability of a credit economy. Third, the distinction between Hawtrey's monetary theory and that of other writers, such as Hayek, was often one of degree. Hawtrey dealt with the effects of monetary changes upon the stocks of merchants and produced a stock or inventory cycle theory whereas other writers concentrated upon the effects of monetary changes upon fixed capital formation. The distinction therefore turns upon how far interest rate changes 'bite' into the real economy and it was a distinction which may have turned upon the fact that European banks financed fixed as well as working capital whereas British banks confined their lending to the financing of working capital.

In Hawtrey's analysis fluctuations in economic activity were associated with fluctuations in total money demand. Total money demand came from consumers' income and constituted consumers' outlay with the difference between income and outlay being defined as the *unspent margin*. Hawtrey adopted a broad definition of consumer which embraced spending on investment as well as consumption. He did, however, exclude expenditure by traders (merchants) on the grounds that their spending was not out of income but out of the turnover of their firms. The merchant who bought to sell again was merely an intermediary passing a part of his or her demand to other economic agents.

An increase in economic activity could be brought about by an increase in bank credit. Banks would be willing to lend to merchants because loans would be a means of increasing banks' profits. The willingness of merchants to borrow would come from the fact that an expansion of bank credit would depress the money rate (loan rate) of holding stocks below the profit rate derived from selling stocks. Merchants would therefore increase their stocks and in doing so would increase consumers' incomes. The excess of income or outlay — that is the rise in the unspent margin — would then spill over into consumers' outlay and lead to reductions in stocks. Merchants would then seek to replenish stocks and, sooner or later, under the restrictions of supply, prices would rise. Increase in prices fuelled by increase in bank credit could continue indefinitely but for leakages of cash from the banks' reserves. One source of leakage would arise because wage-earners did not tend to have bank accounts and would insist upon payment in cash. Another leakage would arise because imports would have to be paid for in gold and foreign currencies. The drain of cash from the banking system would therefore call a halt to the credit expansion, interest rates would rise and a recession would set in. Recovery and a further credit expansion would begin when stocks had been depleted and wages and other costs had fallen.

Hawtrey's monetary theory of the trade cycle explained the tendency of booms and slumps to occur in all industries, and not in a few industries, in terms of an expansion of the money supply which affected all industries. And he explained the tendency in the nineteenth century for simultaneous expansions and contractions in the major economies as stemming from the fact that all countries were on the gold standard. But the fulcrum upon which economic activity turned was the sensitivity of merchants' stockholdings to changes in short-term interest rates.

Dennis Robertson

Dennis Robertson was an eclectic. In his earliest work, *A Study in Industrial Fluctuations* (1915) he emphasized the role of real forces such as the influence of climatic change upon agriculture, population growth, technological change and the opening of new territories. In his later work he concentrated upon presenting critical appraisals of Keynes's *General Theory*. In between he devoted his energies to analyzing the interaction of real and monetary forces and the outcome was his important monograph, *Banking Policy and the Price Level* (1926).

Robertson proceeded by means of a set of economies or successive approximations to reality. Two classifications were adopted: first, barter and monetary economies; and second, cooperative and non-cooperative economies. The simplest case was a cooperative barter economy but even in such an economy fluctuations in economic activity might occur because of time lags in production. In a non-cooperative economy the problems might be intensified because employers would hire workers and conflicts could arise over the intertemporal allocation of leisure. Employers would prefer to expand employment in boom periods and contract employment in recessions, whereas workers would prefer continuous employment. A monetary economy could increase output through the division of labour but it could not remove fluctuations occurring in cooperative and non-cooperative economies and if an attempt was made to reduce unemployment due to real forces it could amplify fluctuations in economic activity. It was this interaction of real and monetary forces which formed the basis of Robertson's work and in his more mature expositions was characterized by the introduction of expectations and period analysis.

The simplest exposition of Robertson's ideas on a monetary economy is to be found in 'Theories of banking policy' which was delivered originally as a public lecture at the LSE in 1928 and subsequently published in *Economica* (1928). The substance of the lecture also appeared in the later editions of his book *Money*, and even as late as 1957 in his *Lectures on Economic Principles*. Suppose, we have an economy containing one farmer and one bank. The farmer hires workers to produce corn and to keep the business going until the corn is sold, the farmer borrows from the bank. Three features of the analysis should therefore be noted at this stage. First, there is a time lag (period of production) between sowing and reaping. Second, there is no metallic or hard state money. Robertson concentrates upon the workings of a credit economy and in doing so he follows the line developed by Hawtrey who in his *Currency and Credit* gave his first chapter the provocative title, 'Credit without money'. Third, there is no fixed capital in the model which reflected the prevailing practice of British banks of only lending on a short-term basis.

Until the corn had matured it could be regarded as working capital and it was against this working capital that the farmer borrowed. The farmer would then pay the farm workers from the loan and the workers would, in turn, deposit their wages at the bank. Thus, every loan would create a deposit and working capital would be equal to bank deposits. Hence, we can write:

$$B = C$$

where B denotes bank deposits and C stands for working capital. Now the quantity of corn per unit of time would be equal to the community's real income (R) and some portion of that income (K) would be held as bank deposits with the result that:

$$KR = C \,(= B)$$

But not all bank deposits are used to finance working capital and we can denote the portion used for that purpose as a. Moreover, working finance might also be financed by means of real saving, as well as bank deposits, and we can denote that portion financed by bank deposits by b. Hence, we can write:

$$aKR = bC$$

The next step is to extend the analysis of the real side of the economy by introducing the Jevons' theory of capital in which there is an emphasis upon the period of production D. The process of production can be illustrated by means of Figure 3.1. We assume that the production period is ten days and that in each day labour is used to build up enough working capital to turn out one unit of good per day. On the first day £1 is

54 Prices and production

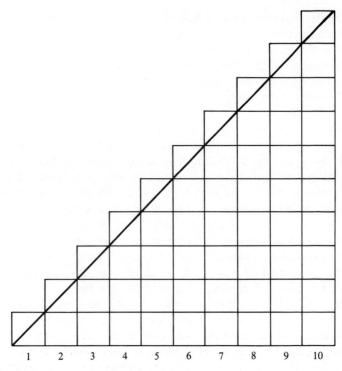

Figure 3.1 The structure of production.

used to treat one unit of good, on the second day a second £1 is applied on further treatment and a further £1 is employed to start another unit, and so on. At the end of ten days the amount spent would therefore be

$$1 + 2 + 3 + 4 + 5 + 6 + 7 + 8 + 9 + 10 = 55$$

On the tenth day, and on each succeeding day, a unit of corn is ready for sale and must sell if it is to cover the costs of £10. The value of the output during the ten days is therefore £100. This is slightly different from the amount spent on building up the working capital, but if the process had been continuous (so that the north west triangles above the diagonal could be neglected, then the value of output would be twice the value of working capital. Hence writing C for circulating capital, D for the period of production and R for real income we obtain

$$C = \tfrac{1}{2}DR$$

and since $aKR = bC$
we have $aK = b\tfrac{1}{2}D$

$$K = \frac{b\tfrac{1}{2}D}{a}$$

The last equation contains Robertson's crucial fractions which govern the inter-relations of the industrial and banking systems and the ability of the policy makers to maintain economic equilibrium. Thus D may be influenced by technological change. A more important feature is that in the upswing of a business cycle it is essential for circulating capital to grow before output increases and before the increase in real saving which the new output generates. Therefore, entrepreneurs may demand extra finance from the banks with the result that C will become greater than aKR. Hence, there will be a period of forced saving imposed by the banking system on the community and the price level will rise. Robertson's use of period analysis provides one source by which real savings and investment might not be equal and why an injection of bank credit may occur in the boom. Robertson divided time into periods which he called 'days'. Thus, savings today would be out of yesterday's income whereas investment today would be governed by today's expectations of future profits. Savings and investment, therefore, might not be equal and the rate of interest would not necessarily bring them into equality.

Robertson's analysis brought together real and monetary forces as determinants of the trade cycle. In *a Study of Industrial Fluctuations* he emphasized the fact that economic progress involved instability resulting from innovations, such as railways, steel, electricity and oil, and that recessions might be caused by a shortage of savings to finance investment or by a temporary saturation of the economy with capital goods. In *Banking Policy and the Price Level* he added a third cause of instability stemming from forced saving imposed on the community by the banking system.

J.M. Keynes

Although Keynes had dealt with monetary matters in *Indian Currency and Finance* (1913) and in *A Tract on Monetary Reform* (1923), the *Treatise on Money* (1930) was his major attempt at dealing with the interrelations of money and economic activity. In *A Tract on Monetary Reform* he had analyzed the theory of the value of money and prices using the Cambridge version of the quantity theory. In the *Treatise* he sought an analysis of the price level in terms of decisions on spending. He introduced a theory of the interrelations between saving and investment which split the interconnections of both money and goods. Goods were divided into consumption and investment goods and money into what was spent and what was saved. Along these lines therefore he was following a path charted by Hawtrey and Robertson.

Keynes's aim was to explain the price level of consumption goods as a function of the ratio of the community's earnings to output:

$$P_c = \frac{E}{O}$$

where P_c stands for the price level of consumption goods, E stands for earnings and O for output. The equation above is no more than the quantity equation. But Keynes added to it the complications of savings and investment. Saving reduces income and the production of capital goods increases income without any immediate increase in output. If investment is greater than savings then prices will rise to generate the required volume of savings and if saving is greater than investment prices will fall. Given the level of efficiency wages the necessary condition for a stable price level is that savings must equal investment and the task of the banking system is to ensure their equality through the control of the rate of interest. But this control must also be exerted upon the price of capital goods as well as upon savings and investment because the price of capital goods can affect the price of consumer goods through the ratio of the cost of investment to saving and through the earnings of the factors of production. If the value of capital goods exceeds their cost then profit will be generated. This profit is not treated by Keynes as part of income and its spending is a source of disturbance. Profit was therefore the 'mainspring of change' and produced an inflationary spiral which lasted until the earnings of agents rose and eliminated profits.

The argument so far expounded can be expressed algebraically as follows. The amended equation for the price level of consumption goods becomes:

$$P = \frac{E}{O} + \frac{I-S}{R}$$

where I stands for investment, S for saving and R is the volume of consumption goods flowing on to the market (that is, $O = R + C$ where C stands for the net increase in investment goods).

The general (average) price level (D) can be written as:

$$\begin{aligned}
D &= PR + P'C \\
&= \frac{PR + P'C}{O} \\
&= \frac{(E-S) + I}{O} \\
&= \frac{E}{O} + \frac{I-S}{O} \\
&= W + \frac{O}{O}
\end{aligned}$$

where *PR* stands for the value of consumption goods, *P'C* for the value of investment goods, *W* for efficiency earnings (E/O) and *Q* represents windfall profits.

Three points should be noted about these equations. First, when savings and investment are equal then the final term in the equations ($I - S/O$) becomes zero and we have the simple quantity theory. Second, profits do not form part of *E*, efficiency earnings. Third, savings ($E - C$) are independent of profits. And, fourth, investment is a determinant of profits.

So far we have set out a series of definitions. Keynes breathed life into them by assuming that the value of consumption depends upon the propensity to save out of income and that investment is determined by the natural rate of interest (what later became dubbed the profit rate) and the 'excess bearish' factor. In introducing the bearish factor Keynes drew a distinction between money used in the industrial circulation and money used in the financial circulation:

> By industry we mean the business of maintaining the normal process of current output, distribution and exchange and paying the factors of production for the various duties which they perform from the first beginning of production to the final satisfaction of the consumer. By finance, on the other hand, we mean the business of holding and exchanging existing titles to wealth (other than exchanges resulting from the specialisation of industry) including stock exchange and money market transactions, speculation and the process of conveying the current savings and profits into the hands of entrepreneurs.[8]

Although the volume of money used in the industrial circulation is influenced by changes in the character of production, in the habits of the public and the business world, it will tend to vary with the volume and cost of production of current output, that is, with aggregate money incomes. In contrast, the amount of money used for financial purposes is determined by different considerations because in 'a modern stock-exchange community the turnover of currently produced fixed capital is quite a small proportion of the total turnover of securities'.[9] Instead the volume of money used for financial circulation is dependent upon the savings behaviour of individuals. Thus some individuals may prefer to hold their savings in securities. Individuals adopting these respective positions may be termed 'bulls' and 'bears'; a bull is one who prefers to hold securities while a bear prefers to hold money.

We are now in a position to pull together the threads of the Cambridge discussion. Starting from the brief treatment of the trade cycle by Marshall, various Cambridge economists sought to tie together an analysis in terms of savings and investment with an analysis in terms of the quantity theory. The principal explorers were Hawtrey, Robertson, and Keynes. However, the ideas of Pigou and Lavington cannot be ignored. In *Wealth and Welfare* (1912), Pigou made two important contributions. First, he introduced into Cambridge thinking the concept of forced savings, although he failed to set out the effects upon final output and prices. Second, he emphasized the importance of the rate of interest as a measure of the marginal convenience of holding money. However, Pigou's contributions were set in the context of a wide ranging study of welfare economics and they were not picked up by reviewers who concentrated their attention on the earlier sections of the book.

What Hawtrey did was to explore the income approach to the quantity theory by conducting his analysis in terms of nominal income, savings and investment and he complemented this with a detailed exposition of the financial operations of the cumulative process. Unfortunately, he did not deal with real forces. For Hawtrey, unemployment was due to high wages and monetary forces were an exacerbating factor. Robertson's contributions were four-fold. First, there was his emphasis upon real forces in *A Study in Industrial Fluctuations* where he looked at the effects of changes in industrial structures. Second, there was the analysis of monetary factors in *Banking and the Price Level.* Third there was the stress upon period analysis and the taxonomy of savings and investment, Fourth, there was his discussion of forced savings. However, Robertson did not trace out the effects of forced saving upon the structure of production – possibly because he felt that monetary forces were less important than real factors.

In his early writings Keynes was less radical than Hawtrey and Robertson. It was the *Treatise on Money* which signalled the radical break with his contemporaries. In the *Treatise* the price levels of consumption and investment goods were distinguished and their determinants were separately analysed. He then introduced the three forces operating upon the demand for money (consumption, investment and convenience) and placed special emphasis upon the rate of interest and expectations. This provided a link with the stock market and brought together the industrial and financial circulations. Hence a reduction in the demand for consumption goods (implying an increase in savings) did not lead automatically to a fall in the rate of interest and an increase in investment. The link between savings and investment, between the fundamental equations and the quantity theory was broken. A change in the amount of money spent on consumer goods, implying a change in the price of consumer goods, does not lead automatically to a change in spending on investment goods, implying a change in the price of investment goods. A change in the quantity of money does not imply a change in the amount of forced saving. Only:

> in equilibrium – i.e. *when the factors of production are fully employed*, when the public is neither bullish nor bearish and is maintaining in the form of savings deposits neither more nor less than the 'normal' proportion of its total wealth, and when the volume of savings is equal both to the cost and to the value of new investments – there is a unique relationship between the quantity of money and the price levels of consumption-goods and of output as a whole.[10]

> the chief inconvenience of the 'Cambridge' Quantity Equation really lies in its applying to the total deposits considerations which are primarily relevant only to the income deposits, and in its tackling the problem as though the same sort of considerations which govern the income deposits also govern the total deposits. . . .[11]

The prominence given to k, namely the proportion of the bank deposits to the community's *income*, is misleading when it is extended beyond the income deposits. The emphasis which this method lays on the point that the amount of real balances held is determined by the comparative advantages of holding resources in cash and in alternative forms, so that a change in k will be attributable to a change in these comparative advantages, is useful and instructive. But 'resources' in this connection ought not to be interpreted as it is interpreted by Prof. Pigou as identical with *current* income.

> . . . when an individual is more disposed than before to hold his wealth in the form of savings deposits and less disposed to hold it in other forms, this does not mean that he is disposed to hold it in the form of savings *at all costs*. It means that he favours savings deposits . . . more than before at the existing price level of other securities. But his distaste for other securities is not absolute and depends on his expectations of the future return to be obtained from savings deposits and from other securities respectively which is obviously affected by the price of the latter – and also by the rate of interest allowed on the former. If, therefore, the price level of other securities falls sufficiently, he can be tempted back into them. If however, the banking system operates in the opposite direction to that of the public and meets the preference of the latter for savings deposits by buying the securities which the public is *less* anxious to hold, then there is no need for the price level of investments to fall at all. Thus the change in the relative attractions of savings deposits and securities respectively has to be met either by a fall in the price of securities or by an increase in the supply of savings deposits, or partly by one and partly by the other.
> . . . The price level of investments as a whole, and hence of new investment (i.e. P') is that price level at which the desire of the public to hold savings deposits is equal to the amount of savings deposits which the is willing and able to create.[12]

In other words, the price level of output as a whole and of profits depend upon the excess of savings over investment and the degree of bearishness of the public which is left unsatisfied by the creation of bank deposits.

Only in equilibrium will the Cambridge and the Fisher equations tell the same story as the fundamental equations.

This then was the difference between Keynes and Robertson and it was summed up in Keynes's rejoinder to Robertson:

> This central difference of opinion is as follows. Mr Robertson quotes me, correctly (p. 400) [in the *Economic Journal*, September 1931], as holding the view that if P, the price level of consumption goods declines owing to an excess of saving over the cost of investment then there *need* be no counterbalancing rise in P', the price level of investment goods, 'even though there is no increase in the disposition to hoard money unspent'. Mr Robertson holds that this result cannot come about 'except as a result of an act of hoarding'. This difference of opinion is evidently a special case of a more general difference as to the character of the forces which determine the price level of investment goods. Mr Robertson is quite right that it is absolutely fundamental to my analysis to distinguish *two* factors at work which I have christened the 'excess-savings factor' and the 'excess-bearish factor'.[13]

The unfortunate feature of the Cambridge debate was that it tended to get bogged down in terminological debates about the relative merits of various definitions of savings and investment. These issues were later clarified by Lutz (1938) who came down in favour of Robertson's definitions. But the central features of Keynes's analysis was that he used the decisions to hold money – at what later came to be called the three-fold margin of consumption, investment and convenience – to draw attention to the possibility that a decision not to consume might not lead automatically to a fall in the rate of interest and an increase in investment. In other words, Keynes had already developed in the *Treatise* a speculative demand for money allied to a liquidity preference theory of the rate of interest before its full-blown emphasis in the *General Theory*.

It was into this Cambridge debate that Hayek intruded for Hayek was also arguing that a monetary expansion was a necessary cause of investment exceeding savings whereas Keynes was maintaining that savings and investment could get out of gear without any departure from neutrality by the banking system merely by the public changing their rate of saving or entrepreneurs their rate of investment and that there was no automatic mechanism to keep savings and investment equal, provided that the quantity of money remained unchanged. Furthermore, Hayek concluded that following a monetary disturbance an economy must be left to unwind and that no attempt should be made to intervene lest further distortions be created. This policy conclusion Keynes could not accept. But before examining the Cambridge response to Hayek it is necessary to recount the public debate which formed the background to the Cambridge discussions.

The public debate

The theoretical work of Hawtrey, Robertson and Keynes cannot be divorced from the public debate which took place in the 1920s and 1930s about the appropriate economic policy for Britain. The postwar boom was followed by a sharp and severe deflation between 1920 and 1921 which carried money wages downwards because – as Hicks was later to observe – there was a general feeling that prices and wages were too high.[14] Nevertheless unemployment persisted and averaged 14 per cent between 1921 and 1925. The fall in money wages and prices was not sufficient to overcome the rise in costs brought about by the postwar reductions in hours of work which took the working week down from 54 to 48 hours. The situation was further intensified by the decision, in 1925, to return to the gold standard at the prewar parity – a decision which put tremendous pressure upon money wages and resulted in the miners' strike and the General Strike. An intense public debate took place concerning the appropriateness of government policy. Monetary and fiscal policy, as it emerged in the 1920s, seemed to have as its objectives the balancing of the budget and reducing government debt and taxes. Balancing the budget led to attempts to cut public expenditure and the return to the gold standard at the prewar parity was seen as a factor contributing to financial soundness. According to the governor of the Bank of England, Montagu Norman: 'The gold standard is the best 'Governor' that can be devised for a world that is still human, rather than divine.'[15] Moreover, there was a remarkable unanimity of agreement on policy by all the political parties. After the abandonment of the gold standard in 1931, Labour politicians expressed surprise that devaluation could be carried out.

However, the persistence of mass unemployment led to demands for a change in policy. In 'The economic consequences of Mr Churchill', published in 1925, Keynes had railed against a policy which made the miners the victims of the economic juggernaut. 'They represent in the flesh the "fundamental adjustments" engineered by the Treasury and the Bank of England to satisfy the impatience of the City fathers to bridge the moderate gap between \$4.40 and 4.86.'[16]

In an article entitled 'How to organise a wave of prosperity', published in the *Evening Standard* of 31 July 1928, he noted that 'we have deflated prices by raising the exchange value of sterling and by controlling the volume of credit; *but we have not deflated costs*' (italics in the original), and he went on to observe that 'The fundamental blunder of the Treasury and of the Bank of England has been due, from the beginning, to their belief that if they looked after the deflation of prices the deflation of costs would look after itself.' Keynes considered the alternatives. Because a general election was imminent a further attack on wages was politically difficult. Rationalization, the elimination of excess capacity, was being attempted in an endeavour to restore profit margins and deflate costs; but rationalization intensified, rather than solved, the problem of unemployment. A second possibility was to run the economy at full steam but that might lead to risks if individual businesses attempted it and to achieve an economy-wide expansion might require an increase in the money supply and lead to possible inflation. Moreover, any expansion would lead to an immediate increase in imports of raw materials. A third possibility was an increase in public spending. In 1928 the Liberal 'Yellow Book', *Britain's Industrial Future*, proposed a public works programme. However, the proposal for a public works programme was opposed by what came to be known as the 'Treasury View' which stated that an increase in public spending could only be accomplished by a reduction of private spending.

The Liberals failed to win the 1929 general election and a minority Labour Government, under Ramsay MacDonald, took office. But one outcome of the agitation for reform was the appointment of the Macmillan Committee on Industry and Finance within which Keynes played an important part and which enabled him to expound the ideas that were to emerge in the *Treatise on Money*. In the *Treatise* the problem of economic stabilization of the price level was to reconcile savings and investment through variation in the rate of interest. But the stabilization of the domestic price level was a problem of internal balance which had, in turn, to be reconciled with the problem of external balance. A rise in the rate of interest might correct an adverse balance of trade, and by inducing an inflow of capital could lead to equilibrium in the balance of payments, but it could also lead to a reduction in investment, a fall in profits, employment and wages. Of course, if wages were flexible then reductions in wages might restore profits, lower prices and increase exports and employment. But if the exchange rate had been set too high then the Bank Rate might be set too difficult a task. There could be resistance to wage reductions and the interest rate mechanism might jam.

In the discussions promoted by the Macmillan Committee the Treasury View was modified. Instead of the emphasis upon crowding out of private spending by increased public spending there was a switch to stressing the administrative and political problems of a public works programme.

However, our interest is in the intrusion of Hayek into the British debate. What Hayek did in *Prices and Production* was to produce an alternative theoretical case against the Keynes–Lloyd George policies. The case was further elaborated in the article. 'Das Schicksal der Goldwahrung' (1932) ('The fate of the gold standard').

Hayek conceded that there may have been a mistake in returning to the gold standard at the prewar parity. He wrote:

> Whether it was wise to return to the pre-war parity with the aid of a difficult process of deflation is extremely questionable. The events which occurred make it seem likely that Britain would have done better to have remembered Ricardo's advice. More than a hundred years previously he wrote that he would never recommend a government to ease back to par a currency whose value had declined by 30 per cent.[17]

Nevertheless, he maintained that Keynes's policy of seeking to stabilize the domestic price level was a mistake and pandered to nationalist sentiments. As an international trading country, Britain could not afford to place its emphasis upon the domestic price level and attempts to reduce unemployment by means of tariffs and public works would lead to increased inefficiency.

Hayek's interpretation of the crisis in the world economy was as follows. The postwar inflations in Europe had led to the abandonment of the gold standard. Only the United States had remained on the gold standard but the operations of the gold standard in prewar Europe provided no obvious policy rules for a country which was, to all intents and purposes, a closed economy. Gold had flowed into the United States and there was therefore a problem of adjusting to the gold inflow and the question arose: should policy concentrate upon price level stability? The problem was further complicated because of America's superior technological progress which resulted in a prolonged boom from 1920 to 1927. It was an innovation wave which led to no increase in the general level of prices and which deluded observers, such as Keynes, into believing that the Americans had sterilized the inflow of gold. But the gold inflow had not been sterilized; it had been allowed to feed through and influence the domestic money supply. After 1927 when the real forces behind the boom started to flag, the money supply started to distort relative prices, spilled over into the financial circulation and prompted the financial crash of 1929.

However, the problems of the gold standard were not caused by strong economies, such as the United States, refusing to play the rules of the game but weak countries, such as Britain, not accepting the rules. In Britain it had been a mistake to go back to the gold standard at the prewar parity and it had produced a painful period of deflation. But the necessity for further price and wage reductions was beginning to disappear at the end of the 1920s when, unfortunately, the world recession began. Moreover, the situation had been complicated by the emergence of new policies sponsored by Keynes which led to a surge of nationalism. Unfortunately, Hayek offered no solution to the search for a new international monetary system and the fact that his ideas were presented in German meant that they exerted no influence upon British economists. They also left open the problem of what should the Americans have done in 1927.

Hayek's analysis of the interwar years differed from that of Keynes. Although in the *Treatise*, Keynes distinguished between the price levels of consumption and investment goods, he did not use the distinction to draw attention to a possible distortion of the structure of production in the 1920s. In June 1931 he contributed to the Harris Foundation lectures with the following economic analysis of the boom and subsequent slump.

> Doubtless, as was inevitable in a period of such rapid change, the rate of growth of some individual commodities could not always be in just the appropriate relation to that of others. But, on the whole, I see little sign of any serious want of balance as is alleged by some authorities. The rates of growth of construction capital, such as houses, of capital for manufacturing production, and of capital for raw material production, or again those of foodstuffs, of raw materials, of manufactures, of activities demanding personal services seem to me, looking back to have been in as good a balance as one could have expected them to be . . . . I am inclined to the view that the part played by inflation was surprisingly small, and true savings kept pace with investment.[18]

In Keynes's view the US boom, and the world boom, came to an end because the most profitable ventures had been exhausted and the rate of interest should have fallen to permit less profitable activities to be undertaken. Unfortunately, the rate of interest was raised in order to check the Wall Street boom. Here lay the unresolved difference between Hayek and Keynes: what was the cause of the upper turning point and the end of the boom?

But although Hayek's article may have had little influence, there can be no doubt that *Prices and Production* did serve to strengthen the position of Keynes's opponents. Economic forces, so the argument ran, must be left to unwind, public works might crowd out private investment. Attempts to stabilize prices were mistaken. These were the policy conclusions stemming from Hayek's lectures.

The Cambridge criticisms

Although published after Keynes's *Treatise on Money,* Hayek used the substance of his theory to criticize the *Treatise* – which presented the spectacle of a conflict between two authors who attributed the lineage of their ideas to Wicksell. Specifically, Hayek was critical of the definitions of savings and investment used by Keynes, the absence of a theory of capital and the notion that the rate of interest could equate savings and investment *and* stabilize the price level. He noted the absence of a theory of supply in the *Treatise* and that although nominal income and factor payments were equal, they need not be equal to the cost of current output except in equilibrium. He observed that Keynes had defined income so as to include all factor payments except windfalls and that it could not remain constant if prices and interest rates changed since changes in interest rates could change payments to lenders and production costs. There was also a clash of opinion about the determination of the rate of interest with Hayek favouring a loanable funds approach in which changes in the money supply interacted with flows of real savings and investment to determine hoarding whereas Keynes emphasized the role of money stocks and hoards.

Keynes was unhappy with Hayek's review of the *Treatise* and responded before Hayek had published the second part of his review. He described *Prices and Production* as 'one of the most frightful muddles' he had ever read. The subsequent exchange between them revealed a failure to agree with both authors talking at cross purposes. But there was a trenchant criticism by Sraffa in which he drew attention to Hayek's emphasis upon money as a medium of exchange and his neglect of its function as a store of value: 'there are no debts, no money contracts, no wage agreements, no sticky prices in his suppositions'.[19] And with all prices being assumed to be flexible, the problems were assumed away. It was a criticism which had its antecedents in Appendix F of Marshall's *Principles* (1924) where it was stated money could not remove all the problems associated with a barter economy. In his reply Hayek confessed: 'I have been assuming that the existing body of pure economic theory demonstrates that, so long as we neglect monetary factors, there is an inherent tendency towards an equilibrium of the economic system.'[20] Later, in 1932, in an article entitled, 'Kapital aufzehrung' ('Capital consumption'), Hayek attempted to accommodate Sraffa's criticisms by arguing that money wage rigidity could be regarded as equivalent to an increase in real wage rigidity and would therefore distort the time structure of production. Unfortunately because of its publication in German it may not have been noted by the Cambridge economists (Hayek, 1932d).

Sraffa produced other criticisms. First, there was a comment on Hayek's treatment of saving and investment:

The essential contradiction is that Dr Hayek must both assume that the 'consumers' are the same individuals as the 'entrepreneurs', and that they are distinct. For only if they are identical can the consumers' decisions to save take the form of a decision to alter the 'proportions' in which the total gross receipts are divided between the purchase of producers' goods; and only if they are distinct has the contrast between 'credits to producers', which are used to buy producers' goods and 'credits to consumers', which are used to buy consumers' goods, have any definite meaning.[21]

To which Hayek responded:

> I do not understand why Mr Sraffa should suggest that a consumer who is not an entrepreneur will not affect the proportion between the demand for consumers' goods and the demand for producers' goods by his decision to save. It is certain that when he invests his savings by lending them out at interest he is instrumental in directing part of his money income to the purchase of producers' goods without himself becoming an entrepreneur.[22]

Second, Hayek assumed that once the boom broke, capital goods brought into existence when the money rate of interest was below the equilibrium rate would lose their value. Sraffa disagreed:

> As a moment's reflection will show, 'there can be no doubt' that nothing of the sort will happen. One class has, for a time robbed another class of part of their incomes, and has saved the plunder. When the robbery comes to an end, it is clear that the victims cannot possibly consume the capital which is well out of their reach. If they are wage-earners, who have all the time consumed every penny of their income, they have no wherewithal to expand consumption. And if they are capitalists who have not shared in the plunder, they may indeed be induced to consume now a part of their capital by a fall in the rate of interest; but no more so than if the rate had been lowered by the 'voluntary savings' of other people.[23]

To this classical type of theorizing Hayek replied:

> That the physical quantity of capital will, for some time, continue to exist does not mean their owners have not lost the greater part, for all, of their capital. It is of very little use for the machine manufacturer to hold on tight to his capital goods when the producer who used to buy the machines is either unable, or finds it unprofitable at the higher rate of interest, to do so now. Whether he likes it or not, the actions of other people have destroyed his capital.[24]

Finally, Sraffa cast doubt on the notion that fluctuations in economic activity arose from a divergence between a money rate of interest and a single real (commodity) rate of interest:

> An essential confusion . . . is the belief that the divergence of rates is characteristic of a money economy. If money did not exist, and loans

were made in terms of all sorts of commodities, there might exist at any one moment as many natural rates of interest as there are commodities, though they would not be equilibrium rates. The arbitrary action of the banks is by no means a necessary condition for the divergence. If loans were made in wheat and farmers (or for that matter the weather) 'arbitrarily changed' the quantity of wheat produced, the actual rate of interest on loans in terms of wheat would diverge from the rate on other commodities and there would be no single equilibrium rate.[25]

To which Hayek responded:

I think that it would be truer to say that in this situation, there would be no *single rate* which, applied to all commodities, would satisfy the conditions of equilibrium rates, but there might, at any moment, be as many 'natural' rates of interest as there are commodities, *all* of which would be equilibrium rates; and which would all be the combined result of the factors affecting the present and future supply of the individual commodities, and of the factors usually regarded as determining the rate of interest. The inter-relations between these different rates of interest is far too complicated to allow of detailed discussion within the compass of this reply.[26]

Hayek did not seem to consider the possibility that the money rate might be higher than some, and lower than, other commodity rates of interest. The issue of own-rates was to receive more detailed treatment in Keynes's *General Theory* and in articles by Kaldor (1939b) and Lerner (1940b).

Among the younger Cambridge economists there was scepticism. At a seminar held in Cambridge, Kahn posed the question: '"Is it your view that if I went out tomorrow and bought a new overcoat, that would increase unemployment?" "Yes", said Hayek. "But pointing to his triangles on the board, it would take a very long time to explain why"'.[27] And although in correspondence with Keynes, Robertson suggested that some of Hayek's ideas had validity, his general position was critical. In *Banking Policy and the Price Level* he had analyzed forced saving. But he was not prepared to castigate forced saving as an evil. Nor was he prepared to let the economy unwind. In a review of Robbins's *The Great Depression* he wrote: 'It seems possible, for instance, to agree with Professor Robbins's diagnosis of the primary phase of the depression without agreeing that no monetary action can usefully be undertaken to counter its secondary phase.'[28]

In his book *The Great Depression* Robbins argued that the slump in Britain and the United States was due to a shift on policy away from the gold standard and towards managed currency systems designed to stabilize price levels. In the United States gold inflows had not been sterilized, as was sometime alleged, but had been allowed to form the basis of credit expansion. This credit expansion had not been inflationary because the general price level had not risen, but relative prices had been disturbed. In Britain the gold outflow had not led to a fall in prices and wages because the authorities had sought to stabilize prices. And wages had tended to become rigid downwards because of the system of national insurance. There had also been a movement towards protectionism which had been advocated by Keynes and vehemently opposed by Robbins. Finally, in 1927 the US Federal Reserve increased the money supply in order to force down money interest rates and provoke an outflow of gold in order to reduce the pressure on sterling. The result was therefore an acceleration of inflationary pressures. Robbins therefore sought a return to the gold standard, the removal of tariffs, the elimination of cartels and the removal of impediments to prices and wages flexibility. In short, Robbins's analysis and prescriptions were the applications of Hayek's theory.

Reviewing Robbins's book Hubert Henderson noted that the analysis and prescriptions stemmed from the 'standpoint of the analytical neo-individualism which has been developing in recent years at the London School of Economics'. But he went on to observe that the 'various analytical theorems which underlay his arguments were 'not set out in full rigour'.[29] However, Henderson accepted some of the points made by Robbins, such as the tendency to inflation before 1929. But, he argued, Robbins's fear of inflation was such that he was reluctant to suggest that creditor countries should allow their price levels to rise. Hence, the burden of adjustment was thrown on to the debtor countries. Clearly this was not obeying the rules of the gold standard. Furthermore, Henderson argued, the postwar disequilibrium was due to many more factors than those instanced by Robbins and he cited reparations and war debts. Henderson also observed that the United States had made wholesale cuts in wages and prices between 1930 and 1933. He stated:

> The obvious moral of the American experience is that a general lowering of wage rates serves to accentuate and perpetuate the vicious circles of depression. Indeed the subsequent adoption by President Roosevelt of policies designed to increases consumers' purchasing power is largely attributable to the widespread belief in the United States that the idea of countering a depression by lowering wages and money incomes has been shown by experience to be a fallacy.[30]

Instability, he concluded, was a worldwide phenomenon due to the disturbances of the balances of international indebtedness (reparations and war debts) and the slowing of population growth which reduced consumer demand. Hence, there might be a need for more state intervention.

In 1925 Hawtrey had presented a reasoned statement of the Treasury view that public spending might displace private spending in an article entitled, 'Public expenditure and the demand for labour' (Hawtrey, 1925). The article was published in the LSE journal, *Economica*. And this article might have been taken to indicate a sympathy with Hayek's case for non-intervention. However, his review of *Prices and Production* was critical of Hayek's theoretical arguments. He did not accept that the boom and slump were caused by an excess demand for capital goods followed by an excess demand for consumer goods. 'The stimulus', he argued, 'is given to all industries.'[31] Hawtrey reached this conclusion because he assumed that monetary disturbances operated primarily upon working capital. Pigou does not appear to have made a public pronouncement upon *Prices and Production*. In his formal works, such as *Industrial Fluctuations* (1927a) and 'Wages policy and unemployment' (1927b) he took the view that an all-round reduction in money wages could reduce unemployment because prices would fall by less than wages. But in his public pronouncements he was in favour of public works and lower interest rates. In a letter in *The Times* of 17 October 1932, when unemployment was over 20 per cent, Pigou, along with McGregor, Sir Walter Layton, Sir Arthur Salter, Sir Hosiah Stamp and Keynes, recommended an increase in public expenditure and attacked the orthodox virtues of saving and frugality, public and private, in a period of mass unemployment. In *The Times* of 19 October 1932, Hayek, Gregory, Plant and Robbins criticized the use of increased government spending to remove unemployment. Thus, all the Cambridge economists were ranged against Hayek and also against the other senior members of the LSE.

Opinions within the LSE

Within the LSE there were divided opinions. The conclusion that prices should be left to unwind seemed to be a reiteration of the opinions of Cannan who took the view that 'any difficulties must be regarded in the same light as those which a spendthrift or drunkard is nightly exhorted by his friends to face like a man'.[32] Subsequently, in his Presidential address to the Royal Economic Society on 'The demand for labour' (1932) he blamed excessive wage demands for mass unemployment and maintained that unemployment would eventually force down wages. Gregory also had propounded a policy of deflation in a series of books, such as *The First Year of the Gold Standard* (1926). He continued the theme in *Gold, Unemployment and Capitalism* (1933) and he was also a signatory of the Macmillan Committee's Report on Finance and Industry. Robbins, as we have noted, took a similar line in *The Great*

Depression. Later, in his *Autobiography*, he expressed regret at the position he had adopted in the 1930s. Shackle, a graduate student, wrote a comparison of the *Treatise* and *Prices and Production* which was favourable to Hayek. In his *The Theory of Wages* (1932c) Hicks drew upon Hayek's analysis in his discussion of the effects of wage increases upon employment and he suggested that unemployment benefits might reduce savings and cause a wastage of capital.

The conclusion that a crisis was not due to underconsumption but was the result of overinvestment fitted in with the prevailing view of the School. In the 1929 *Quarterly Journal of Economics*, Robertson published an article upon the monetary doctrines of Foster and Catchings in which he confessed that after prolonged study he was unable to attach any sense to the statement that money is used twice in succession:

> Money that is once used to bring about the production of goods is again used to bring about the consumption of goods. In other words, it is used twice in succession to create supply whereas if the $100,000 in question, instead of being invested in the production of additional goods had been paid as dividends and spent by the recipients, the $100,000 would have been used alternatively to bring goods to market and take them off the markets.[33]

Hayek also wrote a paper, 'Gibit es einen Wildersinn des Sparens' which was later translated and published under the title 'The paradox of saving' (1931b) in which he drew attention to the lack of discussion of the productivity of capital in the underconsumptionist literature. Underconsumptionists tended to argue that increases in savings would reduce the demand for consumption goods and the increased output of consumption goods could not be bought unless prices fell. But if prices fell below costs then production would be unprofitable and a slump would occur. This result Hayek denied and he argued that the productivity of capital would reduce costs and enable prices to be lowered.

Durbin, along with his friend Gaitskell, both of whom were socialists, were critical of the underconsumptionist literature and its influence on socialist thinking. They therefore sought to produce a model of the trade cycle which did not rely upon that strand of thinking. In 'Consumption and the trade cycle' Robbins (1932b) acknowledged the work done by Durbin and maintained that the trade cycle was due to overinvestment precipitated by credit expansion. He drew a distinction between those theories of underconsumption which assumed that the absolute amount spent on consumption was insufficient and those which asserted that the amount spent on consumption relative to investment was deficient. Into the first category came the ideas of Major Douglas which stated that the amount distributed in any period as final income was insufficient to purchase the output of all financially independent production units. What Robbins then did was to draw attention to the difference between gross and net output and to argue that it was an essential condition of equilibrium that net income had to be less than the value of gross output in a stationary economy and that in a growing economy savings would rise to match investment. On the question of whether prices should fall, Robbins took the same line as Hayek and argued that the productivity of capital might force a fall in prices but that would not spell disaster. On the question of whether a slump would occur because of a failure to achieve an optimum rate of savings, Robbins felt that the concept of an optimum implied that 'there was nothing in economic analysis which would justify the inference that the failure of such an aggregate to reach a maximum has any causal significance for the relation between production and consumption'.[34]

Durbin

However it was Durbin who occupied a significant position in the LSE. He occupied an intermediate position between the senior members, such as Gregory, Robbins and Plant, and the younger assistants, such as Kaldor, Hicks and Lerner. And he had been at Oxford with Robbins. Moreover, Durbin's interests overlapped those of Hayek. He was a socialist and an advocate of planning whereas Hayek favoured the use of markets. And while Hicks, Kaldor and Robbins tended to be interested in value theory, Durbin was, like Hayek, interested in monetary theory. He lectured, like Hayek, on both planning and monetary theory and Hayek's theory seemed to offer some support for his own proposals to nationalize the banks in order to control the money supply. What he sought to do, therefore, was to produce a synthesis of money and cycle theory based upon the writings of the Austrian and Cambridge economists (Table 3.6).

Durbin's ideas were set out in two books, *Purchasing Power and Trade Depression* (1933b) and the *The Problem of Credit Policy* (1935b). The main difference between the two books is that in 1933 Durbin was inclined to allow an economy to unwind to find its equilibrium whereas in 1935 he became more optimistic that something might be done to soften the impact of depressions through the use of consumer credits. Durbin's analysis of underconsumption began by following the lines charted by Robertson, Hayek and Robbins and he emphasized the fact that:

The moment we make the assumption that there are many stages of

72 Prices and production

Table 3.6 Session 1937–8. Modern Trade Cycle and Monetary Theory. Mr. Durbin.

Fifteen lectures. Michaelmas and Lent Terms. Wednesdays beginning M.T. 5 October, L.T. 11 January.
Fee: £2 5s.

SYLLABUS: The course will survey and criticize the postwar economic literature published in England concerned with analyzing the determinants and the equilibrium level of the effective quantity of money (MV).

The course will begin with an account of all the questions that have been asked in modern English monetary theory. From this list five questions are selected for particular consideration: 1. What determines the *form* of the monetary circulation? 2. What determines the size of the monetary circulation? 3. How ought the monetary circulation to behave in order to secure an equilibrium of full employment? 4. How does the monetary circulation in fact behave and why? 5. How can undesirable movements in the monetary circulation be prevented?

Finally some attempt is made to consider the empirical evidence and to answer the central questions.

BOOKS RECOMMENDED: Hawtrey, *Currency and Credit*, **Trade and Credit, The Theory of Capital and Employment*, 'Monetary analysis and the investment market' (*Economic Journal*, 1934); with Keynes and Robertson, 'The definition of saving' (*Economic Journal*, 1934).

Robertson, *Money*, **Banking Policy and the Price Level**, *Theories of Banking Policy*, *The World Slump (republished in *Essays and Addresses* with Prof. Pigou), 'Saving and hoarding' (*Economic Journal*, 1933), 'Industrial fluctuations and the natural rate of interest' (*Economic Journal*, 1934), 'Notes on Mr Keynes' "General Theory"' (*Quarterly Journal of Economics*, 1936), Pigou, 'A contribution to the theory of credit' (*Economic Journal*, 1926).

Keynes, *A Treatise on Money, The General Theory of Employment, Interest and Money*; with Robertson, 'Mr Keynes' *Theory of Money*' (*Economic Journal*, 1930–1); Hicks, 'Mr Keynes' *Theory of Employment*' (*Economic Journal*, 1936).

Pigou, 'Mr Keynes' *General Theory*' (*Economica*, 1936); Lerner, 'Mr Keynes' *Theory of Employment*' (*ILO Quarterly*, 1936); Robinson, *Introduction to the Theory of Employment*.

Hayek, *Monetary Theory and the Trade Cycle, Prices and Production* (2nd edn), 'Prévision de Prix Perturbations' (*Rev. Pol. Econ.* 1935); Robbins, 'Consumption and the trade cycle' (*Economica* 1933).

Source: LSE *Calendar* 1937–8.

---

production of each type of commodity it becomes literally impossible that consumers' income should ever be equal to total payments at all stages of production, for the very good reason that at every moment there are certain monetary payments which cannot in the nature of the case enter into any consumer's income.

But he then went on to observe that: 'A change in the Rate of Saving involves a general disequilibrium as distinct from a partial disequilibrium involved in any other change in the underlying preferences of the consumer. This doctrine appears to be the one contribution to the truth made by the underconsumptionists.' And he suggested that the rate of interest is a sticky element in the economic system and that 'The fraction of the direct costs of producing consumption goods which are immediately affected by a fall in the Rate of Interest must be very small'.[35] However, he felt that a rise in the proportion of savings out of income seemed unlikely because the possibility of producing consumer goods increases right up to the moment of crisis.

Durbin believed that the trade cycle resulted in an oscillation of capital resources brought about by credit instability. It was a conclusion similar to that of Hayek but derived from different assumptions and which therefore tended to contradict the monetary overinvestment theory. Durbin assumed that the upswing of the cycle might be brought about either by credit expansion or technological progress. However, he did not assume that the increase in credit would lead to an expansion of the capital goods sector at the expense of the consumer goods sector. In the long run he agreed that scarcity of resources might meant that the two sectors were in competition but in the short run there might be unemployed resources. Furthermore, the demand for capital goods was derived from the demand for consumer goods, although Durbin did not make use of the acceleration principle.

The upper turning point of the cycle Durbin suggested was brought about by a rising price level and credit restraint arising from cash drains in the manner envisaged by Hawtrey and Hayek. On the downswing of the cycle he exposed a weakness – the asymmetry problem – in Hayek's model. Hayek was unable to explain why the downswing should not mirror the upswing. In other words, why should resources move easily from the consumer goods sector to the capital goods sector but not move so easily in the opposite direction.

Given that the cycle resulted from the instability of credit, Durbin favoured the planning of the money supply. He was not in favour of a constant money supply for the reasons advanced by Davidson; a constant price level in an advancing economy would result in a redistribution of income to profits. Nor did he advocate a constant money supply (MV) along the lines proposed by Hayek because in an advancing economy there would be an increase in the number of stages of production and they would absorb more of the money supply and exert a deflationary pressure.

Durbin had all the ingredients of a trade cycle theory but failed to attract greater support. He sought an eclectic approach based upon rival theories and this led him into inconsistencies. He was critical of the role of the rate of interest in regulating the economy and yet his espousal of credit instability implied that as the banks expanded credit then the money rate would be pushed below the real rate of interest. His interpretation of Hobson led him into arguments which he lost.

Hobson assumed that savings might be related to the distribution of income, the possibility that capitalists had a higher propensity to save than workers, and that savings might be influenced by the degree of monopoly. He also assumed that savings were automatically invested and that there was an optimum savings ratio. If savings rose above the optimum then deflation would ensue, although 'the collapse of demand admittedly shows itself first in a reduced demand for plant and materials in the fundamental production industries into which investment capital has been flowing at a rate now proved to be excessive'. In other words, the crisis could be viewed equally as one of overinvestment or underinvestment.

Durbin followed Robbins in questioning the concept of an optimum savings rate. Hobson replied that the optimum rate of savings was not to be interpreted in the old or new welfare economics sense but as a maximum safe ratio of savings to income. That is, Hobson anticipated Harrod's natural growth rate which was defined as the maximum rate of growth allowed by the increase of population, capital accumulation, technological improvement and the work/leisure preference schedule, and the natural rate was to be contrasted with the warranted rate which would leave agents with the feeling that they had grown neither too fast nor too slow.

Durbin's analysis suffered other defects. To Hawtrey the weakness was that it ignored the effects of interest rates on working capital. To Robertson the problem was that Durbin did not deal adequately with the underconsumptionists (particularly Foster and Catchings), paid 'insufficient attention to the technical obstacles which the use of large, discontinuous and durable instruments of production and transport place in the way of industry's power to make use of a steady rate of saving'[36] and presented a peculiar compound of Hayek, Keynes and Hawtrey with some added features but failed to consider the beneficial effects of forced saving and preferred to allow excess capacity in the capital-making industries slowly and painfully to disappear.

Durbin's analysis of the downswing also suffered from a lack of a theory of the demand for money. It was a curious omission given his desire to reconcile Cambridge with Vienna and it would seem to warrant the comment which Keynes passed on the underconsumptionists:

> Mr Hobson and others deserve recognition for trying to analyse the influence of credit and saving on the price level and on the credit cycle at a time when orthodox economists were content to neglect almost entirely the real problem. But I do not think they have succeeded in linking up their conclusion with the theory of money or with the part played by the rate of interest.[37]

Durbin wanted to be an eclectic but was a poor synthesizer. There is therefore irony in his letter to Keynes congratulating him on the publication of the *General Theory*. 'Perhaps you would allow me', he wrote, 'to repeat how greatly I have enjoyed it. I wish it had come out before I had published my own book. I should have had much to add and some things to alter.'[38] Nevertheless, within the LSE, Durbin's was the first sustained critical response to Hayek. Hayek attempted to deal with the problem of starting a recovery from a situation of unemployed resources in his 1939 book, *Profits, Interest and Investment* but he did not produce a solution to the asymmetry problem.

Summary and conclusions

In 1930 Hayek delivered four lectures at the LSE in which he set out what Haberler was later to describe as a monetary overinvestment theory of the trade cycle. Starting from a position of full employment, Hayek assumed that an increase in the money supply would alter relative prices and since it pushed the money rate of interest below the natural rate there would be an expansion of the capital goods sector. When the money rate rose the boom would come to an end. If unemployment occurred then governments should not interfere but should allow prices to unwind and find new equilibrium values.

The theory and the subsequent application of the theory by Robbins was severely criticized by Cambridge economists. Sraffa drew attention to the lack of a theory of a monetary economy and to the assumption that real forces did not cause disturbances. Kahn could not understand how increased spending during a slump could accentuate the severity of the slump. Keynes thought the theory was a frightful muddle and Henderson believed that Robbins had omitted many important factors contributing to the Great Depression. Even Robertson, the eclectic, found much to criticize. And, obliquely, Pigou found the theory wanting.

Within the School, Cannan, Robbins and Gregory, the Old Austrians, were sympathetic to Hayek's theory. However, Durbin raised two important points of criticism. First, the model did not work if the initial situation were one of unemployment. Second, the model failed to explain the rise in unemployment on the downswing. Unfortunately, weaknesses in Durbin's own model prevented him from pressing home his advantage.

At the end of the first round, therefore, there were several weaknesses in Hayek's theory which were to lead to further debates. First, there was the question of what part money played in economic activity. This issue was taken up by Hicks and Chambers in the School. Second, was it possible to provide a model of an economy in which money was neutral? This issue was examined by Gilbert, Durbin and Barger. Both the demand for money and the neutrality of money are dealt with in the next chapter. Third, if prices should not be allowed to unwind, is it possible to provide a viable theory of state intervention? This issue is taken up in the socialist debate but a more detailed analysis requires some consideration of the nature of the Keynesian avalanche and that is dealt with in Chapter 6. Fourth, was the Austrian theory of capital a sensible way of dealing with investment in durable equipment? This question is dealt with in Chapter 5.

Notes

1. Schorske, C. (1979), *Fin-de-Siecle Vienna*, New York: Knopf, p. 79.
2. Mises, L. (1979), *Notes and Recollections*, South Holland: Libertarian Press, p. 68.
3. Keynes, J.M. (1922, 1971), *Collected Writings of John Maynard Keynes*, Vol. III, *A Revision of the Treaty*, London: Macmillan, p. 34.
4. Hayek, F.A. (1936a), 'Edwin Cannan', *Zeitschrift fur Nationalökonomie*, XXI: 35–7.
5. Keynes, J.M., 'Review of Hawtrey *Currency and Credit*, in *Collected Writings*, Vol. XI (1973), *Economic Articles and Correspondence*, pp. 441–4.
6. Hawtrey, R.G. (1919), *Currency and Credit*, London: Longman, p. 18.
7. op. cit., p. 20.
8. Keynes, J.M. (1930a, 1972), *Collected Writings*, Vol. V, *A Treatise on Money*, p. 57.
9. op. cit., p. 68.
10. op. cit., p. 132.
11. op. cit., p. 207.
12. op. cit., p. 127.
13. Keynes, J.M. (1973), *Collected Writings*, Vol. XIII, *The General Theory and After: Part I, Preparation*, p. 19.
14. Hicks, J.R. (1974), *The Crisis in Keynesian Economics*, Oxford: Blackwell, p. 11.
15. Quoted in Moggridge, D. (1972), *British Monetary Policy*, p. 78.
16. Keynes, J.M. (1931, 1972), *Collected Writings*, Vol. IX, *Essays in Persuasion*, p. 89.
17. Hayek, F.A. (1984), 'The fate of the gold standard', in R. McCloughery (ed.) *Money Capital and Fluctuations: Early Essays*, London: Routledge, pp. 118–35.
18. Keynes, J.M. (1973), *The General Theory and After: Part I, Preparation*, p. 167.
19. Sraffa, P. (1932), 'Dr Hayek on Money and Capital, *Economic Journal*, 42: 44.
20. Hayek, F.A. (1932c), 'Money and capital: a reply', *Economic Journal*, 42: 238.
21. Sraffa (1932), op. cit., p. 45 fnl.
22. Hayek (1932c), op. cit., p. 244.
23. Sraffa (1932), op. cit., p. 48.
24. Hayek (1932c), op. cit., p. 239.
25. Sraffa (1932), op. cit., p. 49.
26. Hayek (1932c), op. cit. p. 240.
27. Hayek quoted in Kahn, R.F. (1984), *The Making of Keynes' General Theory*, Cambridge: Cambridge University Press, p. 56.

28. Robertson, D.H. (1929), 'The monetary doctrines of Messrs Foster and Catching', *Quarterly Journal of Economics*, 43: 473–99.
29. Henderson, H.D. (1935), 'Review of Robbins *The Great Depression*', *Economic Journal*, 45: 117.
30. op. cit., p. 123.
31. Hawtrey, R.G. (1932), 'Review of *Prices and Production*', *Economica*, 12: 126.
32. Cannan, *Economic Journal*, 41: 16.
33. Robertson, D.H. (1929), op. cit., pp 483–4.
34. Robbins, L.C. (1932b), 'Consumption and the trade cycle', *Economica*, 12: 429.
35. Durbin, E.F.M. (1933b), *Purchasing Power and Trade Depression*, London: Cape, p. 68.
36. Hawtrey, R.G. (1935), 'Review of Durbin's *Purchasing Power and Trade Depression*', *Economica*, NS2: 469.
37. Robertson, D.H. (1931), 'Review of Durbin's *Purchasing Power and Trade Depression*', *Economic Journal*, 43: 176.
38. Keynes, J.M. (1979), *Collected Writings*, Vol. XXIX, *General Theory and After: a supplement*', p. 231.

4
Beiträge zur Geldtheorie

Introduction

Edited by Hayek, *Beiträge zur Geldtheorie* (*Essays on Monetary Theory*) introduced the School's economists to contributions on monetary equilibrium and neutral money by European economists. The book was reviewed by Hicks and Gilbert and serves as a peg upon which to hang a discussion of the early writings of Hicks, Chambers, Gilbert and Makower. Hicks commented upon Myrdal's essay on 'Monetary equilibrium' (1933) (of which a revised version was subsequently published in England in 1939) and Fanno's piece on 'The pure theory of the banking system' (Fanno, 1933). Gilbert reviewed Holtrop's (1933) essay on the velocity of circulation and Koopmans' (1933) essay on neutral money. Myrdal's chapter introduced the School to the Swedish writings on expectations and, by the back door, to Keynes's work on expectations because Myrdal had been influenced by Keynes's *Treatise on Probability*. The assimilation of Swedish thought was also assisted by Brinley Thomas who spent a year in Sweden and then gave five lectures at the School on Neo-Wicksellian theory. There was also a visit to the School by Lindahl. Hicks's fiancée, Ursula Webb, assisted in the translation of Lindhal's work which was later published in 1939. Lindahl's ideas also permeated Cambridge because he was in correspondence with, and visited, Keynes. Finally, the Swedish ideas had a profound influence upon Hayek and were, in part, responsible for a change in the direction of his research.

From Wicksell to Myrdal

In the middle of the nineteenth century there was a preoccupation with the workings of the gold standard and its presumption that there was a link between the quantity of money and the price level. However, the last decades of the nineteenth century were dominated by a fall in commodity prices that was not accompanied by a fall in the quantity of money. Wicksell's resolution of the paradox was to draw a distinction between the money rate of interest and the natural rate of interest (a concept which he derived from Böhm-Bawerk's theory of capital and interest) and to assume that the only money available was credit. In a pure credit economy the money supply would not be determined exogenously but by the demands placed upon the banks by businesses. If then businesses demanded more credit then it was a sign that the money rate of interest was below the natural rate of interest which would exist in a money-less or barter economy. Hence, the money rate could be low even though prices were rising. This was an interpretation that overcame Tookes's view that booms were associated with high interest rates.

Wicksell was attempting to explain a twenty year fall in prices and he was not attempting to explain the seven- or nine-year trade cycle. But the Wicksell process was used later by Mises to form the basis of a trade cycle theory and it was the Mises model which Hayek elaborated. There is also a further point to be made. Wicksell did not subscribe to a monetary explanation of the trade cycle and in his pure credit economy it was possible for movements in the price level to be driven by real forces. Another and more important feature of Wicksell's work was that he introduced the concepts of monetary equilibrium and neutral money. He put forward the following three conditions for monetary equilibrium:

1. The money rate of interest should equal the natural rate.
2. The marginal product of capital should equal the natural rate of interest.
3. The price level should remain unchanged.

Which leads on to *Monetary Equilibrium* in which Myrdal (1939) observed that in an economy with many goods the natural rate of interest could only be interpreted as an expected yield in money terms and, as such, introduced expectations about future prices into the analysis. Furthermore, a distinction had to be drawn between *ex ante* and *ex post* savings and investment and it was only in an *ex ante* sense that a difference between savings and investment would show itself. Finally, the reinterpretation of the natural rate as a monetary concept implied that constancy of the price level had to be abandoned because any behaviour of the price level might be consistent with equilibrium if prices were flexible. Hicks began his review of Myrdal by emphasizing that it was 'the most exciting work on monetary theory since Mr Keynes's *Treatise* and

Professor Hayek's *Prices and Production* and marked a very definite step in advance'.[1] But the reinterpretation of the natural rate raised, for Hicks, the disturbing question: 'What is monetary equilibrium for?'[2]

Lindahl and studies in the theory of money and capital

This brings us to the work of Lindahl. In the interwar years there was an intense drive to get to grips with the problem of time. In 1929, in Sweden, Lindahl wrote 'The place of capital in the theory of price'; it was translated into English and published in his book, *Studies in the Theory of Money and Capital* in 1939. In the essay Lindahl sought to integrate capital and interest into price theory by bringing together Walras's general equilibrium analysis with Böhm-Bawerk's theory of capital and interest. However, a significant feature of the analysis was that he set out a theory of intertemporal expectations equilibrium in which he paid particular attention to the problem of expectations. He introduced the assumption of perfect foresight in which he postulated that individuals could know when a future technical change would take place and also its effects in order that they could 'take steps to secure that the apparatus of production could at the same time be completely adjusted to the new technique.'[3] He concluded that the assumption of perfect foresight was useful in analyzing change:

> Under the assumption that the future is perfectly foreseen, all prices in all periods in the dynamic system thus become linked together in a uniform system. The equilibrium of the system is maintained by the same laws as under stationary conditions. Costs of production and prices coincide, and supply and demand are also equal. The real difference from the stationary case lies in the circumstance that the primary factors, there regarded as given, are assumed to undergo change from one period to another period. In this way a movement arises in the system. The task of theory is to elucidate more closely the general conditions on which this movement depends and to give exact expression to its course under all conceivable conditions.[4]

But he also expressed some reservations:

> The assumption that in a given period of time people perfectly foresee the price level that will prevail in this period as a result of their actions during the period is, strictly speaking, a necessary condition for an explanation of a price situation as a state of equilibrium, in the sense that there exists a mutual connection between supply and demand on the one hand and the actual prices on the other, and that, therefore at existing prices exchange can continue until full satisfaction has been attained. This assumption

underlies most theories of price determination. If this abstraction is dropped another method of analysis must be used. It must be imagined that people anticipate a certain price situation and therefore decide upon a certain volume of supply and demand and that these decisions give rise to a price situation *different* from that anticipated. (Even if there should be agreement with regard to prices, the two situations differ with regard to the relation between supply and demand.) The new situation causes people to alter their decisions, and this in turn gives rise to still another situation, again with new decisions, etc. In this case there is no mutual dependence between prices and factors affecting prices at a given moment, but instead a one-sided causal connection in one direction or the other.[5]

That is to say, Lindahl was groping for the distinction between *ex ante* and *ex post* which Myrdal later introduced.

In the 1939 chapter 'The dynamic approach to economic theory', Lindahl showed a preoccupation with disequilibrium analysis and with the possibility of fix-prices:

> The pricing problem is often treated under the assumption of free competition, whereby the prices operating in a certain period can be regarded as the result of the operation of certain given demand and supply functions. This construction is quite appropriate when used for the analysis of the *equilibrium* position of a price or system of prices. But it is not always so appropriate when the pricing problem is analysed from a more realistic point of view. In an actual dynamic case, there is no necessity for equality of demand and supply. But the opposite concept of price as *continuously changing* under the influence of the demand and supply functions is equally not correct.[6]

Brinley Thomas

The *Beiträge zur Geldtheorie* was one means by which Swedish ideas reached the LSE but another and important route arose as a result of Brinley Thomas being sent to Sweden and Germany by Hugh Dalton. Thomas was not by instinct a theorist and most of his work was in applied economics. Beveridge supervised his PhD thesis on population and Carr Saunders asked him to write a chapter on migration. Later he wrote with Hamish Richards a book entitled *Population Movements and Economic Growth* and the ideas which he then developed were expanded into his major work on migration and cycles in economic activity which spanned the Atlantic economy (Thomas and Richards, 1936). However, Dalton did get him to write a chapter for his book on *Unbalanced Budgets* (Thomas, 1934) and he did give six lectures on Swedish monetary theory to a small group of staff and students which included Shackle

Lindahl and the theory of money and capital 83

Table 4.1 Session 1934–5. Neo-Wicksellian Fluctuation Theory in Sweden. Mr. Thomas.

Five lectures. Summer Term. Fridays, 6.00–7.00, beginning S.T. 3 May. Fee: 10s.
SYLLABUS: A review of the developments of the Wicksellian tradition in Sweden, with particular reference to the works of Lindahl, Myrdal and the Ackermans. The course will begin with an account of the controversy between Wicksell and Cassel, Davidson and others. BOOKS RECOMMENDED: D. Davidson, 'Om stabiliseringen av penningens varde' (*Ekonomisk Tidskrift*, 1909); K. Wicksell, *Geldzins und Güterpreise* (1898); 'Penninggränta och varupris' (*Ekonomisk Tidskrift*, 1909); *Vorlesungen* (Vol. II); E. Lindahl, *Penningpolitikens Ma'och Medel* (1929); 'The concept of income' (in *Essays in Honour of Gustav Cassel*); G. Myrdal, *Prisbidnings problemet och Foränderligheten* (1927); *Der Gleichgewichtsbegriff als Instrument der geldtheoretischen Analyse, Beiträge zur Geldtheorie* (ed. F.A. von Hayek, 1933); Johan Akerman, *Konjunkturteoretiska Problem* (1934).

Source: LSE *Calendar* 1934–5.

and Lachmann. From Thomas they got their initial understanding of Myrdal's distinction between *ex ante* and *ex post*, Lindahl's discussion of monetary equilibrium and Swedish stabilization measures (Table 4.1).

Keynes

At this juncture it is useful to see how the Swedish analysis bore upon the work of Keynes. Myrdal said that a lot of Keynes's writings showed signs of unnecessary originality because he was not familiar with Swedish and German writings. Now it is true that Keynes had difficulty with reading German and had no knowledge of Swedish. But that he was unfamiliar with the basic problems was probably wide of the mark and that he was nearer to suggesting more plausible lines of advance seems to be more apposite. In the *Treatise* monetary equilibrium and monetary disequilibrium emerge through possible equalities or differences between investment and savings. By excluding windfall profits from income, Keynes allows for the possibility of monetary disequilibrium.

In Keynes's analysis monetary equilibrium occurred when entrepreneurial income was normal; that is to say, sufficient to maintain the present level of employment and output at current factor prices. But the distinction between normal income and profits presupposed a lag in the adjustment of factor prices. In the *Treatise* Keynes showed little interest in the lag in adjustment except to say that a lag did exist to make his distinction between income and profits useful. As a result he was criticized because of the ambiguity of his treatment of the lag and for his failure to discuss whether the time period of the lag could be expected to vary over the trade cycle. There were two possible lines of defence against these criticisms. First, there could be a complete analysis of the factors influencing lags and the revision of contracts. Second, a timeless or instantaneous analysis could be developed in order to bypass the problems. The first route was that pursued by Robertson and the Swedes; the second path was followed by Keynes in the *General Theory*. The usefulness of the two approaches will be deferred until an examination of the nature of the Keynesian avalanche is made in Chapter 8.

Hayek

In 1976 Lachmann observed that:

> when around 1930 [in Keynes's *Treatise on Money*] expectations made their appearance in the economic thought of the Anglo-Saxon world, the Austrians failed to grasp with both hands the golden opportunity to enlarge the basis of their approach and, by and large, treated the subject rather gingerly. Exploration of the real world only comes in later.[7]

The failure to grasp 'the golden opportunity' was surprising given the emphasis in Austrian economic thought upon the subjective nature of marginal utility analysis. And it was also surprising given that Hayek had, independently of Lindahl, produced an article on intertemporal equilibrium in 1928. But the article assumed perfect foresight of a form more rigorous than that in Lindahl's later work. Hence he was criticized for his failure to include expectations by Myrdal. His initial response was in his article on 'Price expectations, monetary disturbances and malinvestments' published in German in 1933 but not available in an English translation until 1939. In that article Hayek sought to make unanticipated monetary shocks the reason for the trade cycle but he did not deal with the possibility that disturbances might arise from the real side of the economy – that is to say he did not deal with the points of criticism made by Sraffa. And he concluded with the following remarks:

> ... while I cannot quite agree with Professor Myrdal when he alleges that in my theory there is no room for the role played by expectations – to show how important a place they do play was in fact one of the purposes of this lecture – I am on the other hand in complete agreement when he stresses the great importance of this element in the further development of the theory of industrial fluctuations.[8]

The shift in Hayek's views is supposed to come with the publication of his 1937 article 'Economics and knowledge' which Shackle has considered to be one of his most important contributions to economics.

According to Hayek the paper was the result of an LSE colleague poking fun at the use of the word data by economists who were so anxious to assure themselves that there were data that they spoke about *given data*. This gibe made Hayek aware that although economists assumed that facts were given, they never said to whom they were given. But since all knowledge was dispersed and nobody possessed all the knowledge then the data could not exist. Prices, therefore, did not rest upon past events, upon some data given from the past, but were signals about the future. It was this realization that led to the fuller statement about the pricing system in 1945. It also led on to the view of Shackle that there are no objects, no data, until we choose; in choosing we sift and classify and create objects in our act of choosing. But despite the praise heaped upon Hayek's 1937 article it was, by the standards of his day, not a great advance. It was still concerned with equilibrium and equilibrating forces. It did not take account of the stress being placed upon disequilibrium by Myrdal and Keynes and when he reviewed Lindahl's *Studies in the Theory of Money and Capital* he reserved his praise for the 1929 paper.

The demand for money: portfolio analysis

Hicks's review of Myrdal's 'Monetary equilibrium' must be seen in the context of his earlier work in economics and the subsequent publication of his magnum opus, *Value and Capital* (1939a). At school Hicks had been a competent mathematician but when he went up to Oxford he chose to do PPE (philosophy, politics and economics). Because he wanted to be an academic rather than a politician he concentrated upon economics. Oxford economics was however social economics. He did his thesis upon skill differentials in the engineering and building industries and he also did some work on arbitration and conciliation. But he did not encounter Edgeworth's writings until he went to the LSE. Hayek's early impressions of him were that he was a Marshallian.

From 1926 to 1935 he was at the LSE (Table 4.2). He left because, according to Robbins, the Director, William Beveridge, was averse to theorists and would not renew his contract. The years at the School fell sharply into two parts and were separated by the arrival of Robbins in 1929. Before 1929 he was left largely to his own devices, although Dalton suggested, in 1926, that because of his knowledge of Italian he should read Pareto. Later he was to recall that: 'I was deep in Pareto before I got much out of Marshall.' In his second year at the School he took up a temporary lecturership at the University of Johannesburg where he

Table 4.2 Session 1931–2. Problems of Industrial Relations. Mr. Hicks.

Ten lectures. Michaelmas Term. Thursdays, 12.00–1.00, beginning M.T. 8 October.
or (e) Thursdays, 7.00–8.00, beginning M.T. 8 October.
For B.Com. Final. Part I.
Fees: Day: £1 10s.
  Evening: £1.

SYLLABUS: The case for the control of wages examined. The theory of collective bargaining and the minimum wage. Conciliation and arbitration. Wage boards. Hours and conditions.

BOOKS RECOMMENDED: Pigou, *Economics of Welfare* (Part III); Rowe, *Wages in Practice and Theory*; Clay, *Problems of Industrial Relations*; 'The public regulation of wages' (*Economic Journal*, 1920); Hutt, *Theory of Collective Bargaining*; Webb, *Industrial Democracy*; Amulree, *Industrial Arbitration*; Rankin, *Arbitration Principles and the Industrial Court*; Balfour Report on Industrial Relations.

Note: Despite the fact that the course was given at a time when Hicks was still regarded as an industrial relations specialist, the syllabus is strong on analytical works. Years later Schumpeter was to record in his *History of Economic Analysis* that the *Economics of Welfare* marked the furthest advance of a man primarily regarded as a theorist into industrial relations. Rowe, who was a Cambridge lecturer, produced the best discussion of wage determination in practice and Clay's book was an outstanding analysis of the problems posed by wage differentials during the 1920s. The Webbs' *Industrial Democracy* also attempted to impose an analytical framework upon the nature and types of trade unions. Hutt's book was a very instructive work on the adverse effects of collective bargaining and the books by Amulree and Rankin, who were both arbitrators, emphasized the difficulties of establishing principle for the settlement of disputes.

Source: LSE *Calendar* 1931–2.

got a new view of trade unions:

> I began to think of them as monopolists, so that it was by application of monopoly theory that their effects were to be understood. The reservation of skilled jobs to White labour, and the confinement of the best land in the country to White ownership, were the economic obstacles in the way of progress for the Black majority. In a free market system these would wither away, so I became a free market man, even before I left South Africa.[9]

The arrival of Robbins was associated with two changes in Hicks's academic career. First, there was the recognition that he had the ability to become an economic theorist and a mathematical economist. The second event was when Robbins asked him whether it was possible to provide a rigorous mathematical treatment of Hayek's *Prices and Production*. The latter task was to lead him to Hayek's 'Das Intertemporale Gleichgewichtssystem der Preisse und des Bewungen der Geldwertes' in which as we noted in the previous chapter, Hayek had set out the conditions for intertemporal equilibrium.

The outcome was the article 'Gleichgewicht und Konjunktur' ('Equilibrium and the trade cycle') published in 1933. In the article Hicks sought to extend the Paretian system through the incorporation of production in time. To do so it was not sufficient to rely upon present prices to determine the behaviour of economic agents: 'we ought to take account of future (expected) prices as well as current prices on their behaviour.' But present and future prices might not be equal unless there were perfect foresight. This led Hicks to consider the role of money in his intertemporal model – which was an issue ignored by Hayek. He observed that:

> Money as a medium of exchange plays no part in the Lausanne equilibrium . . . the tacit assumption of perfect foresight deprives the numeraire of any monetary function. . . . It is only for future payments that one needs to hold a stock of money. But it is to be noted that it is only to meet uncertain payments that a stock of money is needed . . . thus we cannot escape the conclusion that if the future course of economic data (and the corresponding course of future prices) were exactly foreseen, then there would be no demand to hold money as money. People would lend out all their money holdings.[10]

From which it followed that:

> The Trade Cycle is a 'purely monetary phenomenon' in one sense only; that every large change in economic data affects risk and hence affects the velocity of circulation of money. It has additional real effects through its monetary repercussions. Whatever the *cause causans* of an economic crisis, it is bound to have monetary effects.[11]

Hicks then went on to observe that the existence of risk exerts a significant influence on the way in which a person holds his or her assets and in a severe slump a person would prefer to hold money rather than other assets. He therefore introduced a liquidity spectrum:

> In advanced communities, a representative individual may be considered to hold his assets in innumerable different forms which may, however, be

Table 4.3 Session 1929–30. Theory of Risk and Profits. Mr. Hicks.

Six lectures. Summer Term. Fridays, 6.00–7.00, beginning S.T. 2 May.
For B.Sc. (Econ) Final – Special subject of Economics.
Fee: 12s.

SYLLABUS: A consideration of recent theories of profits, with especial reference to American theories.
BOOKS RECOMMENDED: Clark, *Distribution of Wealth*; Knight, *Risk, Uncertainty and Profit*; Hardy, *Risk and Risk-bearing*.

Source: LSE *Calendar* 1929–30.

broadly classified: cash, call loans, short-term loans, long-term loans, material property (inc shares). Broadly speaking, there is an increasing risk element as we go from left to right; and again, broadly speaking, there is a higher promise of return in the same direction to compensate for increased risk. The distribution of assets among these forms is governed by relative prospects of return and relative risk factors.[12]

What is interesting about Hicks's article is that he was not aware of the difference between Marshallian economics and Paretian economics and that Hayek was not aware of any difference between Austrian economics and Paretian economics. Both Marshallian and Austrian economics tended to be dealing with partial processes in which money exchanged against goods and in which money formed the only link between otherwise decentralized markets. (See Tables 4.3, 4.4, 4.5 and 4.6.)

Table 4.4 Session 1933–4. The Foreign Exchanges and International Trade. Dr. Hicks.

Eight lectures. Summer Term. Thursdays, 11.00–12.00, beginning S.T. 26 April.
or (e) Wednesdays, 6.00–7.00, beginning S.T. 25 April.
For B.Sc. (Econ) Final. 2nd year and B.Com. Honours Final, 2nd year.
Recommended also for postgraduate students.
Fees: Day: £1 4s.
      Evening: 16s.

SYLLABUS: The adjustment of inter-local price differences with a common metallic currency. The complications introduced by different currencies and banking systems. The practical working of the foreign exchanges. Special problems: comparative cost; the terms of trade; the transfer problem.

BOOKS RECOMMENDED: Whale, *International Trade*; Gregory, *The Gold Standard and its Future*; Clare and Crump, *ABC of Foreign Exchanges*; Keynes, *Tract on Monetary Reform* (Chapter 3); Bastable, *Theory of International Trade*; Taussig, *International Trade*; Mises, *Theorie des Geldes* (Part II, Chapters 3–4); Ricardo, *Principles* (Chapter 7); Mill, *Principles* (Bk. III, Chapters 17–25).

The following books are recommended for further reading for economics specialists and other students who wish to pursue more advanced studies in this subject: Foster, *Essay on Commercial Exchanges*; Ricardo, *High Price of Bullion*; Senior, *Cost of Obtaining Money*; Torrens, *Principles of Sir Robert Peel's Act*; Cairnes, *Essays in Political Economy*; Marshall, *Money, Credit and Commerce*; Edgeworth, *Pure Theory of International Values* (Papers, Vol. II); Barone, *Principi dell' economia politica (Grundzuge)* (Chapters 3 and 4); Wicksell, *Vorlesungen* (Vol. II); Angell, *Theory of International Prices*; Haberler, 'Die Theorie der Komparativen Kosten' (*Weltwirtschaftliches Archiv*, 1930); 'Transfer und Preisbewegung' (*Weltwirtschaftliches Archiv*, 1930); Viner, *Canada's Balance of Indebtedness*; Bresciani-Turroni, *Le Vicende del marco ledesco*.

Note: In his autobiographical writings Hicks never refers to his lectures on international trade and in his correspondence with Keynes he stated that he was unfamiliar with monetary theory before 1870. However, the above syllabus would seem to indicate some familiarity with Ricardo's *High Price of Bullion* in which Ricardo did discuss the short run (output) effects of changes in the quantity of money.

Source: LSE *Calendar* 1933–4.

The demand for money 89

Table 4.5 Session 1934–5. Theory of Value. Dr. Hicks.

Ten lectures. Michaelmas Term. Fridays, 5.00–6.00, beginning M.T. 12 October.
For postgraduate students and B.Sc. (Econ) Final – Special Economics.
Fee: £1 5s.

SYLLABUS: The development of the modern theory of value from the time of Cournot and Dupuit. The theory of the utility function, particularly in respect of the relatedness of wants. Market equilibrium: the questions of determinateness, of stability and of formation.
BOOKS RECOMMENDED: A. **Historical classics**: Cournot, *Mathematical Principles of the Theory of Wealth*; Dupuit, *De l'Utilite et de sa Mesure*; Jevons, *Theory of Political Economy*; Menger, *Grunsatze der Volkwirtschaftslehre*; Walras, *Elements d'economie politique pure*; Edgeworth, *Mathematical Psychics*; Böhm-Bawerk, *Grundzuge*; Pantaleoni, *Pure Economics*; Marshall, *Principles*; Wicksell, *Uber Wert, Kapital und Rente*; Pareto, *Manuel d'Economie Politique*.
B. **Modern works**: Wicksell, *Lectures* (Vol. I); Knight, *Risk, Uncertainty and Profit*; Bowley, *Mathematical Groundwork of Economics*; Schonfeld, *Grenznutzen und Wirtschaftsrechnung*; Rosenstein-Rodan, 'Grenznutzen' (in *Handwörterbuch)*; 'La Complentarieta' *(Riforma Sociale*, 1933); Hicks and Allen, 'Reconsideration of the *Theory of Value*' (*Economica*, 1934); Kaldor, 'Determinateness of equilibrium' (*Review of Economic Studies*, 1934).

Source: LSE *Calendar* 1934–5.

Table 4.6 Session 1934–5. Economic Dynamics. Dr. Hicks.

Ten lectures. Lent Term. Fridays, 5.00–6.00, beginning L.T. 18 January.
For B.Sc. (Econ) Final – Special subject of Economics. Also recommended to postgraduate students.
Fee: £1 5s.

SYLLABUS: This course will be concerned with a study of those economic phenomena which appear only in a changing economic system and which drop out when a system is brought to rest in static fashion. An attempt will first be made to lay down certain general principles of the theory of economic change; in some respects this treatment will be parallel to that in Marshall's Book V, but it will be based upon general equilibrium theory of Marshall and Wicksell. Attention will be paid to the theory of risk and on this there will be based some general remarks about the theory of money and fluctuations.
BOOKS RECOMMENDED: Knight, *Risk, Uncertainty and Profit*; Hayek, Das Intertemporale Gleichgewichtsystem (*Weltwirtschaftliches Archiv*, 1928); Fisher, *The Theory of Interest*; Lindahl, *The Concept of Income* (in Cassell Essays); Myrdal, paper in *Beiträge zur Geldtheorie* (ed. Hayek); Hicks, 'The theory of uncertainty and profit' (*Economica*, 1931); 'Gleichgewicht und Konjunktur' (*Zeitschrift für Nationalökonomie*, 1933).

Note: The syllabuses contained in Tables 4.5 and 4.6 contain the ingredients of Hicks' future great book, *Value and Capital*.

Source: LSE *Calendar* 1934–5.

Chambers

Paul Chambers was a graduate student at the LSE in the early 1930s who subsequently went to the Inland Revenue and ultimately became chairman of ICI. In 1934 he was awarded a Master's degree for his thesis on 'The equilibrium analysis of a monetary economy' and in the same year he published an article (based on his thesis) entitled 'Fluctuations in capital and the demand for money' in the *Review of Economic Studies*. In the thesis he set out to discover whether money lay wholly outside equilibrium theory and he acknowledged Hicks's 1933 article as his starting point.

Chambers's extensive survey of British, European and American literature revealed an absence of a systematic analysis of the demand for money. The classical economists, such as Ricardo and Mill, regarded money as a physical commodity and never tackled the problems of a monetary economy. Jevons had nothing original to say about money and Marshall tended to regard cash balances as being available for 'snapping up bargains'. Walras had a similar approach to the Classical economists and looked upon the demand for money as being similar to the demand for final goods. Nor did the other European economists, such as Mises and Holtrop, have much to contribute. Chambers therefore concluded that there were difficulties in introducing money into a general equilibrium framework and that: 'a concept of static equilibrium is needed which does not require perfect knowledge, perfect foresight, infinite divisibility of factors, and other similar refinements which the mathematicians have introduced in order to perfect their models since with those refinements the *raison d'être* of money is eliminated.'[13] To overcome these difficulties he adopted J.B. Clark's concept of a stationary state which enabled him to speak without inconsistency of a static demand for money. Individuals would demand money for future payments and these payments would be foreseen or unforeseen.

Foreseen payments could arise because of a gap between payments and receipts stemming from fluctuations in the demand for and supply of real capital. Even then cash balances might be dispensed with if there were a system of credit transfers – but that would still involve costs in making records of settlements. Optimal cash balances would therefore be determined by comparing interest and investment costs: 'In making his choice the entrepreneur has to balance the costs of making the marginal investment against the additional interest obtained.'[14] In analyzing unforeseen payments, Chambers introduced the risk factor which could be measured by the mean and standard deviation of a probability distribution – an idea which was suggested to him by an unpublished paper written by Hicks. And 'having thus measured the mean and standard deviation of each investment with which an individual investing a marginal unit of capital is confronted, his attitude towards these alternatives can be expressed by a set of indifference curves.'[15] The idea of employing indifference curves to represent risk was another idea Chambers derived from Hicks – and it must be borne in mind that Hicks was lecturing on risk in the early 1930s. Given the indifference curves between risk and return an individual would diversify his or her investments in order to reduce risk. The demand for money would then be influenced by the individual's risk preferences.

Individuals and firms could also reduce risk through insurance and Chambers distinguished between insurable and non-insurable risks and the problems of moral hazard, with insurance being effected either by holding larger cash balances or other assets. Chambers also dealt with the problem of measurable and non-measurable risk. He argued that the distinction was often a matter of degree and that large firms might convert small non-measurable risks into measurable risks by collectively pooling them and invoking the law of large numbers. Furthermore, he argued there were many risks which firms faced which were in fact predictable and which could therefore be insured against, such as earthquakes. He was therefore disinclined to place too much emphasis upon Knight's distinction between risk and uncertainty.

Simplifying the theory of money

In 1935 Hicks published 'A suggestion for simplifying the theory of money' (1935a) and the article was subsequently reprinted in the American Economic Association's *Readings in Monetary Theory* (1952). In the article Hicks said that he came to monetary theory from value theory and was astonished to find that marginal utility theory was not used in monetary analysis: 'We now realise that the marginal utility analysis is nothing else than a general theory of choice . . . people do choose to have money rather than other things, and therefore, in the relevant sense, money must have a marginal utility.'[16] He then went on to observe that he found a useful approach in the bearish motive in Keynes's *Treatise on Money* where Keynes analyzed the determinants of the price level of investment goods and showed that it depended upon the preference of the investor for bank deposits or securities. In other words, an investor would be concerned with a portfolio decision or balance sheet decision involving assets and liabilities. Hicks therefore sought to advance monetary theory by generalizing banking theory.

The question then arose: what are the factors which determine an individual's allocation of his wealth? Why should people hold money when it yields no return? Hicks's answer ran in terms of transactions costs:

> The amount of money a person will desire to hold depends upon three factors: the dates at which he expects to make payments in the future; the costs of investment and the expected return on investment. The further ahead the future payments, the lower the cost of investment and the

higher the expected return on invested capital — the lower the demand for money.[17]

Expected returns would involve risks which would depend upon the expected net yield of the investment and the expected period of the investment with the former being approximated by the mean and standard deviation of a probability distribution. Hicks's analysis was therefore similar to that of Chambers with the main differences being the absence of capital gains and losses from Chambers's stationary state model and the absence of any discussion of insurance in Hicks's theory.

Helen Makower

The second postgraduate thesis to be examined is that of Helen Makower on 'The theory of value on the capital market' and which was submitted in 1937. Makower noted that the theory of relative prices of consumption goods had been well established but that it was necessary to extend the theory of value to the determination of asset prices and that meant incorporating time and risk into the analysis. She observed that Irving Fisher had provided the means for coping with time but had not dealt with asset prices. Hence, there was a need to develop his discussion of time preference and productivity to asset prices and to introduce risk through the use of frequency distributions. Asset prices would then be determined by time, risk aversion and the opportunity to obtain income from assets of varying quality, time horizons and risk. Her analysis was conducted for both competitive and monopolistic markets. Many of her insights were incorporated in an article entitled 'Asset prices and monetary theory' which she wrote with Jacob Marshack in 1938. The article was selected for inclusion in the American Economic Association's *Readings in Price Theory* (1953).

Economists who wrote above their times?

Were Hicks, Chambers and Makower economists who wrote above their times? Were they progenitors of the demand for money and portfolio approach? Were they victims of the Keynesian avalanche? Can their theories be divorced from their existentialist base? Were Baumol and Tobin and the Yale School the true discoverers of the portfolio approach because it was only in the 1950s and 1960s that the 'times were right' for portfolio theory? Now the response to these questions depends upon whether or not there were predecessors of Hicks, Chambers and Makower.

Flushed with his success in developing the ordinal approach to utility theory, Hicks stated in the introduction to 'Simplifying the theory of money' that marginal utility theory was not used in monetary analysis. 'No wonder', he wrote, 'there are such difficulties and differences!'[18] But, as we noted in Chapter 2, Cannan had applied marginal utility analysis to money. And earlier Marshall had also applied marginal utility theory to money. Now Hicks was, on his own admission, ignorant of Cambridge economics but it was strange that he was not aware, through Robbins, of Cannan's work. However, there were also other economists who wrote above their times.

In 1914 Karl Schlesinger (who attended the Mises seminar in the 1920s) published his *Theorie der Geld und Kreditswirtschaft* in which he dealt with the possibilities of holding cash (precautionary balances) as an insurance against liquidity losses stemming from uncertainty in the timing of payments and receipts. He determined the individual's demand for these balances from the equalities of interest forgone and insurance benefits from such a reserve. But in Cambridge the three-fold margin seems to have been propounded at an earlier date by Pigou in *Wealth and Welfare* (1912). And in 1921 Lavington published his *English Capital Market* in which he discussed the motives for holding money in terms of the rate of interest and the state of expectations. After the publication of the *General Theory* Robertson reminded Keynes of Lavington's work and he also drew upon it when he discussed the three-fold margin between consumption, investing and holding money. And yet another twist is added to the history of monetary theory by a letter from Sraffa to Keynes in 1931 in which he spoke of the investor's indifference curve between securities and savings deposits. Sraffa may have been familiar with indifference curves from the work of Pareto. He may even have read Slutsky's article on consumer theory which was originally published in Italian. But it is possible that Keynes was familiar with the idea of indifference curves through his reading of the writings of the Cambridge philosopher, W.E. Johnson from whom he drew inspiration when writing *The Treatise on Probability* (Keynes, 1921).

Schlesinger's book was published in German and adopted a mathematical format. Both characteristics may have reduced its impact since few economists read German and many Austrian economists tended to be averse to mathematics (although this statement cannot be applied to Hayek who was familiar with the calculus and, through his Circle, with the rudiments of more advanced mathematics). But what of Lavington at Cambridge? Was Hicks's success due to his 'promotion' by Robbins whereas Lavington lacked a sponsor at Cambridge? Indeed, Lavington might seem to have been doubly unfortunate since he published an article on vertical integration in *Economica* which anticipated some of the work of Coase and Williamson (Lavington, 1927). But the argument cannot stand close inspection. Lerner presented his famous paper on factor price equalization at a Robbins seminar in the 1930s but it was not published until after the rediscovery of the theorem by Samuelson in 1947 (Lerner, 1952). Furthermore, Lerner had an important paper on capital theory which lay buried until the 1970s (Lerner, 1982). And Lerner as the editor of the *Review of Economic Studies* had the means through which to publish his own work.

Neutral money

Gilbert who had been an undergraduate at the School and was appointed as an assistant (Lecturer) until the Geddes axe fell and he went to the newly formed Dundee School of Economics, reviewed Holtrop's (1933) 'Die Umlaufsgeschwindigkeit'. It dealt with the factors determining the velocity of circulation of money which Holtrop considered to be the central problem of monetary theory. Gilbert disagreed and took the view that: 'the most important problem with which monetary theorists have to deal is surely the relationship between money and economic equilibrium.'[19] He also took exception to Holtrop's rejection of the demand to hold approach on the grounds that a money balance in itself had no positive utility − which was a point of view opposite to that suggested by Holtrop.

However, it was the essay by Koopmans (1933) on neutral money which was to attract the greatest attention within the School and which was to be revived in the late 1950s. The concept of neutral money goes back at least to Hume's essay on money in which he maintained that in the long run the quantity of money would affect the price level but would not affect economic activity. From this insight there was then a search for the conditions under which the results derived from a barter economy would remain applicable when the existence of money was taken into account. Of course, it was recognized that the introduction of money into an economy would lead to some reallocation of resources. Money would overcome the disadvantages of barter and permit an increase in the division of labour and an increase in output. Even the work/leisure relationship would be affected. Hence, a money economy would not be exactly similar to a barter economy although it was assumed that the disturbances due to money would be minimized. In other words, money would be a veil or a lubricant. From which it followed that a neutral money economy would be one which combined the advantages of money without the disadvantages of inflation or deflation. Or as Hayek put it, a neutral money economy would be one in which relative prices remained constant. In Koopmans's analysis a neutral money economy would result when the quantity of money was held constant and any new hoarding or dishoarding would be offset by appropriate changes in the quantity of money. This was similar to the definition proposed by Hayek in *Prices and Production*: 'any change in the velocity of circulation would have to be compensated by a reciprocal change in the amount of money in circulation.'[20]

The concept of neutral money seemed to suggest that there would be no fluctuations in economic activity and on this point Barger, a graduate student, expressed reservations in his article 'Neutral money and the trade cycle' (1935). However, Barger did not explore the conditions which must obtain in the real economy for money to be neutral and only limited progress on this issue was made in the School in the early 1930s. Thus, there was an inconclusive debate between Gilbert and Durbin about the problem of effective credit policy when there was an autonomous increase in savings which was mediated through the banking system. Gilbert took the view that the quantity of money (M) must be kept stable and that Durbin's policy of keeping MV (money velocity) stable would mean that the money rate of interest would be pushed below the equilibrium rate. Durbin was forced to concede that with flexible prices equilibrium would be maintained but denied that inflation would result from his policy. Gilbert's model assumed absolute flexibility of prices in the sense that: 'whenever there is a change in data, prices would move as soon as the impact takes place.'[21] Neutral money therefore meant a constant quantity of money. In Durbin's model the quantity of money could be increased to offset a decline in the income velocity of circulation with a money rate equal to the equilibrium rate. The difference between the two models lay therefore in the absolute level of prices in the new equilibrium. However, the issues involved in the controversy were complicated and the problem was not completely resolved. But it is interesting to note that it was Gilbert's first attempt to formulate the condition for neutral money in a highly abstract model.

Summary and conclusions

The *Beiträge zur Geldtheorie* marked an important step forward in monetary theorizing in the School because it forced attention on the concepts of monetary equilibrium and neutral money in the analysis. It also introduced the School's economists to the Swedish work on expectations. As such the discussions called into question Hayek's work on the trade cycle and, in particular, the lack of attention to real forces and the attempt to postulate a natural rate of interest that was in some sense independent of monetary factors. Hicks had been forced to consider the role of expectations when he was asked by Robbins to provide a more rigorous treatment of the model contained in *Prices and Production*. Beginning, as he assumed Hayek had done, from a Lausanne formulation of intertemporal equilibrium he noted that in such a model there was no place for money. Money was therefore associated with imperfect foresight and Hicks went on to develop a portfolio approach to the holding of money and other assets. His line of approach was then elaborated by Chambers and Makower. However, it has to be noted that there were forerunners in Schlesinger and Lavington.

Four points therefore need to be noted about this theorizing. First, Hicks's conclusions went beyond Sraffa's verdict that money seemed to play no important part in *Prices and Production*, but Hicks went further and seemed to suggest that there was no money at all. Second, not only had Hicks and Chambers arrived at conclusions which were similar to those of Sraffa but their discussion of portfolio choice reiterated points which Lavington had made earlier and which were neglected by Keynes. Third, Hayek's failure to develop a monetary economy as a prelude to his analysis of the trade cycle seems to have stemmed from a mistaken belief that there was a body of economic thought which was commonly accepted by all European economists and he failed to appreciate the difference between Vienna, Lausanne and Cambridge. Fourth, Robbins's role in setting out a research strategy in *The Nature and Significance of Economic Science* and in pointing Hicks in the direction of unravelling the part played by money in Hayek's theory needs to be recognized. The emphasis upon scarcity and choice in Robbins's monograph were adumbrated by Hicks in his work on ordinal utility and in his portfolio approach to money.

In the main areas of analysis represented in the *Beiträge* there was less advance and more obvious faltering footsteps. The nature of Myrdal's attack on monetary equilibrium was only dimly perceived and its relationship to the work of Keynes was not fully grasped. Thus, an interesting insight into the compartmentalization of the School which was still persistent, despite the efforts of Robbins, was that Hicks was directed to the bearish factor in the *Treatise* by Barratt Whale who was not in the theoretical economics section of the School.

Notes

1. Hicks, J.R. (1934a), 'Review of Myrdal in *Beiträge zur Geldtheorie*', ed. F.A. Hayek, *Economica*, NS1: 480.

2. op. cit., p. 483.
3. Lindahl (1939), *Studies in the Theory of Money and Capital*, London: Allen and Unwin, p. 285.
4. op. cit., p. 330.
5. op. cit., pp. 339–40.
6. op. cit., p. 60.
7. Lachmann, L. (1976), *Journal of Economic Literature*, 14: 54–62.
8. Hayek, F.A. (1933a), 'Preiserwartungen, Monetare Storungen und Fehlinvestitionen', translated as 'Price expectations, monetary disturbances and malinvestments', in *Profits, Interest and Investment* (1939), London: Routledge, pp. 155–6.
9. Hicks, J.R. (1933), *Collected Essays on Economic Theory*, Vol. III, *Classics and Moderns*, Oxford: Blackwell, p. 357.
10. Hicks, J.R. (1933), *Collected Essays*, Vol. II, *Money Interest and Wages*, p. 31.
11. op. cit., p. 35.
12. op. cit., p. 36.
13. Chambers, S.P. (1934), 'Fluctuations in capital and the demand for money', *Review of Economic Studies*, 2: 38.
14. op. cit., p. 42.
15. op. cit., p. 45. Note that Hicks lectured on risk in the session 1931–2.
16. Hicks, J.R. (1933), reprinted in *Collected Essays*, Vol. II, *Money, Interest and Wages*, p. 48.
17. op. cit., p. 52.
18. op. cit., p. 44.
19. Gilbert, J.C. (1934a), 'Review of Holtrop in *Beiträge zur Geldtheorie*', ed. F.A. Hayek, *Economica*, NS1: 483.
20. Hayek, F.A. (1931c), *Prices and Production*, London: Routledge, p. 28.
21. Gilbert, J.C. (1934a), op. cit.

5
The capital controversy

Introduction

'God knows what the Austrians mean by the "period of production". Nothing in my opinion. *Vide* Knight's article in the forthcoming March *EJ*', wrote Keynes to Robertson on 20 February, 1935.[1] Keynes's outburst was a response to Robertson's comments on a draft chapter of the *General Theory* in which he had attempted to counter Hayek's criticisms of a lack of a theory of capital in the *Treatise on Money*. In his reply to Hayek, Keynes had admitted the lack of a theory of capital and interest and said he would remedy the defect in a later publication.[2] Keynes had followed Marshall in his critique of Austrian capital theory: 'Lengthy processes are not physically efficient because they are long. Some, probably most, lengthy processes would be physically inefficient, for there are such things as spoiling or wasting with time.'[3] In his comment on the draft chapter, Robertson wrote:

> While holding no particular brief for the Austrian jargon, I can't help feeling that in your criticism of it you are thinking too much of what you and I have called the 'period of production' – viz. the 'working capital' period with no fixed instruments given. I would heartily agree that improvements in efficiency to shorten the period, e.g. by making it possible to sow 2 crops a year, to reduce inventories, etc. But if by 'starting up' one means as the Austrians mean, mining the ore which is going to make the . . . reaping machines to harvest the crops then surely it is a different story.[4]

In sending the draft chapter to Robertson, Keynes was continuing the lengthy discussions which had begun with the preparation of

Robertson's *Banking Policy and the Price Level* (1926) and his (Keynes's) *Treatise on Money* (1930).

But there was added significance. In *A Study of Industrial Fluctuations* (1915) Robertson had explored long swings in economic activity and fixed capital formation. In *Banking Policy and the Price Level* he had experimented with different definitions of saving and investment and in 'Industrial fluctuations and the rate of interest' (1934) he had developed an Austrian type of trade cycle theory. Later, in his *Lectures on Economic Principles* (1957), Robertson was to affirm his belief in the usefulness of an Austrian approach to capital theory. In the lectures on income distribution he devoted a chapter to capital theory and built on the notion of an average period of production. In the lectures on the trade cycle he accepted that the period of production lengthened in the boom.

In his reply to Robertson, Keynes was also introducing into the discussion the debate between Knight and Hayek on the nature of capital and interest and which recalled an earlier clash between J.B. Clark and Böhm-Bawerk. The controversy, or controversies, involved a contrast between a productivity theory of interest, a distinction between original and produced means of production and a rejection of the idea that the average period of production measures an economy's heterogeneous stock of capital per head in homogeneous units of time. The debate, which also attracted other writers, such as Machlup and Gifford, was surveyed by Kaldor who began by being sympathetic to Hayek but subsequently shifted to an appreciation of Knight's ideas. The capital controversy also attracted Lerner, who in an unpublished paper of 1931–2, anticipated Hayek's 1934 article in the use of three-dimensional diagrams to illustrate the interrelations of capital, investment and interest. Subsequently, Lerner adapted his analysis to clarify the relationship between capital and interest in Keynes's *General Theory*.

Responding to both Knight and Kaldor, Hayek sought to clarify the nature of his ideas. Unfortunately, what he said failed to convince his critics. He was trying to continue the analysis of his 1928 paper on intertemporal equilibrium by incorporating capital and then considering the effects of disturbance on the capital structure. But what he did not make clear, or what his critics failed to grasp, was that he wished to concentrate upon the effects of disturbances upon the structure of capital. In contrast, Knight assumed that capital was substitutable over time and therefore it was permissible to speak of a revolving fund. Hayek regarded such a fund as a relic of the discredited wages fund. Hayek was therefore prepared to dispense with the notion of an average period of production but he still gave the impression that it was possible to speak meaningfully about capital intensity.

Between writing to Robertson and the publication of the *General Theory* Keynes did not waver in his view of the Austrian theory of capital and accepted Knight's ideas. Thus, he wrote:

> In a very recent discussion of these problems ('Capital and the Interest Rate', by Prof. F.H. Knight, *Economica*, August 1934), a discussion of which contains many interesting and profound observations on the nature of capital, and confirms the soundness of the Marshallian tradition as to the uselessness of the Böhm-Bawerkian analysis, the theory of interest is given precisely in the traditional, classical mould.[5]

These issues form the substance of this chapter. We begin with a reiteration of Hayek's treatment of capital and the time structure of production as outlined in his *Prices and Production* and foreshadowed in Figure 3.1 of our discussion of Robertson's *Banking Policy and the Price Level*. The diagrammatic treatment is then elaborated to take account of the rate of interest and the need to transform the physical measure of capital into value terms, along the lines suggested by Lerner and Hayek. Then follows Knight's critique of the Austrian theory of capital, the survey of the debate by Kaldor and Hayek's defence of his ideas. This is followed by a discussion of Hayek's 'Ricardo effect' and Kaldor's criticisms.

The time structure of production

In *Prices and Production* Hayek analyzed the effects of an unanticipated increase in the money supply upon the time structure of production using the Austrian theory of capital as derived from Böhm-Bawerk (although Edelberg was to show that the Austrian theory of capital and the notion of an average period of production were similar to Ricardo's theory which recognized that the labour theory of value had to be qualified by allowing for the effect of differences in the time required to bring to market the products of equal quantities of labour). The diagram used by Hayek was similar to that employed in Chapter 3 (Figure 3.1) except that in Figure 5.1 it is turned on its side. The hypotenuse of the diagram represents the successive applications of the original means of production which are needed to bring forth an output of consumer goods. The value of the original means of production are measured along the left-hand ordinate which is the projection of points on the hypotenuse. The right-hand side measures the value of current output. Hence the area of the triangle shows the number of production stages through which the original means of production pass before they are converted into consumer goods. The value of the intermediate goods is represented by

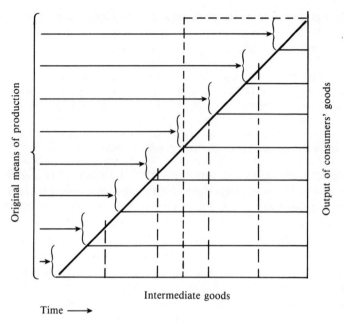

Figure 5.1 The structure of production.

Table 5.1 Session 1936–7. Capital and Interest. Professor Hayek.

Ten lectures. Lent Term. Tuesdays, 10.00–11.00, beginning L.T. 12 January; or (e) Thursdays, 7.00–8.00, beginning L.T. 14 January.
For postgraduate students and B.Sc. (Econ) Final – Special subject Economics.
Fees: Day: £1 10s.
　　　Evening: £1.

SYLLABUS: The duration of the process of production and the durability of goods in their relation to the investment period and the quantity of capital. The productivity of capital and interest. Interest and price relationships in a state of equilibrium. Renewal and maintenance of capital. Free and invested capital. Determination of the supply of free capital. The rate of saving and time-preference. The formation and consumption of capital.

BOOKS RECOMMENDED: I. Fisher, *Theory of Interest*; E. von Böhm-Bawerk, *Positive Theory* (preferably the third or fourth German edition); W.S. Jevons, *Theory of Political Economy*; F.W. Taussig, *Wages and Capital*; K. Wicksell, Wert, *Kapital and Rente and Lectures* (Vol. I); W. Eucken, *Kapitaltheoretische resuchungen*; R. Strigl, *Kapital und Produktion*; H. Kirchmann, *Studien zur Grenzproduktivatstheorie des Kapitalzinses*; J.R. Hicks, *Wages and Interest*; 'The dynamic problem' (*Economic Journal*, 1935); F.A. Hayek, 'Prices and production, investment and output' (*Economic Journal*, June 1934) and 'The maintenance of capital' (*Economica*, 1935); 'The metology of capital' (*Quarterly Journal of Economics*, 1936); 'Utility analysis and interest' (*Economic Journal*, March 1936).

Source: LSE *Calendar* 1936–7.

a rectangle half as high as the triangle and is indicated by the dotted line. Along the horizontal axis is measured the absolute period of production from which the average period of production can be derived. As the length of time increases, so the production processes become more capitalistic (that is to say, more roundabout).

Hayek used the triangles to illustrate the effects of an increase in real saving and an unanticipated increase in the money supply. The effect of an increase in real saving would be to reduce consumption, contract the length of the right-hand ordinate and extend the time scale as more roundabout methods are introduced. A similar procedure would occur with an unanticipated increase in the money supply which produced a state of forced saving, but the end result would be different because in the case of an increase in real saving the change would be permanent whereas forced saving would produce a temporary change.

The Hayek–Lerner elaborations

The original Hayek diagram had one important defect, it did not incorporate, in an explicit manner, the rate of interest. But Austrian theory, as expounded by Böhm-Bawerk, sought to explain not only the period of product and its relationship to the quantity of capital, but also the causes of the rate of interest being paid. In the Austrian model interest was the price paid for waiting, it has to be paid to overcome the preference for present as opposed to future goods. And it was this emphasis upon time preference which distinguished the Austrian theory from the Anglo-American approach which stressed that interest has to be paid because investment is thought to be productive.

In his article 'On the relationship between investment and output' (1934b), Hayek attempted to remedy some of the shortcomings of the diagrammatic treatment he presented in *Prices and Production*. But during the LSE academic session 1931–2, Lerner had written a paper in which he had employed similar diagrammatic techniques in order to incorporate the rate of interest. Lerner's paper was not published until 1973 when it was presented as a commentary upon Hicks's neo-Austrian capital theory as presented in his book *Capital and Time* (Hicks, 1973). In the foreword to the collected papers of Lerner, edited by David Colander, Irvin Sobel observed that:

> What this recently discovered work, published herein under the title of 'Paleo-Austrian Theory' demonstrates, is his [Lerner's] early ability through imaginative three dimensional analysis, to generalise and extend the particular Hayekian version of the average period of production upon

which it is based. Had the article been published then it would have removed the Hayekian formulation from subsequent criticism by Frank Knight and the subsequent reformulation by Sir John Hicks.[6]

Now this argument seems to be strained. Sobel showed no awareness of Hayek's 1934 article nor his book, *The Pure Theory of Capital*, in both of which three-dimensional analysis was employed. Furthermore, he failed to note that Knight had rejected the notion that there was any correlation between the period of production and the quantity of capital and that in his paper Lerner conceded that attempts to talk in a meaningful manner about capital intensity were fraught with difficulty. Finally, it has to be noted that Hicks was at the LSE in the period 1930–4 and would have been familiar with both Lerner's and Hayek's papers. However, Hicks did not, as his later work *Value and Capital* revealed, place much significance on them.

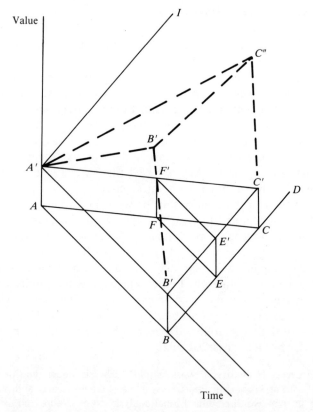

Figure 5.2 Lerner's time structure of production.

In Figure 5.2 the analysis contained in Figure 5.1 is extended by introducing a third dimension which measures a unit of value, say one pound. The flow of inputs is now represented not by ABC but by the area $AA'C'BB'$ and the flow of output is represented by $BB'C'C$. Along the line marked I is measured total net input and as in the previous figure working capital increases along the time axis.

The next step is to introduce the rate of interest and recalculate the average period of production and the capital intensity of the process. In equilibrium the marginal efficiency of investment will be equal to the positive rate of interest. If the interest rate is constant then the value of the inputs will increase over time. Hence in the vertical dimension the input surface $A'B''C''$ will be rising.

Knight's critique of Austrian capital theory

The capital controversy began with Knight's article, 'Capitalistic production, time and the rate of return' in the Cassel *Festschrift* (1933) and culminated with his article 'Capital and Interest' in the *Encyclopaedia Britannica*, 1946. Interspersed between these landmarks were several articles by Knight, Hayek and Kaldor and contributions by non-LSE economists, such as Boulding, Gifford and Machlup.

Knight raised several issues in his criticism of the Austrian theory of capital and interest. First, he argued, it was impossible to distinguish between original and produced means of production or between the services of those resources. Second, it was impossible to distinguish between spending on maintenance and replacement. Third, there was no obvious correlation between the period of production and the quantity of capital. Of the three points, the third is the most important because it challenged the notion that the stock of capital could be measured and it led Knight to propound the notion that the rate of interest does not depend upon the quantity of capital. These theses had obvious attractions for Keynes and they surfaced in the capital controversy of the 1960s between Cambridge, England, and Cambridge, Massachusetts. The third point was expressed most forcibly in Knight's 1936 article, 'The quantity of capital and the rate of interest':

> The problem of capital as a quantity is obviously another view of the problem of the rate of interest. Difficulty and complexity arise because the relation between capital and interest takes different forms and especially because of the danger of circular reasoning. On the one hand, capital is usually and properly defined as 'income' 'capitalized' at some 'rate of return'. But the interest rate is usually thought of as the ratio between the net annual yield and a quantity of capital. On the face of it, this is a

vicious circle; interest cannot be a rate of return; i.e. a ratio to a principal, unless the terms of the ratio are definable independently of the rate of return itself; yet in the same units for both numerator and denominator.

This situation led long ago to the development and fairly wide acceptance of a theory of interest which explained the rate in psychological terms not involving the concept of yield ratio or productivity of capital. Capital quantity was held to be simply the sale value, at the present moment of future income stream – an exchange ratio determined in the market by demand and supply and ultimately by comparisons of gives and takes and the competitive equalization, at the margin, of the appeal or utility of the two magnitudes.

The ultimate meaning of the interest rate does not involve a quantity of capital at all, but only a dynamic relation between an instantaneous rate of investment and a resultant instant rate of growth in income; i.e. in the return to be had by stopping the investment at a given point of time.

The psychological preference of present to future wealth is merely the reflection of the fact that wealth in hand now will grow into a larger amount of wealth in the future.[7]

In Knight's view all resources were capital. Capital was, in fact, a fund or homogeneous mass which had to be maintained. Thus, land had to be maintained lest it lose its fertility. Labour had to be educated and trained or it would lose its usefulness. At points of time the fund might be invested in particular assets but over time it could be transformed. Hence the distinction between maintenance and replacement became meaningless. Most maintenance took the form of replacement. A tyre might be replaced on a truck and if it were not then the truck could lose all its value. And because capital was a fund which was continually being transformed then the notion of a period of production also became meaningless. It could either be infinite or zero. It could be infinite because the knife which was used to cut the meat was made from steel which had been produced from pig iron in a furnace which had been derived from iron ore which had been smelted in a blast furnace and the iron ore had been dug from a mine by a machine which had been made from steel . . . and so on. It could be zero, as in a stationary state, where production and consumption might be simultaneous.

Knight's critique of capital theory was associated with his attack on the classical (what he called Ricardian) theory of production and distribution. This theory, he observed, stemmed from the workings of an agrarian society. Production was assumed to be carried out by labour applied to land. The land and the labour were regarded as original factors of production. And in the theory it was convenient to regard capital as both a source of food and a raw material; in other words, capital was corn. Thus, each year the workers would plant some of the corn and consume the remainder between sowing and reaping. And on the assumption that labour and corn were used in fixed proportions then there would be a positive correlation between the period of production and the quantity of corn employed. This was the essence of the wage fund theory which stated that, ignoring rent, the income of the economy was paid out annually to the workers. The theory was then extended to the entire economy by assuming that a two-year cycle would require twice as much capital as a one-year cycle.

Capital was therefore a produced factor of production and stood in sharp contrast to land and labour which were the original means of production. And corresponding to the factors of production were three owners who derived three distinct types of reward. Landlords owned land and their reward was rent which was due to the bounty of nature since land had no costs of production. Workers received wages and capitalists received interest on their loans of corn. Now Knight's insistence that all resources were capital paved the way for a reconstruction of the rewards of owners of productive resources as follows:

1. A current reward consisting of two elements:
    (a) the payment necessary to keep a factor in its current employment – its transfer earnings;
    (b) a possible surplus over transfer earnings – rent.
2. In terms of the initial outlay incurred in creating the resource its reward can be considered to consist of:
    (a) the interest on the original outlay – that is the payment necessary to transfer resources from possible consumption in the past to increase consumption in the future;
    (b) the profit or loss arising from the decision to invest in resources in a particular activity whose outcome is clouded in uncertainty.

Knight's theory was a long run theory. But he was prepared to concede that there might be a problem of mobility and that capital might not always be transformable: '. . . there is no problem of mobility', he wrote, 'if the time and conditions of transfer are anticipated when an investment is made'. And he concluded:

> a depression, in its critical aspect of serious unemployment (of persons and property) no doubt generally involves more or less mistaken commitment of resources, human or non-human, sustained by immobility. But it is *essentially* a matter of price maladjustments, sustained by price stickiness. If labour were mobile and wages were flexible, no fixity in the capital structure would give rise to unemployment, of labour or of capital, though efficiency might be greatly reduced. . . . The role of capital durability and production period is limited to contributing toward the

wrong commitment and immobility of a relatively small fraction of the productive resources of a system.[8]

Unfortunately Knight's concession, which lay at the heart of Hayek's trade cycle theory, did not become the focal point of the controversies.

Hayek's defence

'The mythology of capital' (1935c) was remarkable not only for the concessions which Hayek made to Knight but also for the firmness with which he rebutted what he considered to be misunderstandings of the Austrian theory and also (and more importantly) misunderstandings of his own advances over the original contribution of Böhm-Bawerk. 'In my opinion', he wrote, 'the oversimplified form in which he (and Jevons before him) tried to incorporate the time element into the theory of capital prevented him from cutting himself finally loose from the misleading concept of capital as a definite "fund" and is largely responsible for much of the confusion which exists on the subject; and I have full sympathy with those who see in the concept of a single or average period of production a meaningless abstraction which has little if any relationship to anything in the real world.' He accepted that Knight had produced 'a masterly exposition of the relationship between productivity and the "time preference" element in the determination of the rate of interest.' But, he maintained, Knight had retarded further analysis by introducing the pseudo-concept of a mystical fund which maintains itself automatically. 'I do indeed hold', he wrote, 'that, firstly all the problems which are commonly discussed under the general heading of "capital" do arise out of the fact that part of the productive equipment is non-permanent and has to be replaced on economic grounds . . . and that an increase of capital will always mean an extension of the time dimension.'[9]

Concessions and clarifications were necessary because of the brevity of key passages in *Prices and Production* and because of a failure of the critics of Böhm-Bawerk, to understand what he had said in the earlier debate with J.B. Clark. Thus, Böhm-Bawerk had not only denounced the concept of a fund but he had also repudiated the view that the period of production had to be treated in an absolute sense as something which stretched back to Adam or even to some non-human hand plucking a banana from a tree:

> A strict interpretation of what has been said above would require us to consider the period of production as beginning at the moment when the first finger is stirred in the production of the good in question, and as

continuing until its final completion. In modern times non-capitalist production has virtually disappeared, and one generation continues to build on the intermediate products created by earlier generations. By a strict accounting, the production period of almost every product would have its beginnings in centuries far beyond us. The boy who whittles a willow whistle with his pocket knife is, strictly speaking, only continuing an operation begun by the miner who centuries ago dug up the first shovelful of earth for the sinking of the mine shaft that was used to bring up the iron for the blade of the boy's pocket knife. That initial work of a bygone century admittedly benefited today's finished product only to an infinitely small degree, neither possible to compare, nor worth comparing if it were. It would therefore result in a badly distorted picture of the degree to which capitalism plays a part in the carving of the willow whistle, if it were to be governed by the absolute interval between the first iota of labour applied and the final completion of the product.[10]

What Böhm-Bawerk's analysis drew attention to was the point that it was not the absolute but the average period of production that was important and that in calculating the average period, the period since a given contribution was made the weight attached to contributions made long ago would be negligible.

But Hayek went further in the 'Mythology' article. First, he argued the technical changes involved in changing the time structure of production were not due to changes in technical knowledge. Second, the periods which lengthened were periods for which particular factors were invested and the 'period of production' (or, as Hayek preferred to call it, the 'period of investment') was a forward and not a backward looking concept. Third, the range of periods for which different factors were invested could not be reduced to a single time dimension and even if it were possible to measure the aggregate of all periods of production it would be irrelevant to the problems of capital theory. Fourth, the fact that the investment of £1,000 in a machine could be thought of as an investment in return for a perpetual annuity, with the assumption that the machine will be scrapped and replaced as often as is necessary, is not incompatible with thinking of a finite series of yields from a physical object in which that value is embodied. In the 'Mythology' article Hayek therefore rejected any attempt to link his view of capital theory with that of Böhm-Bawerk's theory but he also made it clear that his interest was not in a stationary state nor in some equilibrium growth path of the kind that interested Knight, but that he was preoccupied with the problems that could arise if there were any possibilities of unforeseen disturbances to investment decisions. In Knight's analysis there might be uncertainty but the fact that all prices were flexible made the concept of a fund seem plausible. In effect, Knight had a Walrasian auctioneer who was ready

110 The capital controversy

to adjust prices instantly so as to maintain markets. Of course, Knight did concede that uncertainty could exist and prices might not be flexible and resources might not be mobile, but he did not regard those issues as part of capital theory. They were aspects of money and trade cycle theory. Hence, there was a lack of engagement between Knight and Hayek and their debate could not be concluded.

Kaldor and the capital controversy

Nicholas Kaldor was born in Budapest, Hungary in 1908 and attended the Minta (Model) Gymnasium which was a large private school managed directly by the University of Budapest rather than by the Ministry of Education. In 1925 he went to the University of Berlin. Finally, he arrived at the LSE in 1927 and graduated in 1930. In 1932 he was appointed to an assistantship then promoted to a lectureship in 1934. In 1937 he began to lecture on capital theory (Tables 5.2 and 5.3) and a by-product was an article on the capital controversy. Later he went on to investigate Hayek's theory of the trade cycle. Kaldor began his LSE career as an admirer of Hayek but became increasingly disenchanted. In a debate with Colin Clark he defended Hayek's views. However, one of his early tasks (with Honor Croome) was to translate into English

Table 5.2 Session 1937–8. Capital and Interest. Mr. Kaldor.

Ten lectures. Lent Term. Mondays, 5.00–6.00, beginning L.T. 10 January.
(To be given in the evening in 1938–9.)
For postgraduate students and B.Sc. (Econ) Final – Special subject of Economics.
Fee: £1 10s.

    SYLLABUS: The 'Austrian' theory of capital and the concept of the investment period. The present discussion on the nature of capital. The problem of the maintenance and renewal of capital goods. The process of saving and investment. The classical theory of the rate of interest. The Liquidity-preference theory of interest. The question of interest and prices.
    BOOKS RECOMMENDED: I. Fisher, *The Nature of Capital and Income*; *Theory of Interest*; E. von Böhm-Bawerk, *Positive Theory of Capital*; W.S. Jevons, *Theory of Political Economy*; F.W. Taussig, *Wages and Capital*; K. Wicksell, *Lectures on Political Economy*, Vol. I; *Uber Wert, Kapital und Rente*; *Interest and Prices*; Lindahl, *Concept of Income* (in Cassel Essays); Hicks, 'Wages and interest; the dynamic problem' (*Economic Journal*, Sept. 1935); Keynes, *The General Theory of Employment, Interest and Money*; Hawtrey, *Capital and Employment*; Hayek, 'The maintenance of investment and output', (*Economic Journal*, 1934); 'The maintenance of capital' (*Economica*, 1935); 'Einietungen einer Kapitaltheorie' (*Zeitschrift fur Nationalökonomie*, 1937); Knight, 'Capital, time and the interest rate' (*Economica*, August 1934); 'The quantity of capital and the rate of interest' (*Journal of Political Economy*, 1936); Kaldor, 'Annual survey of economic theory; the controversy over the *Theory of Capital*' (*Econometrica*, July, 1937).

Source: LSE *Calendar* 1937–8.

Knight's critique of Austrian capital theory 111

Table 5.3 Session 1938–9. Advanced Problems of Economic Theory (Statics and Dynamics). Mr. Kaldor.

Ten lectures. Lent Term. Mondays, 5.00–6.00, beginning L.T. 9 January.
Fee: £1 10s.

SYLLABUS: Starting with the pure theory of value, these lectures will give an analysis of the assumptions underlying economic statics and compare them with the method of treatment adopted in dynamics. The question of anticipations uncertainty, markets, the quantity of given resources and the velocities of adjustment with respect to change. The problem of 'determinateness'. The place of money in pure theory. The concept of a dynamic equilibrium relating to a point of time and the analysis of dynamic processes according to the theories of the Swedish (neo-Wicksellian) School. The conditions of stability under static and dynamic assumptions. The interpretative value of static and dynamic generalizations.

BOOKS RECOMMENDED: Walras, *Elements*; Edgeworth, *Mathematical Psychics*; Wicksell, *Lectures* (Vol. I); Knight, *Risk, Uncertainty and Profit*; Rosenstein-Rodan, 'The role of time in economic theory' (*Economica*, 1934); Kaldor, 'Determinateness of equilibrium' (*Review of Economic Studies*, 1934); Hicks, '*Gleichgewicht und Konjunktur*' (*Zeitschrift fur Nationalökonomie*, 1933); 'Wages and interest: the dynamic problem' (*Economic Journal*, 1935); Lindahl, *The Concept of Income* (in Cassel Essays); Myrdal, 'Der Gleichgewichtsbegriff' (in *Beiträge zur Geltheorie*, ed. by Hayek); Keynes, *The General Theory of Employment, Interest and Money*; Hart, 'Anticipations, business planning and the cycle' (*Quarterly Journal of Economics*, 1937); Lundberg, *Economic Expansion*; Ohlin, 'Some notes on the Stockholm theory of savings and investment' (*Economic Journal*, 1937).

Source: LSE *Calendar* 1938–9.

Hayek's *Monetary Theory and the Trade Cycle* (Kaldor and Croome, 1934). The experience led him to doubt the validity of Hayek's theory because, as he observed later, when you translate a work you pay more attention to the author's meaning.

In his survey of the capital controversy Kaldor was sympathetic to the Austrian theory and critical of Knight's theory. He therefore began by attempting to undermine Knight's views on factors of production and to attempt to resurrect the distinction between capital and other factors. He conceded that 'there can be no doubt that resources as defined and differentiated by the market are augmentable to a certain degree. Labour can be improved by training, the amount of hydro-electric power can be augmented by the use of yet unexploited waterfalls.' But he noted that:

> Professor Knight appears to overlook one distinction which survives the strictures levelled against the traditional classification. Even if all resources require to be maintained and the services of all resources contribute to the production of new resources, it is still not true that *all* kinds of resources can be *produced*. It is not possible to produce 'land'; and in a capitalist economy which no longer knows the institution of slavery, it is not even possible to 'produce' labour. The quantity of labour, through a change in the birth rate, can certainly be increased, but to regard this quantity as being a function of saving or the rate of interest is turning an analogy into a falsehood.[11]

Factors of production were therefore distinct and could only be substituted for each other at increasing cost. And even augmentation of a factor could occur at increasing cost. Hence 'the law of roundaboutness is merely a roundabout way of expressing non-proportional returns.' Kaldor therefore felt able to introduce the concept of a production function and two inputs, one of which was capital, and the investment period was merely the ratio of capital to other factors (labour):

> The purpose of the 'investment period' is to reduce the production function to two variables, substituting 'waiting' for the services of all produced (or variable) factors, with interest as the price of 'waiting'. In this way – and only in this way – can *capital as capital* be treated as a factor of production, commensurate with 'labour'. This however can only be done so long as the services of the 'fixed' factors can themselves be regarded as homogeneous, or at any rate sufficiently homogeneous to leave their relative scarcity unaffected by changes in the amount of the services of other resources. . . . [But if] we assumed three factors, say the services of machines, labour and land, among which only the services of machines could be increased in quantity by capital accumulation, neither the investment period of the services of land nor the investment period of the services of labour would have afforded an unambiguous measure of the amount of machine capital.[12]

Kaldor concluded his survey of the controversy by observing that even under static assumptions the investment period runs into difficulties once allowance is made for the possibility that the relative prices of factors and goods might change as a result of a change in the quantity of capital and that for dynamic problems the investment period could hardly be of any use. However, he took the view that Austrian capital theory was relevant even though capital might not be measurable.

In 'Capital intensity and the trade cycle' (1939c) Kaldor returned to the problems of capital theory. He emphasized the point that the investment period represented an attempt to measure the capital–labour ratio but that there could be no unique measure of capital and therefore no obvious measure of the capital–labour ratio. But, Kaldor, suggested it might be possible to produce an index or ordinal measure of the capital–labour ratio in order to indicate whether it was moving up or down. Some measures were ruled out because they could be affected by a change in factor and goods prices; for example, the ratio of the value of output to inputs or the ratio of wage costs to interest costs. In the end Kaldor came down in favour of an index of the ratio of initial cost to annual cost in the production of output:

> In planning an investment, entrepreneurs expect a certain prospective stream of net receipts, which is obtained by deducting from the sale of its planned output, the corresponding stream of expenditures. It is generally possible to reduce the size of the expenditure-stream, per unit of receipts-

stream (i.e. the size of the investment) per unit of output. Hence, the relation between initial outlay and annual outlay can be regarded as a measure of the proportion in which capital and other factors are combined in a particular productive unit, i.e. of its 'capital intensity' of production.[13]

But will capital intensity vary over the trade cycle in the manner predicted by Hayek? To answer this question Kaldor employed Keynes's marginal efficiency of capital concept combined with a supply curve of investible funds under the assumption that both product and capital markets were characterized by imperfect competition. For each method of production there would be a different marginal efficiency of capital curve. In order to maximize profits an entrepreneur would choose that technique which would maximize the difference between the marginal efficiency of capital and the supply of investment funds. Thus, the capital intensity of new investment will be determined. But actual capital intensity will depend upon the difference between product prices and costs. Actual capital intensity would then fall in a boom and rise in a slump and because of capital being fixed in the short run the only way that output can be increased is to employ more labour. But, Kaldor asked, what would happen to normal capital intensity? That is, does the character of newly constructed capital vary over the cycle? Kaldor believed that the same relationship held with normal capital intensity falling in the boom, although he noted that there could be no certainty. But if real wages fall in the boom and the rate of interest rises then techniques will become more labour-intensive. The explanation was that the greater the capital intensity, the smaller the increase in potential output created by a given volume of investment. Therefore, if the capital intensity of investment falls during a boom and rises in a slump then newly created investment productive capacity increases faster than the rate of investment in the boom and falls faster than the rate of investment in the slump. And it is this high rate of increase in productive capacity in the boom, with capital intensity falling, which can then lead to the end of the boom if consumption does not rise in line with the increase in the ability of the economy to produce goods. The problem was therefore to increase investment to match the rise in savings; that is to say there must be a switch from capital widening to capital deepening. Kaldor thought that there might be difficulties in effecting such a transition. His conclusion was that:

> in arguing that investments undertaken during a boom are doomed to failure because they involve the adoption of *excessively* roundabout methods, the Austrian theorists got hold of the wrong end of the stick [but they certainly *did* get hold of a stick – which is not always realized].

It would certainly be more correct to say that investments during the boom are doomed to failure, or that the boom is doomed to failure, because the investments undertaken in a boom are *insufficiently* roundabout.[14]

According to Kaldor there was a delay in the publication of his article on capital intensity and the trade cycle because Hayek wished to write a reply. The reply introduced the Ricardo effect.

In 1940 Kaldor presented his own model of the trade cycle. The basic principle was sought in 'a proposition that is really derived from Mr Keynes's' *General Theory*, although not stated there in this form – that economic activity always tends towards a level where savings and investment are equal.'[15] But the proposition was not Keynes's; it was Robertson's, although Kaldor's subsequent use of the concepts of *ex ante* and *ex post* suggested a Swedish influence. In the model he made both *ex ante* savings and investment functions of the level of activity. Making investment a function of the level of activity was an attempt to avoid the mechanical application of the acceleration principle and could be construed as an Austrian or classical influence. According to Thirlwall, 'Keynes expressed surprise that Kaldor meant investment is a function of the level of output.'[16] It was a linkage that was appropriate for gross investment but not net investment and it meant that Kaldor's model contained no explicit dynamic factor. However, his discussion was not always clear. On occasions he suggested that an increase in the current level of profits increases investment demand and that could be compatible with the idea of a flexible accelerator. Of course, what Kaldor was trying to achieve was a model of the trade cycle in which the upper turning point was not brought about by credit scarcity nor by a mechanical application of the multiplier–accelerator model. In his model both investment and savings were functions of the level of output but the functional relationships varied with the level of income. It was an ingenious approach but it never caught on and came to be superseded by models which embodied specific constraints in the form of floors and ceilings.

Edelberg

Not all the staff at the LSE were critical of Hayek's discussion of capital theory, although they sometimes acknowledged their intellectual debts to others. In his highly mathematical treatment of *Wages and Capitalist Production*, Victor Edelberg (1936a) inscribed his Ph.D. thesis to Irving

Knight's critique of Austrian capital theory

Fisher and began with a series of mottoes drawn from the great:

Menger	'The idea of causal connection is inseparable from time.'
Kant	'Time is the formal condition a priori of all phenomena whatsoever.'
Wittgenstein	'The passage of time there is no such thing.'

Edelberg sought to produce a thesis which would take explicit account of time. He noted that the classical economists attacked the problem by studying the relation between profits and wages or wages and capital. In their analysis capitalists advanced wages to workers before final output was produced. Hence the need to study the equilibrium between wages and interest. But the main work done on the subject was by Böhm-Bawerk, Irving Fisher and J.B. Clark (whose ideas were adopted by Hicks in his *Theory of Wages* (1932c). Edelberg rejected Böhm-Bawerk's approach which he thought was backward-looking and thought that Fisher's analysis of output streams was undetermined. Hicks's analysis was also rejected because he treated capital as homogeneous and any lags in production were assumed to be unimportant. Finally, he noted that Knight had pronounced capital theory to be incomprehensible.

Although Edelberg's supervisor was Robbins and although he acknowledged help with mathematics and statistics from Bowley and Frisch, Edelberg did have discussions with Hayek. Therefore, despite differences in techniques – with Hayek preferring geometry and Edelberg employing calculus – there were similarities in their approaches. Edelberg assumed that each entrepreneur had a bundle of resources and was confronted by a variety of production plans with each plan requiring a given amount of investment and yielding a given output – which carried the implication that there were different input and output functions associated with each plan. Given the rate of interest the task of the entrepreneur was to maximize the present value of profits by considering the various production plans and equating the present value of the future marginal product with the present value of future marginal cost. Thus, Edelberg incorporated production into his analysis. Substantial portions of his work was published as articles including 'The Ricardian theory of profits' (1933), 'An econometric model of production and distribution' (1936b), and 'Elements of capital theory' (1936c).

The Ricardo effect

In 1939 Hayek introduced the Ricardo effect as an explanation of the upper turning point and as an argument which showed 'why under certain conditions, contrary to a widely held opinion, an increase in the demand for consumers' goods will tend to decrease rather than increase the demand for investment goods.' For ease of exposition he assumed the following:

1. In the short run there was no mobility of labour between the industrial groups.
2. Money wages could not be reduced.
3. Existing equipment was fairly specific to the purposes for which it was made.
4. The money rate of interest remained constant.

He then suggested that 'at a point somewhere half-way through a cyclical upswing, when excess stocks of consumers' goods have been absorbed, and employment in the consumers' goods industries is high [then] any further rise in demand for consumers' goods will lead to rise in their prices and a fall in real wages.'[17] The effect of the fall in real wages would then lead to a switch to labour intensive methods of production and investment would fall.

Hayek illustrated his argument by means of Table 5.4. Suppose that for a particular product there are several methods of production available which differ with respect to the time which must elapse before the commodity reaches the market. The length of the production periods are two years, one year, six months, three months and one month respectively. It is also assumed that initially these methods are equally profitable on the margin at 6 per cent per annum. Next the product price is assumed to rise by 2 per cent with all other things assumed to remain unchanged. Hence, the annual rate of profit will rise but it will rise by more for the shorter than for the longer periods of production. Therefore the Ricardo effect implies that an increase in consumer demand that leads to a rise in prices and a fall in real wages may bring about a reduction in investment.

Hayek then related his argument to the acceleration principle which

Table 5.4 The Ricardo Effect.

	2 years	1 year	6 months	3 months	1 month
Initial amount of profit per turnover at 6% p.a.	12	6	3	1.5	0.5
Add 2% profit due to rise in product price	14	8	5	3.5	2.5
Final rate of profit p.a. neglecting compound interest	7	8	10	14	30

assumes a constant relationship between increases in final demand and increases in investment. Under the acceleration principle the demand for capital goods is the result of final demand (the multiplicand) and the capital–output ratio (the multiplier to use Hayek's unfortunate term which is not to be confused with Keynes's multiplier). Now in Hayek's theory the multiplier of the acceleration principle depends upon the profit rate (which term he had substituted for the natural rate of interest which he used in *Prices and Production*) under the assumption that the money rate of interest was constant. If the profit rate rises then the multiplier will tend to diminish and if the profit rate falls then the multiplier will tend to increase. What happens in the boom will depend therefore upon the relative strengths of the multiplier and the multiplicand. When final demand increases then the multiplicand will rise, but Hayek maintained that sooner or later the multiplier will fall with the result that the product of the multiplier and the multiplicand will fall. The reason that the multiplier will fall is that profits in the later stages of production (those nearest to final demand) will rise and they will rise because each increase in investment cause consumers' expenditure to rise. The rise in consumers' expenditure could be offset by an increase in voluntary saving but this possibility is excluded by the assumption of a constant money rate of interest.

Given the assumption of a constant money rate of interest there is a problem of how the funds available to an individual firm can be restricted so that no firm attempts to increase output by both quick and longer production methods and so maintaining capital intensity or increasing it. In *Profits, Interest and Investment* (1939) he suggested several alternative constraints. First, it was assumed that: 'there is no lending money of any kind during the period with which we are concerned: entrepreneurs either owning all the capital they employ and being effectively prevented from lending any of it, or being limited by a strict rationing of credit' (Hayek, 1939: 12). Second, he assumed that a firm might be faced by an upward sloping supply curve of credit. Given these restrictions Hayek concluded that the rise in the internal rates of return would lead to the use of less capitalist methods of production.

Another important assumption was that concerning the mobility of labour, where Hayek emphasized the problems that are raised by specific skills: 'the results of the more generally employable labour [due to transfers to the more direct production of consumers' goods] will be unemployment of certain kinds of labour – that which is highly specific to the production of certain kinds of machinery' (Hayek, 1939: 16).

The strongest criticism of the Ricardo effect was presented by Kaldor in his article 'Professor Hayek and the concertina effect' (1942). Kaldor argued:

> (1) that the operation of the 'Ricardo effect' presupposes certain special conditions as to the position of individual firms which are clearly inapplicable to the major firms of modern industry; (2) that even in those cases where the 'effect' does operate, its quantitative importance must be small, and is not likely to exceed the equivalent effect of a small change in the interest rate; (3) that quite apart from (1) and (2), the operation of this 'Ricardo effect' is wholly irrelevant to Professor Hayek's central thesis – i.e. that a demand for capital consumers' goods will lead to a fall in the demand for capital goods – since *under no circumstances can* total investment demand become smaller in consequence of a rise in the rate of profit.[19]

Kaldor's analysis was, however, based upon a comparison of comparative equilibrium positions. He suggested that entrepreneurs would not switch from one method of production to another but would try to invest more in each and every project. If before the rise in product prices the returns on all methods were equal to the firm's cost of capital, then in the next equilibrium position the scale of the firm would increase because it would invest in all its methods of production until each internal rate of return was restored to equality with the cost of capital. Hence Kaldor concluded that Hayek committed the same fallacy as those who argued that a rise in demand will cause a rise in price and the rise in price will cause a fall in demand and therefore an increase in demand will lead to less being bought:

> No doubt the rise in price will make the increase in purchases [following upon the increase in demand] less than it would have been if the price had not risen. But it cannot make it less than before, since the price has only risen because amount bought has gone up. In the same way the reduction in capital intensity will make the rise in investment expenditure less than it would have been if capital intensity had remained constant. But it cannot eliminate it altogether because capital intensity would not have fallen if investment expenditure had not risen.[20]

Kaldor argued that Hayek had assumed that the substitution effect was greater than the scale effect – which a comparative static analysis indicated was impossible.

Hayek countered the criticisms by claiming that Kaldor had applied the perfect competition model which was most inappropriate to the circumstances and that the Ricardo effect should not be evaluated within a comparative static framework. What Hayek was analyzing was a disequilibrium situation before the new equipment becomes available and during which firms have to decide the relative amounts which they will spend on renewing or adding to fixed and circulating capital. In this situation profits will be higher on the method with the higher rate of turnover, *not* because they accrue at a higher rate *after* the new equilibrium envisaged by Kaldor had been established . . . but because the profits on the less capitalistic method will *begin to accrue* earlier than those on the more capitalistic method.[21] That is to say, the eventual equilibrium is time dependent because it depends upon the behaviour of the firms in the transition. Hayek was therefore dealing with a hysteresis process of the kind which later became more familiar in the analysis of unemployment and of the consumption function.

The validity of the Ricardo effect under conditions of not-quite-perfect competition was accepted by Robertson (1957) who wrote:

> There seems to be only one case where the argument fails, namely that in which producers are both willing and able to borrow the whole of their capital in an outside capital market, at a rate of interest which remains unchanged however much or little they want to borrow. In this case the rate of profit on capital employed will be the same at the margin whatever the method of production, i.e. will in all cases tend to equality (after allowing for risk etc.) with the market rate of interest, and the rise in real wages (whether occurring through a fall in prices or a rise in money wages) will only affect the *scale* of production and not the method. This may be what those writers have in mind who have argued that a rise in wages will only lead to a substitution of capital for labour if it is accompanied by a fall in the rate of interest.[22]

And this same emphasis upon disequilibrium behaviour and not-quite-perfect competition also applies to Hicks's criticism of the Ricardo effect which was as follows:

> When the market rate of interest is reduced below the natural rate, what will happen to the *quantities* of inputs and outputs? The correct answer on these assumptions, is very simple: The effect will be nil. Prices will rise uniformly; and that is that. When the Wicksell model is taken strictly (as it was taken strictly), it is in *neutral equilibrium*. The whole *real* system, of quantities and of *relative* prices, is completely determined by the supply and demand equations in particular markets; in this *real* system *the* rate of interest is included. There can only be one rate of interest when the markets are in equilibrium; a market rate that is equal to the natural rate. The 'reduction' of the market rate below the natural rate must therefore be regarded as a disequilibrium phenomenon; a phenomenon that can only persist while the markets are out of equilibrium. As soon as equilibrium is restored, equality between the market rate and the natural rate must be restored. Thus there is no room for a discrepancy between the market rate and the natural rate if there is an instantaneous adjustment of prices (to what – the 'real' data only) money prices will rise *uniformly*; and that is that.[23]

Therefore, argued Hicks, the Ricardo effect could only work if there was some lag in the system. But Hayek responded by saying that:

> the conception of a 'lag' does not seem to be very useful. There is certainly no assignable interval of time between the first change of a price due to changes in the quantity of money and the moment when all prices have changed in the same proportion, because, unless the monetary change (the inflow or outflow of money in the system) continues, the first price change will have been partly reversed before most of the other prices are affected. Nor is the relevant change in the price structure dependent on a rapid change in the price level.[24]

Although Hayek's emphasis upon a disequilibrium situation is important, it did ignore the fact that the assumption of a constant money rate of interest can cause other complications. Hayek ruled out the possibility that the market for loanable funds is perfect and hence the firm cannot expand in all directions. He assumed that there may be credit rationing but he cannot overcome the persistent tendency for the money supply to expand and create inflationary conditions. Indeed, he did recognize that his model is:

> the classical instance of a cumulative process with which we are dealing; the perfectly elastic supply of credit at a rate of interest lower than the internal rate of return of all or most firms will be the cause of continuous change of prices and money incomes where each change makes further changes necessary.[25]

But Hayek did not accept the inevitability of inflation:

> The problem is merely whether there is no limit to the extent to which, and the period of time for which, the price structure is determined by the 'real' factors can thus be distorted, or whether the fact – that the extra money which has first raised the group of prices will soon work round to affect the other group of prices in the same direction does set a limit to the possible degree of distortion. [Hayek took the view that the] speed at which an increase of incomes leads to an increase in the demand for consumer goods limits the extent to which by spending more money on the factors of production we can raise their prices relatively to those of the products.[26]

But Hayek failed to consider the possibility of hyperinflation, such as that of Germany in the 1920s, when people may still concentrate upon producing capital goods. 'In the acutest phase of the inflation', wrote Bresciani-Turroni, 'Germany offered the grotesque, and at the same time tragic, spectacle of a people which, rather than produce food, clothes, shoes and milk for its babies, was exhausting its energies in the manufacture of machines or the building of factories.'[27] In the German hyperinflation it was monetary, and not real, factors which were responsible for the distortion of production. Now Hayek seemed to concede the limitations of his model when, in his article, 'Three elucidations of the Ricardo effect' (1969), he wrote:

> unless credit expansion is continued progressively an inflation-fed boom must sooner or later be reversed by a decline in investment. This theory never claimed to do more than account for the upper turning point of the typical nineteenth-century business cycle. The cumulative process of contraction likely to set in once unemployment appears in the capital-goods industries is another matter which must be analysed by conventional means. It has always been an open question to me as to how long a process of continued inflation, not checked by a built-in limit on the supply of money and credit, could effectively maintain investment above the volume justified by the voluntary rate of savings. It may well be that this inevitable check only comes when inflation becomes so rampant – as the progressively higher rate of inflation required to maintain a given volume of investment must make it sooner or later – that money ceases to be an adequate accounting basis. But this cannot be discussed further without raising the problem of the effect of such changes on expectations – a problem which I do not wish to discuss here.[28]

The German hyperinflation provided one piece of empirical evidence which did not support the Ricardo effect. Other writers (e.g. Tsiang, 1947 and Haberler, 1989) have cited the tendency of real and money wages to move together as evidence against the Ricardo effect. Unfortunately, these tests are not conclusive. In Hayek's theory real wages refers to product wages whereas many of the early tests dealt with cost of living wages and the two real wage series may not move together. But there is a further point. The tests tended to use simple linear regression techniques which ignored the fact that Hayek's thesis referred to the later stages of the upswing of the cycle. Thus, in Figure 5.3 it is possible to distinguish four phases of the cycle: early upswing, late upswing, early downturn and late downturn. Now a simple regression test would yield a positively sloping regression line. But what is required in order to isolate the Ricardo effect is that dummy slope and dummy intercept terms be introduced. Unfortunately, there may not be enough observations in each of the four phases of the cycle to provide a conclusive test.

Another method of testing the Ricardo effect is to consider the movement of unemployment in the United States and Western Europe in the 1980s. According to Haberler (1989) the higher unemployment rates in Western Europe suggested that real wages were high and causing employers to introduce capitalist methods whereas lower unemployment in the United States indicated lower real wages. A final piece of evidence is the movement of overtime and shiftworking. Wilson (1937) suggested

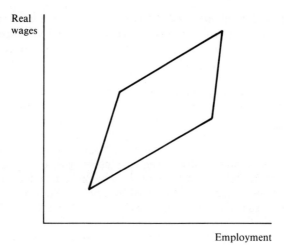

Figure 5.3 Cyclical movement of real wages and employment (after Sampson, 1979).

that Hayek's example of turnover periods was unrealistic but Hayek countered by indicating that shiftworking and overtime working were possible ways of substituting labour for capital and both tend to increase in boom periods.

The pure theory of capital

In his survey of Hayek's contribution to economics, which was written for the Nobel Prize Committee, Machlup said:

> If I had to single out the area in which Hayek's contributions were most fundamental and pathbreaking, I would cast my vote for the theory of capital. As I said before, when I reviewed Hayek's book on *The Pure Theory of Capital*, it is 'my sincere conviction that this work contains some of the most penetrating thoughts on the subject that have ever been published.[29]

Yet the book failed to capture the imagination of the profession.

The Pure Theory of Capital was planned as a two-volume book but the second volume which was intended to deal with dynamic issues was never produced. Later Hayek gave two reasons for the failure to complete the project. In 1978 he said that he found it difficult to deal with dynamic problems. Böhm-Bawerk's theory of capital expressed the simple and powerful idea that time was important in the analysis of capital problems. But the Böhm-Bawerk model was hedged around with a considerable number of qualifications which, once they were relaxed, led to the dissolution of the central message. The Böhm-Bawerk model was applicable to a one-commodity world in which labour was the only factor of production. In a multi-commodity world in which capital goods were produced by other capital goods and labour it was difficult to sustain the conclusions. In 1983, the centenary of Keynes's birth, Hayek gave as a reason for not completing his book that he did not wish to distract from Keynes's efforts to deal with inflation.

What readers of the *Pure Theory* got was a reiteration of many of the ideas presented in the earlier controversies. Hayek wrote:

> Our main concern will be to discuss in general terms what type of equipment it will be most profitable to create under various conditions, and how the equipment at any moment will be used, rather than to explain the factors which determined the value of a given stock of productive equipment and of the income that will be derived from it.[30]

By means of Table 5.5 he set out the main differences between the Austrian and Anglo-American theories of capital. Some of the differences might be regarded as matters of emphasis rather than substance. Durable capital might differ from working capital because it took longer to be used up – although there might be the troublesome problem of joint supply from durable goods which could produce a stream of services over time. 'Productivity' and 'waiting' might be deemed to be complementary explanations of interest with one force representing the demand side for funds and the other indicating supply constraints although Hayek acknowledged that in the long run productivity would be the dominant influence.

But both the Austrian and Anglo-American theories did not deal with what Hayek thought were the important issues which were 'the inter-relations between the different parts of the material structure of the process of production and the way in which it will adapt to changing conditions.'[31] This was a subject which was normally dealt with in the two theories but in a manner which obscured rather than clarified the need to consider the various dimensions of the structure of productive

Table 5.5 Theories of Capital.

	Anglo-American		Austrian
1(a)	Stress is laid exclusively on the role of fixed capital as if capital consisted only of very durable goods.	1(b)	Stress is laid on the role of circulating capital which arises out of the duration of the process of production, because this brings out particularly some of the characteristics of all capital.

(*continued*)

124 The capital controversy

Table 5.5 (*Continued*)

	Anglo-American		Austrian
2(a)	The term capital goods is reserved to durable goods which are treated as needing replacement only discontinuously or periodically.	2(b)	Non-permanence is regarded as the characteristic attribute of all capital goods, and the emphasis is accordingly laid on the need for continuous replacement of all capital.
3(a)	The supply of capital goods is assumed to be given for the comparatively short run.	3(b)	It is assumed that the stock of capital goods is being continuously used up and reproduced.
4(a)	The relevant time factor which we need to consider in order to be able to understand the effect of changes in the rate of interest on the value of a particular capital good is assumed to be its individual durability.	4(b)	It is not the individual durability of a particular good but the time that will elapse before the final services to which it contributes will mature that is regarded as the decisive factor. That is, it is not the attributes of the individual good but its position in the whole time structure that is regarded as relevant.
5(a)	The technique employed in production is supposed to be unalterably determined by the given state of technological knowledge.	5(b)	Which of the many known technological methods of production will be employed is assumed to be determined by the supply of capital available at each moment.
6(a)	The need for more capital is assumed to arise mainly out of a *lateral* expansion of production, i.e. a mere duplication of equipment of the kind already in existence.	6(b)	Additional capital is assumed to be needed for making changes possible in the technique of production (i.e. in the way in which individual resources are used), and to lead to *longitudinal* changes in the structure of production.
7(a)	The changes that will initiate additions to the stock of capital is sought in an increase in *absolute* demand, i.e. in the total money expenditure on consumers' goods.	7(b)	Changes in the stock of capital are supposed to be determined by changes in the *relative* demand for demand for consumers' and producers' goods.
8(a)	In order to make a lateral expansion of production appear possible the existence of unemployed resources of all kinds is postulated.	8(b)	In order to stress the changes in productive technique connected with an increase of capital, the existence of full employment is usually postulated.
9(a)	The demand for capital goods is assumed to vary in the same direction as the demand for consumers' goods but in an exaggerated degree.	9(b)	The demand for capital goods is assumed to vary in the opposite direction from the demand for consumers' goods.
10(a)	The analysis is carried out in monetary terms, and a change in demand is assumed to mean a corresponding change in the size of the total money stream.	10(b)	The analysis is carried out in 'real' terms, and an increase in demand somewhere must necessarily mean a corresponding decrease in demand somewhere else.

Source: Hayek, F.A. (1941) *The Pure Theory of Capital*, pp. 47–8.

equipment and the relative prices which might obtain. Thus the attempt to explain interest by analogy with wages and rent had led to the unfortunate effect of treating capital as a homogeneous quantity which could be taken as given. In the Clark–Knight approach capital was an 'integrated organic conception'. But by treating all capital as substitutable in time this approach suggested that it was irrelevant which piece of equipment was destroyed in a war. Houses could be bombed because they might become tanks. And all swords could be turned into ploughshares – and vice versa. Hayek was also critical of the Marshall–Keynes verdict on Austrian theory:

> . . . there will almost always exist potential but unused resources which could be made to yield a useful return, but only after some time and not immediately; and that the exploitation of such resources will usually require that other resources which could yield a return immediately or in the near future, have to be used in order to make these other resources yield any return at all. This simple fact fully suffices to explain why there will nearly always be possibilities of increasing the output obtained from the available resources by investing some of them for longer periods.
>
> It has never been asserted that *every* investment for a longer period will necessarily yield a larger product, although the critics have sometimes attacked the theory on these grounds. All that is important is that, so long as there are possibilities of increasing the product by investing for a long period, only such prolongations of investment periods will be chosen as will actually give a greater product.[32]

For Hayek the problem was that the interrelatedness of productive processes suggested that the analysis must be grounded in general equilibrium theory but not in the stationary state which was the customary framework of general equilibrium analysis. What was required was the study of non-stationary equilibria in moderately dynamic economies in which equilibrium meant that agents saw no reasons to revise their plans. The problem of planning lay in the fact that time was not irreversible and the correction of mistakes could be costly. Intertemporal coordination of economic activities meant therefore that all the plans of producers had to be compatible and to be consistent with the available resources. But coordination was made difficult because of the various dimensions of capital goods. Complementarity was often present because the plans of one producer to invest in a particular piece of machinery might require the availability of raw materials being forthcoming from other producers. Investment might also be in specific capital goods with limited alternative uses. The various dimensions of capital goods could give rise to capital goods being tied up for varying lengths of time and the degree to which resources were committed would be influenced by the rate of interest.

In *The Pure Theory of Capital* Hayek sought to place capital theory on firmer foundations by taking into account the various criticisms of the Austrian approach. But he was not wholly successful. He conducted most of his analysis on the assumption that full employment existed. This meant that the demand for capital goods moved in the opposite direction to the demand for consumer goods because it was not possible to increase the supply of both simultaneously. It also implied that complementarity of capital goods would be important and might dominate substitution between capital goods. Hence, the Keynesian unemployment situation in which there was unemployment of both capital and labour was excluded from his analysis. In Keynesian analysis it was complementarity of idle labour and capital that was important and not complementarity of capital goods. Moreover, because of his assumption of full employment he ruled out of consideration the acceleration principle which stipulated that the demand for capital goods was stimulated by the demand for consumer goods and by ruling out the acceleration principle he avoided getting involved in dynamic analysis.

In *The Pure Theory of Capital* Hayek conceded the primacy of productivity as the long-run determinant of investment. In 1945 he reconsidered the role of time preference. At the top of the boom the sharp change in monetary conditions might leave some investment projects half-completed or abandoned and if many (physically) completed projects depended for their profitability upon complementary (but abandoned) projects then completed investments might show a low return. In such circumstances when interest rates had risen the trend in the marginal productivity of investment might develop a kink or displacement and time preference could become the dominant influence. Hayek did not however link his analysis to Keynes's concept of liquidity preference even though the disturbance had a monetary origin and holders of money would be looking at returns for several periods in the future.

Capital and its structure

Hayek failed to complete *The Pure Theory of Capital* but said that Lachmann had expressed many of the ideas he would have incorporated in a book devoted to dynamics. Lachmann began by attempting to present a clear statement of Austrian capital theory which would be free from the objectivist and macroeconomic aspects with which Böhm-Bawerk enveloped his theory. What Lachmann sought, therefore, was a theory which expressed the subjectivism, the methodological individualism, which ran through the writings of Menger, Mises and Hayek.

This enabled him to dispense with the average period of production which was a macroeconomic concept applicable in a one-commodity world in which labour was the only factor of production.

For Lachmann capital was a heterogeneous stock of material resources which gave rise to income stream. The stock included land as well as non-permanent resources – whereas Hayek had excluded land from the stock of capital. But land had alternative uses and needed to be maintained. And the fact that capital goods yielded a stream of income over time meant that period analysis was the appropriate method of investigation. Lachmann therefore followed Lindahl. But in looking forward Lachmann rejected Shackle's theory of expectations. Shackle's theory, he thought, tended to stress the individual and ignored the market whereas a comprehensive theory required both. Lachmann also rejected certainty equivalents and in their place introduced the concept of a range of expectations. There would be an inner range of expectations in which prices might fluctuate within a range which was acceptable as normal and there would be an outer range in which action would have to be undertaken. And the fact that capital was heterogeneous meant that complementarity as well as substitutability had to be considered in planning. Each individual would seek to achieve plan complementarity between the various pieces of capital equipment at his or her disposal. But equilibrium, the reconciliation of the plans of all individuals, required market or structural complementarity. Lachmann's emphasis upon complementarity, and here he was following Hayek, was in contrast to its exclusion by Keynes who concentrated upon substitution. In the *General Theory* capital was taken as given and was considered to be homogeneous. Hence, any addition would depress the marginal efficiency of capital. In Austrian theory the presence of complementarity meant that investment could raise the return on existing equipment.

The reconciliation of plans would be brought about by the market but Lachmann recognized that disequilibrium, structural maladjustment, might occur because of price inflexibility and he cited the demise of the wholesaler as a possible reason for price inflexibility. He also went on to question Keynes's interpretation of the stock market. In Keynes's analysis the marginal efficiency of capital was defined in terms of the prospective yield and supply price of capital assets with the latter referring to the cost of a newly produced asset and not to the market price of an existing asset. Stock exchange prices of existing assets were excluded from the scope of the definition of the marginal efficiency of capital and this reflected the fact that Keynes thought that the stock market was not an efficient means of reconciling long-term expectations. This, in turn, was due to the absence of a stock market without forward trading. Keynes's views on the stock market have tended to colour more recent assessments of the stock market and the verdict that short-termism dominates the market. But such short-termism as exists may reflect the nature of the environment within which the stock market operates. In postwar Britain there have been considerable changes in the tax regime governing post-tax profits and these changes have often rendered it difficult for investors to make sensible calculations; the costs of making calculations have been considered too high when considered in the light of the mass of tax legislation. Inflation has also been a factor leading to an emphasis upon short-term gains.

Lachmann's approach to capital theory enabled him to provide a more suitable framework for analyzing the role of money in economic activity and the nature of the trade cycle. Hicks brought money into portfolio theory as a result of moving from consumer theory into monetary theory. But, argued Lachmann, 'a theory of assets cannot be framed on the static model of the General Theory of Consumption. The composition of asset holdings and its changes make sense only as a response to change, expected and unexpected.'[33] Lachmann therefore grounded his approach to money as an asset in the theory of business finance in which assets were classified according to their relevance for planning and action.

Shackle

In 1978 Hayek stated that he had failed to provide a dynamic theory of capital but he thought that Lachmann had managed to provide a useful account in *Capital and its Structure*. However, Lachmann took the view that Shackle was more familiar with Hayek's ideas – Lachmann had been one of Shackle's research students. Unfortunately, Shackle rejected Hayek's ideas. Shackle drew a distinction between two approaches to capital theory. On the one hand there was the point of view expressed in Austrian theory that productive resources could be viewed as a linear sequence. On the other hand, there was the perspective provided by Leontief in his input–output table in which all activities were interrelated with the result that it was difficult to disentangle when each sector made its contribution to the production of a particular good. Austrian theory, he thought had the great merit that it seized upon one bold and brilliant idea: capital is time. However, it suffered from a number of disadvantages which tended to blur the usefulness of that vision. First, it had difficulty in handling durability of machines. Many pieces of equipment lasted for a long time and certainly longer than the time span represented by the trade cycle; ships, for example, were not bought with an eye on their prospective profits over seven or nine years. And once long time horizons entered into the analysis then consideration had to be given to expectations. Shackle noted that there was an absence of discussion of expectations in *Prices and Production* and that the few references to expectations and the role of money which were made in *The Pure Theory of Capital* were devoted to Keynes's analysis. Shackle also thought that Hayek's rejection of the concept of an average period of production meant that he could not say anything about capital intensity over the trade cycle except that when an economy is subject to a disturbance it may be expected that the structure of production will change. And how the structure of production might change and the period over which such a change would be effected might be investigated by means of the input–output table.

The maintenance of capital

So far we have concentrated upon the controversy between Knight and Hayek and that between Hayek and Kaldor. There was however a more prosaic interchange between Pigou and Hayek with contributions by Fowler and Hicks on the practical measurement of capital. This controversy was unresolved and surfaced again in the capital debate of the 1960s and 1970s. It was a subject which was, of course, present in the Sraffa and Hayek debate and in the discussions of the wastes of capitalism as compared with socialism. Hayek argued that in a boom there was malinvestment and the equipment created in the boom lost its value in the slump. Sraffa took the opposite point of view and suggested that capitalists would still have their machines whereas workers would have nothing. Sraffa had in mind a physical concept of capital whereas Hayek looked at a value concept of capital. Robertson took up an intermediate position and argued that as long as machines covered their running costs they would be used.

Running parallel with the debate in the *Economic Journal* were attempts to measure national capital. In 1935 Stamp capitalized aggregate profits and goodwill of companies. Shortly afterwards Daniels and Campion also attempted to measure national capital by using the valuation of estates assessed for death duties and taking into account the death rate among property owners as compared with the population at large. Their measure gave a lower and more satisfactory estimate than that of Stamp. Morganstern used the Stamp measure, but in reverse, by measuring the total value on the Stock Exchange of the shares of the major Austrian companies in 1931 as compared with their value in 1913 and thereby demonstrated that most of Austria's capital had disappeared in 1931. Morganstern's estimates had a strong influence upon the Austrian School of economists and were transmitted to the London School of Economics where they had an even bigger influence upon the course of events in Britain by suggesting that expansionary policies would cause a persistence of unemployment and a waste of resources.

The problem of how capital should be measured had of course been considered by Pigou. In the third edition (1924) of the *Economics of Welfare* he had used a value measure of capital but switched to a physical measure in the fourth edition (1932). This switch in emphasis was commented upon by Fowler (1934) in his little, but perceptive monograph, *The Depreciation of Capital*. Fowler started from the stationary state where investment equalled disinvestment and then considered the time which would be taken to reach equilibrium after additional investment took place; this time interval was found to depend upon the ratio between the period of construction of capital goods and their durability. He also examined the relationship between durability of capital goods, the rate of interest and the average period of investment. Finally, he looked at the depreciation policies of public utilities in the United States and drew attention to the confusions in valuation practices.

However, the main dispute was between Hayek, Pigou and Hicks. Pigou sought to measure the capital stock by comparing the physical units in use at two dates with the different capital goods being reduced to a common measure by using their relative values at the second date. Hayek raised an objection on the grounds that a firm producing fashion goods might decide to scrap its equipment before it was physically worn out. If the second of the two dates was taken just before the equipment was scrapped then the firm would have to have amortization allowances for almost the whole of the value of the equipment if it were to maintain its capital intact.

But Hayek did not provide an alternative method of dealing with obsolescence. In *The Pure Theory of Capital* he abandoned the idea of maintaining capital intact and its corollary net income and chose to work with gross income. His reasons for doing so were that he believed that outside the stationary state the notion of maintaining capital intact had no meaning and, furthermore, it was a concept of which the economist had no need. The difference in outlook stemmed from the fact that Pigou was interested in welfare economics, whereas Hayek was more concerned with disequilibrium processes in which aggregate concepts could be eschewed.

Pigou's definition of net social income in real terms was as follows:

Net income = Consumption + Net investment.

Now net investment was defined as the difference between the value of the capital stock at the beginning and the end of a period and it is only in the case where relative prices remain constant that it is possible to measure the money value of real net investment by the increase in the money value of the capital stock. Usually prices will have changed and an index number problem would arise. There is also an added complication. The prices at the beginning of a period are expected prices. What Hicks therefore suggested was that Lindahl's distinction between *ex ante* and *ex post* be adopted and used to provide a measure of obsolescence. But he did concede that there were other reasons for measuring national income than that pursued by Pigou and of course there still remained the problem of whether Hayek would have conceded any interest in a macroeconomic aggregate such as net social income.

Summary and conclusions

The capital controversy contained many strands. First, there was the debate between Hayek and Knight. Knight assumed that Hayek was reopening an earlier debate between J.B. Clark and Böhm-Bawerk. That earlier controversy centred on the relative merits of a productivity approach versus a time preference approach to capital and interest and the appropriateness of a concept of an average period of production. Knight followed Clark in assuming that capital was a revolving fund and that its embodiment in particular assets at particular points of time was relatively unimportant because all assets were substitutable over time. Hayek followed Böhm-Bawerk in rejecting the notion of a revolving fund but he also rejected the notion of an average period of production. What Hayek was interested in was the medium-term implications of capital being embodied in specific assets. In Hayek's theory the period of production was a forward-looking concept and Hayek looked at the length of time over which capital might be locked in specific assets. Knight conceded that there might be short-run problems with capital assets but thought that the problems were the subject matter of money and business cycle theory and no capital theory and did not develop his ideas.

The second debate was between Kaldor and Hayek. Kaldor began by being sympathetic to Hayek but then shifted his ground and became Hayek's fiercest critic. Kaldor rejected the Ricardo effect which Hayek produced in order to obtain a self-reversing model of the trade cycle arising out of the movement of real wages. This debate also proved inconclusive because both contestants used different methodologies. Kaldor employed comparative statics while Hayek used a less familiar dynamic approach. However, the German inflation of the 1920s suggested that Hayek's thesis was refuted under hyperinflationary conditions.

Hayek's attempts to build a theory of capital were handicapped by his failure to develop a dynamic theory. However, Lachmann presented the most comprehensive account of neo-Austrian capital theory. Capital, he considered, was a heterogeneous stock of material assets which yielded a stream of income. Individuals made decisions as to which assets they would embody their money capital. These decisions were forward looking and involved paying attention to both complementarity and substitutability between assets. Individual decisions would then have to be reconciled through the market.

The unsatisfactory nature of the capital controversy, its lack of conclusiveness, helps to explain the success of Keynes's *General Theory*. The *General Theory* embodied a short-run model which placed the emphasis upon investment decisions. It assumed that the capital stock was homogeneous and that there might be idle capital and labour. Hence the problem of complementarity seemed to disappear. What was emphasized was the possible depressing effect of investment on the existing capital stock when the market rate of interest was known and might be jammed and when the profit rate was dominated by pessimistic expectations. Furthermore, Hayek's emphasis upon complementarity was swamped in the slump by the fact that as long as assets earned an amount sufficient to cover their running costs then further investment might not take place. The Marshallian distinction between prime costs and supplementary costs seemed to take care of Hayek's emphasis upon the problems posed by the stock of capital. When longer-run issues started to surface, as in the Harrod and Solow growth models, then attention was concentrated upon equilibrium growth models. Later, as we shall see, the problem of moving from one growth path to another, the traverse, seemed to call for a revival of Austrian capital theory, although alternative approaches were also advanced.

Notes

1. Keynes, J.M. (1973), *The Collected Writings of John Maynard Keynes*, Vol. XIII, *The General Theory and After: Part I, Preparation*, London: Macmillan, p. 90.
2. op. cit., p. 253.
3. Keynes, J.M. (1936, 1973), *Collected Writings*, Vol, VII, *The General Theory of Employment, Interest and Money*, p. 173, fn3.
4. Robertson, D.H. (1973) in *The Collected Writings of John Maynard Keynes*, Vol. XIII, *The General Theory and After: Part I, Preparation*, p. 253.
5. Keynes, J.M. (1973), *The General Theory*, p. 173, fn3.
6. Sobel, I. (1973), in D. Colander, *The Collected Papers of Abba, P. Lerner*, New York: University of New York Press, p. i.

7. Knight, F. (1936), 'The quantity of capital and the rate of interest', *Journal of Political Economy*, 44: 434–5.
8. Knight, F. (1935), 'Professor Hayek and the theory of investment', *Economic Journal*, 45: 94.
9. Hayek, F.A. (1935c), 'The mythology of capital', *Quarterly Journal of Economics*, 50: 203.
10. Böhm-Bawerk (1959), *Capital and Interest*, Vol. II, *Positive Theory of Capital*, South Holland: Libertarian Press, p. 73.
11. Kaldor, N. (1937), 'Annual survey of economic theory: the recent controversy on the theory of capital', *Econometrica*, 5: 218.
12. op. cit., p. 232.
13. Kaldor, N. (1939c), 'Capital intensity and the trade cycle', *Economica*, NS6: 43.
14. op. cit., p. 60.
15. Kaldor, N. (1940), 'A model of the trade cycle', *Economic Journal*, 50: 78.
16. Thirlwall, A.P. (1987), *Nicholas Kaldor*, Brighton: Wheatsheaf, p. 50.
17. Hayek, F.A. (1942), 'The Ricardo effect', *Economica*, NS9: 1.
18. op. cit., pp. 147–8.
19. Kaldor, N. (1942), 'Professor Hayek and the concertina effect', *Economica*, NS9: 363–4.
20. op. cit., p. 375.
21. Hayek (1942), op. cit.
22. Robertson, D.H. (1957), *Lectures on Economic Principles*, London: Fontana, pp. 274–5.
23. Hicks, J.R. (1967b), 'The Hayek story', in *Critical Essays in Monetary Theory*, Oxford: Oxford University Press, p. 266.
24. Hayek, F.A. (1969), 'Three elucidations of the Ricardo effect', *Journal of Political Economy*, 77: 281.
25. Hayek (1942), op. cit., p. 141.
26. op. cit., p. 142.
27. Bresciani-Turroni, C. (1937), *Economics of Inflation*, p. 197.
28. Hayek (1969), op. cit., p. 282.
29. Machlup (1971), 'Professor Hayek's contribution to economics', *Swedish Journal of Economics*, 76: 528.
30. Hayek, F.A. (1941), *Pure Theory of Capital*, London: Routledge, p. 3.
31. op. cit., p. 60.
32. op. cit., p. 1.
33. Lachmann, L. (1956), *Capital and its Structure*, London: Bell, p. 35.

6
The socialist debate

Introduction

Both in his inaugural lecture, 'The trend of economic thinking' (1933a) and in his editing of the book on *Collectivist Economic Planning* (1935d), Hayek introduced English-speaking economists to the European discussions of the economics of socialism. In doing so he provoked a debate not only on the relative merits of socialism and capitalism but he also pronounced on the relative merits of two approaches to economic analysis. The immediate outcome of the debate was the production of a theoretical model known as market socialism, which had all the advantages of appearing to be a practicable proposition and to fit into Robbins's definition of economics as the study of the allocation of scarce resources between competing ends. Hayek conceded that such a model had not been considered by the apologists of capitalism and admitted that they had assumed that socialism meant planning without markets.

Subsequently Hayek developed his criticism of socialism in his 'Economics and knowledge' (1937a) and in his *The Road to Serfdom* (1944) but by then the tide of public opinion was running strongly in favour of some planning. And the distinction between two approaches to economic analysis, which may be called Mengerian and Walrasian respectively, was not appreciated in the 1930s. Hayek had assumed that he belonged to a community of scholars who shared a common approach to economics problems. Of course, by a common approach to economics he did not mean Marshallian economics which he thought drew a confused distinction between real costs and opportunity costs. He also thought that the Marshallian partial equilibrium approach was not particularly well suited to the analysis of socialism and capitalism – although Marshall was in fact aware of general equilibrium analysis and had discussed socialism. Furthermore, Pigou wrote a book on the relative merits of the two systems and Dobb, another Cambridge economist, was responsible for a number of important articles on socialism. Keynes, of course, pronounced himself not in favour of socialism, but neither was he prepared to be a conservative, and Robertson did write a book on the control of industry. However, the main problem was that Hayek had conflated different European methods of analysis and this did not become apparent until later when what was revealed was that Austrian economics was different from that put forward by the Lausanne School of Walras and Pareto.

Collectivist economic planning

The Austrian critique

Because the substance of 'The trend of economic thinking' and the introductory chapter to the *Collectivist Economic Planning*, which was entitled 'The nature and history of the problem', are similar in content and are closely linked in time, it will be useful to take them together while examining their contents (see Table 6.1). Hayek began by noting that there was a belief that the deliberate regulation of economic and social affairs must be more successful than the apparent haphazard interplay

Table 6.1 Session 1937–8. The Problems of a Collectivist Economy. Professor Hayek.

Six lectures. Summer Term. Thursdays, 5.00–6.00, beginning S.T.
For postgraduate students and optional for B.Sc. (Econ) Final – Special subject of Economics.
Fee: 18s.

   SYLLABUS: Types of collectivist economies. Meaning of the question of their 'possibility'. The conditions of rational planning. The problem of *Wirtschaftsrechnung*; is the problem of the pricing of factors of production necessary and possible? Suggested 'competitive' solutions.
   BOOKS RECOMMENDED: L. von Mises, *Socialism* and *Kritik des Interventionismus*; F.A. Hayek, N.G. Pierson, L. von Mises, G. Halm and E. Barone, *Collectivist Economic Planning* (with full bibliography of the earlier literature); R.L. Hall, *The Economic System in the Socialist State*; A.P. Lerner, 'Economic theory and the socialist economy' (*Review of Economic Studies*, 1935); 'Statics and dynamics in socialist economics' (*Economic Journal*, 1937); F.H. Knight, 'The place of marginal economics in a collectivist system' and A. Gourvitch, 'The problem of prices and valuation in the Soviet system' (both in the *American Economic Review*, March 1936, Supplement); O. Lange, 'On the *Economic Theory of Socialism*', (*Review of Economic Studies*, Vol. IV, Nos. 1 and 2); E.F.M. Durbin, 'Economic calculus in a planned society' (*Economic Journal*, December 1936).

Source: LSE *Calendar* 1937–8.

of independent individuals and he traced the origins of the belief to a variety of causes. First, there was the growth of revulsion against the social misery which seemed to be associated with the market–capitalist system. Later, in *Capitalism and the Historians* (1954), he was to challenge the view that the Industrial Revolution had increased misery. Second, there was the belief that the classical economists had failed to provide acceptable solutions to the problems posed by industrial–market capitalism. But, he argued, the classical economists had distinguished between positive and normative economics and he went on to observe that:

> The attitude of the classical economists to economic policy was the outcome of their scientific conclusion. The presumption against government interference sprang from a wide range of demonstrations that isolated acts of interference definitely frustrated the attainment of those ends which all accepted as desirable.[1]

Third, he pointed to the apparent success of the Historical School in arguing that: 'the laws of economics could only be established by the application to the material of history the methods of the natural sciences.'[2] But Hayek rejected the approach of the Historical School on the grounds that it degenerated into mere record and description. Fourth, he emphasized the fact that, following Marx's example, most socialists had not described the workings of socialist economies lest it should lead them into the wild fantasies of the Utopian socialists (such as Fourier) but had concentrated upon analyzing the workings of historically-given capitalist societies. In effect, Marxian economists followed the path charted by the Historical School.

Hayek took the view that the economic problem of how to allocate resources among competing ends would exist independently of the economic system and what was important to bear in mind was that the economic problem might not be capable of resolution by the methods of the natural sciences. The economic problem was not to be confused with an engineering problem. Planners and:

> most of the planners do not yet realize that they are socialists, assume that there exist given ends, given means and given knowledge whereas the resolution of the economic problem seems to depend upon the spontaneous interplay of the actions of individuals producing something which is not the deliberate object of their actions but results from an organism in which every part performs a necessary function for the continuance of the whole, without any human mind having devised it.[3]

Hayek concluded: 'From what we have seen and demonstrated hitherto, it is obvious how fantastic those doctrines are which imagine that production in the collectivist regime would be ordered in a manner substantially different from that of "anarchist" production.'[4] In a private capitalist economy incomes and output are simultaneously determined by the market process, but in a socialist economy income distribution is first determined and then production and consumption are determined. Hence, the demands for consumer goods and the supplies of labour and saving are derived and these demand and supply functions, taken in conjunction with given technologies, serve to determine the outputs of consumer and investment goods. And in Barone's model individuals had freedom of choice as regards consumption, saving and employment. Therefore, a set of equations could be generated for a socialist economy which would be analogous to those generated in a capitalist market economy.

In the most celebrated critique of socialism, 'Economic calculations in the socialist commonwealth', which was translated and reprinted in *Collectivist Economic Planning*, Mises accepted that the distribution of consumer goods could be independent of their production because the state may own resources but cannot consume them (Mises, 1920, 1935). The state might therefore decide to give everyone equal shares of consumer goods without reference to differences in individual preferences. This could lead to saving or waste but was most likely to lead to exchange and the use of money. Therefore rational calculation, involving the measurement of subjective value through the use of money, might be possible in a socialist economy. However, no such rational calculation might apply to the production and allocation of producer goods. In capitalist societies the valuations of producer goods would be generated by individuals acting as both consumers and producers. But such valuations would be based upon the private ownership of productive resources. Furthermore, the labour theory of value could provide no basis for rational calculation because it assumed that labour was homogeneous which was an argument that ignored the fact that utility might not be homogeneous and that, as a good Austrian might have observed, it is the structure of wants that is important.

In concluding *Collectivist Economic Planning* Hayek took the view that Russian experience suggested that rational economic planning was not possible in a socialist society. He also noted that the Cambridge Marxist economist, Maurice Dobb, had suggested that freedom of choice and planning might be incompatible and that in the absence of competition it was impossible to make public monopolies charge competitive prices.

The socialist response

Although Hayek's last essay in *Collectivist Economic Planning* was entitled 'The state of the debate', there had been no real debate but only an assertion that socialism would not permit of rational calculation in the production of capital goods. The debate really began when Lange and Lerner attempted to refute Mises's critique. Lange opened his article 'On the economic theory of socialism' (1937a) with the observation that:

> Socialists have certainly good reason to be grateful to Professor Mises, the great *advocatus diaboli* of their cause. For it was his powerful challenge that forced socialists to recognize the importance of an adequate system of economic accounting to guide the allocation of resources in a socialist economy. Even more it was chiefly due to Professor Mises's challenge that many socialists became aware of such a problem . . . Both as an expression of recognition for the great service rendered by him and as a memento of the prime importance of sound economic accounting, a statue of Professor Mises ought to occupy an honourable place in the great hall of the Ministry of Socialization or of the Central Planning Board of the Socialist State.[5]

Lange noted that Barone had said that a solution was possible but had not indicated how it could be done. He did however refer to the fact that an American economist, Fred M. Taylor, had suggested that a solution might be obtained through a process of trial and error. What Lange did was to demonstrate how the process of trial and error would operate by extending the use of the Walrasian auctioneer from his place in the competitive general equilibrium system through the creation of a central planning board for the determination of the prices of capital goods and resources other than labour. Individuals would then obtain their incomes from two sources: first, from the sale of their services in the labour market; and second from the receipt of a social dividend. Incomes from these two sources could then be spent on consumer goods.

The central planning board would then lay down two rules to guide producers. First, the output of an industry must satisfy the condition that price must equal average cost of production. This rule replaced the competitive markets injunction to maximize profits and ensure an optimal allocation of resources. The second rule was that managers should equate marginal cost with price and this rule would control the scale of output of the size of an industry and would replace the competitive mechanism which governed the entry and exit of firms from an industry. In this system prices would perform a parametric function and would be set by trial and error; that is to say, the accounting prices would be raised or lowered in order to reconcile demand and supply.

By way of a parenthesis Lange added some comments upon the social dividend and the rate of interest. Recognizing that the social dividend might affect the work–leisure choice, Lange proposed that it be paid as a fixed percentage of the wage. Later Lerner (1937) was to suggest that it be paid as a lump sum which was independent of the wage. In the short run Lange noted that the amount of capital was a constant and the rate of interest would be determined by the condition that the demand for capital would be equal to the amount available. However, in the long run the amount of capital could be increased by capital accumulation and the rate of accumulation could be set arbitrarily by the planning board who might aim to make the marginal net product of capital zero (an objective which could be interrupted by technical progress). Under prodding from Lerner, Lange did concede that the time preference of consumers could be incorporated into the determination of the rate of capital accumulation.

The Austrian reaction

Confronted by the Lange–Lerner solution to the economic problems of socialism, Hayek conceded during the course of a review of Lange and Taylor's book, *On the Economic Theory of Socialism* (1939), and Dickinson's *Economics of Socialism* (1939), that:

> On the whole the books are so thoroughly unorthodox from a socialist point of view that one wonders whether their authors have not retained too little of the traditional trappings of socialist argument in order to make their proposals acceptable to socialists who are not economists.[6]

This conclusion was interpreted as an admission of Hayek's defeat by the followers of Lange and Lerner. But it could also be taken as a criticism of the Lange–Lerner solution by those who equated socialism with physical planning.

But the overall impression given was that Lange and Lerner had shown that a market form of socialism was possible. Why then did the Austrian critique fail to take this possibility into account? In 1978 Hayek argued that the reason why Mises did not succeed was because of his very use of the term *calculation*. People just did not see why calculation should be necessary. They assumed that we have the technical data and we know what we want. Therefore there was no need to calculate. What Mises failed to stress was that without markets we do not know what we want. But this criticism of Mises by Hayek could also be applied to Hayek's own position in the 1930s. It was not until Hayek had published 'Economics and knowledge' in 1937 and not until after he had elaborated the theme of that article in his article 'The use of knowledge in society' (1945), did Hayek indicate that the problem of centralizing the information in society was impossible. What happened in the 1930s was that Hayek had assumed that the Austrian approach to the economic problem was similar to that proposed by Walras and Pareto and elaborated by Hicks and the other exponents of general equilibrium theory in the LSE. Indeed, the sharp contrast between ends and means — both of which could be assumed to be given — seemed to flow from the delineation of the economic problem by Robbins in *The Nature and Significance of Economic Science* (1932a)

In the 1970s and 1980s there has been a revival of the criticisms of socialism which were first advanced by Mises and Hayek. The essence of the neo-Austrian position is that the Austrians emphasize choice in the context of an economy subject to change and uncertainty whereas Lange and Lerner confined their attention to a stationary economy. Thus, in the market prices are continually altering as new knowledge emerges and a central planning board would, because of the slow speed with which a bureaucracy operates, impart disturbances and probably cycles into the movements of prices and outputs. Moreover, the lack of standardization of capital goods might make the setting of accounting prices difficult.

However, the fundamental criticism of the Lange–Lerner model derived by Vaughn (1981) from Hayek is that Lange ignored the role of the price mechanism as an aggregator of different bits of information possessed by different individuals and the dissemination of that information to others. Furthermore, it is alleged that Lange had ignored the role of competition in driving prices and costs to minima. This argument had previously been put by Wiseman (1957) who stated that the marginal cost pricing rule was an equilibrium condition derived from the outcome of market forces. That is to say, if firms were successful and survived it would be as if they had equated price with marginal cost *ex post*. But it would not be possible to equate marginal cost with price *ex ante* because no one could be sure what the market clearing price would be. Now many of the comments rely upon a reading of Part One of 'On the economic theory of socialism' and excluded the analysis presented in Part Two. But Lange was fully aware of the role of the price mechanism in a competitive capitalist economy:

> The system of free competition [Lange wrote] is a rather peculiar one. Its mechanism is one of fooling entrepreneurs. It requires the pursuit of maximum profit in order to function, but it destroys profits when they are actually pursued by a large number of people. However, this game of blindman's buff with the pursuit of maximum profit is only possible as long as the size of the business unit is small and the number of entrepreneurs is consequently large. A return to free competition could only be accomplished by splitting up the large-scale business units to destroy their economic and political power. This could be attained only at the cost of giving up large scale production and the great achievements of mass production which are associated with it. Such an artificially

maintained system of free competition would have to prohibit the use of advanced technology.[7]

Lange assumed that capitalist economies were in the stage of monopoly capitalism and that price competition had ceased because firms entered into collusive agreements. As a result of these agreements technological progress was steered towards cost-reducing and not output-expanding innovations with the result that prices would not fall but profits would increase. Prices, however, might fall if there were product innovations. But because of the lack of competition there was a check to investment which led to depression and economic stagnation. Lange was therefore presenting the case for socialism in the context of a particular historical stage in the evolution of capitalism. Consequently, he drew upon the writings of Joan Robinson and E.H. Chamberlin to emphasize the wastes of competition. He also appears to have been aware of the work of Berle and Means on the modern corporation and the literature which discussed the divorce of ownership from control:

> There is also [he wrote] the argument which might be raised against socialism with regard to the efficiency of public officials under socialism as compared with private entrepreneurs as managers of production. Strictly speaking, these public officials must be compared with corporation officials under capitalism and not with private small-scale entrepreneurs. ... By doing so we do not mean, however, to deny its great importance. It seems to us that the real danger of socialism is that of bureaucratisation of economic life and not the impossibility of coping with the problem of the allocation of resources. Unfortunately, we do not see how the same or even greater danger can be averted under monopoly capitalism.[3]

Finally, Lange incorporated Keynes's analysis of economic stagnation into his case for socialism.

The Lange–Lerner rules were therefore based upon the assumption that firms were not operating at minimum points on their average cost curves. Hence, the rules could be designed to push them towards such minima. This interpretation does, of course, reduce the possibilities of financing the social dividend out of the monopoly rents of firms, but the parametric function of prices becomes increasingly important when monopoly capitalism has supplanted competitive capitalism.

Part Two of Lange's article also disposes of the arguments of Hayek, and Roberts (1971) who states that his version of socialism was incompatible with the views of the founding fathers of socialism. Thus Roberts states that: 'The famous "socialist controversy" among Western economists is not about socialism but about the logical consistency of the models of market simulation, their determinacy, their stability and their convergence towards equilibrium.'[9] It did not, he asserts, deal with alienation, exploitation and the concept of labour as a commodity. But Lange did provide ample quotations from Marx, Engels, Kautsky and Lenin to confirm the ancestry of his ideas.

Durbin on socialism

Lange and Lerner were not the only LSE critics of Hayek and Mises. In addition there was Durbin who, like Hayek, lectured in the LSE on socialism and planning in the 1930s (Table 6.2). Durbin's theoretical work – he tended to emphasize average cost pricing – was shown to be defective and incurred trenchant criticism from Lerner. However, his great strength lay in the fact that as a member of the Labour Party and a future politician, he was more concerned with the scope and limitations of British political institutions. He was therefore much more optimistic about the ability of the community to control planners than Hayek who saw in planning the road to serfdom. A notable feature of Durbin's lectures was that he did draw upon the practical experiments in planning in the Soviet Union and the United States in order to shed light upon the problems of planning.

The Cambridge contribution

So far we have concentrated on the debate within the LSE but there were also interesting contributions from Cambridge. Indeed, it would have been surprising if Pigou, the author of *Wealth and Welfare* (1912) had not intervened in the controversy. But his *Socialism versus Capitalism* (1937) was a curious and modest affair. In *Wealth and Welfare* he had followed Marshall in distinguishing between increasing and decreasing returns industries. And taxes and subsidies had also been proposed for externalities. Hence, it might have been assumed that we would have recommended the extension of such policies and produced a result similar to that of Lange. But in *Socialism versus Capitalism* he reached a pessimistic conclusion. 'In planning the difficulties are formidable, so formidable that so far as one can see no attempt has been made in a capitalist society to use bounties and duties for bringing about adjustments of the kind I have been describing.'[10] And even 'a central planning authority would find it no more easy than the government of a capitalist state to obtain the data required for these calculations.'[11] Nevertheless, in an attempt at a balanced and dispassionate analysis of the merits of socialism and capitalism he did conclude that socialism was more likely to reduce unemployment and promote a more equitable distribution of

144 The socialist debate

Table 6.2 Session 1938–9. Economic Planning in Theory and Practice. Mr. Durbin.

Eight lectures. Lent and Summer Terms. Wednesdays, 5.00–6.00, beginning L.T. 15 February, S.T. 26 April.
Fee: £1 14s.

SYLLABUS: 1. Economic theory and economic institutions. The meaning of the terms 'economic institutions' and 'economic system'. Analysis of the economic institutions of capitalist and pre-capitalist economies. The historical development of capitalist institutions. Planning as an emergent system.

2. The meaning of 'planning' – terminology and practice. Types of planned economy. Types of contemporary economic society. The common element in all meanings of the term 'planning'. The principle of 'large scale survey'. The rationale of 'large scale control'. The logical and psychological case against large-scale control. Democratic and authoritarian planning.

3. The problem of 'economic calculus' in a planned economy. The nature of 'directives' to be issued by the supreme economic authority. The relation between the general directives and the machinery of control.

4. The problem of monetary policy and of international trade for a planned economy. The nature of monetary equilibrium. The instruments of a policy necessary to maintain it. The position of the planned economy. The relation between monetary policy, the trade cycle, the volume of international trade and the probable size of exchange fluctuations.

5. The problem of 'machinery and incentive'. The organization of the representative production unit. The nature of the central planning machinery. The general problem of incentive. The particular problem of 'workers' control'. The analysis of the types of psychological assumption upon which policy can be based.

6. An analysis of the recent economic policies and institutional developments in Great Britain, Russia and America in so far as they throw light upon the practical problems of Planning.

BOOKS RECOMMENDED: *General*: Mises, *Socialism*; Hayek, Halm, Mises etc., *Collectivist Economic Planning*; Hall, *The Economic System in a Socialist State*; Wooton, *Plan or No Plan*; Cole, *The Principles of Economic planning*; Robbins, *Economic Planning and International Order*.

Relevant economic theory: Harrod, 'Notes on supply' (*Economic Journal*, 1930); 'Laws of increasing returns' (*Economic Journal*, 1931); Mrs Robinson, *Economics of Imperfect Competition*; Chapter 7; Chamberlain, *Theory of Monopolistic Competition*, Chapter 5; Kaldor, 'Market imperfections and excess capacity' (*Economica*, 1935); Kahn, 'Notes on ideal output' (*Economic Journal*, 1935).

Applications to the problems of a planned economy: Dickinson, 'Price formation in a socialist economy' (*Economic Journal*, 1933); Dobb and Dickinson, 'The problems of a socialist economy' (*Economic Journal*, 1933); Lerner, 'Economic theory and the socialist economy' (*Review of Economic Studies*, 1935); Dobb and Lerner, 'Economic theory and the socialist economy' (*Review of Economic Studies*); Durbin, 'Social significance of the theory of value' (*Economic Journal*, 1935); 'Economic calculus in a planned economy' (*Economic Journal*, 1936); Lerner, 'Statics and dynamics in socialist economics' (*Economic Journal*, 1937); Durbin, 'A note on Mr Lerner's "Dynamical Propositions"' (*Economic Journal*, 1937); Lange, 'On the *Economic Theory of Socialism*' (*Review of Economic Studies*, 1937).

Recent development of economic policy: Great Britain: Robbins, *The Great Depression*; Horrobin, *The Pleasures of Planning*; Robbins, *The Planning of British Agriculture*; Dalton, *Practical socialism for Britain*, *For Socialism and Peace*, *A Programme for Britain* (Labour Party Official Publications); Morison, *Socialisation of Transport*; Robson, ed., *Public Enterprise*; Joy, *The Case for Socialism*.

Russia: Dobb, *Russian Economic Development*; Hoover, *The Economic Life of Soviet Russia*; Reddaway, *The Russian Financial System*, *Summary of the Fulfilment of the First Five Year Plan*, *Summary of the Second Five Year Plan* (Russian Office Publications); Warriner, 'Soviet Agriculture' (*New Fabian Research Bureau Quarterly Journal*, 1937).

America: Steel-Maitland, *The New America*; Radice and Jones, *An American Experiment*; Brogan, *The American Political System*; A group of American Economists, *The Recovery Programme*; reports of Recovery Administration, Agricultural Administration; Reports by the National Bureau of Economic Research on Cotton and Wheat.

Source: LSE *Calendar* 1937–8.

income and wealth. And in the spirit of *Wealth and Welfare*, but incorporating ideas developed in his unpublished thesis on pricing in the short run, as well as the ideas developed by Joan Robinson in *The Economics of Imperfect Competition* (1933), Kahn produced in his article. 'Some notes on ideal output' (1937), an analytical framework which was comparable to that developed by Lerner.

Cambridge did, however, produce a varied response to the socialist debate. While Pigou and Kahn might be regarded as advocates of some form of market system, Dobb presented a more orthodox Marxist approach. 'It is more or less agreed now', he wrote, 'that free choice of the consumer [and presumably also free choice of occupation] and planning from the centre are incompatible items.'[12] He also questioned whether the market socialists had disposed of the possible conflict between efficiency and equity:

> If carpenters are scarcer or more costly than scavengers, the market will place a higher value upon their services, and carpenters will derive a higher income and greater 'voting power' as consumers. On the side of supply the extra 'costliness' of carpenters will receive expression, but only at the expense of giving carpenters a differential 'pull' as consumers and hence of vitiating the index of demand; on the other hand, if carpenters and scavengers are to be given equal weight as consumers by giving them equal incomes, then the extra costliness of carpenters will find no expression in costs of production. Here is the central dilemma. Precisely because consumers are also producers, both costs and needs are precluded from receiving simultaneous expression in the same system of market valuations. Precisely to the extent that market valuations are rendered adequate in one direction they lose significance in the other.[13]

The nature of the firm

During the 1930s the general equilibrium model was introduced into the LSE and its properties were explored. The conclusion of that research programme was the publication of Hicks's *Value and Capital* (1939a) and Lerner's *Economics of Control* (1944). In the years that preceded the publication of the two books there was also an examination of anomalies. One anomaly was the place of money in such a model and the resulting discussion led to debates with Cambridge. Another puzzle was the socialist economy and it was shown by Lange and Lerner that the socialist economy was compatible with the general equilibrium model. In contrast, Hicks chose 'to consider the pure logical analysis of capitalism to be a task in itself, while the survey of economic institutions is best carried out by other methods, such as those of the economic historian (even when the institutions are contemporary institutions).'[14] And within that issue of how to analyse institutions was the problem of the firm.

For the paradox of the general equilibrium model was that it laid a great deal of emphasis upon the price mechanism but it threw little light upon the nature of competition of the organization of firms. These peculiar features arose because the model attempted to provide a rigorous underpinning to the eighteenth debate concerning the limits of government. Adam Smith had suggested that the pursuit of self-interest in a decentralized market economy would lead to an efficient allocation of resources. That allocation would not be brought about by conscious authority or command but by prices. Hence, the model need throw no light upon the workings of a socialist economy nor upon the existence of firms.

In 1937 Coase published his article on 'The nature of the firm'. It drew attention to the lack of a theory of the firm and the fact that markets did not operate costlessly. In Coase's explanation firms exist because of the cost of using markets and the limits to the size of a firm (what prevents the firm becoming so large that it becomes a command economy) is that there are costs associated with the exercise of managerial control. In effect the size of a firm results from the balancing at the margin of the costs of using the market as against the costs of extending the sphere of managerial control. And Coase's article also clarified the concepts of 'entrepreneurship', 'combination' and 'integration':

> Initiative means forecasting and operates through the price mechanism by the making of new contracts. Management proper merely reacts to price changes, rearranging the factors of production under its control. That the business normally combines both functions is an obvious result of market costs.[15]

> There is a combination when transactions which were previously organized by two or more entrepreneurs become organized by one. This becomes integration when it involves the organization of transactions which were previously carried out between entrepreneurs on a market.[16]

Coase did not explore in any great depth the factors which lay behind the issue of managerial control and which account for the differences in the structures of firms. Knight's book, *Risk, Uncertainty and Profit*, was a set book at the LSE and was referred to by Coase. But the problems of moral hazard and risk which were mentioned by Knight were not dealt with by Coase. Nor did Coase refer to an earlier article by Kaldor on the equilibrium of the firm. In fact, Coase's article is interesting for the light that it throws upon the organizational structure of the LSE – a structure which Robbins had sought to overcome. For, although he had been a student at the LSE and later a junior member of staff, Coase was, on his own admission, 'not fully aware of what was going on. Furthermore, although my appointment at the LSE was in the Economics Department, I had taken a B.Com degree and had worked, and continued to work more closely, with Plant than with Robbins.'[17] He had been taught to think of marginal cost as the cost of the marginal firm but was dissatisfied with that way of looking at the concept. Plant suggested that he should think in terms of the cost of additional units of output to all firms. Later he discovered that Pigou in *The Economics of Welfare* had worked out the relationship between average and marginal cost. And although Hicks referred to the Harrod curve (marginal revenue) in his lectures, the significance of the concept was not appreciated until the publication of Joan Robinson's *The Economics of Imperfect Competition*. However, Coase did acknowledge the influence of Hayek: 'Unassertive, Hayek nonetheless exerted considerable influence through his profound knowledge of economic theory, the example of his own high standards of scholarship and the power of his ideas.'[18]

Eastern Europe

The leap to socialism did not come in the advanced economies but in the backward areas of Europe, and it marked a shift not to market socialism but to centrally planned economies whose characteristics were conditioned by political factors as well as economic problems. After 1917 there was always a fear that the Soviet Union might be invaded and fears of invasion were also present after the Second World War. Between 1917 and 1924 there was a period of War Communism in the Soviet Union whereby planning was concerned with distribution, with the task of feeding and equipping the Red Army. Factories and mines were nationalized and the rest of industry and commerce was gradually brought under control. Foreign trade was also monopolized. Consumer goods were rationed, output norms were set for factories and the peasants were forcibly compelled to deliver their crops. But War Communism was undermined by peasants revolts and the Kronstadt mutiny. The market was then re-established under the New Economic Policy. However, the policy was short lived and controls were re-introduced in 1924.

After Lenin's death, Stalin extended the scope of planning and made its objectives growth and catching-up with the West. The ownership of all the means of production led to the development of yearly and five-year plans and to the belief that shortages were essentially short-run problems which would be solved by growth. The implications of the policy were, however, masked by the abundance of labour and raw materials and so the price mechanism as a means of reconciling demand

and supply could be ignored. After Stalin's death the policies were denounced by Kruschev, but many of Kruschev's policies were to prove ineffective. The virgin lands of the central Soviet Union were ploughed up and the wheat acreage was doubled. But soil erosion and lack of fertilizers led to falling yields. The failure of agriculture was a major factor in the downfall of Kruschev. Brezhnev succeeded Kruschev and he sought to introduce greater devolution. Unfortunately, the effects of moves towards greater liberalization led to a rise in expectations in the rest of Eastern Europe which threatened to undermine Soviet control of the region. The result was a move back to a command economy. There was an attempt to achieve military parity with the United States, exploit the mineral resources of Siberia, increase consumption, and narrow income differentials between town and country. But lagging productivity meant that increased money wages led to rising prices and food shortages.

Soviet statistics are now admitted to be unreliable. But even on the basis of published data there is clear evidence of a deceleration which meant that the Soviet Union could not catch up with the United States and other advanced countries. And it was faced with the task of being forced to export perpetually raw materials in return for Western technology. The slow-down has been revealed by comparisons of purchasing power parity. Between 1950 and 1973 the gap between the Soviet Union and the United States narrowed. After 1973 the gap remained constant for a decade. But there were other signs of declining living standards, such as the fall in longevity with life expectancy falling by about two years between 1970 and 1990. Even Soviet official statistics continued to report that the Soviet GNP was two-thirds that of the United States throughout both the 1970s and the 1980s.

The slowing down of the Soviet economy has been remarkable given the promising start in the 1950s and 1960s. And it is easy to jump to the conclusion that the cause can be ascribed in a simple fashion to the absence of the price mechanism and the prevalence of central planning. But the success stories of the 1970s and 1980s — Japan, Taiwan, South Korea, Hong Kong and Singapore — have all relied upon some measure of planning from the centre. Furthermore, the Soviet Union was successful in recovering from the Second World War without the assistance of Marshall Aid and in spite of appalling losses of manpower.

The Stalin model was applied in varying degrees, and with the notable exception of Yugoslavia, throughout Eastern Europe. But from the 1950s onwards there were attempts at reform in Hungary. Indeed, Hungary was the most open of the Eastern European economies. In 1950 exports formed 14 per cent of the Net Material Product (the socialist equivalent of national income) and were 21 per cent in 1988. As a result movements in the balance of trade tended to serve as a guide to the effectiveness of policies for the planners. And there were balance of payments crises in 1953, 1955, 1961, 1980 and 1988. A major cause of the crises was the practice of operating the economy on a 'soft budget' enhanced by foreign borrowing. Soft budgets led to excess demand and had the advantage of reducing unemployment; in 1988 there were five vacancies for every person unemployed. But soft budgets had the effect of creating cycles, especially in investment, which were similar to those analyzed by Hayek but which led to greater distortions because of the lack of price flexibility in markets. These soft budgets were located in the interface between government departments and public enterprises. In effect, each public enterprise was under the tutelage of a ministry from which it received assistance. The nature of that assistance varied according to the bargaining powers of the ministry and the department and in the absence of market discipline the changes in policies were apt to appear arbitrary.

The solution to the distortions in the economy has been seen to lie in the creation of property rights and markets through a process of privatization. Already many sectors of the economy have been privatized. For example, 40 per cent of agriculture and 30 per cent of catering are in private hands and in 1988 14 per cent of all taxpayers had a secondary (private) income. However, there are problems in privatizing manufacturing and mining. The procedures being followed by the authorities do not insist upon the valuation of the enterprise's assets by the market nor do they stipulate that income derived from the sale of assets should be handed over to the state. In fact, responsibility for asset disposal is left to the enterprise council. This contrasts with the policy now being attempted in Poland which is to offer shares in the enterprises to the public through the medium of an auction. To enable citizens to buy shares the state is prepared to offer loans. In effect, the policy is one of attempting to combine equity with the conscious attempt to convince the public that they are not getting something for nothing.

The transition to a market economy

Which brings us to the fundamental problem of how do centrally planned economies make the transition to becoming market economies. The problem invites comparison with the situation facing Western Europe at the end of the Second World War and with that confronting the Latin American countries in the 1980s and 1990s. At the end of the Second World War the major Western economies sought to move from wartime planning to peacetime structures based upon some form of mixed economy. The move to greater use of markets was not achieved overnight but took a decade to introduce. In Britain the final bonfire of controls took place in 1955 and coal was derationed in 1957. This slow transition was an important factor in the golden age equilibrium attained in the world economy in the 1950s and 1960s. In making the transition the West European economies were assisted by Marshall Aid through which the United States provided $65 billion dollars over four years. Millward (1985) has cast doubt upon the necessity of the aid and has argued that the balance of payments difficulties encountered by the European countries were the result of strong growth and the need to import large amounts of raw materials and manufactures from the United States and the deficits would have been corrected as exports gradually expanded. The argument is controversial and rests upon an assessment of what politicians should have done in the context of the severe winter of 1947.

Sixty-five billion dollars is the same amount of aid that would seem to be required by Eastern Europe but there are some differences between Western Europe at the end of the Second World War and Eastern Europe in the 1990s. The West European countries had some markets in operation throughout the War but in Eastern Europe markets have been suspended for forty years and, in the case of the Soviet Union, for seventy years. Of course, black markets have existed and have been a means of promoting an allocation of resources, but black markets have been confined to some consumer goods. Furthermore, the West European economies operated in international markets which were highly regulated and trade liberalization did not become significant until the middle of the 1960s. And even then, capital markets did not start to become liberalized until the 1980s. The East European countries face, therefore, the problems of deregulating their economies in the context of a world economy characterized by free trade in goods and resources. It is these features which underline the relevance of the experiences of the Latin American economies in the 1980s.

Since the 1930s the Latin American countries had been highly regulated and had pursued import-substitution-industrialization policies. But as a result of the oil price rises in the 1970s they borrowed heavily. When the world recession began in 1979 and interest rates rose they were faced with severe debt problems. As parts of their aid programmes the World Bank and the International Monetary Fund insisted upon the deregulation of their economies. Unfortunately, the financial markets responded much more quickly than the goods and factors markets and many of the countries experienced credit expansion, rising consumption and capital flights as high exchange rates encouraged capital inflows and then uncertainty as to the maintenance of currency values.

Summary and conclusions

The socialist debate concerned the question: 'could a socialist economy provide an efficient allocation of resources?' In the nineteenth century Austrian economists had cast doubt upon the labour theory of value by advocating a utility approach to value. However, the debate which emerged in the 1930s was one in which supporters and opponents accepted marginal utility theory and the associated, and very Austrian, concept of opportunity cost. Mises began the debate with an article in which he claimed that a socialist economy was incapable of rational calculation. This argument was rejected by Lange and Lerner who were able to provide a mechanism by which rational calculations could be achieved. The state could own assets but markets could be used to co-ordinate their usage. In the markets the authorities would announce accounting prices and adjust them until demands and supplies were equated.

The socialist economy designed by Lange and Lerner rested upon the Walrasian theory of general equilibrium. In Walras's theory an auctioneer would announce prices; in the Lange–Lerner model a central planning board would announce prices. However, Hayek later argued that resources were not allocated in capitalist economies in the manner proposed by Lange and Lerner. Unfortunately, he weakened his argument by confessing that he had always assumed that a socialist economy would always be a centrally planned economy. It was not until the late 1930s and early 1940s that Hayek managed to provide a more reasoned critique of the socialist model by drawing attention to the fact that the information which the central planning board would require did not exist in the relevant form in a society where knowledge was dispersed. But by then the Keynesian avalanche had overwhelmed the debate by suggesting that governments would have to control aggregate demand.

The East European economies did not adopt market socialism at the end of the First and Second World Wars but followed the centrally planned model. This model did seem to provide a basis for success in the 1950s and 1960s but in the 1970s the centrally planned economies underwent deceleration. The fundamental problem of how centrally planned economies can move to some form of market system remains one of the major problems of economic policy in the 1990s.

Notes

1. Hayek, F.A. (1933a), 'The trend of economic thinking', *Economica*, 13: 125.

2. op. cit., p. 128.
3. op. cit., p. 130.
4. op. cit., p. 135.
5. Lange, O. (1936), 'On the economic theory of socialism', Part One, *Review of Economic Studies*, 4: 53.
6. Hayek, F.A. (1948), *Individualism and Economic Order*, London: Routledge, p. 208.
7. Lange, O. (1937), 'On the economic theory of socialism', Part Two, *Review of Economic Studies*, 4: 131.
8. op. cit., p. 134.
9. Roberts, P.C. (1971), 'Oskar Lange's theory of socialist planning', *Journal of Political Economy*, 74: 35.
10. Pigou, A.C. (1937), *Socialism versus Capitalism*, London: Macmillan, p. 42.
11. op. cit., p. 43.
12. Dobb, M. (1933), 'On economic theory and socialism', *Economic Journal*, 43: 537. (Reprinted in *On Economic Theory and Socialism* (1973), London: Routledge.)
13. op. cit., p. 592 (p. 38).
14. Hicks, J.R. (1939a), *Value and Capital*, Oxford: Clarendon, p. 7.
15. Coase, R.H. (1937), 'The nature of the firm', *Economica*, NS4: 405.
16. op. cit., pp. 397–8.
17. Coase, R.H. (1983), 'LSE in the thirties', *Atlantic Economic Review*, 8: 27.
18. op. cit., p. 29.

7
The open economy

Introduction

The first director of the LSE was W.S. Hewins who supported Joseph Chamberlain in the Tariff Reform Movement and it was not until Cannan's appointment that the School began to take up the free trade cause. Cannan is, in fact, important in several respects. In 'A student's recollections of Edwin Cannan' (1935), Lionel Robbins wrote:

> So great was his contempt for the belief that there was any difference between trade within and trade across frontiers that he always steadfastly refused to lecture on international trade and rather ostentatiously chose his examples of inter-regional exchange from counties rather than countries.[1]

Another notable feature of his teaching was his emphasis upon the gold standard – a feature which derived from his belief that many of the economic disturbances, and particularly those of the interwar years, stemmed from monetary disturbances. Now both aspects of his teaching were interrelated because a crucial feature of interregional trade is that it takes place under a regime of fixed exchange rates. Nevertheless, it was not until the end of the 1930s that these two aspects were addressed when Barratt Whale asked the question 'why are there balance of payments problems between countries but not within countries?' It was then that Barratt Whale, Hayek, Robbins and Gilbert started to unravel the nature of interregional trade. Over most of the 1930s thinking tended to be dominated by world events and the new theorizing in Cambridge.

The international monetary disturbances after the First World War were quite unlike those that followed other wars in the nineteenth century and Cannan's reliance on the *Bullion Report* tended to lead astray. In the nineteenth century the gold standard had operated to provide a basis for international trade and domestic stability. Despite the occasional crisis, such as the Napoleonic Wars and the Crimean War, there was a presumption in Britain that disruption would be followed by a speedy return to stability. However, such a state of affairs seemed to be precluded by the belligerents in the First World War. Most countries suspended convertibility and financed wartime activities by printing money. The decision to adopt floating exchange rates also led to a slackening of monetary discipline. And the result was a flow of gold from Europe to the United States. Following the practice of the nineteenth century it was expected that after the War the European countries, and especially Britain, would restore convertibility at the old parity. And the situation might have eased if the gold inflows into the United States had exerted an effect upon the domestic price level. There was, of course, a rise in the US price level even though the United States continued to adhere to the gold standard. But the overvaluation of the dollar was only partly corrected by the postwar deflation which left gold undervalued by some 30 per cent. In effect, in the 1920s all currencies were overvalued against gold and the pound was overvalued relative to the dollar. Hence, the problems were not confined to some countries but were prevalent in all countries; there was a systemic problem in the 1920s and world deflation was inevitable unless there was a revaluation of gold or the adoption of flexible exchange rates (which were not introduced until the 1930s) or the creation of a new form of liquidity through the medium of a world bank. But most remedies lay outside the intellectual thinking and the political climate of the period. Hence, the views of the Cunliffe Committee on Currency and the Foreign Exchanges came to nought. The Committee took the view that: 'Nothing can contribute more to a speedy recovery from the effects of the war, and to the rehabilitation of the foreign exchanges than the re-establishment of the currency upon a sound basis.'[2] It also set out the classic statement on the workings of the gold standard:

> When the exchanges were favourable, gold flowed freely into this country and an increase of legal tender money accompanied the development of trade. When the balance was unfavourable and the exchanges were adverse, it became profitable to export gold. The would-be exporter bought gold from the Bank of England and paid for it by a cheque on his account. The Bank of England obtained the gold from the Issue Department in exchange for notes taken out of its banking reserve, with the result that its liabilities to depositors and its banking reserves were reduced by an equal amount, and the ratio of reserve to liabilities consequently fell. If the process was repeated sufficiently often to reduce

the ratio in a degree considered dangerous, the Bank raised its rate of discount. The raising of the discount rate had the immediate effect of retaining money here which would have been remitted abroad and of attracting remittances from abroad to take advantage of the higher rate, thus checking the outflow of gold and even reversing the stream.

If the adverse condition of the exchanges was due not merely to seasonal fluctuations, but to the circumstances tending to create a permanently adverse trade balance, it is obvious that the procedure described above would not have been sufficient. It would have resulted in the creation of a volume of short-term indebtedness to foreign countries which would have been in the end disastrous to our credit and the position of London as the financial centre of the world. But the raising of the Bank's discount rate and the steps taken to make it effective in the market necessarily led to a general rise of interest rates and a restriction of credit. New enterprises were therefore postponed and the demand for constructional materials and other capital goods was lessened. The consequent slackening of employment also diminished the demand for consumable goods, while the holders of stocks of commodities carried largely with borrowed money, being confronted with an increase of interest charges, if not with actual difficulty in renewing loans and with the prospect of falling prices, tended to press their goods on a weak market. The result was a decline in general prices in the home market which, by checking imports and stimulating exports, corrected the adverse trade balance which was the primary cause of the difficulty.[3]

Admirable as the statement was by the Cunliffe Committee on the workings of the prewar gold standard, it did not indicate the nature of the changed circumstances which prevented the classic mechanism from working. In effect, the prewar gold standard had been successful only to the extent that adjustments had to be made by only one country. When, as in the interwar years, all countries were in disequilibrium *vis-à-vis* gold then there was less scope for easy adjustments. The Committee did note that there had been a considerable expansion of credit during the War and it took the view that if the gold standard was to be restored then government borrowing must cease at the earliest possible moment, the Bank of England discount rate must be used to safeguard reserves, differences in interest rates at home and abroad should be removed, and the issue of fiduciary notes should be limited by law. The restoration of the gold standard was subsequently endorsed by two international committees, that of Brussels (1920) and that of Genoa (1922), in the latter of which Hawtrey played an important part. However, the proposals were never implemented.

The question of whether the UK should return to the gold standard or adopt a managed currency was the subject of Keynes's *Tract on Monetary Reform* (1923) (as we noted in Chapter 2). Keynes argued against its restoration and Cannan and Gregory advocated its restoration. In the upshot Britain returned to the gold standard at the prewar parity in 1925 but then, in 1931, left the gold standard and operated with a managed currency.

The transfer problem

Running parallel to the question of whether Britain should return to the gold standard was the transfer problem which is a special case of the balance of payments adjustment process. The transfer problem arose out of the fact that under the Treaty of Versailles, Germany was required to make reparations to the European countries to which it had surrendered. The discussions which surrounded the determination of the magnitude of the reparations were marked by intense acrimony and in *The Economic Consequences of the Peace* (1919), Keynes portrayed with startling clarity the attitudes of the main negotiators at Versailles. Subsequently, in 1929, he set out what he thought were the main features of the transfer problem. It had been assumed that, with international prices remaining unchanged, Germany would have to divert resources from use at home to the production of exports. But Keynes argued that there would be a secondary burden arising from the fact that her terms of trade would be forced to deteriorate. The result might then be that this secondary burden could be so large as to reduce the value of traded goods produced in Germany to an amount less than the value of the required transfer.

Commenting upon Keynes's argument, Ohlin (1929) suggested that there might be a secondary benefit, an improvement in the terms of trade. What Ohlin drew attention to was the possibility that Germany might have to borrow in order to re-equip its industries and that such borrowing could increase the German demand for goods from the Allied Powers while the latters' demand for foreign goods might be reduced. Furthermore, the demand for German-produced goods by Germans could also lead to a reduction in imports. Ohlin therefore drew attention to what was later to become known as the foreign trade multiplier the leakages from which (e.g. imports) might determine the magnitude of the secondary burden. In 1932 Pigou surveyed the problem and suggested that the outcome would depend upon the sum of the marginal propensities to spend of the Germans and the Allies and that those propensities would, in turn, depend upon real incomes and relative prices.

The transfer problem is a perennial problem because war is endemic and because the transfer problem represents, in a unique manner, the main elements of the balance of payments problem. It was revived after the Second World War when the United States embarked upon its

Marshall Aid programme to Europe and it surfaced again in 1990 when a Marshall Aid programme was being canvassed for Eastern Europe.

Tariffs

The tariff question arose after the return to the gold standard in 1925 and provoked a clash between Cambridge and the LSE with the LSE being in favour of free trade and Cambridge, mainly in the form of Keynes, being in favour of some form of protection. The conditions for such a policy were set by the existence of an overvalued pound and the lack of an early revaluation. At the political level the issue surfaced in the *Report* of the Macmillan Committee on Finance and Industry (1930) and at the academic level in Keynes's *Treatise on Money* (1930a, 1930b) and Beveridge's *Tariffs: the case examined* (1931).

The case for and against tariffs as remedies for unemployment was presented in two appendices to the Macmillan Report. In Appendix I, the case for tariffs was presented by Keynes, Ernest Bevin, Thomas Allen, R. McKenna, Frater Taylor and A.A.G. Taylor. In Appendix III, the case against was signed by Gregory. The first argument considered by Keynes and his associates was that tariffs on imports would reduce foreign purchasing power and hence the demand for British exports. This was rebutted by the suggestion that the tariff revenues might be used to increase domestic investment and employment which would, in turn, lead to increased imports of food and raw materials and would also lead to increased foreign lending. The second argument examined was that a restriction of imports would increase the production costs of exports to which the dissenters said that there could be rebates for exports. The third argument which they considered was the possible effect of tariffs on the cost of living of the working class and which they felt might be avoided by a selective tariff. They also took the view that a tariff would have an immediate effect upon business confidence.

In his note of reservation Gregory observed that if a tariff is unable to remove the fundamental monetary difficulty then it would lead to the permanence and elaboration of the tariff and would cause a fall in living standards. Behind Gregory's comments lay the sharper criticisms of Robbins which were presented in the private sessions and behind the main economic protagonists lay the competing theories of Keynes and Hayek. For Keynes the slump was due to an excess of savings which could be mopped up by imposing a tariff and increasing domestic demand. For Robbins and Hayek, and to a lesser extent, Gregory, the slump was due to an increase in the money supply which had caused an expansion of investment beyond the level which could be sustained by real savings. Attempts to curb the money supply would lead to unemployment but that could be removed if money wages were to fall and so reduce production costs. This clash of ideas spilled over into the book *Tariffs: the case examined* which was edited by Beveridge and represented the collective views of the London economists. In the end the clash was brought to an end by the 1931 devaluation which produced both the import control and the export subsidy. And by way of a parenthesis it may be noted that after editing a book which criticized tariffs, Beveridge proposed to his colleagues that they should write a book setting out the case for tariffs! Years later Hayek was to recall that Beveridge was not an economist.

The conclusion of *Tariffs: the case examined* was that the 1931 devaluation had placed protectionism on the shelf of academic curiosities. However, interest in tariffs continued in the School. In 1934 Benham produced an interesting paper which foreshadowed the 1942 Stolper—Samuelson article on tariffs and the distribution of income. In 'Taxation and relative factor prices' Benham (1935) considered an economy which possessed homogeneous labour and land produced wheat and steel under conditions of perfect competition. Three production possibilities were examined: 'Land and labour may not be (1) substitutable for one another or (2) imperfect substitutes for one another or (3) perfect substitutes for one another.' Only the second case was thought to be of practical importance. Now a tax on one commodity could lead to a contraction of demand and a reduction in the employment of resources. There could then be an expansion in the output of the other commodity:

> . . . if in the new equilibrium the production of wheat has fallen and that of steel contracted the price of land will have risen relatively to that of labour. If the opposite has occurred, the price of land will have fallen relatively to that of labour. The change in the relative prices of wheat and steel will have no direct relevance to the result. The sole criterion will be which industry has expanded and which has contracted. For both land and labour are employed in both industries, so that the earnings and the value of the marginal product of a unit of land (labour) will be the same in both industries.
>
> Suppose that wheat production has expanded. This implies that more labour than before has been combined with a unit of land in both industries. This must be so if the supplies of land and labour remain constant and there is sufficient competition to ensure that all the land and all the labour are employed (unless labour becomes a free good — which would merely be an extreme case of a fall in the relative price of labour). But this in turn implies that the marginal physical productivity of land is greater, and of labour is less, than it was before, in both industries. Therefore, the price of labour must have fallen relatively to the price of land in order to induce the landowners to alter the proportions sufficiently

to employ all the labour. The extent of the relative fall will depend upon the extent of the change in the relative marginal physical productivity of land and labour; the more imperfect a substitute is labour for land the greater will be the relative fall.[4]

Benham had all the ingredients of the international trade model which was developed in the 1940s and 1950s by Samuelson. However, there are some surprising features of his analysis. Having linked together relative factor prices and outputs he failed to link relative commodity prices and outputs and therefore overlooked the possibility of moving directly from commodity prices to factor prices. It was a surprising omission given that Lerner had presented a seminar paper on the factor price equalization theorem. Of course some of the elements in the analyses of Benham and Lerner had been anticipated in an article published by Heckscher in Swedish in 1919 and whose contents only became known at second hand through Ohlin's *Interregional and International Trade* which was published in 1933. Finally, we may note that both Benham (1935) and Kaldor (1940) examined the effect of tariffs on the terms of trade and, although their conclusions reiterated those of Bickerdike (1919), they did serve to qualify the arguments presented in *Tariffs: the case examined* by indicating that a country might gain from the imposition of tariffs even though the total amount of trade contracted.

Fluctuating exchange rates

The devaluation of 1931 seemed to render further discussion of tariffs unnecessary. However, the 1930s were characterized by beggar-my-neighbour policies, such as competitive devaluations and bilateral trade agreements. These weakened the case for fluctuating exchange rates. The case for flexible exchange rates had, of course, been under review since the early 1920s, although the movements in the exchange rates in the 1920s had been caused by factors which were not present in the 1930s. Fluctuations in exchange rates in the 1920s had largely been brought about by the war. Postwar inflation led to large differences in the domestic price levels of various countries and the exchange rate movements of the period were a reflection of those price movements. Indeed, the link between inflation and price differentials led to the popularization of the purchasing power parity theory which associated movements in exchange rates with relative changes in domestic purchasing power. However, the theory did not allow for changes in international demand, capital movements, technological change or any of the other factors which might affect the terms of trade. In the early 1930s when the world depression forced most countries off the gold standard, exchange rates were influenced by the fact that the slump did not affect the demand for all countries' exports uniformly. The 1930s were also affected by large scale capital movements.

Finally, doubts were expressed about the stability of the foreign exchange market. These doubts began in the 1920s and re-emerged in the 1930s after the brief experiment with fixed exchange rates. In 1919 wartime controls were removed and as a result the dollar price of sterling fell dramatically. Most of this depreciation was due to the abnormal demand for imports and the gap which opened up during the War between British and American price levels. Nevertheless, the severity of the price plunge led some observers to conclude that the market for incovertible currencies might be unstable. That is to say, British economists began to doubt whether exchange rate depreciation could correct an unfavourable trade balance. Thus, Bickerdike (1920) emphasized that, in the short run, the foreign and domestic demand elasticities might be small and could therefore produce violent changes in exchange rates. This possibility was reiterated by Joan Robinson in 1937.

Pessimism about the ability of exchange rate adjustments to correct balance of trade problems led to a reappraisal of the workings of the gold standard in theory and in practice. Studies into the workings of the prewar gold standard had been conducted by Williams (1920), Viner (1924), White (1928) and Taussig (1928). These seemed to confirm the effectiveness of the gold standard system but left doubts as to the mechanisms at work. Trade balances adjusted rapidly despite relatively small changes in prices and gold flows.

Fixed exchange rates

Although Britain left the gold standard in 1931 and many other countries followed suit, there was a revival of interest in the workings of the gold standard in the late 1930s. The reasons were two-fold. First, the regime of fluctuating exchange rates seemed inadequate and had led to a variety of secondary devices to control adverse balances of trade, such as competitive devaluation, export subsidies, tariffs and bilateral trade agreements. Second, there was a revival of interest in Cannan's thesis that there was no sharp distinction between interregional and international trade. And the point was emphasized by Ohlin's publication of his important book, *International and Interregional Trade* which drew attention to the general equilibrium model underlying both patterns of trade.

In an article entitled 'Banking policy and the balance of payments'

Fixed exchange rates   161

published in 1936, Paish began by considering the question of interregional and international trade. 'No one', he wrote, 'seems to take any interest in the balance of payments of Devonshire, while on the other hand a great deal of interest is taken in the balance of payments of the United Kingdom or Australia.'[5] He observed that if banks were merely branch banks then there would be a problem of intra-bank indebtedness and only if there were independent banks would there be a problem of inter-bank indebtedness. In the first instance, adverse balance of payments would lead to banks refusing advances rather than varying interest rates. But he then went on to suggest that even the interest rate mechanism might take second place to adjustments brought about by changes in incomes and spending and he drew attention to (what he called) the marginal propensity to import. Thus Paish provided an explanation for the rapid speed of adjustment of trade balances which had puzzled Taussig and he anticipated the later theoretical studies by Harrod and Joan Robinson. But in introducing the possibility of income adjustments Paish moved on too quickly and neglected to study in greater detail the effects of changes in the balance of payments through the banking system.

In *Monetary Nationalism and International Stability* (1937b), Hayek observed that what was an interregional payments problem had been transformed into one involving monetary nationalism which he defined as 'the doctrine that a country's share in the world supply of money should *not* be left to be determined by the same mechanism as that which determines the relative amounts of money in different regions or localities.' He attributed the rise of monetary nationalism to a variety of causes. First, there was a preoccupation with statistics on wages and prices which rested on an 'illusion based on an accident that the statistical measures of price movements are usually constructed for countries.'[6] Second, there was the emergence of banks which had developed on national lines. Third, there was the creation of central banks which were responsible for the regulation of note issue.

In his discussion of banking Hayek referred to a Ph.D. thesis written by one of his students, Vera Smith. Its title was 'Free banking: an exploration of the analytical and historical case for free banking' (1935) and it was subsequently published under the title *The Rationale of Central Banking* (1937). The thesis marked renewed interest in a subject which had been mooted by Mises. Miss Smith noted that the early central banks had been founded for political reasons connected with the exigencies of state finance and that the economic arguments for restricting free entry into the note-issuing industry were never fully set out, but once established the monopolies persisted up to the time when the economic case came to be debated. And her thesis drew attention to the fact that free or competitive banking had been practised in the eighteenth century and its proponents were involved in the controversy between the currency and banking schools.

In 1695 the Bank of Scotland was founded and granted a twenty-one year monopoly of note issue by Parliament. At the end of the period Parliament allowed the monopoly to expire. When the Royal Bank of Scotland was formed in 1729 the Bank of Scotland tried to block its charter, failed, and then attempted to drive it out of business and, finally, attempted a merger. All these strategies failed and in 1820 there were twenty competing banks. While Scotland was developing free banking, England was moving towards a central banking system. The Bank of England was founded in 1694 and was given monopoly rights in return for a loan to the government. Subsequently the monopoly privileges were extended with the result that it became the only note-issuing bank of England and Wales. In 1825 a banking crisis caused many small banks to fail and led to a debate which centred on the question of whether the crisis had been caused by the Bank of England and other note-issuing banks. The debate concluded with the passing of the Bank Charter Act, 1844.

Within the debate on the crisis it is possible to isolate three groups of participants. First, there was the free banking school of Scottish bankers who wished to retain a free banking system and who blamed the crisis on the overissue of notes by the Bank of England. Second, there was the currency school which blamed all banks for the panic and pressed for the regulation of note issue by conferring a monopoly right on the Bank of England. Third, there was a group called the banking school who argued that no bank was to blame for the crisis and that the control of the note issue was irrelevant. The free banking school based its case on the low rate of bank failures in Scotland as compared with those occurring in England. However, the currency school triumphed and its proposals were embodied in the Bank Acts of 1844 and 1845.

Why did central banking replace competitive banking? Miss Smith noted that initially the arguments had been political but when she examined the economic argument she found it to be tenuous. It was not obvious that a central bank would behave efficiently. It might be tempted to overissue and then escape bankruptcy by appealing to the government to bail it out. The second argument she examined was that which involved the possibility of commercial banks becoming bankrupt and that the government should intervene and protect note holders by introducing uniformity in note issue. But she concluded that this argument for spreading risks evenly could not be decided on scientific grounds. The third argument examined was that which stated that a central bank could inspire confidence in a crisis whereas commercial banks would restrict loans. But after surveying all the evidence she concluded that:

> it is unlikely that the choice can ever become a practical one. To the vast majority of people government interference in matters of banking has become so much an integral part of the accepted institutions that to suggest its abandonment is to invite ridicule. One result of this attitude is that insolvency in the sphere of banking has won exception from the rule applied to other lines of business that it must be paid for by liquidation, and it is important also to point out that since the laws of bankruptcy have almost never been applied to banking we should be diffident of drawing the conclusion that actual experiences prove the unworkability of free competition in banking.[7]

However, Miss Smith's book became the victim of her own lack of empirical work and of the Keynesian avalanche. Despite the fact that the proponents of free banking referred to the example of Scottish banking she devoted only three pages to the subject. In the *Treatise on Money* Keynes argued for the central bank to lend freely in a slump. But by 1936 he was coming round to the view that monetary policy might be ineffective and that fiscal policy might be more powerful in dispelling a slump. In the 1940s a compromise was reached. If a central bank had to lend freely then its policies had to be underwritten by government; therefore let it be nationalized. But since the ultimate determinant of the value of money was the trust inspired by government and, in the last resort, that trust rested upon the taxable powers of government, then fiscal policy must be deemed to be more efficient than monetary policy.

After the digression on Miss Smith's thesis we can now return to Hayek's conclusions. He took the view that the ideal arrangement of monetary relations between nations should be one which reproduced the relations which normally existed between parts of the same country. In such a system a change in demand would bring about a change in money flows which would affect various markets differently and bring about a new equilibrium of prices. The trouble with the contemporary arrangements was that they allowed for interference by governments.

Hayek's thesis was criticized by Barratt Whale who drew attention to several features overlooked by Hayek. First, there was the fact that balance of payments adjustments took place much more rapidly than was predicted by the theory. Second, he drew attention to the usefulness of exchange rate adjustments in situations where there were non-traded goods and some prices were sticky. In 'The working of the pre-war gold standard' (1937), Whale argued that the effect of a fall in the exports of a country on the gold standard was not a rise in interest rates but a fall in incomes leading to a spontaneous contraction of credit and a subsequent outflow of gold as a result of low interest rates. In other words, his analysis was Keynesian in content, although he attempted to link his analysis to the concept of a natural rate of interest while admitting in a footnote that: 'in the case where there is a general unemployment of productive factors, this does not mean any more than the rate which equalizes savings and investment at the existing level of income.'[8]

However, Whale's analysis was incomplete. He noted that there were no obvious balance of payments problems in a country with a unified banking system. But he then went on to observe that England and Scotland had separate banking systems and that raised a further question: 'is there any evidence that price equilibrium between Scotland and England is maintained by Scottish banks varying their interest rates in response to their reserves?'.[9] Whale's question was answered by Gilbert in a much neglected article entitled, 'The mechanism of interregional redistributions of money' (1938). Gilbert noted that both England and Scotland had separate banking systems but that it was not possible for banks in either country to raise their rates in isolation because of the high degree of mobility of short- and long-term capital between the two countries from which he concluded that: '*If there is perfect mobility of short-term capital redistribution of money between separate reserve banking systems cannot cause monetary disturbances.*'[10] (italics in the original).

Summary and conclusions

International trade theory is the second oldest part of economic theory and may be deemed to be the oldest part if it is acknowledged that taxes on imports and exports were the commonest form of raising revenue for the monarch. Hence, when discussing trade, economists tend to put their best foot forward. Trade problems were, in fact, dominant in the interwar years. They lay behind the decision to return to the gold standard at the prewar parity. They lay behind the preoccupations with floating exchange rates and the stability of foreign exchange markets. They involved the unravelling of the relationships between international and interregional trade. And there was a clash between Cambridge and the LSE over the use of tariffs as a means of reducing unemployment. The conflict was damped down by the devaluation of 1931 but issues of trade persisted and led to the production of a remarkable series of research papers on the relationships between international and interregional trade which did not make their impact until the postwar discussions of optimal currency areas led to their rediscovery. The ideas were of course old ones; they had been canvassed at the time of the formation of the United States when there was an active discussion of payments problems between the states of the Union. But their independent discovery in the 1930s was an achievement of the LSE.

Notes

1. Robbins, L.C. (1935), 'A student's recollections of Edwin Cannan', *Economic Journal*, 45: 397–8.
2. *Report of the Committee on Currency and the Foreign Exchanges*, chairman Lord Cunliffe.
3. op. cit., pp. 23–4.
4. Benham, F.C. (1935), 'Taxation and relative prices of factors of production', *Economica*, NS2: 201.
5. Paish, F.A. (1936), 'Banking policy and the balance of payments', *Economica*, NS3: 405–06.
6. Hayek, F.A. (1937b), *Monetary Nationalism and International Stability*, London: Longman, p. 10.
7. Smith, V.C. (1937), *The Rationale of Central Banking*, London: Routledge, p. 33.
8. Whale, P.B. (1937), 'The working of the pre-war gold standard', *Economica*, NS4: 19.
9. op. cit., p. 30.
10. Gilbert, J.C. (1938), 'The mechanism of interregional redistributions of money', *Review of Economic Studies*, 15: 190.

8
The nature of the Keynesian avalanche

Introduction

There were intimations of the *General Theory* before 1936 and there were muted protests in the LSE after its publication. In 1935 Robert Bryce, a Canadian and a postgraduate student at Cambridge, was invited to give a lecture on Keynes's ideas to Lerner's seminar. Bryce sent a copy of his lecture to Keynes and, in his accompanying letter, said that there had been a preoccupation with definitions. In his reply Keynes praised Bryce for the accuracy of his summary of the *General Theory* but was critical of the scholasticism prevailing in the LSE.[1] Bryce's importance, however, stretched beyond the seminar because he shared a London flat with Lorie Tarshis, another Cambridge postgraduate student and the flat was also frequented by Lerner. Moreover, Lerner used his Leon Fellowship to spend some time at Cambridge in 1935 and he came into contact with Joan Robinson who was anxious to win him over to the new economics. Lerner was also responsible for the joint LSE/Cambridge seminars at which Keynes's ideas were expounded by Joan Robinson and Richard Kahn. Finally, Hicks went to Cambridge in 1935; his departure from the LSE being due to Beveridge's hostility to theorists and his refusal to renew Hicks's contract.

But the surprising feature of 1936 was the lack of response by the senior members of the LSE to the publication of the *General Theory*. Hicks reviewed the book in the *Economic Journal* but it was at the invitation of Keynes who thought that Hicks would be appreciative of the ideas he was expounding. Indeed, it was Pigou who reviewed the book in *Economica*. Pigou had begun his own analysis of the unemployment problem in *Wealth and Welfare* (1912) and his analysis was subsequently extended in his book *Industrial Fluctuations* (1927a) which he followed up with the *Theory of Unemployment* (1933). Pigou recognized the importance of expectations and price rigidities but he assumed that in the long run classical theory would generate full employment. In his evidence to the Macmillan Committee (1931) he had argued that changes in relative wages were necessary to remove unemployment. 'You cannot', he stated, 'shift people out of coal to other occupations because there is no vacancy for them at the present rates of wages, so that unless you alter not only the distribution but also the wage rates, you may not do any good.'[2] In contrast Keynes stressed the effect of a fall in real wages upon aggregate demand. In the *General Theory* Keynes used Pigou's *Theory of Unemployment* as the basis of his attack upon the classical theory because: 'his is the only attempt with which I am acquainted to write down the classical theory of unemployment precisely. Thus it has been incumbent on me to raise my objections to the theory in the most formidable presentment in which it has been advanced.'[3]

The analytical core of the *General Theory* was based upon comparative statics and it was the conclusions from that analysis which Pigou chose to attack when he explored the effect of a fall in wages and prices upon the real value of cash balances; an effect which later came to be called the 'Pigou effect'. The Pigou effect was first suggested by Haberler in his 1937 edition of *Prosperity and Depression* but it was Pigou who provided a detailed exposition. In the *General Theory* Keynes suggested that at low rates of interest the volume of savings might exceed the expected amount of investment and unemployment would ensue. What Pigou drew attention to was the importance of Keynes's assumption of rigid money wages. If wages and prices were allowed to fall then the real value of money balances would rise and stimulate an increase in consumption. Thus, the problems posed by a liquidity trap or by pessimistic investment expectations could be bypassed.

Pigou presented his analysis as a defence of classical theory and not as a policy prescription: 'the puzzles we have been considering . . . are academic exercises of some slight use perhaps for clarifying thought but with very little chance of being posed on the chequer board of actual life.'[4] And in his 1950 Cambridge lectures published as *Keynes's 'General Theory': A Retrospective View*, he concluded:

> There are very serious limitations – limitations of which it is specially proper to remind ourselves when attempts are made to apply Keynes's apparatus directly to the solution of practical problems. This is in no sense to attack Keynes or to decry his achievement. When a man has devised a new way of tackling an unclimbed mountain, we may, indeed, regret that his way has not led him to the top. But for the effort which

has advanced him *towards* the top nothing is due but praise. . . . Whatever imperfections there may be in his working out the fundamental conception embodied there the conception itself is an extremely fruitful germinal idea. In my original review-article on the *General Theory* I failed to grasp its significance and did not assign to Keynes the credit due to it. Nobody before him so far as I know, had brought all the relevant factors, real and monetary at once together in a single formal scheme, through which their interplay could be coherently investigated. His doing this does not to my mind, constitute a revolution. Only if we accepted the myth — as I regard it — that earlier economists ignored the part played by money, and even when discussing fluctuations in employment, tacitly assumed that there weren't any, would that word be appropriate. I should say, rather, that in setting out and developing his fundamental conception, Keynes made a very important, original and valuable addition to the armoury of economic analysis. Any economist afterwards elaborating or refining on that conception is, so far, a follower of Keynes. All economists whether followers or not, owe to the stimulus to thought which his book gave, even the controversies that it aroused, a very great debt.[5]

Pigou chose to attack the *General Theory* within the context of its comparative static framework for its omission of the effect of falling prices upon the real value of money balances. Robertson chose to attack the *General Theory* for its lack of a dynamic framework, for its vision of society which did not correspond to that which Robertson had worked out in his own theories. He was interested in the trade cycle which emerged in a growing economy characterized by technical change, population growth, changing tastes and monetary disturbances. In such an economy unemployment was inevitable; it was part of the price of progress. There were lags in the adjustment of economic variables to disturbances. This was the substance of Robertson's book, *A Study in Industrial Fluctuations* (1915) and which was given greater precision in his *Banking Policy and the Price Level* (1926). In contrast Keynes was interested in the short run and in an economy in which unemployment seemed to be permanent rather than transitory. In his earlier works Keynes had analyzed conditions which were similar to those which interested Robertson and it was this earlier relationship in ideas, plus the fact that Keynes was both his teacher and colleague, which caused Robertson so much distress when the *General Theory* emerged. In the introduction to the 1948 reprint of *A Study of Industrial Fluctuation* Robertson wrote: 'To one so drenched with the vision of eternal ebb and flow, relapse and recovery, Keynes's final attempt in his *General Theory* to deal with the savings—investment complex in terms of a theory of static and stable equilibrium was bound to seem a step backwards.'[6] In the preface to the 1949 reprint of *Banking Policy and the Price Level* he commented:

> While Keynes must at the time have understood and acquiesced in my step-by-step method, it is evident that it never, so to speak, got under his skin; for in two successive treatments of the savings–investment theme in his two big books (*A Treatise on Money* and the *General Theory*) he discarded it completely. This was naturally a great disappointment to me, and it is, I think, being increasingly recognized that it was a misfortune for the smooth progress of theory.[7]

Robertson's stress upon the workings of a dynamic economy led him to emphasize the instability of some economic variables and the importance of lags in adjustment processes. Thus investment and saving might not be automatically equated because investment depended upon 'today's' expectations about future profits while savings might depend upon 'yesterday's' income. If investment were greater than savings then the extra savings required might have to be generated through credit creation. And the resulting excess demand for resources could then lead to a rise in prices and forced savings. Robertson's discussion of forced savings had therefore similarities with that conducted by Hayek and also with the discussion of the credit cycle in Keynes's *Treatise on Money*.

But in the *General Theory* Keynes adopted the method of comparative statics whereby one equilibrium position could be compared with another and the transition phase could be ignored. And he dismissed forced savings because it could not occur under conditions of unemployment. A rise in investment would lead via the (instantaneous) multiplier to a rise in incomes out of which the savings necessary to finance investment would accrue. Robertson was reluctant to accept a stable multiplier and he also questioned the banishment of the financial problem and under prodding from Robertson, Keynes introduced the finance motive. Robertson's emphasis upon finance and his questioning of the stability of the multiplier were responsible for his reluctance to dispense with the quantity theory of money in its Cambridge form of a demand for money to hold.

In the 1960s Hayek stated that he did not respond to the *General Theory* because he feared that Keynes would change his mind in much the same way that he did after the publication of the *Treatise on Money*. And we now know that Keynes's ideas were undergoing change because in 1937 he was considering the usefulness of the Swedish period analysis. Yet Hayek was, in fact, attempting a form of criticism in his preparation of *The Pure Theory of Capital* (1941). Unfortunately he never got round to writing the dynamic aspects of the subject. In 1978 he confessed that he had been unable to conduct the dynamic analysis because he found the subject intractable.[8] On other occasions he said that his desire to help

Keynes in the fight against wartime inflation led him to draw back upon criticizing other aspects of Keynes's work. He also stated that 'to proclaim my dissent from the near unanimous views of the orthodox phalanx would merely have deprived me of a hearing on other matters about which I was more concerned at the time' – this was a reference to his work on theory of knowledge and the framework of political constitutions.[9] But the fundamental reason why Hayek was unable to respond was that he had no solution to the problem of secondary deflation – to the intense contraction of incomes and output which the multiplier process could produce following the cessation of a boom. This phenomenon took Austrian economists by surprise when it emerged following the collapse of the *Kreditanstalt* in Vienna. And the term secondary deflation was coined by Röpke and its implications for Austrian theory, and in the light of Keynes's analysis was explored by Lachmann.[10]

Robbins's problem was different. In his article 'Two types of mind' Hayek (1975a) drew a distinction between the encyclopaedist and the puzzler and, on occasions, he applied the distinction to Robbins and himself. Robbins was an encyclopaedist whereas he was a puzzler. Robbins was familiar with English, European and American literature but he was not a theorist and his preoccupation was with value theory. Hence, his double misfortune. He was not well informed on monetary theory and the newly emerging field of macroeconomics. He could not therefore fall back upon a frame of reference with which to criticize Keynes. Not being a theorist, Robbins was incapable of constructing a model in order to solve the puzzle of the 1930s. He had translated Hayek's *Prices and Production* into English and he had applied the over-investment model to the British economy in his book *The Great Depression* (Robbins, 1934a). But later, in his *Autobiography* (Robbins, 1971), he acknowledged that he was wrong in opposing increased public spending as a means of combating the slump in the 1930s. 'I shall always', he wrote, 'regard this aspect of my dispute with Keynes as the greatest mistake of my professional career, and the book, *The Great Depression*, which I subsequently wrote, partly in justification of this attitude, as something which I would willingly see forgotten.'[11]

There remained Gregory. Gregory had been in the Department of Money and Banking but in the mid-1930s the title of his chair was changed to a Chair of Economics with special reference to money and banking. The translation marked a step towards bringing the various branches of applied economics into conjunction with theoretical economics within the LSE. And Gregory had served on the Macmillan Committee and had an intimate knowledge of the City and international monetary problems. But he had two weaknesses. First, he was always short of money brought about as a result of marital problems. He spent a lot of time in the City and, increasingly, little time in the School at seminars. Students who brought him problems might find him anxious to disengage himself. His second weakness was that he may have been willing to see merit in some of Keynes's arguments.

What transpired at the LSE therefore was prevarication, obstruction and filibustering. Kaldor was told by Robbins that he should not lecture on controversial topics. There were rumours that Lerner was refused a seminar room in which to discuss the *General Theory*, although he seems to have avoided the embargo by combining meetings of the executive board of the *Review of Economic Studies* with seminars on Keynes's work. Furthermore Scitovsky has recounted the occasion when students invited Keynes to give a lecture but were refused the use of one of the large lecture theatres. Keynes therefore lectured in a small room on the fourth floor of the School and as a result there was a large audience which listened outside. Scitovsky stood on the staircase of the second floor.[12] In mitigation it must be said that a similar state of affairs occurred at Cambridge. Robertson avoided Hicks when he went for his interview because he feared that the knowledge that he and Hicks were old friends might result in Hicks not getting a lectureship. And when Gregory retired and Robertson was asked to be an assessor for the chair he volunteered to take up the vacant post, although he did not move to London because the School was transferred to Cambridge in 1939. In both institutions differences in research programmes spilled over into personal conflicts. The notion that scholars were pursuing in a disinterested fashion their ideas has to be rejected.

Scholarship

But to construe the Keynesian avalanche solely in terms of reactions to the *General Theory* is to take too narrow a view of the transformation of economics wrought by Keynes and we need to go on and consider other aspects of his work.

It is customary to draw a distinction between LSE scholarship and Cambridge creativity. It is a view which has been fostered by both institutions. Cannan, Gregory, Hayek and Robbins are known for their histories of economic thought whereas Lavington, Shove and Pigou gave the impression that everything was in Marshall. Hicks, for example, has recalled that: 'what we [LSE] economists thought we were doing was not only to bring to life the inheritance of the British Classical economists, but also to widen the horizons of the British economists of our time by bringing in a refreshment from what was being done, and has been done in other countries.'[13] But such distinctions ignore the fact that Keynes was familiar with the writings of both British classical economists, European economists and American economists and that his grasp of past and current thinking informed the nature of the Keynesian avalanche.

Austrian monetary theory

There is no evidence that Keynes had read Menger's article, 'On the origin of money' which was published in the *Economic Journal* in 1892 and which emphasized the saleability motive for holding money but his early lectures reveal that his reading lists included Knapp's *Staatlichte Theories des Geldes* (1905) (*State Theory of Money*). In 1914 he reviewed Mises's *Theorie des Geldes und Unlaufsmittel* (1912) (*Theory of Money and Credit*) and in 1927 he reviewed Helfferich's *Geld* (1911) (*Money*) in the *National and Athanaeum*. His comments upon Mises were devastating and those cast upon Helfferich were disparaging:

> Dr. von Mises' treatise is the work of an acute and cultivated mind. But it is critical rather than constructive, dialectical and not original. The author avoids all the usual pitfalls, but he avoids them by pointing them out and then turning back rather than surmounting them. Dr. Mises strikes an outside reader as being the very highly educated pupil of a school, once a great eminence, but now losing its vitality. There is no 'lift', but on the other hand, an easy or tired acquiesce in the veils which obscure the light rather than a rending away of them. One closes the book with a feeling of disappointment that an author so intelligent, so candid, and so widely read should, after all, help one so little to a clear and constructive understanding of the fundamentals of his subject.[14]

The conclusion is surprising in view of the importance which has been attached to Mises's work by later economists. It can be explained as the result of a substantial change between the first and second editions of *Money and Credit*. In 1912 Mises came to the conclusion that: 'the primary impulse of a boom does not come from the action of banks',[15] but in the 1924 edition he came to the opposite conclusion that fluctuations in economic activity depended upon changes in the availability of credit. Later, in the *Treatise on Money*, Keynes stated that a copy of the 1930 translation of *Money and Credit* and the 1928 monograph *Geldwerstabilisierung und konjunkturpolitik* were received when his own proofs were being passed through the press. But did it matter? The theory of forced saving had already been developed in *A Tract on Monetary Reform* (1923) and in Robertson's *Banking Policy and the Price Level* (1926).

Swedish theory

There is no evidence that Keynes had read Wicksell's 'The influence of the rate of interest on prices' published in the *Economic Journal* in 1907, and in his 1937 article 'Alternative theories of the rate of interest' Keynes stated that he regarded:

> Mr Hawtrey as my grandparent and Mr Robertson as my parent in the paths of errancy and I have been greatly influenced by them. I might also meet Professor Ohlin's complaint by adopting Wicksell as my great grandparent if I had known his works in more detail at an earlier stage in my own thought and also if I did not have the feeling that Wicksell was trying to be too 'classical'. As it is, so far as I am concerned, I find looking back that it was Professor Irving Fisher who was the great-grandparent who first influenced me strongly towards regarding money as a 'real' factor.[16]

But did it make a great deal of difference? Was it necessary for him to have been familiar with the writings of the Swedes. The evidence suggests not. In his first book *Price Formation and Economic Change* (*Prisbilningsproblem och foranderligheten*), published in 1928, Myrdal acknowledged that his discussion of expectations was strongly influenced by Keynes's *Treatise on Probability*. And Myrdal's book was reviewed in the *Economic Journal* by Lindahl who was then in correspondence with Keynes. Moreover, Winch has drawn attention to the interest of the Swedes in Keynes's ideas as expressed in popular tracts, such as the Liberal Yellow Books. In a letter written to Lindahl in 1934 he stated that his (Lindahl's) 'way of dealing with time leads to undue complications and will be very difficult to apply or generalise about.'[17] Lindahl acknowledged the force of Keynes's argument. Later, in a letter to Ohlin, written in 1937, he stated that he used:

> to speak of the period between expectation and result as 'funnels of process' but the fact that the funnels are all different lengths and over-lap one another meant that at any given time there was no aggregate desired result capable of being compared with some aggregate expectation at an earlier date. You will be quite familiar with the difficulty I have in mind.[18]

However the denouement came in the 1939 edition of Myrdal's *Monetary Equilibrium* in which Myrdal confessed that he no longer accepted the highly abstract period analysis and saw advantages in the use of comparative statics.

American monetary theory

Irving Fisher's *The Purchasing Power of Money* (1911) was the first book reviewed by Keynes and in his early lectures there were extensive references to Fisher's writings. In 1913 he presented a paper to the Political Economy Club entitled: 'How far are bankers responsible for the alternations of crisis and depression?'. In the paper Keynes criticized Fisher's credit theory of the trade cycle because it was based upon a 'temporary lack of caution in bankers in the matter of the proportion of cash to liabilities.'[19] It presumed that bankers would be willing to allow their reserves to run down when they might be reasonably expected to have to replenish them a year later. By way of a parenthesis we may note that many years later Lachmann drew attention to the fact that the credit theory rested upon the assumptions of an elastic supply of credit and myopic behaviour by businessmen. Mises accepted the criticisms but also pointed to other factors which affected the money supply.[20]

In the *Treatise* Keynes was critical of Fisher's equation of exchange and expressed a preference for the Cambridge demand for money to hold approach. But Keynes did come to regard money as a real factor as a result of Fisher's treatment of the marginal efficiency of capital. In addition to Fisher, Keynes corresponded with Bullough, Snyder and Sprague on the question of whether there was overinvestment and inflation in the United States in the 1920s.

The English economists

Keynes wrote critical biographical essays on the major English economists. They were mainly the neoclassical economists, although he did write an essay on Malthus whom he regarded as the first of the Cambridge economists. Of Jevons's *Theory of Political Economy* (1905) he wrote that it was 'the first modern book on economics' and he praised his statistical work. He also emphasized the importance of Jevons's theory of capital which was 'measured on the supply side by the amount of the present utility forgone and on the demand side by the discounted value of the future utilities expected from it.'[21] But it was Marshall for whom he reserved the greatest praise: 'As a scientist, he was, within his own field, the greatest in the world for a hundred years.'[22] In his monetary theory he singled out the following contributions:

1. 'The exposition of the Quantity Theory of Money as part of the General Theory of Value.'
2. 'The distinction between the "real" rate of interest and the "money" rate of interest and the relevance of this to the credit cycle, when the value of money is fluctuating.'
3. 'The causal train by which, in a modern credit system, an additional

supply of money influences prices, and the part played by the rate of discount.'
4. 'The enunciation of the "Purchasing Power Parity" theory as determining the rate of exchange between countries with mutually inconvertible currencies.'
5. 'The "chain" method of compiling index numbers.'
6. 'The proposal of paper currency for the circulation based on gold and silver symetallism as the standard.'
7. 'The proposal of an official tabular standard for optional use in the case of long contracts.'[23]

Posterity has not accorded Marshall so many firsts. For example, Henry Thornton appears to have been the originator of the distinction between real and money interest rates. Yet what may be significant is that it was from Marshall, and not from Wicksell, that Keynes derived the distinction.

Which brings us back to Thornton. The weight of Hayek's criticisms of Keynes rests upon two foundations. First, Keynes was not familiar with the European literature on monetary economics. Second, that he was not familiar with the English monetary literature of the first half of the nineteenth century. In particular, he was not familiar with the work of Thornton. Now the importance of the first half of the nineteenth century was that it was, as a result of the French wars, a period of turbulence. In contrast, the late nineteenth century was relatively uneventful. Hence, Marshall, from whom Keynes derived most of his education in monetary economics, was set by his facts, a dull examination paper. And there are few references to the early nineteenth century in Marshall's writings and none to Thornton. Yet Hayek's criticisms may be misplaced for, as Hicks has noted, Hayek failed to recognize that in the *Paper Credit* Thornton (1802) developed his analysis for a credit economy and he recognized that such an economy would have to be managed. Although Keynes does not appear to have read *Paper Credit*, he did, in *A Tract on Monetary Reform* and in the *Treatise on Money*, analyze the workings of a credit economy. Furthermore, he did stress, as Thornton had done, that in a crisis the central bank must be willing to act as lender of last resort and must be prepared to spend freely. Where Keynes differed from Thornton was that Thornton could assume that money wages were flexible downwards whereas Keynes could not.

Methodology

In a draft (unpublished) preface for the *General Theory* written in 1934

Keynes stated that:

> ... when we write economic theory, we write in a quasi-formal style; and there can be no doubt, in spite of the disadvantages, that this is our best available means of conveying our thought to one another. But when an economist writes in a quasi-formal style, he is composing neither a document verbally complete and exact so as to be capable of a strict legal interpretation, nor a logically complete proof. Whilst it is his duty to make his premises and his use of terms as clear as he can, he can never state all his premises and his definitions are not perfectly clear-cut. He never mentions all the qualifications necessary to his conclusions. He has no means of stating, once and for all, the precise level of abstraction on which he is moving, and he does not move on the same level all the time. It is, I think of the essential nature of economic exposition that it gives not a complete statement, which, even if it were possible, would be prolix and complicated to the point of obscurity but a sample statement, so to speak, out of all the things which could be said, intended to suggest to the reader the whole bundle of associated ideas, so that if he catches the bundle, he will not in the least be confused or impeded by the technical incompetentness of the mere words which the author has written down, taken by themselves.
>
> This means, on the one hand, that an economic writer requires from his reader much goodwill and intelligence and a large measure of cooperation; and, on the other hand, there are a thousand futile, yet verbally legitimate, objections which an objector can raise. In economics you cannot convict your opponent of error; you can only convince him of it. And even if you are right, you cannot convince him if there is a defect in your own powers of persuasion and exposition or if his head is already so filled with contrary notions that he cannot catch the clues to your thought which you are trying to throw to him.[24]

At first glance Keynes's preface appears to contain echoes of his pencilled comments on Hayek's review of the *Treatise*:

> Hayek has not read my book with that measure of 'good will' which an author is entitled to expect of a reader. Until he can do so, he will not see what I mean or know whether I am right. He evidently has a passion which leads him to pick on me, but I am left wondering what this passion is.[25]

But further reflection suggests that it summarized the approach to epistemology and methodology which he had laid down in the *Treatise on Probability*, elaborated in discussions with Ramsay and incorporated in the final draft of the *General Theory*. It therefore raises interesting questions concerning the respective approaches of Keynes and Hayek to economics with Keynes, in his early years being influenced by Johnson,

Russell and Moore and in his later years being influenced by Ramsay and Wittgenstein, whereas Hayek was associated with the Vienna Circle and later with Wittgenstein (who was a distant cousin) and Popper. Furthermore, both Keynes and Hayek acknowledged a debt to Burke. For Keynes, as the draft preface underlined and subsequent correspondence with Harrod confirmed:

> Progress in economics consists almost entirely in a progressive improvement in the choice of models. The grave fault of the later classical school, exemplified by Pigou, has been to overwork a too simple model; whilst Marshall often confused his models, for the devising of which he had great genius, by wanting to be realistic and being unnecessarily ashamed of lean and abstract outlines.[26]

But model building involves two problems. First the point made in the draft preface, it is impossible for an economist to be precise about all the terms which he uses. Second, 'unlike the typical natural science, the material to which it [the model] is applied is, in many respects, not homogeneous through time.'[27]

Which brings us to the question of how Keynes assessed models. The starting point for his ideas seems to have been his reaction to Hume's work on induction and causality. According to Hume:

> The idea of cause and effect is derived from experience, which informs us, that such particular objects, in all past instances, have been constantly conjoined with each other. . . . According to this account of things . . . probability is founded on a presumption of a resemblance betwixt those objects, of which we have had experience, and those, of which we have had none; and therefore 'tis impossible this presumption can arise from probability. . . . When we are accustomed to see two impressions conjoined together, the appearance or idea of the one immediately carries us to the idea of the other. . . . Thus all probable reasoning is nothing but a species of sensation.[28]

Keynes noted that in an endeavour to escape from Hume's conclusion, mathematical economists had invoked the concept of frequencies. But Keynes was concerned with those situations where events were infrequent and he also wished to retain a logical approach to probability. In the *Treatise on Probability* he sought to clarify different types of expectation and he concentrated upon those events which required the establishment of logical relationships between the premises (h) and the conclusion (a) and he attached considerable importance to what he called the weight of the evidence, by which he meant that it was possible to compare arguments, not only in terms of their probabilities, but also according to how much evidence was involved:

> As the relevant evidence at our disposal increases, the magnitude of the argument may either decrease or increase, according as the new strengthens the unfavourable or favourable evidence; but something seems to have increased in either case – we have a more substantial basis upon which to rest our conclusions. I express this by saying that an accession of new evidence increases the weight of an argument. New evidence will always increase its 'weight'.
>
> The weight, to speak metaphorically, measures the sum of the favourable and unfavourable evidence, the probability measures the difference.[29]

And under conditions of uncertainty, as Keynes observed in the *General Theory* we may fall back on convention – by which we assume that 'the existing state of affairs will continue indefinitely, except in so far as we have specific reasons to expect a change' (Keynes, 1921: 77 and 84). Keynes therefore had a theory of rational expectations but not the Lucas approach in which the evaluation of probabilities predominates. But it was a theory of rational expectations in which people attempted to use all the available evidence and attempted to establish logical connections between the evidence and the outcome.

The discussion in the *Treatise on Probability* appears to be absent as a formative influence upon *A Tract on Monetary Reform* and the *Treatise on Money* and it might be legitimately argued that no significance should be placed upon a work whose origins lay in Keynes's early thinking around 1904. Such an argument seems to gain support from the exchange with Ramsay which is referred to by Braithwaite in his preface to the 1973 edition of the *Treatise on Probability*. According to Braithwaite Ramsay persuaded Keynes to switch to probabilities. However, this argument does not stand up to close inspection. In *Essays in Biography* (1933) Keynes wrote:

> Ramsay argues, as against the view which I put forward that probability is not concerned with objective relations between propositions but (in some sense) with degrees of belief, and he succeeds in showing that the calculus of probabilities simply amounts to a set of rules for ensuring that the system of belief which we hold shall be a consistent system. Thus the calculus of probabilities belongs to formal logic. But the basis of our degrees of belief – or the a priori probabilities, as they used to be called – is part of our human outfit, perhaps given to use merely by natural selection, analogous to our perceptions and memories rather than to our formal logic. So far I yield to Ramsay – I think he is right. But in attempting to distinguish 'rational' degrees of belief from belief in general he was not yet, I think, quite successful. It is not getting to the bottom of the principle of induction merely to say that it is a useful habit.[30]

What Keynes may be alluding to is the fact that Ramsay's individuals formed their probabilities independently of each other whereas, as Keynes revealed in the *General Theory*, there may be interdependencies.

This yields a plausible explanation of the apparent disappearance of the substance of the *Treatise on Probability* and its subsequent appearance in the *General Theory* in terms of Keynes's changing appreciation of the deepening and prolonged depression which resulted in a shift from the role of expectations under certainty to darker shades of uncertainty. Thus the weight of evidence plays an important part in the discussion of the marginal efficiency of capital (where confidence is all important) and in the desire for liquidity and its influence on the rate of interest. Furthermore there is a distinction in the treatment of expectations in Chapters 11 and 12 which deal with the marginal efficiency of capital and the state of long-term expectation. In Chapter 12 there is a greater emphasis upon the weight of evidence, the importance of confidence and the employment of the convention.

Which brings us to the matter of testing theories and to the approaches of Hayek and Popper. Hayek, in fact, has very little to say about the testing of theories. In his treatment of the Ricardo effect he is content to draw attention to the problems of obtaining the appropriate statistical material for testing and despite being involved in the supervision of Tsiang's thesis, which was critical of Hayek's discussion of the Ricardo effect, he offered no comments. His own theories he regarded as 'algebraic' – meaning that they employed no constants – and were presumably not meant to be tested in a formal manner. And as a result of his association with Wesley Clair Mitchell and other economic statisticians in the United States in the 1920s he was wary of statistical evidence.

Yet Hayek was attracted by the ideas of Popper. What Popper did was to extend Hume's argument on induction by suggesting that theories be constructed so as to enable the hypotheses to be refuted. Refutation rather than verification became the criterion of testing. However, Popper was cautious about applying his ideas to the social sciences:

> In physics, for example, the parameters of our equations can, in principle, be reduced to a small number of natural constants – a reduction which has been successfully carried out in many important cases. This is not so in economics – here the parameters are themselves in the most important cases quickly changing variables. This clearly reduces the significance, interpretability, and the testability of our measurements.[31]

All of which sounds like Keynes:

> Economics is a science of thinking in terms of models joined to the art of choosing models which are relevant to the contemporary world. It is compelled to be this, because, unlike the typical natural science, the

material to which it is applied is, in too many respects, not homogeneous through time.[32]

But, unlike Robbins, and to some extent Hayek, Keynes did not lapse into apriorism. 'The object of statistical study', he wrote in a letter to Harrod, 'is not so much to fill in missing variables with a view to prediction, as to test the relevance and validity of models.'[33]

Most of Hayek's ideas on epistemology and methodology were developed after Keynes's death and at this stage we shall touch on them briefly and, in particular, the special place in his ideas of Popper's writings. Hayek invited Popper to the LSE in 1942 and in the same year he published his three-part article 'Scientism and society' in which he criticized the 'slavish imitation of the method and language of Science', although he raised no objections to the use of 'the methods of Science in their proper sphere.' Subsequently, he modified his views in his collected essays, *Studies in Philosophy, Politics and Economics* (1967):

> A slight change in the tone of my discussion of the attitude which I then called 'scientism.' The reason for this is that Sir Karl Popper has taught me that scientists did not really do what most of them not only told us what they did but also urged representatives of other disciplines to imitate. The difference between the two groups of disciplines has thereby been greatly narrowed and I keep up my argument only because so many social scientists are still trying to imitate what they wrongly believe to be the methods of the natural sciences.[34]

Hayek put forward three reasons for a distinction being drawn between the natural sciences and the social sciences. First, the 'facts' of the social sciences are 'opinions – not opinions of the student of social phenomena, of course, but opinions of those whose actions produce his object.'[35] Second, those 'opinions' cannot be observed directly but must be inferred from what people do and say 'because we have a mind similar to theirs.'[36] Third, there is the problem of spontaneous order:

> If social phenomena showed no order except in so far as they were consciously designed, there would indeed be no room for theoretical sciences of society and there would be, as is often argued, only problems of psychology. It is only in so far as some sort of order arises as a result of individual action but without being designed by any individual that a problem is raised which demands theoretical explanation.[37]

Moreover, this 'order cannot be stated in physical terms, for if we define the elements in physical terms no such order is visible, and that the units which show an orderly arrangement do not (or at least need not) have any physical properties in common.'[38]

In his article 'Degrees of explanation' Hayek (1978b) adopted

Popper's refutation criterion to the needs of the social sciences by distinguishing between an explanation of the principle by which a phenomenon is produced and explanation which enables us to predict the precise results. Explanation in principle serves to exclude some explanations; it therefore refutes some possible explanations. In contrast, the prediction of precise results is something that can only be pursued, with confidence, in the natural sciences. This distinction appears to have been operating in his discussion of the Ricardo effect where he suggested that the customary tests of predictions might be difficult to apply.

Hayek's approach is therefore reminiscent of that of Keynes when he advocated the examination of the weight of the evidence which supports an argument and when, in his correspondence with Harrod and disagreements with Tinbergen, he commented upon the usefulness of econometrics:

> I think it most important, for example, to investigate statistically the order of magnitude of the multiplier, and to discover the relative importance of the various facts which are theoretically possible.
>
> My point against Tinbergen is a different one. In chemistry and physics and other natural sciences the object of experiment is to fill in the actual values of the various quantities and factors appearing in an equation or a formula; and the work when done is once and for all. In economics that is not the case, and to convert a model into a quantitative formula is to destroy its usefulness as an instrument of thought. Tinbergen endeavours to work out the variable quantities in a particular case, or perhaps in an average of several cases, and he then suggests that the quantitative formula so obtained has general validity yet in fact, by filling in figures, which one can be quite sure will not apply next time, so far from increasing the value of his instrument he has destroyed it. This implies that the skills required of an economist are different from those needed to be a natural scientist or engineer – a point on which Keynes and Hayek were in agreement.
>
> Good economists are scarce because the gift for using 'vigilant observation' to choose good models, although it does not require a highly specialized technique, appears to be a very rare one.[39]

Vision

Keynes's scholarship matched that of Hayek with the main difference being Keynes's preference for analyzing the writings of the nineteenth century (especially the late nineteenth century) economists whereas Hayek concentrated upon the late eighteenth and early nineteenth century writers. And in their approaches to methodology there are strong similarities with the main difference being Hayek's interest in psychology and its insights into the acquisition of knowledge whereas Keynes displayed greater interest in the philosophical aspects of epistemology and methodology. Which leaves us with their respective visions of society. 'In practice' wrote Schumpeter, 'we all start from the work of our predecessors, that is we hardly ever start from scratch. But suppose we did start from scratch', he went on, 'what are the steps we should have to take? Obviously, in order to be able to posit to ourselves any problems at all, we should first have to visualize a distinct set of coherent phenomena as a worth-while object of our analytical efforts. In other words, analytical effort is of necessity preceded by a pre-analytic cognitive act that supplies the raw material for the analytic effort. In the book, (*The History of Economic Analysis*), this pre-analytic act will be called Vision'.[40]

Hayek's vision was of an economy which might be in intertemporal equilibrium in the sense that all economic agents had no desire to change their plans. Unemployment might result from the interplay of changing demands and supplies being superimposed upon a capital structure whose various characteristics – durability, specificity and complementarity – as well as lags in the adjustment of factor prices, might create problems. Such unemployment might be called frictional. However, unemployment associated with the trade cycle resulted from unanticipated changes in the money supply leading to changes in relative prices which, in turn caused changes in the time structure of production (that is, the outputs of consumer and capital goods). Thus Hayek's model of the trade cycle emphasized the fact that unanticipated changes in the money supply do not necessarily produce changes in total output, but changes in the composition of output. Reductions in the money supply would then lead to a reversal in the time structure of production. This vision had its origins in the histories of small open economies operating on the gold standard in the nineteenth century, in the attempts of European governments to promote economic growth by means of forced saving in the late nineteenth century and in the experiences of the European inflations after the First World War. What Hayek did was to provide an explanation of how booms might start and how they were brought to an end. When countries were operating on the gold standard booms would be brought to an automatic end by gold outflows to cover trade deficits.

According to Schumpeter:

> Keynes's work presents an excellent example of our thesis that, in principle, vision of facts and meanings precedes analytic work which, setting in to implement the vision, then goes hand in hand with it in an unending relation of give and take. Nothing can be more obvious than that in the beginning of the relevant part of Keynes's work stood his vision of England's ageing capitalism and his intuitive diagnosis of it

(which he followed up without the slightest consideration of other possible diagnoses): the arteriosclerotic economy whose opportunities for rejuvenating venture decline while old habits of saving formed in times of plentiful opportunity persist.[41]

This vision was clearly formulated in the first few pages of *The Economic Consequences of the Peace* (1919) and adumbrated with increasing clarity in *A Tract on Monetary Reform* and *The Treatise on Money*, and then in *The General Theory*.

Increasing clarity becomes more apparent after 1931. Before 1931 Keynes's preoccupation was with both internal and external balance. As a result of the return to the gold standard at the prewar parity in 1925 the export industries were depressed. Attempts to stimulate foreign demand by deflation ran up against wage rigidity. Various solutions were offered to the Macmillan Committee and spelled out in the *Treatise on Money*. Devaluation was a possibility but by 1930 the opportunity was lost. An incomes policy, a National Treaty, was proposed by Keynes in 1925 but rejected in 1930 because 'its feasibility is almost a matter of psychological and political, and not economic factors.' And in both 1931 and 1936 an incomes policy was seen as more feasible in an authoritarian state. A third solution was the rationalization of industry but that was seen as leading to increased unemployment. Tariffs were mooted and resulted in a clash of opinion between Keynes and Robbins. Finally, a public works programme was suggested but Hawtrey said that if it were financed by borrowing then it might require a credit expansion and if an increase in the money supply were needed then its effects might not be confined to the public sector.[42]

After 1931 some of the problems posed by the need to achieve external balance were removed. The floating of the pound achieved the results sought previously in devaluation and tariffs. After 1931 the problem of public and private investment competing for a limited amount of saving was resolved by the recognition that investment, via the multiplier, could lead to an increase in incomes and savings. After 1931 there was a preoccupation with the domestic forces which might promote unemployment and these were seen to lie on the demand side rather than the supply side. Hence, the emphasis in the *General Theory* upon aggregate demand.

Summary and conclusions

There were critical reactions to the *General Theory* from the older Cambridge economists, Pigou and Robertson; there was silence by the older members of the LSE, Hayek, Robbins and Gregory. In both institutions there were appreciative responses by the younger economists. Pigou accepted Keynes's use of comparative statics but then pointed out that he had failed to allow for the possibility that falling prices would increase the real value of cash balances and stimulate consumption. Robertson chose to emphasize the dangers of applying comparative statics to the workings of a dynamic economy. Hayek chose to excuse his failure to respond by pointing out that Keynes might change his mind but the more important reasons for his lack of response were his failure to produce a theory of capital and his inability to foresee and provide a solution to the problem of secondary deflation. He also tended to attribute to Keynes doctrines which he did not hold, such as the belief that investment depended on final demand whereas Keynes emphasized the importance of expectations. Robbins's failure to respond may have been due to the fact that he was not a macroeconomist nor, indeed, a monetary theorist. During the 1930s Gregory began to develop interests outside the LSE.

But behind the *General Theory* lay other factors which may have contributed to the success of the Keynesian avalanche. First, Keynes did possess a considerable knowledge of the writings of earlier economists. Second, he possessed a well developed and well articulated approach to the problems of epistemology and methodology. Third, he had a vision of the workings of the economy which was more closely attuned to the circumstances of the 1930s.

Notes

1. Keynes, J.M. (1979), *The Collected Writings of John Maynard Keynes*, Vol. XXIX, *General Theory and After: a supplement*, London: Macmillan, p. 150.
2. Pigou, A.C. (1931), *Minutes of Evidence of the Macmillan Committee on Finance and Industry*, p. 259.
3. Keynes, J.M. (1936, 1973), *Collected Writings*, Vol. VII, *The General Theory of Employment, Interest and Money*, p. 279.
4. Pigou, A.C. (1947), 'Economic progress in a stable environment', *Economica*, NS14: 185–8.
5. Pigou, A.C. (1950), *Keynes's 'General Theory': a retrospective view*, London: Macmillan, p. 65.
6. Robertson, D.H. (1915, 1948), *A Study of Industrial Fluctuations*, London: LSE reprint, p. 65.
7. Robertson, D.H. (1926, 1949), *Banking Policy and the Price Level*, London: P.S. King, p. xi.
8. Cleaver, E. (ed.) (1978a), *F.A. Hayek: Nobel Prize Economist*, Berkeley, Ca.: University of California, p. 88.
9. Hayek, F.A. (1960), *The Constitution of Liberty*, London: Routledge, p. 87.

10. Lachmann, L. (1939), 'On crisis and adjustment', *Review of Economics and Statistics*, 7: 62–9.
11. Robbins, L.C. (1971), *Autobiography of an Economist*, London: Macmillan, p. 153.
12. Scitovsky, T. (1980s) in *Conversations with LSE Economists in the 1980s*, conducted by N. Shehadi, London: LSE archives.
13. Hicks, J.R. (1983), 'The formation of an economist', *Classics and Moderns, Collected Economic Essays*, Vol. 3, Oxford: Blackwell, p. 56.
14. Keynes, J.M. (1914), 'Review of Mises's Theories des Geldes und des Umlaufsmittel', in *Economic Journal*, XIV: 417. (Reprinted in J.M. Keynes (1973), *Collected Writings*, Vol. XII, *Economic Articles and Correspondence: Academic*, pp. 400–1.)
15. Mises, L. (1943), *The Theory of Money and Capital*, London: Cape, p. 58.
16. Keynes, J.M. (1973), *Collected Writings*, Vol. XIV, *The General Theory and After: Part II, Defence and Development*, p. 167.
17. Keynes, J.M. (1979), *The General Theory and After: a supplement*, p. 131.
18. Keynes, J.M. (1973), *Defence and Development*, p. 54.
19. Keynes, J.M. (1973), *Collected Writings*, Vol. XIII, *The General Theory and After: Part I, Preparation*, p. 19.
20. Mises, L. (1943), 'Elasticity of expectations', *Economica*, NS10: 251.
21. Keynes, J.M. (1933, 1972), *Collected Writings*, Vol. X, *Essays in Biography*, p. 132.
22. op. cit., p. 187.
23. op. cit., p. 191.
24. Keynes, J.M. (1973), *General Theory: Preparation*, p. 469.
25. op. cit., p. 243.
26. Keynes, J.M. (1973), *Defence and Development*, p. 296.
27. op. cit., p. 297.
28. Hume, *Treatise on Human Nature*, pp. 126–7.
29. Keynes, J.M. (1921, 1973), *Collected Writings*, Vol. VIII, *Treatise on Probability*, p. 77.
30. Keynes, J.M. (1933, 1972), *Essays in Biography*, pp. 338–9.
31. Popper, K. (1944), *Poverty and Historicism*, London: Routledge, p. 68.
32. Keynes, J.M. (1973), *Defence and Development*, p. 296.
33. op. cit., p. 296.
34. Hayek, F.A. (1967), *Studies in Philosophy, Politics and Economics*, London: Routledge, p. 27.
35. op. cit., p. 63.
36. op. cit., p. 72.
37. op. cit., p. 75.
38. op. cit., p. 78.
39. Keynes, J.M. (1973), *Defence and Development*, p. 299.
40. Schumpeter, J.A. (1954), *History of Economic Analysis*, Oxford: Oxford University Press, p. 1151.
41. op. cit., p. 1152.
42. Hawtrey, R.G. (1925), 'Public expenditure and the demand for labour', *Economica*, 5: 38–48.

9

The neoclassical synthesis: Hicks and Lerner

Early impressions

The publication of the *General Theory* posed problems for the LSE's economists who had been brought up on a diet of Lausanne and Vienna. They were pressed to reject or accept the new ideas or effect a synthesis. It is therefore interesting to observe the reactions of two of the School's leading theorists – Hicks and Lerner – both of whom went on to produce syntheses which were to become the building blocks of the neoclassical synthesis whereby the *General Theory* was deemed to be applicable to slump conditions and neoclassical theory was applicable to the full employment situation and fiscal policy could be used to ensure that aggregate money demand was maintained at the full employment equilibrium level.

Lerner's invitation from the International Labour Office (ILO) to write an article review of the *General Theory* for a general audience is interesting because in his previous work he had concentrated on value theory, international trade theory, welfare economics and the economics of socialism. He had, however, received in 1935, a research fellowship which enabled him to move from the LSE to Cambridge and he was involved in the joint LSE–Cambridge seminars in which the ideas of the *General Theory* were canvassed as well as being the editor of the *Review of Economic Studies* which catered for younger economists. But an early draft of the review article which he submitted to Keynes for comment revealed his lack of understanding of the essential elements of the *General Theory*. 'I think your article splendid', wrote Keynes, 'you have succeeded in getting a most accurate and convincing story into a small space.'[1] However, he then went on to make two fundamental criticisms.

188 The neoclassical synthesis

First, Lerner had failed to grasp the significance of Say's Law for the classical economists. Second, Lerner had not emphasized the importance of the growing gap between consumption and real income created by a marginal propensity to consume which was less than unity. This gap had to be filled by spending on capital goods but such spending would not be forthcoming automatically. These omissions were removed in the final draft.

In the published version Lerner cleared up the omissions and presented a well-rounded summary of the main arguments of the *General Theory*. He noted that there was an emphasis upon involuntary unemployment as opposed to voluntary employment and that involuntary unemployment occurred when the supply of labour at the previously money wage was greater than the demand for labour and that the unemployed might be willing to work for a lower real wage if brought about by an increase in prices but that workers would resist a cut in real wages engineered by a fall in money wages. Money wages were however sticky downwards but even if they were flexible then there might be no guarantee that employment would increase. What determined an increase in employment was not merely the effect on costs and the possibility of substituting labour for other resources but also the impact upon demand. Hence he emphasized the importance of hoarding, the determinants of the marginal efficiency of capital and the part played by liquidity preference. His conclusion was no doubt acceptable to readers of the ILO review:

> To seek the alleviation of depression by reducing money wages, rather than by directly reducing the rate of interest or otherwise encouraging investment or consumption, is to abandon the high road for a dark, devious, difficult and unreliable path for no better reason than that the dangers that await one at the common destination are more closely seen when it is approached by the broad highway.[2]

In contrast to Lerner, Hicks had been heavily involved in monetary theory, risk and the trade cycle in the early 1930s. In 1935 he published the influential article on 'Simplifying the theory of money' (Hicks, 1935a) and in the same year he went, at the invitation of Pigou, to Cambridge where he renewed his friendship with Robertson and where, between 1935 and 1938, he spent his time writing up *Value and Capital* (1939a) – which was very much a product of the LSE and reflected the influence of Pareto and Walras but in which Hicks also acknowledged the work of Keynes. When therefore he was invited by Keynes to review the *General Theory* for the *Economic Journal* he came to the task with an awareness of the underlying issues but equipped with a different analytical framework.

In his first impressions Hicks noted that the *General Theory* was:

1. A theory of employment 'in so far as the problem of employment and unemployment is the most urgent problem' to which the new theoretical apparatus was relevant.
2. A theory of output in general whereas Marshall dealt with a single industry.
3. A theory of shifting equilibrium as compared with the static theories of general equilibrium of Ricardo, Böhm-Bawerk and Pareto.

Unlike the *Treatise on Money*, savings and investment were defined as equal by definition because there is now no norm by which deviations of saving from investment can be judged. But the identity, Hicks observed, had the more fundamental point that savings and investment were brought into equality by unanticipated variations in stocks. Expectations could then be classified into short-term and long-term expectations with the latter not being closely connected with current receipts. Having explored previously the problems associated with expectations, Hicks was sympathetic to Keynes's discussion.

However he was critical of two issues in the *General Theory* and both criticisms also surfaced in his later work. The first point was the assumption that an increase in consumer spending, stemming from the increase in income resulting from investment, would need to be marked by an increase in the supply of consumer goods. According to Hicks, the absence of a high elasticity of supply of consumer goods would lead to a rise in the rate of interest. In reply, Keynes argued, that a high elasticity was not required. All that was necessary was that the price elasticity of output in general was not zero and be redefined full employment in terms of the supply elasticity:

> If I were writing again I should indeed feel disposed to define full employment as being reached at the same moment at which the supply of output in general becomes inelastic. It is perfectly true that a great part of my theory ceases to be required when the supply of output as a whole is inelastic.[3]

Hicks withdrew the point about 'high' elasticity but chose to invent an 'Austrian' qualification when he replied:

> I do not want to give up my substantial point, that output may have reached a short-period maximum, even when there are a considerable number of unemployed specialized to the investment goods industries. But I take it that you would not accept this and redefine full employment to cover this case.[4]

Keynes did not accept Hicks's argument.

The ISLM diagram

Hicks's article, 'Mr Keynes and the "Classics"' (1937) represented one of the first attempts to provide a neoclassical synthesis of Keynesian and pre-Keynesian ideas. It was presented at the 1937 Oxford meeting of the Econometrics Society where similar papers were presented by Harrod and Meade. Before the meeting Hicks had been permitted to see their papers and the main advantage of his own contribution was that it incorporated a simple diagram. The *ISLM* diagram contained two curves in interest rate/real income space. One curve, the *IS* curve traced out a locus of which yielded equilibrium in good markets; the other curve, the *LM* curve, was a locus of equilibrium in money markets. The intersection of the two curves yielded simultaneous equilibrium in goods and money markets. Variations in the elasticities of the two curves provided insights into, for example, the polar cases of neoclassical and Keynesian theory.

Did the *ISLM* diagram provide an adequate interpretation of the 'Classics'? Commenting upon the paper Keynes wrote:

> From one point of view you are perhaps scarcely fair to the classical view. For what you are giving is a representative belief of a period when economists had slipped away from the pure classical doctrine without knowing it and were in a much more confused state of mind than their predecessors had been. The story that you give is a very good account of the beliefs which, let's say, you and I need to hold. But if you were to go further back, how much I am not quite sure, you would have found a school of thought which would have considered this an inconsistent hotch-potch.[5]

In his reply Hicks confessed that his knowledge of the classics was restricted to the period after 1870. Subsequently, he sought to remedy his deficiency. In 'Monetary theory and history: an attempt at perspective' (1967a) he noted that classical theory, pre-1870, contained several strands. Ricardo had tended to concentrate upon long-run theory whereas Hume and Thornton had considered the short-run effects of monetary disturbances. Ricardo had also sought to treat a credit economy as if it were a metallic commodity system and could therefore be controlled by rules which tied credit to gold. In contrast, Thornton was much more aware that a credit economy had to be managed. In 'Monetary experience and the theory of money' the analysis of monetary history was extended to embrace Wicksell and Keynes. Ricardo and Keynes had looked at the problems of readjustment afterwards; Thornton and Wicksell had examined credit economies. In *A Market Theory of Money* (1989) Hicks contrasted Keynes and Marshall and also sought to relate the evolution of monetary economies to changes in real forces where fix-price markets began to supplant flex-price markets.

But did Keynes give an accurate picture of the classics? Did he provide Hicks with false clues? We shall have more to say on this question in the next chapter and merely note the following points. First, Keynes overlooked the point that, although Ricardo did concentrate upon long-run analysis, there were hints in, for example, the *High Price of Bullion* of short-run analysis and an awareness that the demand function for money might be subject to shifts. Thus, in the *High Price of Bullion*, Ricardo wrote:

> I do not dispute that if the Bank were to bring an additional sum of notes into the market, and offer them on loan, but that they would for a time affect the rate of interest. The same effects would follow the discovery of a hidden treasure of gold or silver coin. . . . It is only during the interval of the issues of the Banks, and their effects on prices that we should be sensible of an abundance of money; interest would, during the interval, be under its natural level; but as soon as the additional sum of notes or of money became absorbed in the general circulation, the rate of interest would be as high.[6]

An interesting point to note is that Hicks's syllabus for his lectures on international monetary problems which he delivered at the LSE in 1933 contained the *High Price of Bullion* as required reading (see Table 4.4).

Second, Keynes did not appreciate the distinction between real and money capital in classical theory and, as a consequence transferred the quantity theory from being a theory of the price level to becoming a theory of the interest rate. Third, both Robertson and Hawtrey were highly critical of what they considered to be Keynes's distorted interpretation of the classics.

Value and capital

'Mr Keynes and the Classics' was a response to the *General Theory*; *Value and Capital* was an LSE book, inspired by discussions at the School in the 1930s (see Table 9.1) but written up at Cambridge between 1935 and 1939. It was influenced by the *General Theory* but it was not a Cambridge book. It contained a two-pronged inquiry into first, static theory involving the interactions of many markets, and second, dynamic economics – where quantities and prices are dated – and where the emphasis is upon capital and interest (see Table 9.2).

The treatment of static economics opened with the theory of subjective value as it had been developed by Hicks and Allen in their article,

192 The neoclassical synthesis

Table 9.1 Session 1934–5. Theory of Value. Dr. Hicks.

Ten lectures. Michaelmas Term. Fridays, 5.00–6.00, beginning M.T. 12 October.
For postgraduate students and B.Sc. (Econ) Final – Special Economics.
Fee: £1 5s.

SYLLABUS: The development of the modern theory of value from the time of Cournot and Dupuit. The theory of the utility function, particularly in respect of the relatedness of wants. Market equilibrium: the questions of determinateness, of stability and of formation.
BOOKS RECOMMENDED: A. **Historical classics**: Cournot, *Mathematical Principles of the Theory of Wealth*; Dupuit, *De l'Utilite et de sa Mesure*; Jevons, *Theory of Political Economy*; Menger, *Grunsatze der Volkwirtschaftslehre*; Walras, *Elements d'economie politique pure*; Edgeworth, *Mathematical Psychics*; Böhm-Bawerk, *Grundzuge*; Pantaleoni, *Pure Economics*; Marshall, *Principles*; Wicksell, *Uber Wert, Kapital und Rente*; Pareto, *Manuel d'Economie Politique*.
B. **Modern works**: Wicksell, *Lectures* (Vol. I); Knight, *Risk, Uncertainty and Profit*; Bowley, *Mathematical Groundwork of Economics*; Schonfeld, *Grenznutzen und Wirtschaftsrechnung*; Rosenstein-Rodan, 'Grenznutzen' (in *Handwörterbuch*); 'La Complentarieta' (*Riforma Sociale*, 1933); Hicks and Allen, 'Reconsideration of the *Theory of Value*' (*Economica*, 1934); Kaldor, 'Determinateness of equilibrium' (*Review of Economic Studies*, 1934).

Source: LSE *Calendar* 1934–5.

Table 9.2 Session 1934–5. Economic Dynamics. Dr. Hicks.

Ten lectures. Lent Term. Fridays, 5.00–6.00, beginning L.T. 18 January.
For B.Sc. (Econ) Final – Special subject of Economics. Also recommended to postgraduate students.
Fee: £1 5s.

SYLLABUS: This course will be concerned with a study of those economic phenomena which appear only in a changing economic system and which drop out when a system is brought to rest in static fashion. An attempt will first be made to lay down certain general principles of the theory of economic change; in some respects this treatment will be parallel to that in Marshall's Book V, but it will be based upon general equilibrium theory of Marshall and Wicksell. Attention will be paid to the theory of risk and on this there will be based some general remarks about the theory of money and fluctuations.
BOOKS RECOMMENDED: Knight, *Risk, Uncertainty and Profit*; Hayek, Das Intertemporale Gleichgewichtsystem (*Weltwirtschaftliches Archiv*, 1928); Fisher, *The Theory of Interest*; Lindahl, *The Concept of Income* (in Cassel Essays); Myrdal, paper in *Beiträge zur Geldtheorie* (ed. Hayek); Hicks, 'The theory of uncertainty and profit' (*Economica*, 1931); 'Gleichgewicht und Konjunktur' (*Zeitscrift für Nationalökonomie*, 1933).

Note: The syllabuses contained in Tables 9.1 and 9.2 contain the ingredients of Hicks's future great book, *Value and Capital*.
Source: LSE *Calendar* 1934–5.

'A reconsideration of the theory of value' (1934). Indifference curve analysis was presented as an advance over Marshall's assumption of cardinal utility and a recognition of Pareto's emphasis upon ordinal utility. In his UCLA interview, in 1978 Hayek suggested that he may have been responsible for introducing Hicks to the indifference curve technique and that he (Hayek) had been struck by the fact that the same geometric technique could be used to illustrate both consumer (indifference curve) and producer (isoquant) behaviour. But this raises the intriguing question:

why did both Hicks and Hayek ignore the limitations of an approach which slurred over the reservations expressed by both Menger and Marshall? In the hands of Hicks the consumer was assumed to be capable of maintaining a given level of utility while substituting indefinitely one good for another. This assumption was not adopted by Menger and Marshall. Menger had an explicit discussion of the hierarchy of wants with its implication that utility was not homogeneous. Marshall confined his use of marginal utility theory to inessential goods (handkerchiefs) and recognized that the utility from some goods might be infinite.

Given the revised theory of value Hicks went on to rework the general equilibrium analysis of Walras and Pareto. In his review Morganstern (1941) severely criticized Hicks for assuming that general equilibrium was guaranteed by ensuring that there were as many equations as there were unknowns and that he had overlooked the work of Von Neuman (1937). However, Hicks was explicit that he wished to transcend the mere counting of equations and unknowns, and to lay down general laws for the workings of a price-system with many markets. 'This is the main thing which needed to be done in order to free the Lausanne theory from the reproach of sterility brought by the Marshallians. I believe I have done it.'[7]

Hicks's interest in the analysis of general equilibrium under static conditions was a mere bridgehead to the study of the instability which is characteristic of a dynamic economy. Therefore his preoccupation was in the conditions necessary for the stability of a static system. Stability could be perfect or imperfect. A market would be stable if a fall in price resulted in an excess of demand over supply at the new price even after all other prices in the system have adjusted to the price change. And a market would be imperfectly stable if a fall in price below equilibrium led to an excess of demand over supply at the new price only after all other prices have been readjusted to the new price. In the stable market case the market for one commodity was not only stable taken by itself but this stability is not disrupted by changes in other prices arising from the change in the first commodity. In the unstable case, the market for the first commodity is not stable taken by itself but it is rendered stable by side-effects of changes in other prices promoted by the change in the price of the first commodity. In the case of product markets, Hicks came to the conclusion that if the market for a commodity taken by itself was stable then it was unlikely to be affected by changes in other prices. The only factor likely to lead to instability was the income effect of a fall in price but this was thought to be unlikely. In the case of an imperfect stability Hicks doubted whether a market which was unstable by itself would be rendered stable by repercussions from other markets. And, in a nutshell, Hicks thought that multiple products would be perfectly stable.

Income effects were considered to be unimportant in the markets for direct services and intermediate goods and both would therefore be stable. But labour markets might give rise to large income effects and income effects could give rise to instability. However, there might be other stabilizing elements in the system which could swamp the destabilizing income effects. Hicks assumed that if each market were stable then the whole system would also be stable. This conclusion was later criticized by Samuelson (1941) and Metzler (1945) who demonstrated that the analysis of the stability conditions of equilibrium could only proceed as part of the development of dynamic economics. However, in the second edition of *Value and Capital* Hicks argued that his approach enabled him to say more about expectations whereas Samuelson's approach concentrated on the mechanics of dynamic theory.

The dynamic part of *Value and Capital* contained several influences. In 1931 Hayek had lectured on *Prices and Production*, and directed attention to his 1928 paper on intertemporal equilibrium and also to Böhm-Bawerk's work on capital theory. Subsequently, he introduced Hicks to Wicksell and, through his editing of *Beiträge zur Geldtheorie*, to Myrdal. The Wicksellian influence was strong in Hicks's *Theory of Wages* (1932c) where Hicks analyzed the effects of high wages on an economy. Since he had taken over the stationary state from Wicksell he concluded that high wages would lead to income effects on profits and saving and result in capital consumption. Later Robertson was to chide him for not casting his analysis in terms of a progressive economy in which high wages would lead to a slackening of the growth rate.

Wicksell's model concentrated upon price movements whereas Hayek's model assumed that there were real effects arising from monetary disturbances. But in *Prices and Production* Hayek had provided no reasons why real distortions should occur, although he had hinted in his 1928 article that disequilibrium could arise from frustrated expectations. And if expectations were uncertain then there might be a demand for money. Hence, the writing of the article 'A suggestion for simplifying the theory of money' (1935a). What that article did was to clarify the relationship between money and interest-bearing securities in the point-of-time equilibrium. About the same time Hicks was also reviewing Myrdal's *Monetary Equilibrium* (1939) which subsequently led him to the problems of change over time and to Lindahl's discussions of income and temporary equilibrium.

In the 'Simplifying' article Hicks elaborated a point of time or balance sheet equilibrium between money and other assets and the next step was to examine the problems of flow equilibrium. Myrdal provided some assistance through his distinction between *ex ante* and *ex post* but it was not enough. What Hicks then did was to introduce the concept of temporary equilibrium whereby decisions were made at the beginning of the 'week' (Monday) and as new decisions were made until the next 'week'. Within the 'week' therefore the distinction between stocks and flows became unimportant and within the week *ex ante* saving and investment were equal. Furthermore, the distinction between loanable funds and liquidity preferences theories of interest rates was removed even though during the week additional saving might take place.

Many of the ingredients of *Value and Capital* therefore pre-dated the *General Theory*, although Hicks did acknowledge that the latter half of his book would have been very different if he had not had the *General Theory* at his disposal when writing and he confessed amazement:

> at the way [Keynes] manages, without the use of any special apparatus to cut through the tangle of difficulties that beset him and to go straight for the really important things. He succeeds in doing so because he makes free use of his superb intuition and acute observation of the real world, in order to go straight for the essentials.[8]

Yet, he thought, Keynes's methods could have their drawbacks.

In his discussion of dynamic economics Hicks as we have noted, employed the method of temporary equilibrium whereby the progress of an economy was sliced up into units of time during each of which no change was assumed to take place. These slices of time, or rather the prices and quantities emerging in these slices of time, were linked through the creation of spot and futures markets. In spot markets current prices were determined; in futures markets prices were created for the quantities likely to emerge in the successive slices of time. The future prices depended, of course, upon expectations of future demands and supplies. The link between your prices and expected future prices was then established through the rate of interest. In other words, all transactions could be reduced to a spot transaction, a forward transaction and a loan (interest rate) transaction. Thus, if the loan rate were 5 per cent and the future price of copper for delivery twelve months hence were 3 per cent above the spot price then it would be possible to lend copper for one year by selling copper on the spot market, lending the money proceeds and covering the sale by a purchase on the forward market. The resulting set of transactions would then establish a rate of interest in terms of copper. One unit of copper would exchange for 105/103 units of copper to be delivered twelve months hence so that the rate of interest in terms of copper would be 2 per cent. The copper rate of interest would then equal the money rate of interest minus the contango (percentage excess of the futures price over the spot price).

196 The neoclassical synthesis

Having established a relationship between spot and future prices and interest rates Hicks considered the stability of the system. Disturbances to present prices could affect future prices but future prices were expected prices and he introduced the concept of an elasticity of expectations in order to analyze the effect of spot price changes upon future prices. Thus, a less than unit elastic expectations would denote a less than proportionate effect of spot price changes upon future price changes. And having mapped out the intertemporal pattern of prices and the effects of price changes Hicks went on to the production plan and the effect of interest rate changes upon the capital intensity of production. Given the intertemporal price pattern firms would choose production plans which maximized the net present value of the income stream. Changes in interest rates would then cause a change in production plans. Hicks accepted that the Böhm-Bawerk theory of capital and interest was valid for simple cases of point-input/point-output but for the cases where there might be continuous inputs or outputs he acknowledged the crushing objections raised by Knight to the concept of an average period of production. 'But what sort of average is it? What are the weights?'[9] he asked. Hicks's solution was to define the average period as the average length of time for which the various payments were deferred from the present, when the times of deferment were weighted by the discounted values of the payments although he acknowledged that: 'The reader may perhaps be angry with me for appropriating the term "Average Period" to this quantity, since he may have in his head what appears to be a very definite meaning of the term.'[10] He also recognized that:

> ... even when we are considering the effect of changes in the rate of interest on the production plan, we must not allow the rate of interest which we use in the *calculation* of the average period to be changed. What we must do is to start with a certain rate of interest, a certain production plan drawn up in view of the rate, and an average period calculated from this production plan at this rate of interest. Then we must suppose the rate of interest to fall, and the production plan to be varied in consequence. Finally, we must calculate the average period of the new plan, using the same rate of interest in its calculation as before — that is to say, the old rate of interest. Then our proposition is that the new average period, calculated in this way, must be longer than the old. A fall in the rate of interest lengthens the average period.[11]

Hicks's approach then was to base his concept of an average period upon the average length of time for which surpluses were deferred. That is to say, the stream of surpluses (output minus inputs) were discounted to the present. The absolute length of the true average period of production was deemed irrelevant. Instead the emphasis was upon the change in the average period as interest rates changed. Hicks's approach did, of course, represent a productivity approach to the extent that the stream of surpluses was calculated upon expected returns from various lines of activity. Given the production plans of producers Hicks then went on to consider the temporary equilibrium of an economy and to analyze the effects of disturbances. At this juncture he took into account Keynes's *General Theory*.

Value and Capital was an LSE product but was not reviewed in the School's journal, *Economica*. However, Lerner reviewed it in the *Quarterly Journal of Economics* and began:

> To say that Professor Hicks' 'Value and Capital' is the most important publication for economic theory since the appearance of Mr Keynes' 'General Theory of Employment, Interest and Money' does not quite do it justice. For not only do some of the important 'Keynesian' results, reached independently and earlier by Professor Hicks, appear in their final form in this volume, but the elegance and precision with which fundamental notions are presented and the astonishingly simple way in which the intricate argument unfolds itself make it certain that the book will remain a classic for students to read and re-read long after Mr Keynes' book has been rendered absolute by a more careful presentation of its arguments at the hands of other writers.[12]

Lerner's comment was remarkably prescient for, *Value and Capital*, along with 'Mr Keynes and the Classics' did become the starting point for most of the research in the postwar period. And it was the work for which he was awarded a Nobel Prize. Yet it did omit many things. It contained nothing on economies of scale, it had nothing to say about government and it made only slight references to money. Some of these issues were taken up by Lerner and some were taken up by Hicks in writings which he said in his Nobel lecture he would like to have been remembered for.

The economics of control

Value and Capital and 'Mr Keynes and The Classics' represent one approach to the problem of reconciling the *General Theory* with the ideas prevailing in the LSE during the 1930s. A second attempt was provided by Lerner in *The Economics of Control*. The book was published in 1944 but had its origins in the early 1930s and was presented as a PhD thesis in 1942. The book began life as an attempt to demonstrate that a socialist economy in which private ownership of the means of production was abolished could achieve an efficient allocation of resources provided money and markets were retained. Consumers would spend their incomes as they liked and the managers of socialist enterprises would be instructed to meet the demands for all goods and services unit costs and prices were equal. A socialist, or collectivist, could therefore be as efficient as a *laissez-faire*, capitalist economy. But the histories of Russia and Germany in the 1920s and 1930s convinced Lerner that the maintenance and extension of democracy deserved more attention than collectivization and that collectivization could represent a threat to democracy. Lerner's awareness of the dangers of collectivization coincided with Hayek's publication of *The Road to Serfdom*.

Growing awareness of the dangers of collectivization and increasing appreciation of the message of the *General Theory* led therefore to a change of plans. The initial design had been to solve each economic problem for a collectivist economy first and then to compare the results with those for a capitalist economy. But the problem of the slump of the 1930s and the message of the *General Theory* produced a new type of economy, the controlled economy, in which the main objective was to achieve and maintain full employment. In the controlled economy there would be the deliberate application of whatever policy would serve the public interest and there would be no attempt to prejudge the issue of collectivism versus *laissez-faire*. *The Economics of Control* approached the problems of socialism versus capitalism in the same spirit that had inspired Pigou's earlier studies but did not pursue the problems of externalities even though Lerner spent a period as a research fellow at Cambridge in the middle of the 1930s.

The book began with an examination of the principles which might govern the optimum distribution of goods (what was later to be called the optimum conditions of exchange). Such an optimum involved the equalization of marginal rates of substitution between goods by different individuals. The optimum could be achieved in a barter society but the inconveniences of barter meant that it was preferable to introduce money and achieve an equalization of the ratios of money prices of goods to be marginal rates of substitution between these goods. The discussion of the optimum conditions of exchange leaned heavily upon Lerner's earlier work and also that of Kaldor and Hicks both of whom were at the LSE in the 1930s. And in subsequent chapters Lerner went on to examine the optimal conditions for production.

In achieving the optimal conditions of production Lerner laid considerable emphasis upon the rule that, price should measure marginal cost. This was fairly straightforward under competitive conditions but he went on to consider also the problems which could arise when there were indivisibilities so that marginal cost was less than average cost and where the application of the marginal rule seemed to break down. The first part of *The Economics of Control* therefore dealt with microeconomics and represented a synthesis of ideas developed in the

LSE during the 1930s and to which Lerner was a major contributor. The difference from Hicks's *Value and Capital* lay in the fact that Lerner concentrated upon welfare economics. And in its treatment of welfare economics the emphasis was, as was the original intention, upon the collectivist economy with capitalist and controlled economies both receiving slight treatment. Where the book broke new grounds was in its discussion of the relations between the marginal efficiency of capital and the marginal efficiency of investment, and in the introduction of the concept of functional finance.

The marginal efficiency of investment

In the *General Theory* Keynes discussed the inducement to invest in terms of the marginal efficiency of capital and the rate of interest. Now the marginal efficiency of capital is essentially a static concept but, in the context of the *General Theory*, it was appropriate because the analytical core was one of comparative statics in which a comparison was made between alternative equilibrium situations. As Shackle emphasized: 'At each curtain rise the *General Theory* shows us, not the dramatic moment of inevitable action but a tableau of posed figures. It is only after the curtain has descended again that we hear the clatter of violent scene-shifting.'[13] There were however asides devoted to economic dynamics which Lerner took up and attempted to integrate with his earlier discussion of capital theory and also that provided by Hayek. The distinctions can best be appreciated by means of Figure 9.1.

In the second quadrant of Figure 9.1 the marginal productivity of capital curve of a typical firm is D_{k0}. Along the horizontal axis is measured the stock of capital while the vertical axis measures the price of capital and the marginal productivity of capital. The marginal productivity curve slopes downwards from left to right because of diminishing returns to successive additions to the capital stock. Now suppose that the rate of interest falls from i_0 to i_1. The marginal productivity of capital curve will shift upwards from D_{k0} to D_{k1}. With an unchanged capital stock, OK_0, the price of machines will rise from OP_0 to OP_1 and generate quasi-rents of $OK_0P_0P_1$. The emergence of quasi-rents will then generate a flow of new orders (investment) for new machines. The rate of investment will then depend upon two factors. First, there will be the conditions of supply in the machine-making industry. If the supply of machines is perfectly elastic OK, machines will be installed. However, in the first quadrant of the diagram the supply curve of the machine-making industry is less than perfectly elastic. And for simplicity we assume that the equilibrium price is OP_2. Hence, quadrant one shows a flow demand

200 The neoclassical synthesis

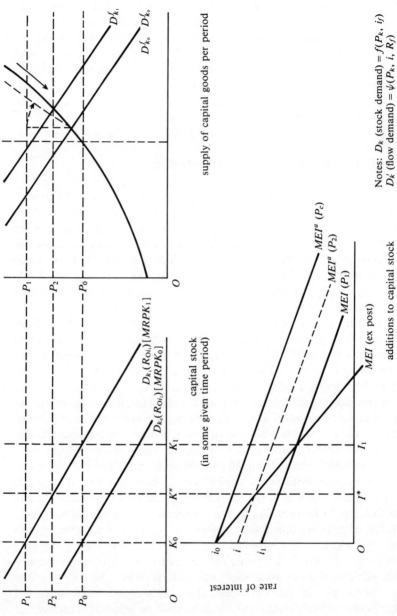

Figure 9.1 The relationship of marginal efficiency of capital to marginal efficiency of investment.

curve $D'K_0$ intersecting the supply curve at OP_0. When the rate of interest falls the flow demand curve shifts upward to D_{k2}. There is a temporary equilibrium at A and a final equilibrium at price OP_2.

The third quadrant shows the marginal efficiency of investment curve. It is an *ex ante* investment curve, denoted by the superscript a, which links investment to the rate of interest. The curve $MEI^a(P_0)$ shows the curve which a business would move along if the rate of investment fell but the price of machines remained constant at OP_0. Now the effect of the rise in the price of machines to OP_1 is to cause the MEI curve to shift downwards to $MEI^a(P_1)$ and to choke off investment despite the fall in the rate of interest. But this choking off is temporary because quasi-rents have risen and because the machine industry can supply machines at less than OP_0. The industry can supply K_0K, machines at a marginal cost of OP_2.

When the rate of interest falls a business would like to move along $MEI^a(P_0)$ but because the fall in the interest rate and the rise in demand applies to all firms the price will initially rise to OP_3 and then fall back to OP_2. Hence, the business will move along the curve $MEI^a(P_2)$. The fact that the business cannot move along $MEI^a(P_0)$ is due to the difference between *ex ante* and *ex post* factor demands. The *ex post MEI* curve cuts across the *ex ante* curves.

The analysis contained in Figure 9.1 illustrates Lerner's distinction between the marginal efficiency of capital and the marginal efficiency of investment but elaborates his treatment by also incorporating the distinction between *ex ante* and *ex post*. In some of his writing in the 1930s Lerner had expressed some scepticism concerning the appropriateness of the distinctions between *ex ante* and *ex post* saving and investment and exhibited a preference for Keynes's tendency to treat their relations as an identity but his discussion was sometimes at odds with his analysis of capital and investment which had showed the influence of Hayek. The final point to observe is that by explicitly acknowledging the importance of the supply curve of the machine industry, Lerner enabled a bridgehead to be formed to Hayek's discussion of the various dimensions of capital. Specificity and complementarity of resources are, in effect, locked into the supply curve of machines.

Shackle's elaboration

Lerner's resolution of the concepts of marginal efficiency of capital and marginal efficiency of investment were dealt with in the previous chapter. However, Shackle (1946) made a significant amendment to that analysis when he sought to reconcile the findings of the *Oxford Studies in the*

Price Mechanism (Wilson and Sayers, 1951) with Keynesian economics. What the *Oxford Studies* did was to undermine the role of the price mechanism as a means of allocating resources. Thus, one study suggested that businesses tended to ignore changes in interest rates when making investment decisions. What Shackle did was to draw attention to the impact of interest rate changes upon short- and long-term investment decisions. Thus, the interest elasticity of investment is the proportional change in investment associated with a given proportional change in investment:[14]

$$e_{Ir} = \cdot \frac{\Delta I}{r} \cdot \frac{\Delta r}{I}$$

This elasticity is the product of two elasticities. One is the elasticity of the demand price of machines with respect to the interest rate change and the other is the elasticity of investment with respect to changes in the price of prices; that is:

$$e_{Ir} = \frac{\Delta I}{r} \cdot \frac{\Delta r}{I} = \frac{\Delta P_m}{r} \cdot \frac{\Delta r}{P_m} \cdot \frac{\Delta I}{P_m} \cdot \frac{\Delta P_m}{I}$$

Now the elasticity of investment with respect to changes in the price of machines is dependent upon the elasticity of supply of capital goods from the machine-making industry and depends upon cost conclusions in this industry. In contrast the elasticity of the demand price of machines with respect to the interest rate can be strongly influenced by the expected length of life of machines. For example, if two machines have returns of £100 per period but one machine has a life of two years and the other machine has an indefinite life and the rate of interest is 5 per cent, then these respective demand prices will be:

$$\text{machine 1} = \frac{100}{1.05} + \frac{100}{(1.05)^2} = 192.9$$

$$\text{machine 2} = \frac{100}{0.05} = 2{,}000.0$$

Now if the rate of interest is doubled to 10 per cent then the demand prices of the machines will become:

$$\text{machine 1} = \frac{100}{1.10} + \frac{100}{(1.10)^2} = 174.24$$

$$\text{machine 2} = \underline{100} = 1{,}000.0$$

Hence a change in the rate of interest has a small effect on the demand price of the short-lived machine and a large effect on the demand price of the long-lived machine. That is to say, the elasticities of the demand prices of the two machines with respect to the interest rate are:

$$\text{machine 1} \quad \frac{18.66}{0.05} \cdot \frac{0.05}{192.9} = 0.096$$

$$\text{machine 2} \quad \frac{1{,}000}{0.05} \cdot \frac{0.05}{2{,}000.0} = 0.50$$

Now if entrepreneurs are uncertain about returns beyond a given period then they may adopt a fixed payoff period and truncate the period of return with the result that investment decisions become insensitive to changes in the rate of interest. Shackle's analysis provided an explanation of some of the findings of the *Oxford Studies* as well as providing an elaboration of Lerner's discussion of the marginal efficiency of investment economy that Lerner's book was to have a significant influence in the early postwar years because it directed attention to the price policies of nationalized industries. But there were two other issues which had an important influence upon theory and policy. Lerner's discussion of the marginal efficiency of investment had its antecedents in the discussion of Austrian capital theory but was transformed to provide a dynamic basis for the *General Theory*. And in the process it provided a link between Knight's discussion of capital as an organic entity and Keynes's discussion of investment. Lerner's marginal product of capital diagram depicted, in aggregate, the productivity of Knight's organic entity. While his marginal efficiency of investment was the dynamic counterpart of Keynes's marginal efficiency of capital. But given the nature of the diagram, and its obvious similarities to those presented in Hayek's 1934 article, it provided a link between Hayek and Keynes, except that Hayek in 1935 had repudiated any attempt to handle capital as an aggregate. Lerner's analysis, however, exercised a significant influence upon all the discussions of investment which began to emerge in the 1960s and 1970s.

Functional finance and the debt burden

Lerner's other significant contribution was his doctrine of functional finance and his assertion that a national debt was not a burden because we owe it to ourselves. Lerner argued that government had strong and efficient tools with which to maintain full employment and prevent inflation but their use was hindered by prejudice. These instruments become recognizable once it is realized that debt is not a burden unless it is externally held debt. The instruments which were available to governments were borrowing, taxing and printing money. Given these instruments a government could use them to vary private sector or public sector spending on public works. As a general rule Lerner advocated that the respective sizes of the two sectors could be determined by the rule that marginal social benefits from spending in the two sectors including the marginal social benefit from increased employment. And generalizing he suggested that the marginal social benefits from spending and the marginal social costs of taxes should be equal.

Lerner's doctrine of functional finance implied that there was no need for the budget to balance except in the long run. Instead, the budget deficit or surplus should be varied so as to maintain full employment and prevent inflation. Functional finance was therefore an application of marginalist principles to fiscal stabilization policy. It provoked considerable controversy in the 1960s when government borrowing expanded and the precise relations between taxing and borrowing and the effects of taxing and borrowing upon present and future generations were unravelled. Thus an individual might be indifferent between tax finance and loan finance if the present value of discounted future tax liabilities is equal to the present value of present scheme. But for this to be the case it is required not only that the capital market be perfect so that those who prefer to pay taxes in the future rather than the present can do so by raising personal loans at the government's borrowing rate, but also that either people expect to live for ever, paying known taxes, or that they treat the known liabilities of taxpayers in the future as their own. The foregoing assumes that the level of taxation at a point of time is of no importance. But, as Meade (1945), observed in his review of the *Economics of Control* taxes may distort the choice between work and leisure. Furthermore, equity considerations may underlie the impact of liabilities on present and (unborn) future generations.

Although expressing some reservations as to the practicalities of functional finance, Keynes's verdict was favourable and he was prepared to give it an airing:

> It is a grand book [he wrote to Lerner] worthy of one's hopes for you. A most powerful piece of well organized analysis with high aesthetic quality, though written more perhaps than you see yourself for the cognoscenti in the temple and not for those at the gate . . .
> In the second of the two books which you have placed within one cover, I have marked with particular satisfaction and profit three pairs of chapters – chapters 20 and 21, chapters 24 and 25, chapters 28 and 29. Here is the kernel of yourself. It is very original and grand stuff. I shall have to try it when I hold a seminar for the heads of the Treasury on Functional Finance.[15]

Summary and conclusions

The publication of the *General Theory* forced the LSE's economists to come to terms with Keynesian economics. The reactions were varied and not always instantaneous. Lachmann remained faithful to Austrian economics and made the fewest concessions, Kaldor, Shackle and Lerner seemed to have been early converts. Gilbert's conversion seems to have occurred after the Second World War. But there were two attempts to produce syntheses. Hicks produced the most notable synthesis in his book *Value and Capital* which was based upon ideas distilled from Hayek and Pareto, Marshall and Keynes. Lerner's *Economics of Control* owed much to discussions within the LSE in the 1930s about general equilibrium and welfare economics, capitalism and socialism, international trade and the *General Theory*. *Value and Capital* had a profound effect in the United States where it was adopted as a box of tools by the emerging generation of mathematical economists, such as Samuelson and Metzler. It was Hansen and Samuelson who popularized Hicks's *ISLM* diagram and neoclassical synthesis. And although there was a Hayek influence in the discussion of capital theory, Hicks's treatment of Austrian theory was not taken up – except by Hicks (!) in the 1970s.

In contrast, Lerner's book exerted its influence in other directions. There was its apparent paradoxical conclusion that capitalist and socialist economies were similar in that their efficiency rested upon the adoption of marginalism. Socialism might be preferable to capitalism in terms of its democratic character, although the Russian record did not suggest that it was inevitable. What Lerner's conclusion omitted was any reference to Hayek's emphasis upon the impossibility of centralizing all information – except by, possibly, suggesting that a mixed economy might be preferable to either controlled or socialist economies. Indeed, it was through his discussion of the mixed economy that Lerner exerted a significant influence upon postwar discussions in the LSE. In the pages of *Economica* in the late 1940s and early 1950s, Thirlby, Coase, Lewis and Nordin engaged in a controversy over the relative merits of various pricing rules for nationalized industries. Coase advocated the use of two-part tariffs and Lewis pursued the same theme. Later Wiseman was to emphasize the Hayek point that the condition 'marginal cost should equal price' was an outcome of competition and not a guiding rule. If firms attempted to maximize profits and survived the rigours of competition then it would be found that price would cover marginal cost. But it was not possible to impose such a rule in advance (*ex ante*) because costs were subjective opportunity costs and the manager of a

206 The neoclassical synthesis

nationalized firm, being in a monopoly position, could always make the firms costs equal price – if only by being inefficient.

In the field of macroeconomics *The Economics of Control* exerted an influence through its astringent treatment of fiscal stabilization policy and its provocative assertion that a national debt need not be a burden. The clarification of the relationship between capital and investment served as an essential building block in the neoclassical synthesis and his treatment of international monetary economics expanded the treatment in Gilbert's 1939 article.

Notes

1. Keynes, J.M. (1979), *The Collected Writings of John Maynard Keynes*, Vol. XXIX, *General Theory and After: a supplement*, London: Macmillan, p. 214.
2. Lerner, A.P. (1936a), 'Mr Keynes' "General Theory of Employment"', *International Labour Review*, p. 286.
3. Keynes, J.M. (1973), *Collected Writings*, Vol. XIV, *The General Theory and After: Part II, Defence and Development*, p. 71.
4. op. cit., p. 73.
5. op. cit., p. 79.
6. Ricardo, D. (1951), 'The High Price of Bullion' in *The Collected Works and Correspondence of David Ricardo*, Vol. III, *Pamphlets 1809–1811* (ed. P. Sraffa), Cambridge: Cambridge University Press.
7. Hicks, J.R. (1939a), *Value and Capital*, Oxford: Clarendon, p. 161.
8. op. cit., p. 4.
9. op. cit., p. 218.
10. op. cit., p. 186.
11. op. cit., p. 187.
12. Lerner, A.P. (1939–40), 'Review of Hicks Value and Capital', *Quarterly Journal of Economics*, 54: 298.
13. Shackle, G.L.S. (1967), *The Years of High Theory*, London: Cambridge University Press, p. 182.
14. Shackle, G.L.S. (1946), 'Interest rates and the pace of investment', *Economic Journal*, 56. (Reprinted in T. Wilson and R.S. Sayers (1951), *Oxford Studies in the Price Mechanism*, Oxford: Clarendon.
15. Keynes, J.M. (1974), *Bretton Woods: Shaping the post-war world*, in *Collected Writings*, Vol. XXVI, *Activities*, p. 244.

10
The thaw

Introduction

The neoclassical synthesis provided by Hicks and Lerner left many loose ends which stemmed from the attempt to provide complementarity of neoclassical theory with the comparative statics core of the *General Theory*. Among the issues neglected were: the treatment of money, the unresolved dispute over loanable funds and liquidity preference theories of the rate of interest and the extension of the ideas of the *General Theory* to the long run.

The demand for money

In 'The demand for money: the development of an economic concept' (1953) Gilbert sought to establish that the demand for money was a genuine demand in the sense that holding money conferred benefits to the holder which could be subsumed under the two headings of time and uncertainty as to the future value of a fixed interest bearing asset called a bond. That such a task was necessary in the early 1950s stemmed from the still prevailing confusions surrounding money. The early marginal utility theorists had shown a reluctance to admit that utility theory could be applied to money even though some could write of a demand for money.[1] Later European economists, such as Schumpeter and Holtrop, attributed holding money to accidents or institutional factors; thus, we might receive our incomes on Saturdays but not be able to spend them until Mondays. Cambridge writers could speak of a veil of money with the suggestion that money might not admit of demand analysis or be intertwined with the real economy. Furthermore, Keynes tended to place the emphasis upon the speculative demand and played down the importance of the transactions and precautionary motives. Therefore, Gilbert had to establish that those writers who had produced varying reasons as to why there might be a genuine demand for money could have their arguments classified under the headings of time and uncertainty about the rate of interest on bonds.

The 1953 lecture notes state that: 'It all boils down to the question of whether time is involved in exchange.' But time did not necessarily indicate an accident or institutional factor: a Saturday to Monday problem. Gilbert was prepared to admit a conventional element in the holding of money but maintained that at the margin choices were made. Likewise indivisibilities might be responsible for money holdings but were not essential and a clear distinction could be drawn between indivisibilities and transactions costs. The fact that human action takes time also leads to a possible lack of synchronization between payments and receipts but lack of synchronization need not be a reason for holding money because with perfect foresight it would be possible to anticipate all future transactions and, borrowing from Chambers's 1934 article, there would be 'no need for records of any kind and hence no money transactions. Unforeseen dishonesty cannot occur.'[2]

Perfect foresight could eliminate money while uncertainty might obscure analysis. What was required therefore was Lindahl's distinction between general and specific expectations. We may know that a biscuit packing machine will be invented but we may not know what form it will take because that would mean that it could be produced now. The time factor therefore must encapsulate the minimum expectation required for money to exist before it slipped away and a barter economy re-emerged.

Given expectations concerning technological progress, what of expectations concerning bond prices? And what of the subsequently inserted finance motive which has come to play a large part in post-Keynesian economics? Tavlas (1981) has emphasized that the modern quantity theory, as put forward by Friedman, took into account expected prices and he criticized Gilbert for the following statement: 'it is often said that money is held because of the uncertainty of future prices, some people thinking that prices will fall. I do not regard this as a fundamental reason.'[3] Unfortunately, Tavlas then took no account of the succeeding sentence: 'If an individual thinks prices will fall he can postpone purchases; but this does not of itself lead to the holding of money, since the alternative of holding a bond is open to him.'[4] Monetarists of course, tend to emphasize the precautionary motive rather than the speculative motive and until recently the evidence, as surveyed by Laidler (1985) and Cuthbertson (1985) on the speculative motive and the liquidity trap, was mixed but did not constitute an outright rejection. But following the stock market crash of October 1987, the percentage of cash holdings of the investment funds of large institutional investors rose from 3 per cent in September 1987 to 8 per cent in March 1988 (Sarjeant, 1988).[5]

This brings us to the Keynesian and post-Keynesian positions. Hicks was a contemporary of Gilbert at the LSE and began to develop his portfolio approach to the demand for money at the School. But in more recent years his emphasis has been on the speculative motive to almost the exclusion of the transactions motive. In his *Critical Essays* he argued that the transactions demand is not a true demand: 'It is the amount needed to *circulate* a certain volume of goods at a particular level of prices.'[6] It is a point of view at odds with Gilbert. In its emphasis upon the mechanical problem of transporting goods around the economy it contains echoes of Schumpeter and the *Treatise on Money*. The inclusion of 'particular level of prices' suggests that in some sense it is a real demand with money holdings falling during hyperinflation. It is also possible to assert that what appears to be a production function approach to the demand for money would admit of the rate of interest and the price level.

Expectations, uncertainty and causality

Time and uncertainty raise questions concerning expectations and causality. In 1931, in his article 'The theory of uncertainty and profit', Hicks had been an exponent of an objective approach to probabilities but by 1939, in *Value and Capital*, he had moved to considering expectations in terms of subjective probabilities – with (in a footnote) some attention being paid to the skewness of the distribution. In the post-Keynesian period Hicks's expressed reservations about the mean-variance approach. Thus, in his article 'The pure theory of portfolio selection' Hicks (1967) posed the following problem:

> There is one portfolio which offers a 90 per cent chance of an outcome of 4 and a 10 per cent chance of an outcome of 14; the mean value of the prospect is 5 and the standard deviation is 3. There is another prospect which offers a 90 per cent chance of 6 and a 10 per cent chance of -4; the mean value is again 5, and the standard deviation is again 3. It is implied in (E, S – expected mean, standard deviation) theory that the investor would be indifferent between these two outcomes, which are skewed in opposite ways. But it is not by any means obvious that we are justified in assuming that he would be indifferent, though it is not easy to say straight off which would be preferred. Though the two prospects are equally *uncertain*, common parlance would say one was more *risky* than the other.[7]

Hicks therefore expressed reservations about the mean-variance approach to expectations. In his book *Causality in Economics* Hicks (1979) moved closer to the position adopted by Keynes in the *Treatise on Probability*:

> The more characteristic economic problems are problems of change, of growth and retrogression, and of fluctuation. The extent to which these can be reduced into scientific terms is rather limited; for at every stage in an economic process new things are happening, things which have happened before. We need a theory that will help us with these problems; but it is impossible to believe that it can ever be a complete theory. . . . As economics pushes on beyond 'statics', it becomes less like science and more like history.
>
> The probability calculus, which is a powerful tool of discovery in the sciences, has seemed in recent years to be carrying all before it in economics also. No piece of research, in economics, seems now to be regarded as respectable unless it is decorated with least squares and confidence intervals. It is my belief that the relevance of these methods to economics should not be taken for granted; before they are applied their use should be defended. There is evidence that this was the view of Keynes.[8]

The strongest opponent of a frequency approach to expectations has been Shackle who, in his *Expectation, Investment and Income* (1938), had adopted *equivalent certainties*. But in the subsequent years, under the impact of mature reflection on the message of the *General Theory* he rejected the relative frequencies (probabilities) and mathematical expectation in favour of his own concepts of potential surprise and focus gains/focus losses. In his theory Shackle replaces probabilities by potential surprise and assumes that an individual will consider gains and losses separately. However, his theory has not attracted a great deal of attention – possibly because Shackle provides few examples of its use in economics. Coddington (1976) classified Shackle as a fundamentalist Keynesian in contrast to those neoclassical economists who pursued a policy of reductionism whereby market phenomena were reduced to stylized individual choices on which were based the theories of markets and general equilibrium. According to the fundamentalists Keynes emphasized that the basis of choice lies in vague, uncertain and shifting expectations of future events and that those expectations have no firm foundation.

Loanable funds v. liquidity preference

The insertion of money into an economy required the simultaneous determination of the money rate of interest and the price level. But what determined the money rate of interest? Keynes suggested, in the *General Theory*, that the rate of interest was determined by the demand for and supply of money — with demand being determined by liquidity preference, by the need to reward people for parting with liquidity. Apparently opposed to this theory was a classical theory which emphasized the importance of the real forces of productivity and thrift and which in a monetary economy came to be known as the loanable funds theory. A version of the loanable funds theory appeared in Hayek's writings but the most vigorous exponent of the theory was Robertson. Robertson was a visiting lecturer at the LSE in 1930–1 and was appointed to a chair in 1938. In the later period he exerted an influence upon Tsiang and Wilson.

The two theories could, of course, be regarded as complementary. Robertson wrote:

> We may start by regarding the rate of interest ruling during any short period of time as the price which equates the flow of loanable funds, which some people are prepared to put on the market during that short period of time, with the flow which other people are prepared to take off it. For this procedure, it can be said that it accords well both with the ordinary language of the newspapers, and with the tendency of modern economic theory to exhibit the hire-prices of the several factors of production as special cases of a general law of pricing. Alternatively, we may start by regarding the rate of interest as something which in monetary theory was contrasted with money, namely real resources.[9]

And he noted Keynes's tendency to introduce hybrid concepts, such as 'the supply of finance' and the 'supply of liquidity' which became interchangeable with savings or the supply of money. Classical theory tended to regard the rate of interest as being the amount paid for funds (capital) borrowed directly from savers or through an intermediary such as a bank or finance house. They distinguished capital from money and capital from credit. The role of money was the determination of the price level and they allowed for short-term effects of variations in the quantity of money on the rate of interest. In a passage devoted to Marshall's theory of the rate of interest Keynes demonstrated his confused interpretation of classical theory when he quoted from the *Principles*:

> Interest being the price paid for the use of capital in any market, tends towards an equilibrium level such that the aggregate demand for capital in that market, at that rate of interest, is equal to the aggregate stock.[10]

and offered the following comment upon the passage.

> It is to be noted that Marshall uses the word 'capital' not 'money' and the word 'stock' not 'loans'; yet interest is a payment for borrowing *money*, and 'demand for capital' in this context should mean 'demand for loans

of money for the purpose of buying a stock of capital goods.' But the
equality between the stock of capital goods offered and the stock
demanded will be brought about by the prices of capital goods, not by the
rate of interest. It is equality between the demand and supply of loans of
money, i.e. of debts, which is brought about by the rate of interest.
(italics in the original)[11]

Keynes failed to understand Marshall's use of the word 'capital' and as a result transformed the quantity theory of money and the price level into a quantity theory of the rate of interest.

In Robertson's analysis the rate of interest was determined by the demand for and supply of loanable funds. In the long run demands and supplies would be determined by the real forces of productivity and thrift although in a money economy those real forces would be expressed in money terms. In the short run, as in the analysis contained in *Banking Policy and the Price Level* those real forces could be distorted by unanticipated increases in the money supply created by the banking system and could lead to a condition of forced savings. In his criticisms of Keynes's interest rate theory, especially in 'Mr. Keynes and the rate of interest', Robertson emphasized that productivity considerations could lie behind the concept of liquidity preference since an individual exercised choice on a three-fold margin of consumption, buying a bond or purchasing a machine. He also took exception to the view that investing created its own savings. He conceded in a comparative statics model without a period of transition from one equilibrium to another, 'We can declare the problem of the finance of the process of investment to be self-solving.'[12] But once time lags were introduced then the equality of saving and investment became uncertain.

The problem of the equality of saving and investment cropped up in the interchange between Ohlin and Keynes. Keynes rejected the concept of *ex ante* savings on the grounds that it was a very dubious concept and because period analysis was complicated. Yet he was prepared to concede the necessity of a finance motive and for that motive to be a determinant of the rate of interest:

> Planned investment – i.e. investment *ex ante* – may have to secure its financial provision before the investment takes place; that is to say, before the corresponding saving has taken place. . . . This service may be provided either by the new issue market or by the banks: – which it is makes no difference. . . . I have no objection at all to admitting the demand for finance as one of the factors influencing the rate of interest. For 'finance' constitutes, as we have seen, an additional demand for liquid cash in exchange for a deferred claim. It is, in the literal sense, a demand for money.[13]

Yet despite Robertson's criticisms and Keynes's concessions, confusion still existed. Both Lerner and Hicks attempted to reconcile the liquidity preference and loanable funds theories of the rate of interest and to minimize the importance of the classical theory. Lerner combined his attempt to provide the equivalence of the two theories with a proof that saving and investment did not affect the rate of interest. In Figure 10.1 the S-curve and the I-curve show saving and investment as functions of the rate of interest. If there were neither hoarding nor increased bank lending then the rate of interest would be APc. The L-curve shows hoarding (assumed to be positive) as a function of the interest rate and the M curve shows the increase in the quantity of money (which is assumed to be independent of the rate of interest). If the hoarding curve is added to the investment curve we obtain the $I + L$ curve and if new credit is added to the savings curve we get the $S + M$ curve and the interest rate will then be given by the intersection at P_1.

Lerner rejected this approach for two reasons. First, at the interest rate P_1B saving is greater than investment whereas both must be equal according to Keynes's definitions. Second, the increase in the quantity of money DE is not equal to the hoarding DF because an individual can only increase his or her hoarding at someone else's expense if the total

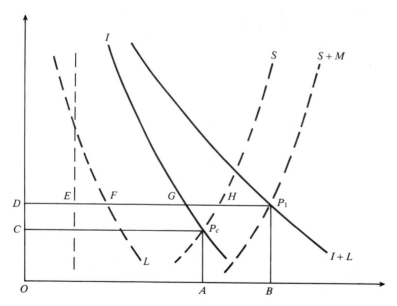

Figure 10.1 Lerner's reconciliation of liquidity preference and loanable funds theories of the interest rate.

quantity of money remains unchanged. With an unchanged money supply there cannot be a net excess of hoarding. Therefore, net hoarding can take place only if new money is created.

Lerner then proceeded to provide an alternative, and in his opinion, correct interpretation by means of Figure 10.2. In the diagram all points on the *SI* curve are equilibrium points at which saving and investment are equal. Behind the curve lies the notion that at any given rate of interest there corresponds a level of income at which the amount saved is equal to the amount invested. These amounts are then plotted against the rate of interest. The $L(Y_1)$ curve represents the hoarding of new money at the income level Y_1 and OO^1 shows the increase in the quantity of money. The curves $S + M$ and $I + L$ are obtained by summation as in Figure 10.1. According to Lerner it is convenient to regard OO^1 as measuring the total amount of money (and not the increase) and to consider the *L* curve as signifying the total demand for money (and not the increase in the demand for money). The interest rate is then P_2B.

Lerner's diagram can be regarded not only as an attempt to present the determinants of the interest rate but also as an alternative to Hicks's

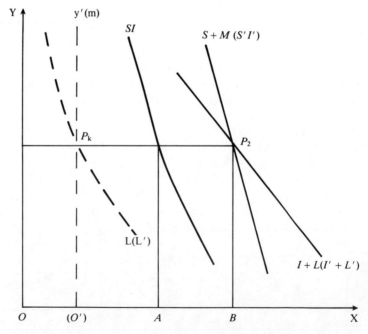

Figure 10.2 Lerner's reconciliation of liquidity preference and loanable funds theories of the interest rate.

ISLM curve diagram (referred to in the previous chapter). However, it does contain some errors. First, the *L* curve is a demand curve in the sense that it refers to the demand for money at different interest rates when the *level* of income is given. But the *IS* curve refers to the equilibrium points of savings and investment which correspond to *different* levels of income. Adding the two curves together seems to be an incorrect procedure. Second, saving and investment do not, in Lerner's analysis, affect the rate of interest because he assumed initially that Y_1 was the equilibrium level of income. But given Y_1 is the equilibrium level of income then it follows that P_2B can be the only compatible rate of interest.

As we observed in the previous chapter Hicks attempted to prove that the two theories were equivalent in a general equilibrium framework. This approach met with the comment, ascribed to Lerner: what happens if instead of leaving out the money equation or the bond equation we drop the equation for peanuts? In other words, in a general equilibrium framework all the independent equations are required for the determination of each individual price, including the rate of interest. The rate of interest could be determined with the money equation if the bond equation were eliminated but no more so than it would be determined by the presence of the equation for peanuts or any other commodity equation. Furthermore, even if the current rate of consumption of goods were equal to the current production of goods, that need not mean that the existing stock of goods was equal to the current demand. In equilibrium not only must the rate of consumption equal the rate of production, but total demand must equal total supply. Any commodity must therefore be represented by two equations and not one.

Under the influence of Robertson and recognizing the importance of the finance motive conceded by Keynes, Tsiang, in a series of articles, sought to resolve the conflict between the loanable funds and liquidity preference theories. In a monetary economy there is a continuous circular flow of money in the form of spending of incomes and with a part of this flow being diverted in the form of loanable funds which are absorbed by the demand for loans. It is the circular flow which accounts for the loanable funds theory of the interest rate. Of course, some of the flow can be temporarily trapped in a stagnant pool. But neither the flow nor the stagnant pool have any influence upon the money market unless attempts are made to change the flow of reactive idle balances.

The flows are measured per unit of time; in Robertson's case the period was defined as one during which, at the outset of our inquiry, the stock of money changes hands once in final exchange for the constituent's of the community's real income or output and in Tsiang's analysis the unit period was defined as one during which, at the outset, the stock of money changes hands once in exchange for *all* goods and services. But irrespective of the unit period adopted it is still possible for funds borrowed or realized from the sale of assets to be spent during the same period.

At the beginning of a period an individual faces a budget constraint in that he or she can spend only his or her disposable income and his or her idle balances and any money he or she can borrow from the money market. Hence, the demand for loanable funds comprises:

D_1 funds required to finance current investment;
D_2 funds required to finance expenditure on maintenance and replacement of capital;
D_3 funds required to be added to idle balances;
D_4 funds required to finance current consumption in excess of disposable income.

On the supply side we have:

S_1 current savings defined as disposable income minus current consumption spending;
S_2 current depreciation allowances for capital derived from gross revenue of the preceding period;
S_3 dishoarding from previously held idle balances;
S_4 new bank money.

What the money market does is to reconcile the flow demands for loanable funds with the supply of loanable funds. In the resulting flow equilibrium there appears to be a place for the total stock of money. However, D_1, D_2 and D_4 constitute Keynes's finance motive and S_1 and S_2 constitute reductions in the demand for finance by other households and finance. Hence, D_1, D_2 and D_4 constitute Keynes's finance motive and S_1 and S_2 constitute reductions in the demand for finance by other households and finance. Hence, $D_1 + D_2 + D_4$ minus $S_1 + S_2$ must equal the increase in transactions balances which the community wishes to make. In a similar vein D_3 minus S_3 represents the net increase in idle balances which the community wishes to make. Hence the flow equilibrium condition for loanable funds is:

$$D_1 + D_2 + D_3 + D_4 = S_1 + S_2 + S_3 + S_4$$

or

$$D_1 + D_2 + D_4 - (S_1 + S_2) + (D_3 - S_3) = S_4$$

which states that the increase in the demand for transactions balances (the finance motive) and for balances equals the current increase in the money supply created by the banks. If the previous stock demand and stock supply were equal and the current flow changes in demand and supply are the full adjustments to their new equilibrium values then the flow equilibrium must imply a new stock equilibrium.

Nevertheless, the Robertson three-fold margin does leave open the question as to whether one margin is more significant than another. This is a subject upon which Hicks attempted to shed some light in his posthumously published book, *A Market Theory of Money* (1989). In the late nineteenth century the trend of the rate of interest was downwards; there was no great demand from the private sector, such as the railways had prompted earlier and there was no great demand from the public sector. In the 1930s the external problem had seemed to be resolved when Britain went off the gold standard. The problem of government debt seemed to have been resolved by debt conversions and the rate of interest had fallen. But the fall in the interest rate had been recent and there was uncertainty as to whether it might rise again. Hence, the emphasis upon the margin between bonds and money.

There is a further problem. The liquidity preference theory appears to contain no reference to a normal rate of interest whereas the loanable funds theory does. This was expressed forcibly by Robertson as follows: 'the rate of interest is what it is because it is expected to become other than it is. The organ which secretes it has been amputated, and yet it somehow still exists – a grin without a cat.'[14] The factors governing the normal rate were, in Robertson's opinion, productivity and thrift and Robertson noted that Keynes had not been successful in banishing productivity because it crept back under the finance motive. But although productivity crept back there was no reference to a normal rate because it was not clear to Keynes that the turmoil of the interwar years offered any guide as to what a normal rate was supposed to be. It had been amputated.

Productivity and the price level

The insertion of money into an economy required the analysis of the simultaneous determination of the money rate of interest and the price level. But how should the price level behave in a progressive economy? Wicksell argued that as productivity increased the price level should remain constant and wages should increase as productivity increased. Davidson took the opposite point of view and stated that wages should remain constant and prices should fall as productivity increased. The debate remained inconclusive because Wicksell and Davidson failed to clarify the assumptions underlying their respective arguments. The debate surfaced in the 1920s when Robertson came down in favour of a falling price level. Harrod asserted that a stable or falling price level was compatible with equilibrium and Hayek argued that Wicksell's discussion of monetary equilibrium was inapplicable to a progressive economy. In 1957 Gilbert resolved the dispute by demonstrating that any behaviour of the price level was compatible with equilibrium. As long as the price level was foreseen and foreseeable then that trend could be incorporated into the money rate of interest.

Gilbert's paper anticipated the rational expectations models of the 1970s and 1980s but because it carried over from the 1953 paper the assumptions necessary for the existence of money it dealt with a monetary economy. The crucial assumption was the payment of interest on money balances in order to correct for changes in real balances as the price level altered. It was written within one year of Solow's real growth model and Tobin's money growth model (with which it expressed some difference) and it was written five years before Samuelson reached similar conclusions in his evidence to the 1962 Canadian Royal Commission on Banking and Finance. Subsequently, Samuelson repeated his conclusions in his 1963 obituary notice on Robertson when he criticized Robertson's advocacy of a falling price level.

But why did Wicksell propose a constant price level, Davidson and Robertson advocate a falling price level and Hayek criticize the extension of Wicksell's discussion of monetary equilibrium to a progressive economy? In an earlier article, published in 1956, entitled 'Changes in productivity and the price level in a closed economy', Gilbert maintained that the different conclusions stemmed from different assumptions:

> The most favourable assumptions for Wicksell are that productivity
> increases at the same rate in all industries and demand conditions are such
> that the resulting increased supplies of the various commodities constitute
> an equilibrium output; relative prices remain unchanged. . . . With
> imperfect foresight and different rates of technological progress,
> Davidson's policy would cause less disturbance than Wicksell's.[15]

But Robertson did not assume different rates of technological progress. Instead, he advanced two arguments. First, the equity argument was, with diffidence, put forward: people on fixed incomes should be allowed to benefit from economic progress. To counter this proposal Samuelson suggested the provision of a pay-as-you-go bond system which could be purchased by the public. Second, the economic argument: if increasing productivity were due to organizational improvements rather than increased factor supplies, then an increase in the money supply would result in forced savings and a redistribution of income to entrepreneurs. But, as Gilbert noted in his 1956 article, and Samuelson observed in his 1963 obituary notice on Robertson, there may be a rate of fall in the price level which will give rate of return on money which is higher than the rate of return on capital and this is not tenable. And, finally, Hayek's criticisms of Wicksell were found to be based upon a lack of explicit assumptions in Hayek's analysis: 'if he [Hayek] had used the same expectations assumption in his discussion of Wicksell as in his analysis of a producer's credit inflation he would have been less critical of Wicksell.'[16]

Gilbert also set limits to the movement of the price level before the monetary system breaks down.

> If a rate of rise in the price level is assumed which reduces the net advantages of holding money to zero, the advantages of convenience being offset by the disadvantages of an asset depreciating in real terms at the assumed rate, no money is held.[17]

> If a rate of fall in the price level is assumed which eliminates the net advantages of using money for transactions because the appreciation of money in real terms at the assumed rate offsets the inconveniences of doing without the medium of exchange, no money is spent.[18]

Although formally correct Gilbert's analysis overlooks the tremendous gains from using a monetary system rather than barter. What seems more plausible is that in the event of a breakdown it is not the monetary system which breaks but the money-thing. There would be a substitution of one kind of money for another in order to retain the advantages of a monetary system.

In 1934 Gilbert dealt with the problem of an increase in autonomous saving mediated through the banking system and in 1956 and 1957 he returned to the general problems of productivity advance and the price level. There remained one unresolved issue and it was one which had a bearing upon the efficiency of the Keynesian investment multiplier (as well as having affinities with the underconsumptionist literature). The problem: what should be the appropriate policy when there is technological progress in the capital goods sector and there is a lag in the output of consumer goods? If resources move to the capital goods sector then resource owners will receive increases in incomes and will seek to purchase consumer goods. Given the time lag in the production of consumer goods then there will be inflation and forced saving. Of course, the problem can be resolved by drawing upon stocks of consumer goods if they exist and in an open economy it might be possible to increase imports and run a temporary deficit. (These two possibilities provide a link with Hicks's discussion of the multiplier in which he raised the question of whether there would be a net expansion of employment as a result of a housebuilding programme. Housebuilding requires bricks and if there are no surplus stocks of bricks then there can be no housebuilding.)

Another possibility, the fiscal alternative, is that consumers are given credits (enhanced because of the waiting) which they can spend when the consumer goods become available. But in the absence of a fiscal alternative and on the assumption that technological change is mediated through the banking system then, as the real interest rate rises, the money rate and the price levels must move so as to persuade consumers to postpone purchases.

The 1934, 1938, 1956 and 1957 articles were important contributions to the analysis of neutral money and supply-side economics.

Capital, growth and the traverse

Gilbert's paper contained a fudge; in a footnote he explained that he was assuming that the growth in output was consumed and did not become part of the capital stock. But about the same time that Gilbert was writing, the capital controversy broke out anew and its outcome was to prove fatal to the Austrian theory of capital.

The starting point was Harrod's 1934 article on the expansion of credit in an advancing economy (Harrod, 1934a). In that article Harrod took the view that the Hayek–Keynes controversy of 1931–2 could not be settled in the context of a short-run model, but had to be considered in the context of a dynamic economy. In effect, he resurrected the Wicksell–Davidson controversy but in doing so he introduced the idea of examining the concept of equilibrium in terms of the savings–investment mechanism. Harrod's paper was commented upon by Robertson but was then temporarily submerged under the Keynesian avalanche until Harrod set out to dynamize the Keynesian model.

In the later Harrod model equilibrium was defined in terms of two conditions: first, the savings–investment relationship, and second, the full employment requirement. Savings were then assumed to be determined by the marginal save out of income:

$$S_t = sY_t.$$

Investment was then assumed to be determined by the rate of growth of income:

$$v(Y_t - Y_{t-1}).$$

Hence the condition for equilibrium in the market for goods was:

$$K_t = K_{t+1} - K_t = v(Y_t - Y_{t-1}) = sY_t$$

where K denotes the capital stock.

In the labour market it was assumed that the labour supply (population) grew autonomously and that there was a problem of matching labour supply (L_s) to labour demand (L_d):

$$L_d = L_s$$

Harrod then considered three possible growth paths: an actual growth path, g_a; a warranted growth path which was dictated by savings and technology, g_w; and a desired growth path, g^*.

In Harrod's growth model it was only by chance that the actual growth path dictated by savings and investment would guarantee full employment. Indeed, as a result of the manner in which the model was constructed the economy was conceived of as balanced on a knife-edge equilibrium. If savings were greater than investment then the economy would decline as incomes fell. If investment were greater than savings then the economy would expand continuously. And it was the knife-edge instability of the model that prompted some economists to look for methods of introducing stability — and in doing so they precipitated the capital controversy. Thus, Solow (1957) sought to introduce stability and full employment by inserting a neo-classical production function which allowed for substitutability of labour and capital in response to changing factor prices. In effect, Solow argued that instability was a result of fixed savings and capital–output coefficients and rigidities of factor prices.

Solow's paper produced a reaction from Joan Robinson who challenged the basis of the neo-classical production function by asking how capital was to be measured. In her work on growth, especially *The Accumulation of Capital* (Robinson, 1957) she received a great deal of support from Piero Sraffa, who had challenged Hayek's ideas in the 1930s, and from R.F. Kahn, who had been a pioneer of Keynesian economics. About the same time Kaldor also produced a growth model which had similarities with that developed by Robinson and which also attacked Solow's neoclassical production function.

The essence of the Robinson–Kaldor attack was that once a move was made from the Harrod model then the capital measurement problem had to be addressed. In Harrod's model the problem of capital measurement was locked away in the capital–output ratio where it was taken as given and no substitution between labour and capital was permitted. However, capital was heterogeneous and some method of valuation had to be introduced in order to render it homogeneous. The obvious method was to use a discount factor in order to measure the various income streams. But, in terms of the production function, the discount factor could not be known until the stock of capital was given. In effect both the capital stock and the discount rate had to be simultaneously solved. This argument contained echoes of Knight's criticisms of capital theory which were mentioned in Chapter 5. However, Robinson and Kaldor went further and argued that there was no simple monotonic relationship between the capital stock and the rate of interest. This was the switching issue which was initially considered to be a curiosum and later was recognized to be a fundamental criticism of capital theory.

The switching problem can best be appreciated by means of an example used by Samuelson in his 1966 summing up of the capital controversy. It is assumed that a commodity can be produced in three years by means of technique A or technique B. Technique A employs 7 units of labour in period 2 and technique B uses 2 units of labour in period 1 followed by 6 units of labour in period 3. Both techniques are assumed to be profitable if the rate of interest is either 50 per cent or 100 per cent. This result follows from the fact that the roots of the quadratic equation:

$$7(1 + r) = 2(1 + r)^2 + 6$$

has two roots 0.5 and 1.00. At rates of interest above 100 per cent, A is more profitable than B because 2 units of labour compounded for 2 years plus 6 units of uncompounded labour will be greater than 7 units of labour compounded for 1 year. But at rates of interest above 100 per cent, technique B's use of 6 units of labour in the current period means that the interest bill is less. When the interest rate falls below 50 per cent then it becomes profitable to switch techniques. In effect the switching phenomenon occurs because production processes which use inputs that are staggered over time will yield multiple rates of return.

What does the switching problem imply for the Austrian theory of capital? In the case of the homogeneous capital model the outcome of the switching debate was fatal. But what of Hayek's disaggregated capital model? In an article on the surrogate production function Samuelson (1962) attempted to demonstrate that information on capital, labour and output derived from an economy of heterogeneous capital goods can be regarded as if it were derived from a world of malleable capital; therefore a heterogeneous capital structure is an irrelevance. Samuelson postulated a two-sector economy in which a single consumer good and a single capital good are produced by means of non-reproducible labour and a single produced capital good both of which are combined in fixed proportions. He then assumed that there were a large number of fixed proportions techniques and that the problem was to choose the most efficient given the wage rate or the interest rate. This can be illustrated using trade-off curves (Figure 10.3) for each sector between the real wage and the interest rate. The resulting straight lines will then intersect on the assumption that there are fixed proportions and the same proportions are employed in both sectors. No matter how many capital goods and techniques there are there will be as many straight lines and they will slope downwards. The envelope of the straight lines will

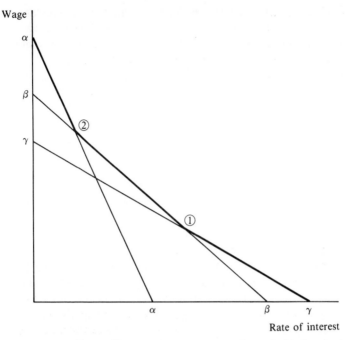

Note: At points ① and ② two techniques are equally profitable but as the interest rate changes one technique becomes less profitable. As the number of techniques increases the envelope (thick black line) loses its kinks and becomes a smooth convex production function.

Figure 10.3 The surrogate production function.

then form a factor–price frontier whose slope along any segment measures the capital–labour ratio and whose elasticity measures the relative shares of capital and labour in the national income.

Unfortunately the surrogate production function assumed that the ratio of capital to labour was the same in all sectors – an assumption that was as realistic as Marx's assumption that organic compositions of capital were everywhere equal. Two further points need to be noted. First, heterogeneity of output may be as important as heterogeneity of capital. Second, there is a contrast between capital which is bought outright and labour which is merely hired. If capital were hired then it is possible that the amount of capital in use could rise or fall without any change in the rate of interest.

How important is the switching issue? Samuelson conceded the logical validity of the argument but doubted its empirical relevance. And in the case of Hayek and the later 'Austrian' writers the position seems to be that they never accepted the idea of capital being homogeneous and they would not accept Samuelson's attempt to reduce heterogeneous capital to malleable capital on the grounds that that was the heresy that J.B. Clark perpetrated. Nevertheless, many Cambridge writers, including Kaldor, were able to use the switching debate to reject Solow's argument that the production function expressed a mere technical relationship. In doing so they revived some of the ideas that Sraffa had used in his criticisms of Hayek in the early 1930s.

Growth and distribution

One way round the problems posed by the switching issue was advanced by Kaldor (and a similar line of analysis was charted by Joan Robinson). He rejected the notion of a production function and made the distribution of income a matter of bargaining subject to two conditions. First, wages could not fall below the subsistence level. Second, profits could not fall below the premium necessary to overcome risk and imperfections in product markets. However, within these limits the distribution of income was left to bargaining. Investment was then considered to be influenced by a variety of factors which were summarized in the expression 'animal spirits' of the entrepreneurs. And given the amount of investment that entrepreneurs sought to carry out then the task of pricing policy was to add a mark-up to wages which would then yield the product price and the amount of savings required to finance that investment. Thus, Kaldor brought to bear several influences from the intense discussions of the interwar years. First, there was the investment–savings relationship which was not influenced in any direct way by the rate of interest. Second, there was the dependence of income shares upon bargaining which was derived from Kalecki (who had spent a brief spell at the LSE) and from Sraffa. Third, there was the rejection of an aggregate measure of capital which stemmed from his own criticisms of Hayek's work as well as the discussions which took place at Cambridge in the 1950s.

The Keynesian links are apparent if we consider an economy without technical change and operating at full employment. If investment tended to exceed savings then incomes would rise and that would cause prices to rise and bring about a shift of income towards profits. If savings exceeded investment then incomes would fall (by means of the multiplier process) until savings were equal to investment. There was therefore no place for a production function and an aggregate measure of capital. And the attack on the production function continued in Kaldor's discussion of an economy experiencing technical change. He argued that it

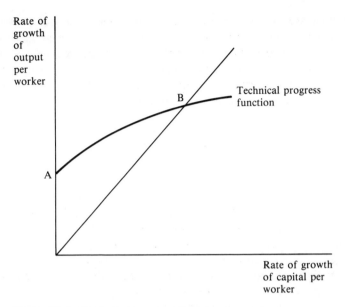

Figure 10.4 Technical progress function.

was difficult to distinguish between movements along an isoquant in response to changing factor prices and shifts of isoquants due to technical change. In a growing economy technical change was likely and Kaldor captured its effects by means of a technical progress function which related the rate of growth of output per worker to the rate of growth of capital per worker (Figure 10.4). The position of the technical progress function would depend upon the rate of technical progress and its shape would depend upon the degree to which capital accumulation embodied new techniques which incorporated labour productivity. Changes in the rate of flow of new ideas would then lead to shifts in the curve. Thus, at point A it may be assumed that technical change had shifted the curve upwards and this would then lead to capital accumulation until equilibrium was reached at B.

Hicks and Gilbert on the trade cycle and growth

In 1949 Hicks attempted to construct a model of the trade cycle which was based upon the work of Samuelson and Harrod. Samuelson produced a typology of possible trade cycle fluctuations based upon interactions of the multiplier and the accelerator but left open the question of which was the most appropriate combination of values for the multiplier and the accelerator. Harrod produced a model of the trade cycle and also a model of growth in which the main characteristic was that there were weak booms. This meant that some external agency was required to provide an impetus to the cycle. In contrast Hicks produced a model in which there were high values for the multiplier and the accelerator and which produced therefore an explosive model of income movements. To provide a cycle Hicks then introduced a floor of autonomous investment and a ceiling set by the growth of the labour force. In the boom the economy would be carried up to the ceiling but once the economy hit the ceiling then it could not grow at a rate greater than the increase in labour supplies. Hence demand would fall and that would cause the economy to turn down and be carried to the floor by the movement of autonomous investment. The model contained no reference to monetary factors on the upswing where there was a reliance upon real forces – although, presumably, the money supply must have been allowed to expand in response to demand. However monetary factors were permitted to complicate the slump where Hicks referred to risk and liquidity.

Hicks's model prompted criticisms from some economists. Both Kaldor and Knox were critical of the reliance upon the accelerator. Robertson also pointed to the fact that autonomous investment was used to promote growth and there was no recognition of the fact that autonomous investment might itself be subject to fluctuations. Lachmann was also critical of Hicks's model on the grounds that it was extremely aggregative in character and that Hicks was forced to concede that the ceiling might not be reached because there were bottlenecks in particular sectors. This last point marked an implicit concession to Austrian thinking. But Hicks's conclusion was that the collapse of the 1930s was a collapse of real forces which impinged upon a 'monetary situation which was quite unexceptionally unstable.'[19] The monetary overinvestment theory of the trade cycle was therefore rejected. Subsequently, in 'The Hayek story' Hicks (1967b: 203–15) went further and argued that the Hayek model failed to explain secondary deflation:

> It is in its application to deflationary slumps that the Hayek theory is at its worst; and it is a terrible fact that it was in just such conditions – in 1931–2 – that it was first propounded. In such conditions its diagnosis was wrong; and its prescriptions could not have been worse.[20]

However Hicks was prepared to concede a Hayek slump might occur at the end of a period of rapid inflation and he thought that such conditions might have been developing in the late 1960s. In other words, Hicks was prepared to conceive of an upper turning point being produced along the lines charted by Hayek – but he was not prepared to accept Hayek's explanation of the downturn and lower turning point of the cycle.

However, the main thrust of Hicks's article 'The Hayek story', was that the model required a consumption lag, and, as such, was more relevant to an economy in which there was an increase in real savings. Hayek responded with his article 'Three elucidations of the Ricardo effect' (1969) which Hicks chose to ignore.

In 1955 Gilbert attempted to rehabilitate Hayek's theory of the trade cycle and to provide an explanation of increasing unemployment which was compatible with Hayek's assumptions and did not assume the presence of wage rigidities and liquidity traps. He accepted the fact that Hayek had only provided an explanation of the upper turning point and that it was not the only possible explanation because there might be underconsumption rather than overinvestment. He therefore thought that progress might be made through attempting to test the two rival hypotheses concerning the upper turning point, and producing a synthesis of the work of Hayek and Keynes (there was an echo of Durbin's attempt to reconcile Keynes's *Treatise on Money* with Hayek's *Prices and Production*). Two aspects of Gilbert's article are therefore worth noting. First, Sraffa had criticized Hayek for assuming that the end of the boom would lead to the destruction of capital values. Sraffa suggested that the capitalists would be left with their machines whereas the workers would have nothing. Echoing Robertson, Gilbert suggested a compromise: machines might still be used as long as they covered their prime costs. Second, Hayek had failed to indicate why the end of the boom should necessarily result in unemployment; this was the Durbin asymmetry problem and Gilbert suggested that resources might be more mobile when the money supply was increasing than when it was constant or contracting. In other words, Gilbert pointed to the possibility of money illusion. Gilbert's paper was read originally at the 1955 meeting of the British Association for the Advancement of Science which was held in Liverpool. It was received in silence; such was the grip that the *General Theory* had upon academic thinking despite the fact that the UK economy was then experiencing inflation.

Hicks on the traverse

At the Corfu conference on capital theory, at which Solow had suggested that the production function was about technical relationships, Hicks also had an interchange with Sraffa about the nature of capital. However, it was not until the publication of the second edition the *Theory of Wages* (1963) that he began to spell out his views on capital and growth. He drew a distinction between materialists and fundists. It was a distinction which had been implicit in the 1930s when he intervened in a controversy over the maintenance of capital between Hayek and Pigou. Materialists, according to Hicks, were those who represented capital in a physical form whereas fundists depicted capital in value terms. Both approaches, thought Hicks, had their place in economics. The materialist approach was useful in empirical work, in estimating, for example, national income per head at a point of time. The materialist approach was essentially a static approach. In contrast, capital viewed as a fund was more appropriate to problems of growth. Unfortunately, Hicks then went on, in later writings, to classify economists according to the approach they used:

> Not only Adam Smith, but all (or nearly all) of the British Classical Economists were Fundists; so was Marx (how else should he have invented 'Capitalism'?) so was Jevons. It was after 1870 that there was a Materialist Revolution. It was not the same as the Marginalist Revolution; for some of the marginalists, such as Jevons and Böhm-Bawerk kept the Fundist flag flying. But most economists, in England and America, went materialist. Materialism, indeed, is characteristic of what is nowadays reckoned to be the 'neoclassical' position. Not only Cannan, but Marshall and Pigou and J.B. Clark, were clearly Materialists. Anyone, indeed, who uses a Production Function, in which Product is shown as a function of labour, capital and technology, supposed separable, confesses himself to be (at least while he is using it) a Materialist.[21]

Hayek was regarded as a 'very sophisticated Fundist'. But the assignments seemed to be strained and even Hicks was forced to make concessions: 'there was at least an American Fundist, F.W. Taussig. Irving Fisher is harder to place, since he, at least sometimes, would see both sides.' Even Jevons in the quotation above could 'see both sides':

> Keynes . . . was brought up as a Materialist, and there are no more than slight signs in the *General Theory*, that he had departed from the Materialist position. So it is perfectly possible to be a Keynesian and yet be a Materialist. But the rethinking of capital theory and of growth theory, which followed from Keynes, and from Harrod on Keynes, led to a revival of Fundism. If the Production Function is a hallmark of modern materialism the capital–output ratio is a hallmark of modern Fundism.[22]

There were other aspects of Hicks's work that called for revision and reappraisal in the light of developments in economic analysis. In the *Theory of Wages* he had classified inventions as either autonomous or induced. Autonomous inventions were not the result of changes in factor prices whereas induced inventions were a response to such changes. However, Hicks had failed to clarify the relationship between induced inventions and substitution along a given isoquant. *Value and Capital* came in for reappraisal because he came to believe that the temporary equilibrium method obscured many aspects of dynamic economics. And a similar verdict was made by him on the *ISLM* diagram.

Capital and Growth represented an intermediate step in Hicks's thoughts on growth theory. It involved a catching up and appraisal of the work of others who had pioneered while he had been engaged in development economics and in writing his *A Revision of Demand Theory* (Hicks, 1956a). The first part of *Capital and Growth* set out an historical review of previous work on growth theory and contained references to Adam Smith, Ricardo, Marshall, Lindahl and Keynes. It drew attention to the problems of defining equilibrium in dynamic economics: 'In statics, equilibrium is fundamental; in dynamics as we shall find, we cannot do without it; but even in statics it is treacherous, and in dynamics, unless we are very careful it will trip us up.'[23] Such an equilibrium required that expectations were appropriate to it and the initial capital stock was appropriate to it; 'both conditions', he stressed, 'are necessary.' But having noted that in dynamics we must give up the notion of a homogeneous capital stock he tended to ignore heterogeneity and the problems of malinvestment.

The historical review also led Hicks to draw attention to a shift in the nature of price fixing arrangements between Marshall's *Principles* and Keynes's *General Theory*. In Marshall's day prices were flexible and were set by merchants but nowadays prices were fixed by manufacturers. The move to fix prices meant that the temporary equilibrium method which Lindahl had pioneered and Hicks had used in *Value and Capital* was no longer useful: 'The fundamental weakness of the Temporary Equilibrium method is the assumption, which it is obliged to make, that the market is in equilibrium – actual demand equals desired demand, actual supply equals desired supply – even in the very short period.'[24]

In *Capital and Time* (1973) Hicks's thoughts on growth and capital theory were brought together in a discussion of the traverse from one equilibrium growth path to another. It was for such a problem, in which there are vertical displacements in the production process, that he believed that Austrian theory came into its own. Indeed, he had already stated that:

> The Hayek Theory is not a theory of the credit cycle, the Konjunktur, which need not work out in the way he describes, nor is it, in fact, at all likely to do so. It is an analysis – a very interesting analysis – of the adjustment of an economy to changes in the rate of saving. In that direction it does make a real contribution which, when it was made, was made out of time. It does not belong to the theory of fluctuations which

was the centre of economists' attention in the 1930s; it is a forerunner of the growth theory of more recent years.[25]

Hicks assumed that there were fully integrated activities which applied 'original factors of production' at various points of time and which gave rise to a later stream of outputs. For ease of exposition he assumed that homogeneous labour produced a homogeneous consumer good and that new activities were being added continuously and that old ones were continually being abandoned. New activities would be chosen so as to maximize the difference between the present values of planned input and output streams with the length of any activity being determined by the discounted value of extra output from the lengthening of a production process being less than the discounted value of the additional inputs required. Figure 10.5 illustrates the typical time profile of inputs and outputs. Initially, there is a construction period in which there is a high level of inputs and this is followed by a period of low inputs and high outputs. If the consumption good is chosen as the numeraire then the wage and interest rate have to be determined. Hicks also adopted the notion of a week and assumed that instead of inputs and outputs flowing continuously they would occur at specific points of time.

Assuming that the process lasted $n+1$ weeks and that a's ($a_1, a_2, \ldots a_n$) were inputs of labour, that b's ($b_1, b_2, \ldots b_n$) were outputs and q's ($q_1, q_2, \ldots q_n$) represented flows of net output in terms of the consumer good then the discounted value of a process of t weeks would be:

$$k_t = q_1 + q_{t+1}R^{-1} + q_n R^{-(n-t)}$$

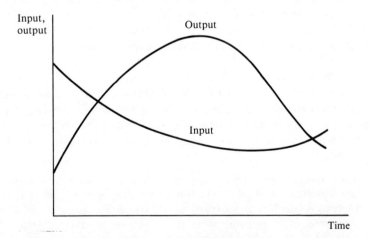

Figure 10.5 The production process profile.

with $R = 1 + r$. Hicks then demonstrated that such an activity could not be shortened whenever there was a rise in the interest rate.

Hicks then began from an equilibrium situation in which the discounted value of a process was zero and there was therefore no gain from starting up another process. In other words, the market for funds was at all times in equilibrium with the rate of return equal to the market rate and any fall in the rate of interest would be offset by a rise in the wage. Hence, it would be possible to draw up an efficiency frontier for any technique. The envelope curve for all the techniques available would then yield the efficiency curve of the technology. At any point in time the level of activity would be determined by the level of employment of labour and the output of the consumer good and in steady state growth savings and investment would be equal.

This then brings us to Hicks's discussion of the traverse from equilibrium growth path to another and for the analysis of which he emphasized the usefulness of the Austrian approach to capital theory. Suppose there is an invention which makes it possible to produce more consumption goods profitably. In order to realize all the gains it would be necessary for the invention to be embodied in new machines and therefore there would have to be investment. Of course there would have been some investment in the absence of the invention and so what occurs is a switch in the nature of investment. But the transformation of the economy does not take place overnight and for some time the rest of the economy will be using old machines. However, the invention will release resources and in order for the double equilibrium conditions of full employment and savings equal to investment those resources will have to be absorbed. There is a further problem. With an increase in output there will be a rise in wages which could check the expansion of the new technique because a rising real wage would lower the profit rate. This could be prevented by the emergence of induced inventions which were not previously profitable but which the change in factor prices could bring into creation.

Capital and Time and its elaborations in *Economic Perspectives* (1977) and *Methods of Dynamic Analysis* (1978) represented Hicks's attempts to present an Austrian approach to growth theory but it was a presentation which rejected the Austrian emphasis upon monetary disturbances:

> The relevance to economic fluctuations of the time structure of production was the discovery of Professor Hayek; that there is such a relevance our present analysis confirms. . . . To have drawn attention to vertical displacements was a major contribution; it is due to Professor Hayek.
>
> Where (I may as well emphasize here) I do not go along with him (or with what he said in 1931) is in his view that the disturbances in question

have a monetary origin. He had not emancipated himself from the delusion (common to many economists, even the greatest economists) that with money removed 'in the state of barter' everything would somehow fit. One of my objects in writing this book has been to kill that delusion. It could not arise because the theory of the barter economy had been insufficiently worked out. There has been no money in my model; yet it has plenty of adjustment difficulties. It is not true that by getting rid of money one is automatically in 'equilibrium' – whether that equilibrium is conceived of as a stationary state (Wicksell), perfect foresight economy (Hayek) or any kind of steady state. Monetary disorders may indeed be superimposed upon other disorders; but the other disorders are more fundamental.[26]

Summary and conclusions

In the postwar period economists who had been at the LSE in the 1930s sought to produce a synthesis of their ideas and those of Keynes and then to elaborate those ideas in order to take account of growth. Thus, Gilbert sought to classify the motives for holding money under the headings of time and uncertainty. And with the introduction of money into an economy there was a simultaneous determination of the money rate of interest and the price level. Building upon Robertson's work Tsiang sought to provide a reconciliation of the loanable funds and liquidity preference theories of the rate of interest. Gilbert took up the question of the behaviour of the price level and equilibrium in an economy undergoing productivity change. In doing so he clarified many of the issues raised by Wicksell, Davidson, Hayek and Harrod.

Interest in money and growth was complemented by a renewed interest in the real forces operating on an economy in the medium and long term. Hicks produced a model of the trade cycle in which change and fluctuations were due to real disturbances and he carried his analysis further by analyzing the movements from one equilibrium growth path to another by means of the Austrian approach to capital theory.

Notes

1. Gilbert, J.C. (1953), 'The demand for money: the development of an economic concept', *Journal of Political Economy*, 64: 144–6.
2. op. cit., p. 151.
3. op. cit., p. 147.
4. op. cit., p. 147.
5. Sargeant, D. (1988), *The Times*, 13 April, p. 12.

6. Hicks, J.R. (1967b), *Critical Essays on Monetary Theory*, Oxford: Oxford University Press, p. 25.
7. op. cit., p. 57.
8. Hicks, J.R. (1979), *Causality in Economics*, Oxford: Blackwell, p. 34.
9. Robertson, D.H. (1940), *Essays in Monetary Economics*, London, P.S. King, p. 14.
10. Quoted in J.M. Keynes (1936, 1973), *The Collected Writings of John Maynard Keynes*, Vol. VII, *The General Theory of Employment, Interest and Money*, London: Macmillan, p. 186.
11. op. cit., p. 186 fnl.
12. Keynes, J.M. (1973), *Collected Writings*, Vol. XIV, *The General Theory and After: Part II, Defence and Development*, p. 68.
13. op. cit., p. 87.
14. Robertson, D.H. (1940), *Essays in Monetary Economics*, p. 56.
15. Gilbert, J.C. (1955), 'Changes in productivity and the price level in a closed economy', *Yorkshire Bulletin of Economic and Social Research*, 8.
16. op. cit., p. 67.
17. Gilbert, J.C. (1957), 'The compatibility of any behaviour of the price level with equilibrium' *Review of Economic Studies*, 24: 182.
18. op. cit., p. 180.
19. Hicks, J.R. (1950), *The Trade Cycle*, Oxford: Oxford University Press, p. 145.
20. Hicks, J.R. (1967b), *Critical Essays on Monetary Theory*, p. 89.
21. Hicks, J.R. (1973), *Capital and Time*, Oxford: Clarendon, p. 115.
22. op. cit., p. 58.
23. op. cit., p. 32.
24. op. cit., p. 46.
25. op. cit., p. 112.
26. op. cit., p. 114.

11
The road from serfdom

Introduction

In 1946 Hayek could consider that he and Keynes were the most well-known economists in the world. Two things then happened. Keynes died and was immediately canonized whereas Hayek found himself discredited for having transgressed the boundaries of his discipline by writing a political tract, *The Road to Serfdom*. There followed three decades in the wilderness until economic circumstances changed and politicians, who as Keynes foresaw were: 'Practical men, who believe themselves to be quite exempt from any intellectual influences, are usually the slaves of some defunct economist. Madmen in authority, who hear voices in the air, are distilling their frenzy from some academic scribble of a few years back.'[1] On 5 February 1981 Mrs Thatcher, speaking in the House of Commons said: 'I am a great admirer of Professor Hayek. Some of his books – *The Constitution of Liberty* and the three volumes of *Law, Legislation and Liberty* – would well be read by some honourable members.'[2] What follows therefore is to examine the content of Hayek's ideas and to consider the extent to which they influenced the Thatcher Administration and to account for differences between policy and precept.

The Chicago programme

The Road to Serfdom was written to counteract the popular view that fascism and socialism were different; that fascism was a capitalist reaction to socialism. On the contrary, urged Hayek, fascism and socialism were both manifestations of a drive towards totalitarianism – of a movement towards regulating economic and social activity in order to free people. But free people for what asked Hayek. To Hayek both ideologies threatened to reduce liberty of the individual and restore serfdom. The book met with a mixed reception in England. Barbara Wooton thought that Hayek had overstated his case and that there had been no serious infringement of liberty.[3] Keynes thought that it was a grand book but qualified his remark by suggesting that what was wanted was not less planning but more planning.[4] It was disliked by William Beveridge. Beveridge was the author of a plan on social security, the Beveridge Plan, which was the foundation stone of the welfare state. He was also the author of *Full Employment in a Free Society* (1944) which was a popular account of Keynesian economics but, in addition, contained an appendix, written by Nicholas Kaldor, which set out a detailed plan of how to maintain full employment in the postwar period. Finally, Beveridge was the Director of the London School of Economics where Hayek was a professor. However, the book was widely acclaimed in the United States and received the highest accolade – condensation in the *Reader's Digest*. It was the beginning of the Cold War and lecture tours were arranged. But to the hostile political climate must be added pressing financial problems which led him to apply for a post at Chicago in 1944. In 1949 Hayek resigned from the LSE and went to the University of Arkansas. In 1950 he moved to a Chair of Moral and Social Sciences at the University of Chicago.

At Chicago Hayek was delivered from the narrow specialisms of the LSE and recaptured the heady atmosphere of his undergraduate and postgraduate days in Vienna where he mixed with philosophers, biologists and scientists. And although many of the ideas he pursued at Chicago had their origins in earlier discussions, there is a sense in which his writings at Chicago set out in a coherent and comprehensive manner his views on the workings of a liberal society. It contained very little on monetary economics because he was preoccupied with the framework within which such issues as unemployment and inflation could be discussed. Moreover, inflation did not become a serious issue until the 1970s. Even the fierce controversy over capital theory with which he had been engaged with Knight had died down and Knight, a colleague of Chicago could endorse the general thesis of *The Road to Serfdom* that:

> general replacement of the free-market organized by a predominance of centralized political control will mean the destruction of democracy and freedom and the establishment of a totalitarian social order. This seems as certain as any general political prediction can be, which of course is not comparable to the status of established scientific laws, to say nothing of logical necessity. [And] what is essential to freedom is the preservation of

the open market in the major part of the field, as the only possible method for setting basic standards of values and efficiency and providing an incentive and improvement.[5]

Knight did not confuse an open market economy with *laissez-faire* but he did observe that 'the great danger to freedom was that people might feel that they enjoyed more freedom under a dictatorship than they might expect under the disorderly processes of democracy and free enterprise.'[6]

In 1951 he published *John Stuart Mill and Harriet Taylor: their Friendship and Subsequent Marriage* in which he explored the idea that Harriet Taylor was responsible for turning Mill's mind to socialism. Between 1942 and 1944 he had published a three-part article on 'Scientism and society' in *Economica* and in 1952 it was published in book form under the title *The Counter Revolution of Science* (1952a). A foray into psychology resulted in *The Sensory Order* (1952b) which contained an elaboration of ideas which had been first mooted in the 1920s. In 1954 he edited *Capitalism and the Historians* which attempted to counter the popular view that living standards had deteriorated in the early decades of the Industrial Revolution. But the main achievement of his period at Chicago was *The Constitution of Liberty* (1960) which was 'a restatement of the basic principles of a philosophy of freedom'. Then in 1962 Hayek returned to Europe as professor of economic policy at the University of Freiburg. During his six year period in the chair he produced an important collection of papers entitled *Studies in Philosophy, Politics and Economics* (1967) and in 1976 a second edition, *New Studies in Philosophy, Politics and Economics* was published (1976a). Becoming professor emeritus in 1968 he accepted an invitation from the University of Salzburg where he began work on his three-volume *Law, Legislation and Liberty* the first volume of which was published in 1973. In 1974 he was awarded a Nobel Prize in Economics. In 1989 he produced a further critique entitled *The Fatal Conceit*.

In examining Hayek's research programme it has to be recognized, at the onset, that Hayek has been participating in one of the historic controversies in philosophies between the empiricists – best represented by Locke, Berkeley, Hume and Adam Ferguson – and the continental rationalist philosophers, represented by Descarte, Leibniz and Rousseau. To these two groups of thinkers Hayek adds the influence of Kant, Mach, Wittgenstein and Popper in order to produce the Chicago programme of thought and action which is set out in the following propositions:

1. The brain cannot know itself.
2. Phenomena can be classified as simple, can be made simple or are complex.

3. Explanation may be in detail or in principle. Refutation may be difficult.
4. Most social phenomena are complex; they are not the product of design but represent the unintended consequences of people's actions.
5. Central planning cannot handle the knowledge of particular circumstances and time.
6. Statute law cannot deal with the knowledge of particular circumstances and time. Therefore, it should not discriminate.
7. Social justice is a mirage.
8. There is a possible conflict between our moral values which were developed in small face-to-face groups and the operations of markets which require impersonal conduct. The case for markets is that not only do they provide for freedom of choice but they are the only form of social organization which can support a larger number of people at a high standard of living.
9. Democracy is the best form of achieving peaceful change of government but suffers from the tyranny of the single representative assembly and interest groups. These defects can be overcome by a properly constituted two – or three – chamber system.
10. Liberty is the means by which we can expand our knowledge but it does not guarantee automatically greater happiness.
11. Markets should, as far as possible, be deregulated in order to improve their efficiency. However, liberalism should not be confused with *laissez-faire*.

The brain cannot know itself

In *The Sensory Order* Hayek provided a bridgehead between the philosophical ideas derived from earlier writers and his critique of planning and socialism (indeed the book contained references to 'Scientism and Society'). It also formed the basis for his subsequently elaborated views on liberty and justice. As with Kant, Hayek viewed the brain, not as a passive, but an active mechanism which classified phenomena encountered by the senses. In other words, the world is viewed not as a series of isolated facts but as a series of orders which have been constructed by the mind itself. Hayek, then, distinguished two facts which account for our knowledge. First, there is the physical world of which each individual's knowledge is imperfect and fragmentary and about which we have no direct evidence but can reconstruct it partially. Second, there is the mental order of sensations about which we may never be able to establish all the relationships which determine its order.

The neural order, as in Kant's analysis, is a means by which we classify information and, unlike Hume, we do not first have sensations which are committed to memory but, instead, the physiological impulses are converted into sensations. Furthermore, Hayek rejected Hume's theory of associations on the grounds that associationism 'is not something additional to the appearances of mental qualities, nor something which acts upon given quantities – it is rather the factor which determines the qualities'.[7] But again, in contrast to Kant, Hayek assumed that the mind can undergo a process of evolution.

Hayek therefore rejected behaviourism in favour of subjectivism. That is to say, he did not accept that mental events or states can be understood as physical processes and that all statements can be reduced to empirical phenomena. Finally, Hayek's theory of knowledge contained an argument which emphasizes the limitations of knowledge and which contains implications for the debate over planning and markets. In a nutshell, any classificatory system must possess a structure of higher order complexity than is possessed by the objects which it classifies. Hence, it followed that the brain can only explain the operations of an order of lower complexity but it cannot explain itself. In the end there must be some things which must be taken as given; there can be no reductionism. On this point Hayek is an agreement with Hume in emphasizing the limits of reason.

Classification, explanation and refutation

Simple phenomena may involve a few variables and are encountered in classical mechanics. Phenomena which *can be made* simple can be so arranged through the use of statistical techniques which involve the use of averages and measures of dispersion. Complex phenomena cannot be so ordered and are characteristic of social phenomena. And it follows from the classification of phenomena that simple phenomena may be explained in detail whereas complex phenomena may only be explained in principle. Hence, detailed explanations may be possible in some of the natural sciences but not in most of the social sciences.

The nature of the classification and explanation also have a bearing upon the testing of hypotheses. Popper's refutation test may be applicable only to simple phenomena. In *The Poverty of Historicism* (1944) Popper was prepared to concede this point but, unfortunately, the point was overlooked by economists in the 1960s. What happened was that it was Hutchison's brand of positivism which was adopted by most economists. Thus, Friedman in his book, *Essays in Positive Economics* (1950) attacked monopolistic competition for its lack of predictions and suggested that the theory of perfect competition had been tested on numerous occasions. Now perfect competition is an example of a phenomena which can only be explained in principle because the amount of knowledge required to describe a market in detail would be horrendous — especially when we would have to take into account possible (unknown) entrants to markets. Unfortunately, Friedman never produced any examples of tests of the competitive model. In his book, *Introduction to Positive Economics* (1963), Lipsey pointed to the lack of tests of economic theories but he provided no statement of how we might proceed in those circumstances where there might be errors of observation.

Spontaneous order

Throughout his writings Hayek has emphasized that social phenomena, complex phenomena, may be characterized by spontaneous order. Borrowing, with approval from Adam Ferguson, he has observed that they are the product of accident rather than design. In 'Scientism and the study of society' he cited the example of a path through 'wild broken country':

> It is only in the very simplest instances that it can be shown briefly and without any technical apparatus how the independent actions of individuals will produce an order which is no part of their intentions; and in those instances the explanation is usually so obvious that we never stop to examine the type of argument which leads to it. The way in which tracks are formed in a wild broken country is such an instance. At first everyone will seek for himself what seems to be the best path. But the fact that such a path has been used once is likely to make it easier to traverse and therefore more likely to be used again; and thus gradually more and more clearly defined tracks arise and come to be used to the exclusion of other possible ways. Human movements through the district come to conform to a definite pattern which, although the result of the deliberate decisions of many people, has yet not been consciously designed by anyone.[8]

Central planning cannot cope with the knowledge of particular circumstance and place

The most complex social phenomena include those concerned with the allocation of resources and for such purposes Hayek finds central planning deficient. The argument goes back to the socialist debate of the 1930s. Mises suggested that socialism would not permit of rational calculation. His assertion failed when Lange and Lerner produced the model of market socialism in which a central planning board alters prices until markets are cleared. This argument seemed to convince Mises's critics. However, Hayek, later, took the view that Mises had erred in emphasizing calculation and that the real problem was that it might not be possible to gather information in a socialist society. The most obvious case is that of research and development where there is no prior knowledge of wants and processes and products and therefore it may not be possible to adjust prices because it is not known what prices are being adjusted to. The emphasis upon (market) competition as a process of discovery, however came in the 1950s.

Statute law cannot deal with the knowledge of particular circumstances and place

Hayek's criticism of central planning can also be applied to centrally planned law; that is to say, to statute law. Because of the lack of detailed knowledge of circumstance and place, Hayek suggests that the primary task of devising detailed rules of conduct should be left to common law – to judge made law. Statute law could then be confined to the drawing up of laws which are explanations in principle and which do not discriminate but are general in intent.

Social justice is a mirage

Hayek's objections to the concept of social justice are based upon the notion that justice is a relationship between human beings whereas society is an abstract concept. Markets cannot intend particular outcomes or favour particular individuals or groups. Now Raymond Plant has argued that Hayek ignores the fact that the outcomes of markets are influenced by the distribution of income and wealth. However, a more important feature of Hayek's analysis is that his liberal society does contain a provision for the payment of a social security benefit – which suggests that he has not exorcised the rationalist – socialist ghost. No doubt he could extricate himself from his difficulty by making social security benefits a parish affair. In effect each citizen would be taxed in his or her parish in order to provide a social income for the needy. If an individual does not like the amount that he or she has to pay then the individual could vote with his or her feet and move to another parish where the contributions were lower. Thus, by a process of competition between parishes, and on the assumption that sturdy beggars were not allowed to migrate from parish to parish, then it might be possible to determine a set of perfectly discriminatory benefits obtaining between parishes.

There is a possible conflict between our moral values and the demands of markets

Hayek argues that our moral values are the product of life in small face-to-face social groups where the injunction 'love thy neighbour' referred to someone who was both visible and needy. But, he maintains, markets require us to serve people we do not know. This is of course, the essence of Adam Smith's parable of the butcher who serves us meat not out of benevolence but one of regard for his own self-interest. However, the problem with Hayek's argument is that it does not tell us why individuals do not renege on contracts. In effect, markets must provide incentives for us to be honest.

Democracy is the best means of achieving peaceful change of government but suffers from the tyranny of the single representative assembly and the simple majority vote

According to Hayek these deficiencies arise from the fact that political parties obtain support by granting privileges to numerous groups with the result that the searching for support can lead to the destruction of democracy. To overcome these deficiencies Hayek proposes a three-chamber system. The first chamber, the legislative assembly, has its membership drawn from people aged between 45 and 60; that is to say, people of experience and some substance. Their task would be to frame rules of just conduct which are abstract and general and whose consequences are unforeseeable. The second assembly would be the *government assembly* and its task would be running the government and making rules of organization. In the event of a conflict between the two chambers then issues might be referred to an arbitration body.

Hayek's objective is clear enough. He wishes to disentangle the procedures for making general rules and those for specific purposes. It is their mix-up which has led to the proliferation of privileges. In Britain the development of a legislative assembly, as distinct from a government assembly might have taken place when the Commons acquired responsibility for the raising of taxes. Unfortunately, the House of Lords was identified as a class-based institution and so was never able to develop into a legislative assembly. In the United States the Constitution attempts to do too much and, in Hayek's opinion, the Constitution should have stopped with the first three articles which defined Congress, the presidency and the courts. Unfortunately, the Constitution took on the character of law – as opposed to an instrument of organization. In America the function of legislation and the function of government were entrusted to a single body (the two houses of Congress) and seems to have arisen out of a compromise between Madison who wanted to limit the powers of government and Jefferson who wanted government to do good.

Attractive though Hayek's proposal appears to be, there is no guarantee that it will overcome the weaknesses that he observes in democracies. For example, it would be possible for parties to capture the legislative assembly and there is no guarantee that his arbitration court could work. Moreover, Hayek seems to underestimate the useful role which interest groups play in the workings of democracies and the possibilities of countervailing power.

Liberty is the means by which we expand our knowledge but it does not guarantee automatic happiness

Attempts have been made to assess whether Hayek is postulating negative freedom (freedom from) or positive freedom (freedom for). Unfortunately, such discussions seem to grind into the dust of desuetude. Hayek is advocating both concepts: freedom from restraints may enable freedom of choice to be exercised.

Hayek traces the idea of liberty and the importance of rules to the emergence of towns and the development of trade. In small face-to-face groups there was an emphasis upon self-sufficiency and the development of moral values. Feudal societies did not materially change this picture of social and economic life because they were created by military conquest. The decisive change came with the emergence of towns as trading posts and within towns there was a freedom from the restrictions imposed by the feudal system.

Hayek's preoccupation with the evolution of institutions came out of his early interest in biology and it raises a number of important points. First, he appears to subscribe to the Darwinian notion of the survival of the fittest. In a free society evolution may throw up an inefficient or evil organization or person but (in the absence of government interference) it will be eliminated. Second, the evolutionary model based upon spontaneous order makes intelligence dependent upon culture and rejects the Descartes–Bentham notion that if our institutions and culture are useful then they must have been deliberately designed. The third aspect of his work is that it draws attention to the fact that small groups are end-oriented whereas modern societies have no obvious goals. Free societies have rules which no one understands but which leave room for freedom of action for the individual. However, it has to be noted that Hayek emphasizes rules which arise out of ignorance and overlooks those rules which arise from disagreements about morals and interests.

Markets need to be deregulated

In the *Constitution of Liberty* Hayek (1960) set out to provide examples of markets which had been regulated and which had resulted in inefficiencies; housing and the labour market were cited as examples.

The fundamental problem with Hayek's social and political philosophy is that it rests upon a distinction between two idealized systems which are presumed to have some basis in history. First, there is an empirical, unsystematic and spontaneously coordinated tradition. Second, there is a rational and speculative tradition. The first tradition is traced to developments in eighteenth century England which led to an emphasis upon the rule of law before which everyone is deemed to be equal while the second tradition emerges with the French Revolution. However, these models of the market and central planning which are generated out of the traditions are idealized and while it is useful to have an awareness of the properties of market and planning systems it is also important to realize that societies are concerned with specific problems rather than generalizations. Hayek's emphasis upon the rule of law obscures the problem that societies may wish to change a rule of law; that is, the political problem which may have to be resolved by a system which involves majority voting. Hayek brushes aside the problems of income and wealth inequality and ignores the association of income inequality with other inequalities. The parents who leave a large sum of money to their children may also provide them with a good education. Furthermore, wealth tends to marry wealth. He ignores the fact that equality before the law may be undermined by the quality of legal advice which is available to the rich and poor.

The re-emergence of Hayek

Towards the end of the 1960s Keynesianism began to be discredited. It could not eliminate inflation. It could not abolish unemployment.

The re-emergence of Hayek 245

It could not explain stagflation – the coexistence of inflation and unemployment. Hayek began therefore to re-emerge as an intellectual force. In 1974 he got a Nobel Prize – but observed in 1978 that no prestigious university gave him an honorary degree. Hayek's views on the causes of booms and slumps had, of course, undergone some changes since he first startled British economists in 1931 with a theory of the trade cycle which contained the following propositions:

1. Booms and slumps were due to monetary disturbances.
2. Monetary changes drove wedges into the structure of relative prices.
3. The changes in relative prices led to a distortion of the vertical structure of production.
4. Booms came to an end when the banks contracted credit because cash reserves were falling.
5. No attempt should be made to counteract the resulting unemployment because that would lead to further distortions. The economy should be left to unwind.

The theory was discredited in the 1930s for the following reasons:

1. It assumed that if there were no monetary disturbances then there would be no booms and slumps. But in an interchange with Sraffa he conceded that he had assumed that an economy without money would always be in equilibrium. However, it was not until the 1950s that the conditions for the existence, stability and uniqueness of equilibrium in a barter economy were derived and were found to be extremely stringent.
2. Hayek's theory failed to take account of the possibility that there would be no monetary disturbances if there were unemployed labour and capital. Mass unemployment of resources was the condition examined by Keynes who recommended intervention to increase aggregate money demand rather than let things unwind.
3. Hayek failed to produce a theory of capital; that is, a theory explaining changes in the vertical structure of production. *The Pure Theory of Capital* published in 1941 was intended to be a two-volume treatise in which the second volume would deal with the workings of a dynamic. But the second volume was never published and later, in 1978, he confessed that he found the problem intractable.
4. Subsequent work by Friedman and Schwartz suggested that the slump of the 1930s was due to a severe contraction of the money supply. Although their work did not support Keynes's belief that the slump was due to a collapse of real forces, it did support his view that there should have been an increase in aggregate money demand.

In the 1970s Hayek took the view that his theory provided a good explanation of booms and slumps in the nineteenth century when countries operated on the gold standard and credit-inspired booms would be brought to a halt by an outflow of gold reserves. But he was surprised by the length of the postwar boom – he thought it would last about five years. He could find no evidence of price distortions in the boom and he thought that his theory no longer provided insights because governments had supplanted banks as creators of money and could inject money into all points of an economy whereas commercial banks had tended to lend to firms and had, thus, distorted the relative prices of consumer and capital goods. But he still believed that unemployment was due to distortions of relative wages. And in 1973 he advocated the denationalization of central banks and the introduction of competitive banking on the grounds that with central banks being monopolies it was impossible to predict their behaviour.

Notwithstanding his lack of an adequate theory of the postwar period, but emboldened by his Nobel Prize, Hayek wrote to *The Times* on 10 March 1980 and stated that, despite the possibilities of some adverse side-effects in the short run, cutting the money supply was the most efficient means of combating inflation. 'After World War One', he wrote, 'the United States brought prices down (August 1920 – February 1921) by one-third. The suffering was great but another six months later another boom was under way.'[9]

Conservative policy

Speaking in the House of Commons on December 1981 Mrs Thatcher said that she was a great admirer of Hayek. Yet the choice of Hayek as a guru needs amplification. Modern British Conservatism traces its foundations to the writings of Burke, and Burke emphasized many features of society which find an echo in Hayek's writings – and also those of Keynes. Burke's opinions rated on three principles: history, society and continuity. He was impressed by the frailty, ignorance and evil present in human nature and conscious of the need for an ordered society in which the best elements in human nature was liberated and the worst elements were restrained. But he was sceptical of attempts of deliberate design. In his *Reflections on the French Revolution* (1989) he pointed to the possibility that the apparently innocuous principles on which the revolution was initially founded could, in the hands of evil men, produce a tyranny. Society, he believed, could not be designed; it was a product of history and evolved slowly.

Burke's ideas find an echo in Hayek's writings and Burke was the founder of modern Conservatism. But Burke's writings could not be used to create a basis for policy and bring about that decisive shift in Conservative policy in the 1980s. Nor was Burke widely quoted in the early postwar years. In so far as there was a Conservative guru in the 1950s then it might have been Oakshott whose writings can be distinguished from those of Hayek by their greater reliance upon instincts and institutions – some of which might mislead. Indeed, Oakshott was critical of Hayek's political theory which relied too much upon economics and did not stress the moral basis of society. In contrast, Hayek's political theory was derived from Mises's prewar critique of socialism and Menger's stress upon the organic and evolutionary nature of society. Therefore, despite publishing *The Road to Serfdom* Hayek was not a guru in the 1950s and, indeed, the predisposition to power meant that the Conservative Party shared, with other parties, a reliance upon Keynesianism as a philosophy of action. It was not until the successive electoral defeats of the 1960s that some Conservatives sought new gods. And the attraction of Hayek – who has never regarded himself as a conservative – lay in the fact that he had predicted that long-run economic and social decline would accompany moves towards planning and socialism. Hayek, therefore, gave the New Right which emerged in the Conservative Party in the late 1960s a full-blooded alternative political philosophy to Butskellism – that compound of Keynesianism and middle of the road pragmatic politics which had been the Conservative party philosophy in the 1950s. It marked an advance over the policies pursued by the Heath government. Disenchantment with the performance of the British economy permitted the new philosophy to be enacted. The Thatcher Government ran a tight fiscal policy, cut public spending and privatized parts of the public sector. It deregulated the labour market by restricting the powers of the trade unions and it reduced the scope and content of minimum legislation. The suffering was great and it was not short lived. Throughout the 1980s unemployment averaged 8 per cent and reached a peak of 11 per cent in 1985; results which stood in marked contrast to the low unemployment levels of less than 4 per cent throughout the 1950s, 1960s and 1970s. The question is whether alternative policies should have been pursued and whether the problems of the economy in the 1980s reflected Hayek's ideas or a misapplication of his ideas.

Unemployment

In a letter to *The Times* (20 November 1980) Hayek presented a *post mortem* upon his policy recommendations. His conclusion that the failure to cope with both unemployment and inflation was due to the fact that the deflation was not sufficiently severe and that Mrs Thatcher had bowed to the wishes of her moderate ministers, such as James Prior. There were, he thought, insufficient bankruptcies and unemployment should have been pushed towards 20 per cent in order to stamp out inflation and produce that wholesale revision of contracts which would have yielded full employment and price stability:

> It is not gentle action that is needed now, but drastic action. . . .
> You can cure inflation suddenly or gradually. Politically it is impossible to do it gradually. To put it crudely I would say that it is possible to cause 20 per cent unemployment for six months if you can hold out a hope that things will be better after that. You cannot have 10 per cent unemployment for three years. Yet that is what the Government's present course asks for and I don't think it can hold out.[10]

Hayek was also critical of Friedman's monetarist approach – not because he (Hayek) did not accept monetary explanations of crises but because Friedman's approach was too aggregative; it was merely an elaboration of the quantity theory approach which he had criticized in *Prices and Production* when he drew attention to the effects of monetary changes upon relative prices and the structure of production. And he concluded by suggesting that Britain would have been much better if there had been bigger and better bankruptcies.

Figure 11.1 reveals the actual course of wages and unemployment in the 1980s. After an initial severe fall the Phillips curve flattens out and, although unemployment continues to increase, the rate of increase of money wages does not fall dramatically. In the middle of the 1980s the Phillips curve would have predicted (on the basis of the evidence from 1867 to 1957) a negative rate of increase of money wages. What then accounted for the persistence of unemployment and the failure of money wages to fall? The levels of unemployment benefit were criticized. It was also suggested that those who were employed would continue to press for wage increases as long as they saw no rise in unemployment which would threaten their job security. This was the insider theory which emphasized the point that where unemployment was based on a last in, first out basis then senior workers would feel that they were insulated from the rigours of the labour market. There was also reference to the fact that the severe deflation of 1979–81 had resulted in many long service workers in the energy-intensive, capital goods industries being thrown out of work and facing a situation for which they were ill-equipped.

Hayek's argument in 1980 has some parallels with that put forward by Keynes in the *General Theory*. Keynes suggested that it was only in a highly authoritarian society, where sudden, substantial, all-round

The re-emergence of Hayek 249

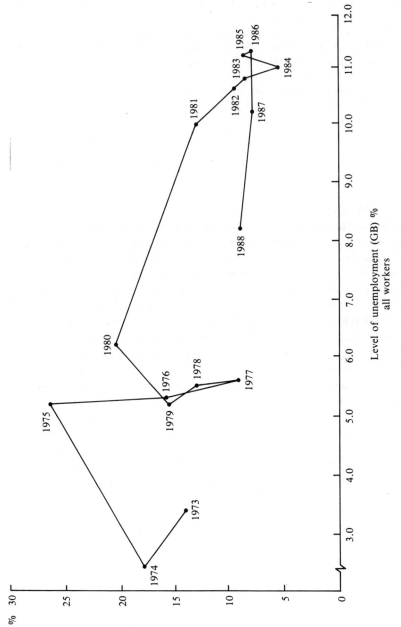

Figure 11.1 Annual rate of change of weekly earnings of all workers. *Source*: Department of Employment *Gazette*.

changes could be decreed that a flexible wages policy could function with success. And he observed that:

> The most unfavourable contingency is that in which money-wages are slowly sagging downwards and each reduction in wages serves to diminish confidence in the prospective maintenance of wages. When we enter on a period of weakening effective demand, a sudden large reduction of money-wages to a level so low that no one believes in its indefinite continuance would be the event most favourable to a strenghtening of effective demand. But this could only be accomplished by administrative decree and is scarcely practical politics under a system of free wage-bargaining.[11]

However, Hayek rejected Keynes's solution of increasing aggregate money demand and pressed for a sharp and severe deflation. He also rejected incomes policies.

Hayek opposed incomes policies because they would promote a distortion of the structure of production. If wages were held down without any corresponding reduction in the quantity of money, then the demand for consumer goods would diminish and there would be a shift of resources into the capital goods sector. In effect, his argument was a variation of his 1931 trade cycle theory. Moreover, his argument could have gained support from the collapse of the Callaghan incomes policy of 1979 when there was an attempt to impose a 5 per cent increase in money wages during a period when prices were increasing at 15 per cent. But he did make two concessions. First, he accepted that he had no solution to the problem of secondary deflation – of calculating the multiplier effects of a reduction of money demand. Second, he accepted that Austria's incomes policies had been successful.

An international comparison of unemployment rates in the 1980s suggests that unemployment in all advanced countries was mainly due to a rise in long-term unemployment; that is, unemployed workers tended to be unemployed for longer periods. In effect, the unemployed became the new serfs. The old serfs did not know from the setting of the sun 'til its rise in the morn that their master required of them. The new serfs knew that their master – the market – did not want them. However, there were substantial differences in the unemployment rates which occurred in different countries. The EC countries tended to have higher unemployment rates than the EFTA countries and Japan had a very low unemployment rate. And in general the differences in unemployment rates seem to have been associated with differences in unemployment benefits, active manpower policies and incomes policies (Figure 11.2).

Countries which had high replacement ratios (the ratio of unemployment benefit to average wage) and indefinite benefit periods tended to have high unemployment rates: for example, Sweden and Switzerland.

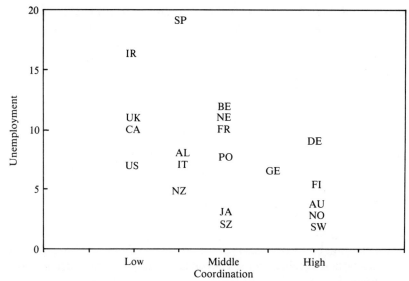

Figure 11.2 Average unemployment rate (1983–8) by level of coordination in wage bargaining. *Source*: Employment Institute (1990) *Economic Report*.

The other major difference lay in the manner in which trade union power was exercised. Where collective bargaining was decentralized then unions could ignore the employment effects of their wage policies. Centralized bargaining is, of course, another name for incomes policies and Austria, Sweden, Japan, the Netherlands and, more recently, Belgium, have incomes policies. And even Germany has had an embryonic incomes policy. Hayek acknowledged the beneficial effects of Austrian incomes policies, although his conclusion was based upon the belief that Austria's trade union leaders were reasonable men.

The case of Austria is complicated. Austria is a small open economy which has tied its currency, the schilling, to the deutschmark and much of its trade is with Germany. Hence, the success of its anti-inflation policy could be due to its observance of a fixed exchange rate policy. But the ability of Austria to maintain a fixed exchange rate policy may be the result of a willingness to observe an incomes policy. Hayek is inclined to allow moral principles to be created out of market practices whereas the reverse may be nearer to the truth with the moral and social framework determining the efficiency of the market. In Austria the willingness of employers and unions to observe an incomes policy has meant that it has been easier to control the effects of monetary changes and prevent those distortions of the structure of production which Hayek anticipated. In a similar manner, the Shunto (Spring Offensive) whereby wage changes tend to be concentrated in May in Japan could enable the authorities to employ efficient monetary and fiscal policies.

In the 1950s Hayek advocated fixed exchange rates as a means of controlling inflation. But, as he later conceded, he failed to consider the possibility of a country on a fixed exchange rate importing inflation. And he concluded that Germany had maintained a fixed exchange rate for too long in the 1960s with the result that it imported inflation from the rest of the world – especially from the United States. His later solution to the problem of inflation was to resurrect the idea of competitive banking and the abolition of central banks. Competition would prevent excessive credit creation and would also permit flexibility of prices. However, this idea has been overtaken by the emergence of an optimum currency area in Europe.

Constitutional politics and the limitations of Hayek's research programme

Hayek's research programme and its policy conclusions seem to suffer from a number of limitations. First, in emphasizing the limitations of human reason he tends to place too much reliance upon spontaneous co-ordination. According to Hayek, 'The dispute between the market order and socialism is no less than a matter of survival. To follow socialist morality would destroy much of present human kind and impoverish much of the rest.'[12] The socialist conceit, the fatal conceit, consists in the belief that humans are able to shape the world around them according to their wishes; 'in fact', he argues 'we are able to bring about an ordering of the unknown *only by causing* it to order itself.'[13] But not all socialists go that far and some, lib–labs, accept a mix of planning and the price mechanism. Second, and stemming from the first point, Hayek produces an admirable survey of the requirements of a liberal constitution but pays scant attention to the need for political parties and interest groups in order to make everyday politics work. Third, in emphasizing the role of prices and aggregators and disseminators of information he tends to overlook those issues for which a price mechanism cannot work. There is therefore a complementarity between his constitution without everyday politics and his price mechanism without a constitution to cover issues for which price signals fail. Fourth, by stressing the point that market rules of conduct tend to predominate as economies expand he has overlooked the influence of religious and moral principles in the two most successful economies of the postwar world: Germany and Japan. In a nutshell, Hayek's philosophy attempted to produce a synthesis from the ideas of Hume, Kant and Popper but he neglected certain aspects of their ideas and he also neglected Weber's work. Kukathas (1988) has noted the tension between the emphasis upon accidents and evolution in Hume and the idealism of Kant and suggested that prominence be given to the ideas of Hume. But Kant's idealism points to certain features present in postwar Germany and Japan. And Kant points the way to Weber's analysis of the importance of the great religions upon economic and social developments. Finally, Hayek has chosen to emphasize Popper's work on methodology but overlooked his views on the requirements of an open society. In effect, Hayek tends to constrain societies within his constitutional requirements. But we review these ideas against the backcloth of the world economy and of the German and Japanese economies in particular.

The world economy

The postwar world economy has been characterized by four phases: a period of reconstruction, 1945–53; a golden age which ran from 1954 to about 1968; a period of high inflation, 1969–79; and a period of stagnation which covered the 1980s. Now what was striking about the golden age was that it was based upon a great deal of deliberate planning. The world did not, as it did after the First World War, rush immediately into abandoning wartime controls with a resulting sharp inflation followed by an equally severe deflation. Instead, controls were dismantled over a decade. And on the international plane there was the UN commitment to full employment (which was endorsed by national governments), there was a commitment to fixed exchange rates, to freer trade and to relief and rehabilitation for devastated Europe and Japan, an well as the provision of aid to the less developed countries. In addition to those policies which were enshrined in a new set of international rates and institutions, there was the dissemination of US technology and production management (sometimes known as Fordism or Taylorism, but owing as much to the ideas of Alfred Sloane of General Motors). And throughout the golden age there were the conscious US policies of providing aid on a generous scale, acting as the world's banker and maintaining the value of the dollar. The golden age of the 1950s and 1960s possessed many of the characteristics set out by Kaldor. There was no deficiency of demand because real wages rose and because the rise in real wages did not bite into profits. The rise in both real wages and profits was ensured by the system of production management, by the absence of increases in raw material costs and by the social cohesion provided by growth of welfare states.

The golden age began to break down around 1968, although conventional wisdom pinpoints the first oil price rise in 1973, OPEC I, as the turning point. But the growth rate of labour productivity had begun to slip in the late 1960s. There was also a squeeze on profits and wages. And what had begun as a growth of demand and output in individual countries began to be subject to international competition which was intensified by international differences in inflation rates in a world of increasing economic interdependence.

The 1970s were marked by an attempt to cope with the increase in oil prices and yet still maintain some form of full employment. But the resulting inflation and erosion of the gains to the oil prices from OPEC I led to a further increase in oil prices, OPEC II, in 1979. Faced with the impossibility of offsetting the rise in oil prices by inflation, the advanced market economies reduced aggregate money demand. The result was an increase in unemployment – but there were international differences in unemployment rates. Part of the explanation was that labour supplies may be growing at different rates. Thus, the number of school leavers in Japan was much greater than in Germany. And setting aside demographic forces we have to acknowledge that a greater proportion of young people went into higher education in the United States, Japan and Germany. But when these factors are taken into account we observe striking differences in unemployment rates. Japan and Switzerland had low unemployment rates while that of Britain was high. Some of the differences are accounted for by differences in the provision of unemployment benefits, and the systems of collective bargaining, but we shall concentrate upon the two most successful economies of the 1970s and 1980s: Germany and Japan.

Japan and Germany

A starting point for analysis is the recognition that there are differences in spending on R&D among the advanced market economies. Japan and Germany tend to be big spenders whereas Britain is a low spender. Furthermore, much of Japan's spending is concentrated on high tech, Germany tends to predominate in medium technologies (although within the medium-tech industries, such as cars, there is a tendency to incorporate many sophisticated ideas) while Britain is notable as a spender on low technologies. These differences in spending on R&D, which are dependent upon attitudes, are linked to methods of finance. Both Germany and Japan, in contrast to Britain and the United States, relied heavily upon bank finance; that is to say they relied upon debt finance as opposed to equity finance raised through the stock market. Now the efficiency of a stock market depends not only upon it providing a means of liquidity for those who wish to sell shares, but also upon the information it is provided with. The criticism of an equity-financed industrial system is that firms may be reluctant to supply the stock market with information because it then becomes available to competitors. In contrast, a bank financed system, with bankers being on management boards, provides a source of insider information – what Dore (1985) has called *relational contracting* as opposed to market price linkage.

German firms are also characterized by a two-tier system of management. On the one hand, there is the supervising board which provides an effective monitoring system that is independent of the shareholders' meeting and contains workers' representatives drawn from the unions through the system of codetermination (*mitbestimmung*). On the other hand, is the executive board which is appointed by the supervisory board.

Finally, German and social policy has been strongly influenced by the Papal encyclicals, *Quadragesimo Anno* and *Reru Novarum* which emphasized the rights of workers. The contents of the encyclicals were incorporated in the political programmes of the Christian Social Democrats (and a similar influence can be traced in the policies of other European Christian Social Democratic parties). In other words, there has been a strong religious and moral influence exerted upon the manner in which markets have operated in the German economy. There have also been other features of the German economy which deserve mention. Since 1967, and as a result of the Stabilization Law, Germany has had an incomes policy which has worked in conjunction with the fact that the Bundesbank, the central bank, has been independent of the government and its object has been to maintain the value of the Deutschmark. Monetary policy has therefore controlled inflation, the incomes policy has tempered the possibilities of unemployment arising from union wage policies and the religious and moral ideas, which have infused welfare policies, have created a high degrees of social cohesion.

Now many of the features we have noted in the German economy can also be found in Japan. There has been a high degree of cooperation within firms as a result of the use of quality circles, job rotation, the system of annual increments (*nenko*) for permanent workers. And inter-firm cooperation has been achieved through the existence of the incomes policy, known as the *Shunto*. In addition there was a high degree of involvement of the banks in the operations of firms – although this influence may have waned in the 1980s when firms began to reduce the amount of debt financing. And behind these formal characteristics of the Japanese economy lies the influence of Confucianism which Dore (1985) has suggested emphasizes original virtue rather than original sin.

But there are other aspects of the 1980s which need to be judged in the light of Hayek's ideas. In the *Constitution of Liberty* he argued for a change in the parliamentary system but no changes were made in the House of Lords. Indeed, what happened in the 1980s was that the United Kingdom produced a state of affairs in which a strong government attempted to create a free market. One consequence of this situation was the attempt to reduce the power of trade unions; workers were given greater freedom and a balance of power was sought in the labour market. Unfortunately, the effects of North Sea Oil plus deflation led to a collapse of companies and managers as well as unions. There was an increase in productivity — some of which was due to the elimination of unproductive plants. But there was no attempt to create a cooperative state of affairs on the shopfloor. Instead, the problems of dismissals, unfair dismissals, were handed over to industrial tribunals which could only offer compensation, but not reinstatement. Furthermore, the absence of an incomes policy meant that when the money supply was expanded after 1985 there was no means of preventing inflation until the decision was made to raise interest rates in 1990 and then to enter the European Exchange Rate Mechanism in 1991. In emphasizing these points we are, of course, drawing attention to the fact that the Thatcher Government was not a slavish follower of Hayek's ideas. Political parties may adopt or adapt the ideas of defunct economists but they possess their own internal logic which requires them to put the pursuit and maintenance of political power above the demands of philosophers.

Summary and conclusions

Through the 1940s and 1950s Hayek devoted most of his efforts to the analysis and development of the social framework within economic activity. The result was the *Constitution of Liberty* and *Law, Legislation and Morals* in both of which he attempted to provide an agenda which would refute socialism and establish the case for liberalism. There were limits to human reason which prevented a complete ordering of society — but which did not preclude intervention. Hayek attempted to infuse his philosophy with a synthesis of the ideas of Hume and Kant although it was the ideas derived from Hume which seemed to provide the most plausible base even though actual societies seemed to be suffused with religious and moral ideas. In advancing his agenda Hayek sought to eliminate the tyranny of the majority present in democratic societies by the creation of political agencies which were divorced from the influence of political parties and interest groups. But Hayek's ideas tended to slur over the part played by parties and interest groups as collectors and disseminators of information on everyday politics.

In the 1970s Hayek's earlier economic ideas underwent a revival and exerted an influence on governments in the 1980s. Keynesianism had been discredited as a result of the experiences of inflation. Inflation was identified with increases in the money supply and it was conceded that unanticipated monetary changes could produce changes in relative prices and the structure of production. Later, under the impact of the oil shocks, it was conceded that unanticipated real shocks could disturb relative prices and the structure of production. But what emerged in the 1980s was a realization that the emphasis upon markets and the price mechanism may have gone too far. The successful economies seemed to have more institutional structure than the propagandists of Hayek's ideas might have allowed; they even had incomes policies. Paradoxically, the emphasis upon transactions costs which the price mechanism sought to address has led to attention being focused on seemingly more important issues, such as the role of property and the role of competition. Hayek did, of course, investigate the nature of competition but his ideas have not been taken up in an intensive manner. It is not so much Hayek's ideas on monetary economics which will prove to be enduring as his questioning of the meaning of what is meant by rationality in an economy where competition serves as a discovery process.

Notes

1. Keynes, J.M. (1936, 1973). *The Collected Writings of John Maynard Keynes*, Vol. VII, *The General Theory of Employment, Interest and Money*, London: Macmillan, p. 383.
2. Thatcher, M. (1981), *Hansard*, 5 February, p. 287.
3. Wooton, B. (1946), *Freedom Under Planning*, Durham, University of North Carolina.
4. Keynes, J.M. (1980), *Collected Writings*, Vol. XXIII, *Activities: Shaping the Post-war World, 1940–46*, pp. 385–8.
5. Knight, F.H. (1946), 'Review of Barbara Wooton *Freedom Under Planning*', *Journal of Political Economy*, 54: 453.
6. op. cit., p. 453.
7. Hayek, F.A. (1952b), *The Sensory Order: An inquiry into the foundations of theoretical psychology*, London: Routledge, p. 121.

8. Hayek, F.A. (1942), 'Scienticism and the study of society', *Economica*, NS9: 289.
9. Hayek, F.A. (1980), *The Times*, 10 March, p. 12.
10. Hayek, F.A. (1980), *The Times*, 20 November, p. 19.
11. Keynes, J.M. (1936, 1973), *The General Theory*, p. 265.
12. Hayek, F.A. (1989), *The Fatal Conceit*, London: Routledge, p. 12.
13. op. cit., p. 25.

12

A summing up

In the 1930s there developed a fierce controversy between John Maynard Keynes and Friedrich August von Hayek. Hayek had been recruited to the LSE in order to improve its intellectual standing following the early and tragic death of Allyn Young. Hence the controversy between Keynes and Hayek cannot be divorced from the intellectual claims of their parent institutions, Cambridge and the LSE. As a result of Alfred Marshall's great intellectual achievements, Cambridge had come to be regarded as the dominant centre of economics in England. And the LSE had been set up as a counterweight. Its first professor of economics, Edwin Cannan, had been critical of Marshall and in the 1920s he had been critical of Keynes. But after Cannan retired and Allyn Young had died there was a need to rebuild and to find a star. Robbins was appointed to the chair of economics at an early age but needed to establish his own reputation. He was attracted to Austrian economics because it seemed to provide him with an approach which was distinct from that of Marshall and that of Cannan. And in Vienna he found a potential star in Hayek.

Hayek was interested in the big issues of the interwar years. He was interested in the economics of socialism. He was interested in money and the trade cycle. He was critical of underconsumptionist theories of the trade cycle – theories which were, incidentally, attractive to many socialists. He was critical of Marshallian economics with its tendency to mix real cost and opportunity cost theories. And he was to become interested in the emerging areas of expectations and uncertainty.

Hayek produced a theory of the trade cycle which emphasized the importance of monetary disturbances. But it was not a simple quantity theory of the trade cycle because he emphasized the importance of monetary shocks upon relative prices and the capital goods sector. He produced a theory of the boom and the upper turning point of the cycle but he had less to say about the slump and the lower turning point except that intervention might create further distortions. And on the basis of his theory Hayek criticized Keynes's *Treatise on Money* for its lack of a theory of capital. Keynes conceded the point but Hayek's ideas came under attack from Cambridge – from Sraffa, from Robertson, from Kahn and from Henderson. And the controversy widened and deepened as the area of disagreement extended to the use of tariffs as a remedy for unemployment and Robbins and Gregory entered the fray. Although the *General Theory* was in the future, the idea of deficient demand being a cause of unemployment was being mooted in Cambridge. And any theory which emphasized the importance of demand constituted an important qualification to Robbins's definition of economics which ran in terms of scarcity.

Within the LSE there were criticisms of Hayek's ideas and these criticisms became more vociferous in the late 1930s and 1940s. However, it would be misleading to dismiss Hayek's influence upon his colleagues. Ideas, such as neutral money and monetary equilibrium, still came to play a part in economics – although in different guises – long after the publication of the *General Theory* and they surfaced as a result of the interest in growth in the 1950s. Furthermore, Lerner and Kaldor did incorporate some of Hayek's ideas into their theorizing. Thus Lerner's work of capital theory bears the hallmarks of Hayek. And for some time there were attempts to produce a synthesis of the ideas of Hayek and Keynes – a combination of the theory of the upper turning point with the theory of the lower turning point.

The failings of Keynesianism in the 1960s and 1970s led to a revival of Hayek's ideas on money and the trade cycle. But he was never able to dominate the stage and he tended to be overshadowed by Friedman. Friedman's work had two ideas which were appealing. First, there was the wealth of empirical testing. Second, his aggregative approach seemed to be in tune with the observation that there appeared to be no expansion of investment at the expense of consumption.

The 1970s and 1980s also saw a revival of interest in Hayek's ideas on the economics of information and on socialism. Hayek emphasized the importance of competition as a discovery process and was critical of the concept of perfect competition. Yet it is not clear that his ideas have been fully absorbed. Prices do not aggregate and disseminate all bits of information. Contracts contain more information than can be compressed into a price. And this point has a bearing upon the deregulation of planned and mixed economies. Although Hayek has been proved right in many of his criticisms of the planned economies, he failed to anticipate that possession of abundant natural resources could enable a planned economy, the Soviet Union, to persist for forty years. Nor did he shed much light upon the problems of transition. And his failure to anticipate the long boom of the market economies complemented his lack of foresight on the strength of a planned economy.

There remains for consideration Hayek's views on methodology and upon the operations of a liberal state. What is surprising is the extent to which Hayek and Keynes have been in agreement (and also one might add, Hicks) on the problems of testing in economics. Hayek may have accepted some of Popper's ideas at an early stage in his career but he then seems to have swung away from them – as did Popper when he came to contemplate the social sciences. What is also remarkable is the consistency of Keynes's views on testing from his early debate with Pearson through to his brush with Tinbergen. On liberalism Hayek is notable for his espousal of a programme for a liberal society which draws upon economics and evolutionary biology and which stands in sharp contrast to the ideas of other writers, such as Oakshott. And if his ideas have not proved wholly acceptable to other thoughtful writers, such as Frank Knight, they have served to reflect the gap between idealism and pragmatism.

Over a long period Hayek has produced many stimulating ideas. He achieved early success with *Prices and Production*. He also suffered early eclipse when Keynesianism became fashionable. But it is a measure of his intellectual toughness that he was able to suffer an early rebuff and to persist with his enquiries into the human condition. For Hayek liberty is an instrument of social progress. Progress cannot be planned, there is too much uncertainty; it must therefore be pursued but within a framework of a rule of law which is both universal and consistent. And within that framework a spontaneous social order will emerge. To have emphasized the relationships between uncertainty, market forces, the rule of law and evolutionary biology may be Hayek's most enduring contribution to the social sciences.

Bibliography

American Economic Association (1952), *Readings in Monetary Theory*, London: Allen and Unwin.
American Economic Association (1953), *Readings in Price Theory*, London: Allen and Unwin.
Barger, H. (1935), 'Neutral money and the trade cycle', *Economica*, NS2: 429–47.
Barry, N.P. (1989), 'The liberal constitution: rational design or evolution', *Critical Review*, 3: 267–83.
Benham, F.C. (1932), 'Review of Pigou and Robertson, Economic Essays and Addresses', *Economica*, 12: 247–8.
Benham, F.C. (1935), 'Taxation and the relative prices of factors of production', *Economica*, NS2: 198–203.
Beveridge, W.H. (1909, 1930), *Unemployment: a problem of industry*, London: Longman.
Beveridge, W.H. (ed.) (1931), *Tariffs: the case examined*, London: Allen and Unwin.
Beveridge, W.H. (1944), *Full Employment in a Free Society*, London: Allen and Unwin.
Bickerdike, C.F. (1919), 'The instability of foreign exchange', *Economic Journal*, 31: 118–22.
Bickerdike, C.F. (1920), 'External purchasing power of paper currencies', *Economic Journal*, 32: 23–38.
Bode, K. and Harberler, G. (1935), 'Monetary equilibrium and the price level in a progressive economy: a comment', *Economica*, NS2: 75–81.
Böhm, S. (1989), 'Hayek on knowledge, equilibrium and prices', *Wirtschafts Politische Blätter*, 36: 201–13.
Böhm, S. (1990), 'Ludwig Lachman (1906–1990) – a personal tribute', mimeo, Austria: University of Graz.
Böhm-Bawerk (1959), *Capital and Interest*, Vol. II, *Positive Theory of Capital*, South Holland: Libertarian Press.
Bresciani-Turroni, C. (1953), *The Economics of Inflation* (translated M.E. Sayers), London: Allen and Unwin.

Burke, E. (1989), *The Writings and Speeches of Edmund Burke*, Vol. 8, *The French Revolution*, ed. L.G. Mitchell, Oxford: Clarendon.
Caldwell, B. (1982), *Beyond Positivism*, London: Allen and Unwin.
Caldwell, B. (1992), 'Clarifying Popper', *Journal of Economic Literature*, XXIX: 1–33.
Cannan, E. (ed.) (1904), Adam Smith's (1776) *The Wealth of Nations*, London: Methuen.
Cannan, E. (1912), *History of Local Rates in England and Wales*, London: P.S. King.
Cannan, E. (1919a), *The Paper Pound of 1797–1821: The Bullion Report*, London: P.S. King.
Cannan, E. (1919b), *A History of Theories of Production and Distribution* (3rd edn), London: P.S. King.
Cannan, E. (1921a), 'The meaning of bank deposits', *Economica*, 1: 28–36.
Cannan, E. (1921b), 'The application of the theoretical apparatus of supply and demand to units of currency', *Economic Journal*, 31: 453–61.
Cannan, E. (1924a), '"Total utility" and "consumer's surplus"', *Economica*, 4: 21–6.
Cannan, E. (1924b), 'Limitation of currency or limitation of credit?', *Economic Journal*, 34: 52–64.
Cannan, E. (1924c), 'Alfred Marshall 1842–1924', *Economica*, 4: 257–61.
Cannan, E. (1929), *Review of Economic Theory*, London: P.S. King.
Cannan, E. (1930), 'The problem of unemployment', *Economic Journal*, 40: 45–55.
Cannan, E. (1932a), 'Review of Robbins' *The Nature and Significance of Economic Science*', *Economic Journal*, 42: 426.
Cannan, E. (1932b), 'The demand for labour', *Economic Journal*, 42: 357–70.
Cannan, E. (1933), 'The need for simpler economics', *Economic Journal*, 43: 367–78.
Cannan, E., Addis, C., Brand, Lord and Hawtry, R.G. (1924), 'Discussion of monetary reform', *Economic Journal*, 34: 155–76.
Chambers, S.P. (1934), 'Fluctuations in capital and the demand for money', *Review of Economic Studies*, 2: 38–50.
Coase, R.H. (1937), 'The nature of the firm', *Economica*, NS4.
Coase, R.H. (1976), 'Marshall on Method', *Journal of Law and Economics*, XVII: 25–32.
Coase, R.H. (1983), 'LSE in the thirties', *Atlantic Economic Review*, 8.
Coddington, A. (1976), 'Keynesian economics: the search for first principles', *Journal of Economic Literature*, 14.
Collard, D.A., Helm, D., Scott, M.F.G. and Sen, A.K. (1984), *Economic Theory and Hicksian Themes*, Oxford: Oxford University Press.
Collini, S. (1983), *That Noble Science of Politics*, Oxford: Clarendon.
Cunliffe, Lord (chairman) (1923), *Interim Report of the Committee on Currency and Foreign Exchanges*, Cmnd 9182, London: HMSO, pp. 17–21.
Cuthbertson (1985), *The Supply and Demand for Money*, Oxford: Blackwell.
Dalton, H. (ed.) (1934), *Unbalanced budgets*, London: Routledge.
Dickinson, H.D. (1939), *Economics of Socialism*, London: Oxford University Press.
Dobb, M. (1933), 'On Economic Theory and Socialism', *Economic Journal*, 43: 537. (Reprinted in *On Economic Theory and Socialism* (1973), London: Routledge.)

Dore, R.P. (1984), *Authority and Benevolence: the Confucian recipe for success*, mimeo, Oxford: Pembroke College.
Durbin, E.F.M. (1933a), '(Underconsumption) a reply to Mr Hobson', *Economica*, 13: 417–25.
Durbin, E.F.M. (1933b), *Purchasing Power and Trade Depression*, London: Cape.
Durbin, E.F.M. (1935a), 'Mr Gilbert's defence of a constant circulation', *Economica*, NS2: 220–22.
Durbin, E.F.M. (1935b), *The Problem of Credit Policy*, London: Chapman and Hall.
Edelberg, V. (1933), 'The Ricardian theory of profits', *Economica*, 13: 51–74.
Edelberg, V. (1936a), *Wages and Capitalist Production*, Ph.D. thesis, London: London School of Economics.
Edelberg, V. (1936b), 'An econometric model of production and distribution', *Econometrica*, 4: 210–25.
Edelberg, V. (1936c), 'Elements of capital theory', *Economica*, NS3: 314–22.
Eshag, E. (1963), *From Marshall to Keynes*, Oxford: Blackwell.
Fanno, M. (1933), 'Die Reine Theorie des Geld Marktes', in Hayek (ed.) *Beiträge zur Geldtheorie*, pp. 1–113.
Fisher, I. (1911), *The Purchasing Power of Money*, New York: Macmillan.
Fowler, R.F. (1934), *The Depreciation of Capital*, London: P.S. King.
Foxwell, H.A. (1913), 'Review of Keynes's *Indian Currency and Finance*, *Economic Journal*, XXIII: 57.
Friedman, M. (1950), *Essays in Positive Economics*, Chicago: University of Chicago Press.
Giffen, R. (1877), *Stock Exchange Securities*, London: G. Bell.
Gilbert, J.C. (1934a), 'Review of Holtrop in *Beiträge zur Geldtheorie*', *Economica*, NS1: 483.
Gilbert, J.C. (1934b), 'A note on banking policy and the income velocity of circulation of money', *Economica*, NS1: 242–5.
Gilbert, J.C. (1935), 'The present position of the theory of international trade', *Review of Economic Studies*, 3: 18–34.
Gilbert, J.C. (1936), 'A rejoinder to Mr Durbin', *Economica*, NS2: 223–6.
Gilbert, J.C. (1938), 'The mechanism of interregional redistribution of money', *Review of Economic Studies*, 15: 187–94.
Gilbert, J.C. (1950), 'Exchange rate adjustments', *Yorkshire Bulletin of Economic and Social Research*, 9: 64–87.
Gilbert, J.C. (1953), 'The demand for money: the development of an economic concept', *Journal of Political Economy*, 64: 144–6.
Gilbert, J.C. (1955), 'Professor Hayek's contribution to trade cycle theory' in J.K. Eastham (ed.), *Dundee Economic Essays*, Dundee: Dundee School of Economics.
Gilbert, J.C. (1956), 'Changes in productivity and the price level in a closed economy', *Yorkshire Bulletin of Economic and Social Research*, 8: 61–79.
Gilbert, J.C. (1957), 'The compatibility of any behaviour of the price level with equilibrium', *Review of Economic Studies*, 24: 177–84.
Gregory, T. (1924), 'Recent theories of currency reform', *Economica*, 4: 163–75.
Gregory, T. (1926), *The First Year of the Gold Standard*, London: Benn.
Gregory, T. (1927), 'Professor Cannan and contemporary monetary theory', in T. Gregory and H. Dalton, *London Essays in Economics*, London: Routledge.

Gregory, T. (1933), *Gold, Unemployment and Capitalism*, London: P.S. King.
Gregory, T. (1934), 'Twelve months of American dollar policy', *Economica*, NS1: 121–46.
Gregory, T. (1935), 'Edwin Cannan; a personal impression', *Economica*, NS: 365–79.
Gregory, T. and Dalton, H. (1927), *London Essays in Economics*, London: Routledge.
Haberler, G. (1937), *Prosperity and Depression*, Geneva: League of Nations.
Haberler, G. (1989), 'Reflections of Hayek's business cycle theory', *Wirtschafts Politische Blätter*, 36: 220–30.
Harris, J. (1977), *William Beveridge: A biography*, London: Macmillan.
Harrod, R.F. (1934a), 'The expansion of credit in an advancing economy', *Economica*, NS1: 287–99.
Harrod, R.F. (1934b), 'Rejoinder to Mr Robertson', *Economica*, NS1: 476–8.
Harrod, R.F. (1935), 'Rejoinder to Drs Haberler and Bode', *Economica*, NS2: 82–4.
Harrod, R.F. (1936), *The Trade Cycle*, London: Clarendon.
Harrod, R.F. (1939), *Towards a Dynamic Economics*, London: Macmillan.
Harrod, R.F. (1952), *Economic Essays*, London: Macmillan.
Hawtrey, R.G. (1919), *Currency and Credit*, London: Longman.
Hawtrey, R.G. (1925), 'Public expenditure and the demand for labour', *Economica*, 5: 38–48.
Hawtrey, R.G. (1932), 'Review of *Prices and Production*', *Economica*, 12: 126.
Hawtrey, R.G. (1935), 'Review of Durbin's *Purchasing Power and the Trade Depression*', *Economica*, NS2: 469.
Hayek, F.A. (1978), 'Die Währungspolitik der Vereinigten Staaten seit der Uberwindung der Krise von 1920', *Zeitschrift fur Volkwirtschaft und Sozialpolitik*, NS5: 25–63 and 254–317. (Pages 255–82 were translated as 'The monetary policy of the United States after the recovery from the 1920 crisis', in R. McCloughery (ed.) (1984), *Money, Capital and Fluctuations: Early Essays/F.A. Hayek*, London: Routledge.)
Hayek, F.A. (1928a), 'Das intertemporale Gleichgewichssystem der Preise und die Bewegungen des "Geldwertes"', *Weltwirtschaftliches Archiv*, 28: 33–76. (Translated as 'Intertemporal price equilibrium and movements in the value of money', in R. McCloughery (ed.) (1984), *Money, Capital and Fluctuations*, London: Routledge.)
Hayek, F.A. (1928b), 'Review of Hans Neisser, Der Tauschwert des Geld (Jena 1928)', *Weltwirtschaftliches Archiv*, 29(1): 103–6. (Translated as 'The exchange value of money in R. McCloughery (ed.) (1984), *Money, Capital and Fluctuations*, London: Routledge.)
Hayek, F.A. (1929), *Geldtheorie und Konjunkturtheorie* (Beiträge zur Konjunturforschung herausgegeben vom Osterreichischen Institut fur Konjunturforschung No. 1), Vienna: Holder-Pichler-Tempsky. (Translated as *Monetary Theory and the Trade Cycle*, by N. Kaldor and H. Croome (1934), London: Routledge.)
Hayek, F.A. (1931a), 'Gibt es einen "Widersinn des Sparens"? Eine Kritik der Krisentheorie von W.T. Foster unde W. Catchings mit einigen Bemerkungen zur Lehre von den Beziehungen Geld und Kapital', *Zeitschrift für Nationalökonomie*, 1: 387–429. (Translated as (1931b) 'The paradox of saving', *Economica*, 11: 125–69.)
Hayek, F.A. (1931c), *Prices and Production* (2nd edn), London: Routledge.

Hayek, F.A. (1931d), 'Reflections on the Pure Theory of Money of Mr J.M. Keynes, Part I', *Economica*, 11: 270–95.
Hayek, F.A. (1931e), 'The Pure Theory of Money: a rejoinder to Mr Keynes', *Economica*, 11, 398–403.
Hayek, F.A. (1932a), 'Reflections on the Pure Theory of Mr J.M. Keynes, Part II', *Economica*, 12: 22–44.
Hayek, F.A. (1932b), 'Das Schicksal der Goldwährung', *Deutsche Volkswirt*, 6: 642–5 and 677–81. (Translated as 'The fate of the gold standard', in R. McCloughery (ed.) (1984), *Money Capital and Fluctuations*, London: Routledge.)
Hayek, F.A. (1932c), 'Money and Capital: a reply to Mr Sraffa', *Economic Journal*, 42: 237–49.
Hayek, F.A. (1932d), 'Kapital aufzehrung', *Weltwirtschaftliches Archiv*, 36: 86–108. (Reprinted in R. McCloughery (ed.) (1984), *Money, Capital and Fluctuations*, London: Routledge, pp. 136–58.)
Hayek, F.A. (1933a), 'The trend of economic thinking', *Economica*, 13: 121–37.
Hayek, F.A. (1933b), 'Uber "Neutrales Geld"', *Zeitschrift fur Nationalökonomie*, 4: 655–61. (Translated as 'On "Neutral Money"', in R. McCloughery (ed.) (1984), *Money, Capital and Fluctuations*, London: Routledge.)
Hayek, F.A. (ed.) (1933c), *Beiträge zur Geldtheorie*, Vienna: Julius Springer.
Hayek, F.A. (1933d), 'Preiserwartungen Monetare Storungen und Fehlinvestionen', *Nationalökonomisk Tidskrift*, 73. (Translated as 'Price expectations, monetary disturbances and malinvestments', in *Profits, Interest and Investment* (1939), London: Routledge.)
Hayek, F.A. (1933e), 'The trend of economic thinking', *Economica*, 13: 125.
Hayek, F.A. (1934a), 'Capital and industrial fluctuations', *Econometrica*, 2: 152–67.
Hayek, F.A. (1934b), 'On the relationship between investment and output', *Economic Journal*, 44: 207–31.
Hayek, F.A. (1934c), 'Carl Menger', *Economica*, NS1: 393–420.
Hayek, F.A. (1935a), 'The maintenance of capital', *Economica*, NS2: 241–76.
Hayek, F.A. (1935b), 'Edwin Cannan', *Zeitschrift fur Nationalökonomie*, 6: 246–50.
Hayek, F.A. (1935c) 'The mythology of capital', *Quarterly Journal of Economics*, 50: 199–228.
Hayek, F.A. (ed.) (1935d), *Collectivist Economic Planning*, London: Routledge.
Hayek, F.A. (1936a), 'Edwin Cannan', *Zeitschrift fur Nationalökonomie*, XXI: 35–7.
Hayek, F.A. (1936b), 'Utility and interest', *Economic Journal*, 46: 44–60.
Hayek, F.A. (1937a), 'Economics and knowledge', *Economica*, NS3: 33–54.
Hayek, F.A. (1937b), *Monetary Nationalism and International Stability*, London: Longman.
Hayek, F.A. (1939), *Profits, Interest and Investment*, London: Routledge.
Hayek, F.A. (1941), *The Pure Theory of Capital*, London: Routledge.
Hayek, F.A. (1942), 'The Ricardo effect', *Economica*, NS9.
Hayek, F.A. (1944), *The Road to Serfdom*, London: Routledge.
Hayek, F.A. (1945), 'The use of knowledge in society', *American Economic Review*, 35: 519–30.
Hayek, F.A. (1946), 'The London School of Economics 1895–1945', *Economica*, NS13: 1–13.

Hayek, F.A. (1948), *Individualism and Economic Order*, London: Routledge.
Hayek, F.A. (1951), *John Stuart Mill and Harriet Taylor: their friendship and subsequent marriage*, London: Routledge.
Hayek, F.A. (1952a), *The Counter Revolution of Science*, New York: Free Press of Glencoe.
Hayek, F.A. (1952b), *The Sensory Order: An inquiry into the foundations of theoretical psychology*, London: Routledge.
Hayek, F.A. (ed.) (1954), *Capitalism and the Historians*, London: Routledge.
Hayek, F.A. (1955), *The Political Ideal of the Rule of Law*, Cairo: Bank of Egypt.
Hayek, F.A. (1960), *The Constitution of Liberty*, London: Routledge.
Hayek, F.A. (1967), *Studies in Philosophy, Politics and Economics*, London: Routledge.
Hayek, F.A. (1968), 'Economic Thought, VI: The Austrian School', in *International Encyclopedia of Social Sciences*, ed. D.L. Shils, New York: Macmillan.
Hayek, F.A. (1969), 'Three elucidations of the Ricardo effect', *Journal of Political Economy*, 77: 274–85.
Hayek, F.A. (1972a), 'Menger, Carl', in *International Encyclopedia of Social Sciences*, ed. D.L. Shils, New York: Macmillan.
Hayek, F.A. (1972b), 'Wieser, Friedrich von', in *International Encyclopedia of Social Sciences*, ed. S.L. Shils, New York: Macmillan.
Hayek, F.A. (1972c), *A Tiger by the Tail: the Keynesian legacy of inflation, a forty years' running commentary on Keynesianism by F.A. Hayek*, compiled and introduced by Sudha Shenoy, London: Institute of Economic Affairs.
Hayek, F.A. (1973a), 'The place of Menger's Grundsatze in the history of economic thought', in J.R. Hicks and W. Weber (eds), *Carl Menger and the Austrian School of Economics*, Oxford: Oxford University Press.
Hayek, F.A., *Law, Legislation and Liberty: a new statement of liberal principles of justice and political economy*, Vol. I (1973), *Rules and Order*; Vol. II (1976), *The Mirage of Social Justice*; Vol. III (1979), *The Political Order of a Free People*, London: Routledge.
Hayek, F.A. (1975a), 'Two types of mind', *Encounter*, 45: 1–6.
Hayek, F.A. (1975b), *Full Employment at any Price*, London: Institute of Economic Affairs.
Hayek, F.A. (1976a), *New Studies in Philosophy, Politics and Economics*, London: Routledge.
Hayek, F.A. (1976b), *Choice in Currency. A way to stop inflation*, London: Institute of Economic Affairs.
Hayek, F.A. (1976c), *Denationalisation of Money: an analysis of the Theory and Practice of Concurrent Currencies*, London: Institute of Economic Affairs.
Hayek, F.A. (1978a), *F.A. Hayek: Nobel Prize Economist*, interviews ed. E. Cleaver, UCLA, Ca.: University of California.
Hayek, F.A. (1978b), 'Degrees of explanation', *New Studies in Philosophy, Economics and Politics*, London: Routledge.
Hayek, F.A. (1980a), Letter to *The Times*, 11 February.
Hayek, F.A. (1980b), 'Monetarism and hyper-inflation', *The Times*, 5 March.
Hayek, F.A. (1980c), 'How to deal with inflation', *The Times*, 27 March.
Hayek, F.A. (1980d), 'Testing time for monetarism', *The Times*, 31 May and 13 June.
Hayek, F.A. (1980e), Letter to *The Times*, 20 November.

Hayek, F.A. (1989), *The Fatal Conceit*, London: Routledge.
Hayek, F.A., Gregory, T.E., Plant, A. and Robbins, L. (1932), 'Spending and savings: public works and rates', Letter to *The Times*, 19 October, (A reply to 'Private spending: money for productive investment', Letter to *The Times*, 17 October 1932, by D.H. McGregor, A.C. Pigou, J.M. Keynes, W. Layton, A. Salter and J.C. Stamp.)
Helfferich, K. (1911), *Geld*, Leipzig: C.L. Hirschfeld. (Translated by L. Infield (1927) as *Money*, 2 vols, London: Benn.)
Henderson, H.D. (1935), 'Review of Robbins's *The Great Depression*', *Economic Journal*, 45: 117.
Hicks, J.R. (1928), 'Wage fixing in the building industry', *Economica*, 8: 159–67.
Hicks, J.R. (1930), 'The early history of industrial conciliation in England', *Economica*, 10: 25–39.
Hicks, J.R. (1931), 'The theory of uncertainty and profit', *Economica*, 11: 170–89.
Hicks, J.R. (1932a), 'Marginal productivity and the principle of variation', *Economica*, 12: 79–88.
Hicks, J.R. (1932b), 'A rejoinder (Marginal productivity and the Lausanne School)', *Economica*, 12: 297–300.
Hicks, J.R. (1932c), *The Theory of Wages* (2nd edn, 1963), London: Macmillan.
Hicks, J.R. (1933), *Collected Essays on Economic Theory*, Vol II: *Money, Interest and Wages*; Vol. III, *Classics and Moderns*, Oxford: Blackwell.
Hicks, J.R. (1934a), 'Review of Myrdal in *Beiträge zur Geldtheorie*', *Economica*, NS1: 480.
Hicks, J.R. (1934b), 'Leon Walras', *Econometrica*, 2: 338–48.
Hicks, J.R. (1935a), 'A suggestion for simplifying the theory of money', *Economica*, NS2: 1–19. (Later reprinted in the American Economic Association's *Readings in Monetary Theory* (1952).)
Hicks, J.R. (1935b), 'Wages and interest: the dynamic problem', *Economic Journal*, 45: 456–68.
Hicks, J.R. (1936a), 'Mr Keynes' theory of employment', *Economic Journal*, 46: 238–53.
Hicks, J.R. (1936b), 'Distribution and economic progress: a revised version', *Review of Economic Studies*, 4: 1–2.
Hicks, J.R. (1937), 'Mr Keynes and the 'Classics': a suggested interpretation', *Econometrica*, 5: 147–59.
Hicks, J.R. (1939a), *Value and Capital*, Oxford: Clarendon.
Hicks, J.R. (1939b), 'The foundations of welfare economics', *Economic Journal*, 49: 696–712.
Hicks, J.R. (1939c) 'Mr Hawtrey on bank rate and the long-term rate of interest', *Manchester School*, 10: 21–37.
Hicks, J.R. (1942a), 'The monetary theory of D.H. Robertson', *Economica*, NS9: 53–7.
Hicks, J.R. (1942b), 'Maintaining capital intact: a further suggestion', *Economica*, NS9: 174–9.
Hicks, J.R. (1943), 'History of economic doctrine', *Economic History Review*, 13: 111–15.
Hicks, J.R. (1945), 'Recent contributions to general equilibrium economics', *Economica*, NS12: 235–42.
Hicks, J.R. (1949), 'Mr Harrod's dynamic theory', *Economica*, NS16: 106–21.

Hicks, J.R. (1950), *The Trade Cycle*, Oxford: Oxford University Press.
Hicks, J.R. (1955), 'Economic foundations of wages policy', *Economic Journal*, 65: 389–404.
Hicks, J.R. (1956a), *A Revision of Demand Theory*, Oxford: Clarendon.
Hicks, J.R. (1956b), 'The instability of wages', *Three Banks Review*, 31: 3–19.
Hicks, J.R. (1957), 'A rehabilitation of 'classical' economics?', *Economic Journal*, 67: 278–89.
Hicks, J.R. (1958), *Essays in World Economics*, Oxford: Oxford University Press.
Hicks, J.R. (1959), "A 'Value and Capital' growth model", *Review of Economic Studies*, 26: 159–73.
Hicks, J.R. (1960a), 'Thoughts on the theory of capital; the Corfu Conference', *Oxford Economic Papers*, NS12: 123–32.
Hicks, J.R. (1960b), 'Linear theory', *Economic Journal*, 70: 671–88.
Hicks, J.R. (1961), 'Prices and the turnpike. The story of a mare's nest', *Review of Economic Studies*, 28: 77–88.
Hicks, J.R. (1962), 'Liquidity', *Economic Journal*, 72: 787–802.
Hicks, J.R. (1965a), 'Dennis Robertson', London: British Academy.
Hicks, J.R. (1965b), *Capital and Growth*, Oxford: Oxford University Press.
Hicks, J.R. (1966a), *After the boom*, London: Institute of Economic Affairs.
Hicks, J.R. (1966b), 'Growth and anti-growth', *Oxford Economic Papers*, NS18: 257–69.
Hicks, J.R. (1967a), 'Monetary theory and history: an attempt at perspective', in *Critical Essays in Monetary Economics*, Oxford: Clarendon, pp. 155–73.
Hicks, J.R. (1967b), *Critical Essays on Monetary Theory*, Oxford: Oxford University Press.
Hicks, J.R. (1969), *A Theory of Economic History*, Oxford: Clarendon.
Hicks, J.R. (1973), *Capital and Time*, Oxford: Clarendon.
Hicks, J.R. (1974), *The Crisis in Keynesian Economics*, Oxford: Blackwell.
Hicks, J.R. (1977), *Economic Perspectives: Further essays on money and growth*, Oxford: Clarendon.
Hicks, J.R. (1978), *Methods of Dynamic Analysis*, Oxford: Clarendon.
Hicks, J.R. (1979), *Causality in Economics*, Oxford: Blackwell.
Hicks, J.R. (1983), 'The formation of an economist', *Classics and Modern, Collected Economic Theory Essays*, Vol. 3, Oxford: Blackwell.
Hicks, J.R. (1989), *A Market Theory of Money*, Oxford: Clarendon.
Hicks, J.R. and Allen R.G.D. (1934), 'A reconsideration of the theory of value', *Economica*, NS1: 52–76 and 196–219.
Hobson, J.R. (1933), 'Underconsumption: an exposition and a reply', *Economica*, 13: 402–17 and 425–7.
Holtrop, M.W. (1933), 'Die Umlaufsgeschwindigkeit des Geldes' in Hayek (ed.) *Beiträge zur Geldtheorie*, pp. 115–209.
Howson, S. (1975) *Domestic Monetary Management in Britain 1919–1938*, London: Cambridge University Press.
Howson, S. and Winch, D. (1977), *The Economic Advisory Council 1930–1939*, London: Cambridge University Press.
Hutchison, T.W. (1938), *The Significance and Basic Postulates of Economic Theory*, London: Macmillan.
Jevons, W.S. (1905), *Theory of Political Economy*, New York: Kelly.
Kadish, A. (1989), *Historians, economists and economic history*, Oxford: Clarendon.

Kahn, R.F. (1937), 'Some notes on ideal output', *Economic Journal*, 45: 1–35.
Kahn, R.F. (1984), *The Making of Keynes' General Theory*, Cambridge: Cambridge University Press.
Kaldor, N. (1937) 'Annual survey of economic theory: the recent controversy on the theory of capital', *Econometrica*, 5.
Kaldor, N. (1939a), 'Welfare propositions of economics and interpersonal comparisons of utility', *Economic Journal*, 49: 549–52.
Kaldor, N. (1939b), 'Keynes' theory of own-rates of interest', in N. Kaldor (1960) *Essays on Economic Stability and Growth*, London: Duckworth, pp. 59–74.
Kaldor, N. (1939c), 'Capital intensity in the trade cycle', *Economica*, NS6: 43.
Kaldor, N. (1940), 'Tariffs and the terms of trade', *Economica*, NS7: 377–80.
Kaldor, N. (1942), 'Professor Hayek and the concertina effect', *Economica*, NS9: 14.
Kaldor, N. (1960), *Essays on Economic Stability and Growth*, London: Duckworth.
Kaldor, N. and Croome, H. (1934), English translation of F.A. Hayek's *Monetary Theory and the Trade Cycle*, London: Routledge.
Keynes, J.M. (1911), 'Review of Irving Fisher's Purchasing Power of Money', *Economic Journal*, XXI: 393.
Keynes, J.M.: *The Collected Writings of John Maynard Keynes*, London: Macmillan.
  Vol. I (1913, 1971), *Indian Currency and Finance*.
  Vol. II (1919, 1971), *The Economic Consequences of the Peace*.
  Vol. III (1922, 1971), *Revision of the Treaty*.
  Vol. IV (1923, 1971), *A Tract on Monetary Reform*.
  Vol. V (1930a, 1972), *A Treatise on Money, 1 The Pure Theory of Money*.
  Vol. VI (1930b, 1972), *A Treatise on Money, 2 The Applied Theory of Money*.
  Vol. VII (1936, 1973), *The General Theory of Employment, Interest and Money*.
  Vol. VIII (1921, 1973), *Treatise on Probability*.
  Vol. IX (1931, 1972), *Essays in Persuasion*.
  Vol. X (1933, 1972), *Essays in Biography*.
  Vol. XI (1973), *Economic Articles and Correspondence*: Various.
  Vol. XII (1973), *Economic Articles and Correspondence*: Various/Academic.
  Vol. XIII (1973), *The General Theory and After: Part I, Preparation*.
  Vol. XIV (1973), *The General Theory and After: Part II, Defence and Development*.
  Vol. XV (1971), *Activities: India and Cambridge, 1906–14*.
  Vol. XVI (1971), *Activities: The Treasury and Versailles, 1914–19*.
  Vol. XVII (1971), *Activities: Treaty Revision and Reconstruction, 1920–22*.
  Vol. XVIII (1978), *Activities: The End of Reparations, 1922–32*.
  Vol. XIX (1981), *Activities: The Return to Gold and Industrial Policy, 1924–29*.
  Vol. XX (1974). *Activities: Rethinking Employment and Unemployment Policies, 1929–31*.
  Vol. XXI (1982), *Activities: World Crises and Policies in Britain and America, 1931–39*.
  Vol. XXII (1980), *Activities: War Finance, 1940–45*.
  Vol. XXIII (1980), *Activities: Shaping the Post-war World, 1940–46*.

Vol. XXIV (1982), *Social, political and literary writing.*
Vol. XXV, *Bibliography and Index.*
Vol. XXIX (1979), *General Theory and After: a supplement.*
Keynes, J.N. (1891), *The Scope and Method of Political Economy*, London: Macmillan.
Knapp, G.F. (1905), *Staatlichte Theories des Geldes*, Leipzig: Hirschfeld. (Translated by H.M. Lucas and J. Bonar (1924) as *The State Theory of Money*, London: Macmillan.)
Knight, F.H. (1921), *Risk, Uncertainty and Profit*, Boston: Hart, Schaffner and Marx. (Reissued in 1948 by London School of Economics as Reprint No. 16.)
Knight, F.H. (1924), 'Some fallacies in the interpretation of social cost', *Quarterly Journal of Economics*, 38: 582–606.
Knight, F.H. (1933), 'Capitalistic production, time and the rate of return', in *Economic Essays in Honour of Gustav Cassel*, London: Allen and Unwin, pp. 327–42.
Knight, F.H. (1935), 'Professor Hayek and the theory of investment', *Economic Journal*, 45: 94.
Knight, F.H. (1936), 'The quantity of capital and the rate of interest', *Journal of Political Economy*, 44: 434–5.
Knight, F.H. (1946), 'Capital and interest' in *Encyclopaedia Britannica*, IV, London, pp. 777–801.
Koopmans, J.G. (1933), 'Zum problem des "Neutralgen" geldes', in Hayek (ed.) *Beiträge zur Geldtheorie*, pp. 211–359.
Koot, G. (1987), *English Historical Economics 1870–1926*, Cambridge: Cambridge University Press.
Kukathas, C. (1989), *Hayek and Modern Liberalism*, Oxford: Clarendon.
Lachmann, L. (1936), 'Commodity stocks and equilibrium', *Review of Economic Studies*, 3: 230–4.
Lachmann, L. (1937), 'Uncertainty and liquidity preference', *Economica*, NS4: 295–308.
Lachmann, L. (1938a), 'Investment and the costs of production', *American Economic Review*, 28: 469–81.
Lachmann, L. (1938b), 'On crisis and adjustment', *Review of Economic Statistics*. 21: 62–8.
Lachmann, L. (1939), 'On crisis and adjustment', *'Review of Economics and Statistics*, 7: 62–9.
Lachmann, L. (1940), 'A reconsideration of the Austrian theory of industrial fluctuations', *Economica*, NS7: 179–96.
Lachmann, L. (1941), 'On the measurement of capital', *Economica*, NS8: 361–77.
Lachmann, L. (1945), 'A note on the elasticity of expectations', *Economica*, NS12: 248–53.
Lachmann, L. (1947). 'Complementarity and substitution in the theory of capital', *Economica*, NS14: 108–19.
Lachmann, L. (1956), *Capital and its structure*. London: Bell.
Lachmann, L. (1976), 'From Mises to Shackle: an essay of Austrian economics and the Kaleidic Society', *Journal of Economic Literature*, 14: 54–62.
Lachmann, L. (1986), *The Market as an Economic Process*, Oxford: Blackwell.
Laidler, D.E.W. (1985), *The Demand for Money* (3rd edn), New York: Harper and Row.

Lange, O. (1936), 'On the economic theory of socialism', Part One, *Review of Economic Studies*, 4: 53–71.
Lange, O. (1937a), 'On the economic theory of socialism', Part Two, *Review of Economic Studies*, 4: 123–42.
Lange, O. (1937b), 'Mr Lerner's note on socialist economics', *Review of Economic Studies*, 4: 143–4.
Lange, O. and Taylor, F. (1939), *On the Economic Theory of Socialism*, Minneapolis: University of Minnesota Press.
Lavington, F. (1921), *English Capital Market*, London: Methuen.
Lavington, F. (1927), 'Technical approaches to integration', *Economica*, 7: 27–36.
Leijonhufvud, A. (1968), *On Keynesian Economics and the Economics of Keynes*, Oxford: Oxford University Press.
Leijonhufvud, A. (1984), 'Hicks on time and money', in D.A. Collard, D. Helm, M.F.G. Scott and A.K. Sen, *Economic Theory and Hicksian Themes*, Oxford: Oxford University Press.
Lerner, A.P. (1934), 'Economic theory and socialist economy', *Review of Economic Studies*, 2: 51–61.
Lerner, A.P. (1935), 'Economic theory and socialist economy: a rejoinder', *Review of Economic Studies*, 2: 152–4.
Lerner, A.P. (1936a), 'Mr Keynes' "General Theory of Employment"', International Labour Review, p. 286.
Lerner, A.P. (1936b), 'A note on socialist economics', *Review of Economic Studies*, 4: 72–6.
Lerner, A.P. (1937), 'Statics and dynamics in socialist economics', *Economic Journal*, 47: 253–70.
Lerner, A.P. (1938a), 'Saving equals investment', *Quarterly Journal of Economics*, 52: 297–309.
Lerner, A.P. (1938b), 'Alternative formulations of the rate of interest', *Economic Journal*, 48: 211–30.
Lerner, A.P. (1938c), 'Theory and practice in socialist economics', *Review of Economic Studies*, 6: 71–75.
Lerner, A.P. (1939a), 'The relation of wage policies and price policies', *American Economic Review* (supplement), 29: 158–69.
Lerner, A.P. (1939b), 'Saving and investment: definitions, assumptions, objectives', *Quarterly Journal of Economics*, 53: 611–19.
Lerner, A.P. (1939c), 'Ex-ante analysis and the wage theory', *Economica*, NS6: 436–49.
Lerner, A.P. (1939–40), 'Review of Hicks *Value and Capital*', *Quarterly Journal of Economics*, 54: 298.
Lerner, A.P. (1940a), 'Professor Hicks' dynamics' *Quarterly Journal of Economics*', 54: 298–306.
Lerner, A.P. (1940b), 'Some Swedish stepping stones in economic theory', *Cambridge Journal of Economics*, 6: 575–91.
Lerner, A.P. (1944), *Economics of Control*, London: Macmillan.
Lerner, A.P. (1952), 'Factor prices and international trade', *Economica*, NS19: 1–18.
Lerner, A.P. (1982), 'Paleo-Austrian capital theory' in D. Colander (ed.) *Selected Economic Writings of Abba P. Lerner*, New York: New York University Press, pp. 563–79.

Liberal Party (1928), *Britain's Industrial Future: being the report of the Liberal industrial future*, London: Benn.
Lindahl (1939), *Studies in the Theory of Money and Capital*, London: Allen and Unwin.
Lipsey, R.G. (1963), *Introduction to Positive Economics*, London: Weidenfeld and Nicolson.
Lutz, F.A. (1938), 'The outcome of the savings-investment discussion', *Quarterly Journal of Economics*, 52: 588–614.
McCloughery, R. (ed.) (1984), (Hayek's) *Money, Capital and Fluctuations: Early Essays*, London: Routledge.
Machlup (1971), 'Professor Hayek's contribution to economics', *Swedish Journal of Economics*, 76.
Macmillan (chairman) (1930), *Report of the Committee on the Finance of Industry and Trade*, Cmnd 3897, London: HMSO.
Makower, H. and Marschak, J. (1939), 'Asset, prices and monetary theory', *Economica*, NS5: 261–88.
Marshall, A. (1924), *Principles of Economics* (8th edn), London: Macmillan.
Meade, J.E. (1945), 'Mr Lerner on "The Economics of Control"', *Economic Journal*, 55: 47–69.
Menger, C. (1892), 'On the origin of money', *Economic Journal*, 2: 239–55.
Menger, C. (1923), *Grundsätze der Volkswirtschaftlehre* (2nd edn), Vienna: Holder-Pichler-Tempsky.
Metzler, L.A. (1945), 'Stability of multiple markets: the Hicks conditions', *Econometrica*, XIII: 1277.
Millward, A. (1985), *The Reconstruction of Western Europe*, London: Allen and Unwin.
Mises, L. (1912), *Theories des Geldes und der Umlaufsmittel*, Munich: Dunker and Humblot. (Translated into English by H.E. Batson (1934) (2nd edn) as *Theory of Money and Credit*, London: Cape.)
Mises, L. (1920), 'Economic calculation in the socialist commonwealth', reprinted in F.A. Hayek (ed.) (1935d), *Collectivist Economic Planning*, London: Routledge. (Originally published in German in *Archiv fur Sozialwissenschaften*.)
Mises, L. (1928), *Geldwersabilisierung und konjunkturpolitik*, Jena: Gustav Fischer.
Mises, L. (1934), *The Theory of Money and Credit*, London: Cape.
Mises, L. (1943) 'Elasticity of expectations', *Economica*, NS10.
Mises, L. (1979), *Notes and Recollections*, South Holland: Libertarian Press.
Moggridge, D. (1972), *British Monetary Policy, 1924–1931*, Cambridge: Cambridge University Press.
Morganstern, O. (1941), 'Review of Hicks' Value and Capital', *Journal of Political Economy*, 49: 361–93.
Myrdal, G. (1928), *Price Formation and Economic Change*, Uppsala: Almqvist and Wicksell.
Myrdal, G. (1933), 'Der Gleichgewichts begriff als instrument der Geldtheorstischen analyse' in Hayek (ed.) *Beiträge zur Geldtheorie*, pp. 361–487.
Myrdal, G. (1939), *Monetary Equilibrium*, London: Hodge (revised and translated version of Myrdal, 1933).
Ohlin, B. (1929), 'The reparation problem: a discussion', *Economic Journal*, 39: 172–8 and 400–4.

Ohlin, B. (1933), *Interregional and International Trade*, Cambridge, MA.: Harvard University Press.
Paish, F.A. (1936), 'Banking policy and the balance of payments', *Economica*, NS3: 405–6.
Patinkin, D. (1958), 'Liquidity preference and loanable funds: Stock flow analysis', *Economica*, NS25: 287–301.
Pennington, J.R. (1829), 'Deposits with Bankers' in T. Tooke, *A Letter to Lord Grenville on the Value of Money*, London: John Murray. Reprinted in R.S. Sayers (1963), *The Economic Writings of James Pennington*, London: London School of Economics.
Pennington, J.R. (1838), Appendix C in T. Tooke, *A History of Prices*, Vol 2, London: Longmans. Reprinted in R.S. Sayers (1963) *The Economic Writings of James Pennington*, London: London School of Economics.
Pheby, J. (1988), *Methodology and Economics: A Critical Introduction*, London: Macmillan.
Phillips, C.A. (1921), *Bank Credit*, New York: Macmillan.
Pigou, A.C. (1912), *Wealth and Welfare*, London: Macmillan.
Pigou, A.C. (1917), 'Value of money', *Quarterly Journal of Economics*, 32: 54.
Pigou, A.C. (1927a), *Industrial Fluctuations* (1st edn; 2nd edn, 1929), London: Macmillan.
Pigou, A.C. (1927b), 'Wages policy and unemployment', *Economic Journal*, 37: 18–27.
Pigou, A.C. (1928), *The Economics of Warfare*, London: Macmillan.
Pigou, A.C. (1933), *Theory of Unemployment*, London: Macmillan.
Pigou, A.C. (1936), 'Mr Keynes' General Theory of Employment, Interest and Money', *Economica*, NS3: 1–10.
Pigou, A.C. (1937), *Socialism versus Capitalism*, London: Macmillan.
Pigou, A.C. (1941), *Employment and Equilibrium* (2nd edn, 1949), London: Macmillan.
Pigou, A.C. (1945), *Lapses from Full Employment*, London: Macmillan.
Pigou, A.C. (1947), 'Economic progress in a stable environment', *Economica*, NS14: 185–8.
Pigou, A.C. (1950), *Keynes's 'General Theory': a retrospective view*, London: Macmillan.
Pigou, A.C. and Robertson, D.H. (1931), *Economic Essays and Addresses*, London: P.S. King.
Popper, K. (1944), *The Poverty of Historicism*, London: Routledge.
Popper, K. (1959), *The Logic of Scientific Discovery*, New York: Harper and Row.
Ricardo, D. (1951), 'The High Price of Bullion' in *The Collected Works and Correspondence of David Ricardo* (ed. P. Sraffa), Cambridge: Cambridge University Press.
Robbins, L.C. (1932a), *An Essay on the Nature and Significance of Economic Science*, London: Macmillan.
Robbins, L.C. (1932b), 'Consumption and the trade cycle', *Economica*, 12: 429.
Robbins, L.C. (1934a), *The Great Depression*, London: Macmillan.
Robbins, L.C. (1934b), 'Remarks upon certain aspects of the theory of costs', *Economic Journal*, 44: 1–18.
Robbins, L.C. (1935), 'A student's recollections of Edwin Cannan', *Economic Journal*, 45: 393–8.

Robbins, L.C. (1971), *Autobiography of an Economist*, London: Macmillan.
Roberts, P.C. (1971), 'Oskar Lange's theory of socialist planning', *Journal of Political Economy*, 74: 35.
Robertson, D.H. (1915), *A Study in Industrial Fluctuations*, (later reprinted in *Money* (2nd edn, 1948)), Cambridge: Cambridge University Press.
Robertson, D.H. (1922), *Money* (2nd edn, 1948), Cambridge: Cambridge University Press.
Robertson, D.H. (1926), *Banking Policy and the Price Level* (2nd edn, 1949), New York: Kelly.
Robertson, D.H. (1928), 'Theories of banking policy', *Economica*, 8: 131–46.
Robertson, D.H. (1929), 'The monetary doctrines of Messrs Foster and Catching', *Quarterly Journal of Economics*, 43: 473–99.
Robertson, D.H. (1931), 'Review of Durbin's *Purchasing Power and the Trade Depression*', *Economic Journal*, 43: 176.
Robertson, D.H. (1934), 'Industrial fluctuations and the rate of interest', *Economic Journal*, 44: 650–6.
Robertson, D.H. (1940), *Essays in Monetary Economics*, London: P.S. King.
Robertson, D.H. (1957), *Lectures on Economic Principles*, London: Fontana.
Robinson, J. (1933), *The Economics of Imperfect Competition*, London: Macmillan.
Robinson, J. (1937), 'The foreign exchanges', in *Essays in the Theory of Employment*, London: Macmillan, pp. 188–201.
Robinson, J. (1957), *The Accumulation of Capital*, London: Macmillan.
Samuelson, P.A. (1941), 'Stability of equilibrium', *Econometrica*, IX: 111–12.
Samuelson, P.A. (1962), 'Parable and realism in capital theory: the surrogate production function', *Review of Economic Studies*, 39: 193–206.
Sampson, A.A., Sedgwick, R. and McCormick, B.J. (1979), 'Real and money wages', *University of Sheffield Discussion Paper*.
Schlesinger, K. (1914), *Theorie der geld und Kreditswirtschaft*, Munich: Dunker and Humblot. (Partial translation as 'Basic principles of the money economy', *International Economic Papers* (1959), 9: 20–38.)
Schorske, C. (1979), *Fin-de-Siècle Vienna*, New York: Knopf.
Schumpeter, J.A. (1954), *History of Economic Analysis*, Oxford: Oxford University Press.
Scitovsky, T. (1940–41), 'Capital accumulation, employment and price rigidity', *Review of Economic Studies*, 8: 25–30.
Scitovsky, T. (1941), 'A note on welfare propositions in economics', *Review of Economic Studies*, 9: 77–88.
Scitovsky, T. (1980s) in *Conversations with LSE Economists in the early 1980s*, conducted by Nadim Shehadi, London: LSE Archives.
Shackle, G.L.S. (1933), 'Some notes on monetary theories of the trade cycle', *Review of Economic Studies*, 1: 27–38.
Shackle, G.L.S. (1936), 'The breakdown of the boom: a possible mechanism', *Economica*, NS3: 423–35.
Shackle, G.L.S. (1937), 'Dynamics of the crisis: a suggestion', *Review of Economic Studies*, 4: 108–22.
Shackle, G.L.S. (1938), *Expectation, Investment and Income* (2nd edn, 1968), Oxford: Oxford University Press.
Shackle, G.L.S. (1946), 'Interest rates and the pace of investment', *Economic Journal*, 56. (Reprinted in T. Wilson and R.S. Sayers (eds) (1951), *Oxford Studies in the Price Mechanism*, Oxford: Clarendon.)

Shackle, G.L.S. (1967), *The Years of High Theory*, London: Cambridge University Press.
Shackle, G.L.S. (1972), *Epistemics and Economics*, London: Cambridge University Press.
Shackle, G.L.S. (1974), *Keynesian Kaleidics*, Edinburgh: Edinburgh University Press.
Shackle, G.L.S. (1987), 'F.A. Hayek 1899–', in D.P. O'Brien and J.R. Presley (eds), *Pioneers of Modern Economics*, Vol. 1, London: Macmillan, pp. 171–98.
Shearmur, J. (1987), *The Political Thought of F.A. von Hayek*, PhD thesis, London University.
Smith, V.C. (1937), *The Rationale of Central Banking*, London: Routledge.
Solow, R.M. (1957), 'Technical change and the production function', *Review of Economics and Statistics*, 39: 312–20.
Spann, O. (1912), *Die Haupttheorien der Volkswirtshaftslehre*, Leipzig: Quelle and Meyer.
Sraffa, P. (1932), 'Dr Hayek on Money and Capital', *Economic Journal*, 42: 42–53.
Stolper, W.F. and Samuelson, P.A. (1941), 'Protection and real wages', *Review of Economic Studies*, X: 58–73.
Taussig, F.W. (1928), *International Trade*, New York: Macmillan, Chapters XX–XXV.
Tavlas, A. (1981), 'Keynes and monetarist theories of the monetary transmission process', *Journal of Monetary Economics*, 7: 317–37.
Thirlwall, A.P. (1987), *Nicholas Kaldor*, Brighton: Wheatsheaf.
Thomas, B. (1934), in H. Dalton (ed.) *Unbalanced Budgets*, London: Routledge, pp. 19–216.
Thomas, B. (1936), *Monetary Policy and Crises: a study of Swedish experience*, London: Routledge.
Thomas, B. and Richards, H. (1936), *Population Movements and Economic Growth*, London: Routledge.
Thornton, H. (1802), *An Enquiry into the Nature and Effects of Paper Credit*, London: Hatchard. (New edition by F.A. Hayek (1939), London: London School of Economics.)
Tobin, J. (1971), *Essays in Economics*, Vol. 1, Macroeconomics, Amsterdam: North Holland.
Torrens, R. (1838), *A Letter to the Right Honourable Lord Viscount Melbourne*, London: Longman.
Tsiang, S.C. (1947), *The Variations of Real Wages and Profit Margins*, London: Pitman.
Vaughn, K. (1981), 'Economic calculation under socialism', *Economic Inquiry*, 18: 535–54.
Vicary, S.J. (1976), *The Monetary Theory of Evan Durbin*, MA thesis, Sheffield University.
Viner, J. (1924), *Canada's Balance of International Indebtedness 1900–1913*, Cambridge, MA.: Harvard University Press.
von Neuman, J. (1937), 'Über ein okonomisches Gleichungssystem und eine verall geimerung des Brouwer 'schen fixpunksatzes', *Ergebnisse Eines Math Kolloquiums*, 8: 73–83. (Translated as 'A model of general economic equilibrium', in O. Morganstern and G. Thompson (1976), *Mathematical*

Theories of Expanding and Contracting Economies, Lexington, MA.: Lexington Books.)
Webb, B. (1926), *My Apprenticeship*, London: Longman.
Webb, S. and Webb, B. (1902a), *Industrial Democracy*, London: Longman.
Webb, S. and Webb, B. (1902b), *The History of Trade Unionism*, London: Longman.
Whale, P.B. (1930), *Joint Stock Banking in Germany*, London: Macmillan.
Whale, P.B. (1937), 'The working of the pre-war gold standard', *Economica*, NS4: 19.
White, H.D. (1928), *The French International Accounts, 1880–1913*, Cambridge, MA.: Harvard University Press.
Wicksell, K. (1898), *Geldzins und Guterpreise*, translated from the German by R.F. Kahn as *Interest and Prices* (1936), London: Macmillan.
Wicksell, K. (1907), 'The influence of the rate of interest on prices', *Economic Journal*, 17: 212–20.
Williams, J.H. (1920), *Argentine International Trade under Inconvertible Paper Money, 1880–1900*, Cambridge, MA.: Harvard University Press.
Wilson, T. (1940), 'Capital theory and the trade cycle', *Review of Economic Studies*, 7: 179.
Wilson, T. and Sayers, R.S. (eds) (1951), *Oxford Studies in the Price Mechanism*, Oxford: Clarendon.
Wiseman, J. (1957), 'The theory of public utility price: an empty box', *Oxford Economic Papers*, NS9: 56–74.
Wooton, B. (1946), *Freedom Under Planning*, Durham: University of North Carolina.
Yeager, L. (1989), 'Reason and cultural evolution. The Fatal Conceit: the errors of socialism', *Critical Review*, 3: 324–36.
Young, A.A. (1913), 'Pigou's Wealth and Welfare', *Quarterly Journal of Economics*, 27: 672–86.
Young, A.A. (1928), 'Increasing returns and economic progress', *Economic Journal*, 38: 527–42.

Index

Acceleration principle, 116–17
Allen, T., 2, 157
American Economic Assoc,
   Readings in Monetary Theory, 91
   Readings in Price Theory, 92
American monetary theory, 174–5
Asset prices, determination, 92
Austria,
   capital theory, 123–4 Table, 125, 222, 223
   see also individual economists
   economic indicators, 42, 43 Table
   fixed exchange rate policy, 251
   growth theory, 231–2
   incomes policies, 250, 251, 252
   monetary theory, 173
Austrian Institute of Business Cycle Research, 44
Austro-Hungarian Empire,
   economic, political and social history, 41–3

Bank Charter Act 1844, 162
Bank credit, economic activity, 51
Bank deposits as money, 22
Bank of England discount rate, 155
Banking, 162–3
Barger, H., 95
Barter economy, 94
Baumol, W.J., 92
Bearish factor, 57, 59, 60
Bears, 57

Benham, F.C., 2, 23, 158–9
Bentham, J., 8, 43
Beveridge, W.H., 13, 31, 158, 236
Bevin, E., 157
Bickerdike, C.F., 159, 160
Black markets, 150
Bohm-Bawerk, E., 26, 115
   capital theory, 47, 48, 122–3, 196
   debate with Clark, 100
   period of production, 108–9
Bond prices, 208
Boom and slump, 8, 64, 66, 157–8, 163
Bowley, A.L., 13
Braithwaite, R.B., 179
Bresciani-Turroni, C., 30
Brezhnev, L.I., 148
Bryce, R., 167
Budget, balancing, 204
Bulls, 57
Burke, E., 246–7

Cambridge,
   criticisms of Hayek, 64–9
   and LSE, 28–9
   research, 30
Campion, H., 129
Cannan, E., 2, 13, 35, 69, 75, 93, 160
   A History of Theories of Production and Distribution, 15

Cannan, E., (*continued*)
  Adam Smith's *Wealth of Nations*, 14
  appointment to LSE, 11
  criticism of Keynes, 259
  criticism of Marshall, 14, 259
  economic outlook, 4, 14–23
    consumer surplus, 14, 15
    demand for money, 15
    monetary theory 4, 18–23
    money supply, 15–18
  editor *Paper Pound of 1797–1821*, 15
  features of his teaching, 153
  free trade, 12
  History of Local Rates in England and Wales, 15
  Review of Economic Theory, 15
  review of Keynes' *A Tract on Monetary Reform*, 22
  value judgements, 27
Capital, measurement of 129–31
Capital goods, 66, 219–20
Capital intensity variation, 113
Cash, precautionary balances, 93
Cassell, G., 21
Catchings, W., 70
Central banks, 161, 162, 176
Centrally planned economies, transition to market economies, 149–50, 151
Chamberlain, J., 11
Chambers, S.P,, 5, 75, 89–91, 96
Chicago programme, 237–43
  summary of propositions, 237–8
Clark, J.B., 100, 115, 125
Classical economists, interests, 26
Coase, R.H., 12, 146–7, 205
Coddington, A., 210
Collectivist economic planning, 136–45
  Austrian critique, 136–8
  socialist response, 138–40
Collectivization, dangers of, 198
Committee on Finance and Industry, report on *window dressing*, 16–17
Comparative statics, 7
Conservative party, 246–7
Consumer, definition by Hawtrey, 51
Consumption and savings, 57

Costs, relationship between average and marginal cost, 147
Credit policy, debate between Gilbert and Durbin, 95
Crick, W.F., 16
Cumulative processes, 48
Cuncliffe Committee on Currency and the Foreign Exchange, 154–5
Cuthbertson, holding money, 208–9

Dalton, H., 13
Daniels, W., 129
Davidson, D., 49, 217, 218
Deflation, 20, 69
Deregulation of markets, 8
Dickinson, H.D., 140
Disequilibrium analysis, 82
Division of labour, 23
Dobb, M., 136, 138, 145
Domestic stability, 22
Dore, R.P., 255
Douglas, Major, 70–1
Durbin, E.F.M., 71–5
  analysis of underconsumption, 70, 71–2
  criticism of Hayek, 75
  lectures, 71, 72 Table, 143, 144 Table
  optimum savings rate, 74
  Purchasing Power and Trade Depression, 71
  The Problem of Credit Policy, 71
Dynamic economy, instability, 193–4

Eastern Europe, 147–9, 151
Econometrics, usefulness, 182
Economic policy for Britain, public debate in 1920s and 1930s, 61–2
Economica, 2
Economics, definition by Robbins, 135
Economics of control, 197–9
Economics as a science, 180–1
Economics of socialism, 6
Edelberg, V., 30, 114–15
Edgeworth, F.Y., 14, 26
Employment, 188, 203–4
English economists, 175–6
Equity-financed industrial system, 255

Index   281

European Exchange Rate
    Mechanism, 256
Evidence, importance of, 179, 180
Ex ante and *ex post*, 80, 82, 83, 114,
    131, 141, 195, 201
Exchange rates,
    effect of inflation, 21, 252
    fixed, 160–4, 252
    floating, 154, 159–60, 164
    stability, 21
Expectations,
    and causality, 209–10
    elasticity 196
    mean-variance approach, 210

Factor price equilization theorem,
    29, 159
Fanno, M., 79
Firm, nature of, 30, 145–7
Fisher, I., 115
    criticism by Keynes, 19–20
    The Purchasing Power of Money,
        18, 174–5
Fix-prices, 82
Forced savings, 58, 170
Forward exchanges 21
Foster, W.F., 70
Fowler, R.F., 129, 130
Foxwell, H.A., 3, 13
Friedman, M., 239–40, 248
Futures markets, 195–6

Gaitskell, H., 30, 70
General equilibrium analysis, 139,
    151, 193
General equilibrium model, 145
Germany, 156, 254, 255
Gilbert, J.C., 7, 94, 153, 227
    demand for money, 207, 208
    motives for holding money,
        208–9, 232
    productivity and the price level,
        218–19, 232
    *The mechanism of interregional
        redistributions of money*,
        164
    trade cycle theory, 227
Gold standard, 153
    abandonment, 61, 156
    causes of problems, 63–4
    pre-war, 160, 163

return to at pre-war parity, 19,
    35, 61, 63, 156, 164
workings, 154–5, 160
Gregory, T., 2, 17, 69, 75, 157–8,
    184
*Gold, Unemployment and
    Capitalism*, 69
lectures, 18 Table
tariffs, 157
*The First Year of the Gold
    Standard*, 69
time at LSE, 171–2
Growth and distribution, 224–5

Haberler, G., 30, 39, 121, 168
Hansen, A., 205
Harrod, R.F., 161, 218, 220–2, 226
Hawtrey, R.G., 30, 50–2, 69, 74,
    184
    Currency and Credit, 19, 50, 51
    quantity theory, 58
    theory of the trade cycle 50–2
Hayek, F.A., 6, 27, 31, 40, 64,
    66–7, 69, 71, 75–6, 84–5,
    86, 94, 95, 120–1, 140–1,
    153, 157, 180, 211, 218,
    219, 252
    acceleration principle, 116–17
    Austrian capital theory, defence
        of Knight's critique, 108–10
    *Banking Policy and the Price
        Level*, 67
    capital, measurement 129, 130
    capital goods, value after boom,
        66
    capital intensity, 100
    Capitalism and the Historians,
        137, 237
    Chicago programme, 237–43
    Collectivist Economic Planning,
        136–8
    Constitution of Liberty, 256
    crisis in world economy, 63
    criticism,
        Cambridge 64–9
        of Keynes, 50, 64–5, 176, 260
        of perfect competition, 260
        of planned economies, 260–1
        of socialism, 135
        of underconsumptionist
            literature, 70
    Degrees of explanation, 181–2

282 Index

Hayek, F.A., (*continued*)
  denationalization of central banks, 246
  difference of opinion with Keynes, 7, 259
  early life history, 37–8
  econometrics, usefulness, 182
  Economics and Knowledge, 84–5, 135, 140
  education at Univ of Vienna, 38–9
  epistemology and methodology, 181
  Geistreisse discussion group, 39
  gold standard, return to, 63
  incomes policies, 250
  influence,
    Mises, L., 41, 43–4
    Rathenau, E., 38
  interest in human psyche, 9
  intertemporal allocation of resources, 46–7
  intrusion into British debate of 1920's and 1930's, 62–4
  John Stuart Mill and Harriet Taylor, 237
  Keynes's *General Theory*, 170–1, 184, 185
  Law, Legislation and Liberty, 237
  Law, Legislation and Morals, 256
  lectures, 48 Table, 136 Table
  LSE,
    appointment as professor, 44
    criticism from, 260
    recruitment to, 28
  LSE syllabuses, 44, 45–7 Tables
  marginal utility analysis, 38
  Marshallian economics, 135
  Monetary Nationalism and International Stability, 161
  monetary relations between nations, 163
  Monetary Theory and the Trade Cycle, 2, 44, 48
  natural and social science, 181
  New Studies in Philosophy, Politics and Economics, 237
  Nobel prize, 3
  political and social theory, 10, 247
  price mechanism, 2
  Prices and Production, 95, 96, 2, 4–5, 48–50, 49–50, 63, 64, 65, 69, 69–75, 86–7, 194, 248, 261
  Profits, Interest and Investment, 117
  Pure Theory of Capital, 30
  research programme, limitations, 252–3
  review of Robbin's *The Great Depression*, 67
  revival of ideas in 1970's and 1980's, 260
  Ricardo effect, 115, 116 Table, 117–18
  savings and investment, 65–6
  similarities to Keynes, 182–3
  Studies in Philosophy, Politics and Economics, 181, 237
  The Constitution of Liberty, 237
  The Counter Revolution of Science, 237
  The Fatal Conceit, 46
  The Paradox of Saving, 70
  The Pure Theory of Capital, 104, 122–6, 130, 170
  The Road to Serfdom, 135, 235–7, 247
  The Sensory Order, 39, 237, 238
  three chamber system for government, 242–3
  Three elucidations of the Ricardo effect, 121
  time in Chicago, 236–7
  time structure of production, 101, 102 Fig, 103
    Lerner elaborations, 103, 104 Fig, 105
  time in USA, 40
  trade cycle theory, 4, 40, 75–6, 183, 226–7, 245, 259–60
  tribute to Robbins, 45
  Two types of mind, 171
  unemployment, 69, 246, 247–52
  vision, 183
Hayek, F.A. & Robbins, L., research programme at LSE, 2–3
Hayeks, 4
Heath, E., 247
Helfferich, K., *Money*, 173
Henderson, H.D., 68, 75, 260
Hewins, W.S., 11, 12, 153

Index 283

Hicks, J.R. & Allen, R.G.D.,
  Reconsideration of the Theory of Value, 30
Hicks, J.R., 2, 5, 28, 61, 91–2, 93, 129, 130, 167, 188–9, 192, 196, 209, 229
  A Market Theory of Money, 190–1, 217
  A Revision of Demand Theory, 229
  arrival of Robbins at LSE, 85, 86
  average period, 196
  Capital and Growth, 229
  Capital and Time, 103, 229, 231, 232
  Causality in Economics, 210
  classification of economists, 228
  classification of inventions, 228–9
  Critical Essays, 209
  criticism,
    of Hayek's trade cycle theory, 75, 226–7, 229–30
    of Ricardo effect, 119–20
  distinction between materialists and fundists, 228
  Economic Perspectives, 231
  equilibrium, defining in dynamic conditions, 229
  general equilibrium analysis, 192–3
  income effects, 194
  instability of dynamic economy, 193–4
  interest rate, factors determining, 213, 215
  ISLM diagram, 190, 205, 213, 215
  lectureship at University of Johannesburg, 85–6
  LSE, time at, 85, 86 Table, 104
  LSE lectures, 87–9 Tables, 191, 192 Table
  Methods of Dynamic Analysis, 231
  Monetary theory and history: an attempt at perspective, 190
  Mr Keynes and the Classics, 190
  portfolio selection, 2, 96, 209–10
  production process profile, 230 Fig, 231
  real disturbances, 8, 226, 232
  relationship between spot and future prices, 195–6
  risk, influence on assets held, 87
  Simplifying the theory of money, 6, 91–2, 188
  static economies, 191
  temporary equilibrium, 195, 197
  The theory of uncertainty and profit, 209
  The Theory of Wages, 70, 115, 194, 227–32
  trade cycle and growth, 225–7
  traverse from one equilibrium growth path to another, 229, 231, 232
  unit period, 215
  Value and Capital, 85, 145, 188, 191–7, 194, 195, 197, 209, 229
Hobhouse, L., 13
Hobson, J.R., 73–74
Holtrop, M.W., 79, 94, 207
Hume, D., 8, 26, 178, 190, 239, 253
Hungary, reform, 148–9
Hutchinson, T.W., 27–8
Hyperinflation, 120–1

Incomes policies,
  absence in Britain, 256
  Austria 250, 251, 252
Indifference curve analysis, 192
Industrial structure changes, 58
Inflation, 120, 252
  effect on exchange rate, 21
  link with price differentials, 159
  revenue maximizing rate, 22
  and short-term gains, 128
Inflation and deflation,
  distribution of wealth, 20
  postwar, 19
Interaction of real and monetary forces, 52
Interest rate,
  divergence and fluctuations in economic activity, 66–7
  and expectations, 58, 59
  factors determining, 210–17
Interest rate changes,
  capital intensity of production, 196
  impact on investment decisions, 202–3
International and interregional trade, 153, 160–1, 164

Intertemporal allocation of resources, 46–7
Intertemporal equilibrium, 81, 84, 86
Investment,
  marginal efficiency, 199, 200 Fig, 201, 203
  rate of interest, 57, 202–3
Investment funds, cash holdings, 209
Investor's indifference curve, 93
ISLM diagram, 190, 205, 213, 215

Japan,
  features of economy, 255–6
  methods of finance, 255
  R&D spending, 254
  Shunto (Spring Offensive), 252
Jevons, W.S., 26, 175

Kahn, R.F., 30, 67, 167, 221
  criticism of Hayek, 67, 75, 260
  socialist debate, 145
Kaldor, N., 28, 40, 114, 159
  Austrian theory of capital, 6, 111–12, 113
  capital controversy, 110–14
  Capital intensity and the trade cycle, 112, 113
  Classificatory Note on Equilibrium, 30
  criticism,
    Knight's capital theory, 111
    Ricardo effect, 117–19, 131
  distribution of income, 224
  index of ratio of initial cost to annual cost in output production, 112–13
  lectureship at LSE, 45, 46, 110–11 Figs
  model of trade cycle, 113
  own-rates, 67
  production function, 224–5
  technical progress function, 225 Fig
  Young's influence 23
Kant, I., 253
Keynes, J.M., 20, 21, 29, 30, 55–7, 58, 62, 68, 74, 157, 178, 190, 219
  A Revision of the Treaty, 42
  A Tract on Monetary Reform, 3, 15, 19–22, 55, 155–6, 173, 176, 179, 184

  government control over resources, 21
  reviews, 22
  Alternative theories of the rate of interest, 174
  analysis of credit economy, 176
  analysis of price level in terms of spending decisions, 55–7
  appraisals, 3
  criticism,
    of Fisher, 175
    of Hayek, 7, 65, 75, 259
  critique of Austrian capital theory, 6, 99, 100, 101
  critiques, 3
  domestic stability, 22
  Economic Consequences of the Peace, 23
  editor of *Economic Journal*, 3, 31
  Essays in Biography, 3, 179–80
  Essays in Persuasion, 3
  forces operating upon demand for money, 58
  functional finance, 204
  General Theory, 3, 30, 50, 52, 60, 84, 168–9, 168, 184, 195, 197, 211, 260
    attack by Robertson, 169–70
    capital as homogeneous, 127
    comparison of responses from Cambridge and LSE, 6–7
    inducement to invest, 199
    lectures by Pigou, 168–9
    own-rates, 67
    review,
      Hicks, 188–9
      Lerner, 187–8
    summary of reactions, 184–5, 205
  incomes policy, 184
  Indian Currency and Finance, 3, 55
  individualism and utility streams of thinking, 8
  influences, 83–4, 177–8
  interest rates, 57, 58, 59, 211–12
  investment, 57, 203, 219
  knowledge of writings of earlier economists, 172–6
  methodology, 176–82, 185
  monetary equilibrium, 83
  policies, discredit in 1960s, 244–5

Keynes, J.M., (*continued*)
  rational expectations, 179
  review of Fisher's *The Purchasing Power of Money*, 18–19
  savings–investment complex, 56–7, 58–9, 169–70
  similarities to Hayek's scholarship, 182–3
  socialism, 136
  stock market, 127–8
  The Economic Consequences of the Peace, 156, 184
  The end of laisser faire, 8
  The Scope and Method of Political Economy, 12
  Treatise on Money, 3, 30, 50, 55, 58, 59, 60, 62, 83, 100, 163, 176, 179, 184, 189, 209
  Treatise on Probability, 3, 79, 93, 177, 178–9
  unemployment, 30–1
  vision, 183–4, 185
Keynesian avalanche, elements, 3
Knapp, G.F., *State Theory of Money*, 173
Knight, F.H., 1, 23, 30, 100, 196, 203, 261
  criticism of capital theory, 221
  critique of Austrian capital theory, 105–10
  problem of mobility, 107–8
  production and distribution, 106–7
  resources as capital, 106, 107
  Risk, Uncertainty and Profit, 146
  The quantity of capital and the rate of interest, 105–6
Koopmans, J.G., 79, 94–5
Kruschev, N., 148

Lachmann, L., 2, 6, 40, 126–8
  Capital and its Structure, 126–8
Laidler, D.E.W., 208–9
Lange, O., 6, 26, 139, 141–2
Lange, O. and Taylor, F., *On the Economic Theory of Socialism*, 140
Lange–Lerner,
  model of market socialism, 241
  solution to economic problems of socialism, 139–40, 145, 151, 241

Austrian reaction, 6, 140–3
Latin American countries, 149, 150
Lavington, F., 2, 6, 13, 58, 93–4, 96
Leijonhufvud, A., 1
Lenin, V.I., 147
Leontief, input–output table, 128
Lerner, A.P., 26, 82, 159, 201, 203
  balancing budget, 204
  capital theory, 260
  distribution of goods, 198
  Economics of Control, 145, 197–9, 205, 206
  Factor Prices in International Trade, 30
  functional finance, 203–4
  interest rate, 213–14 Figs
  joint LSE/Cambridge seminars, 167
  own-rates, 67
  production, 198
  relations between capital, investment and interest, 100
  review of *General Theory*, 187–8
  seminar, 29
  time structure of production, 103, 104 Fig, 105
  see also Lange and Lerner
Lewis, W.A., 205
Liberal Party, *Britain's Industrial Future*, 62
Lindahl, E., 6, 79, 81–2, 131, 229
Lipsey, R.G., 240
Loanable funds v liquidity preference, 7, 210–17
Locke, 8
London Economic Club, 29
LSE,
  Dramatis Personnae, 1920–45, 5 Table
  economic syllabus under Hayek, 44, 45–7 Tables
  establishment, 11
  opinions of Hayek's *Prices and Production*, 69–75
  part-time and mature students, 14
  scholarship compared with Cambridge creativity, 172
  Swedish work on expectations, 95

Machlup, F., 30, 39
McKenna, R., tariffs, 157

Macmillan Committee on Industry and Finance, 62, 69, 168, 171
Makower, H., 92, 96
Marget, A., 30
Marginal efficiency of investment, 199, 200 Fig, 201, 203
Marginal productivity of capital, 199, 200 Fig, 203
Marginal utility theory, 91, 93, 193, 207
Market clearing equation, 20
Market socialism, 135
Marschak, J., 40
Marshall, A., 1, 2, 3, 12, 17, 18, 26, 93, 193
  compared with Webb, S., 12–13
  criticism of Keynes discussion of methodology, 12
  economics as a science, 28
  interest rates, 211–12
  monetary theory, 175–6
  Principles, 65
  review of Keynes *Indian Currency and Finance*, 3
Marshall Aid, 150, 157
Materialists compared with fundists, 228
Mayer, F., 26–7, 38
Meade, J.E., 204
Menger, C., 26, 47, 193
  Grundsatze, 39
  On the origin of money, 173
Metzler, L.A., 194
Mises, L., 5, 30, 175
  criticism by Hayek, 140
  Economic calculations in the socialist commonwealth, 138
  influence,
    on Hayek, 41, 43–4
    on Robbins, 24
  socialism and rational calulation, 240–1
  The Theory of Money and Credit, 48, 173
  trade cycle theory, 49, 80
Model building, 178
Monetary economics, revival in Britain, 18
Monetary theory of the trade cycle 50–2

Money,
  demand for, 3, 15, 20, 207–9
  motives for holding, 93
  neutral, 75, 80, 94–5
Money supply, 8, 15–18
Morganstern, O., 39, 129–30
Multipliers, 16–18, 30, 156, 184, 219
Myrdal, G., 6, 80, 83
  attack on monetary equilibrium, 96
  influence of Keynes's *Treatise of Probability*, 79
  Monetary Equilibrium, 79, 80–1, 174, 194–5
  Price Formation and Economic Change, 174

Namier, L.B., 40
National capital, measurement, 129–30
Natural rate, 80
Neoclassical economics, 26
Neutral money, 75, 80, 94–5
Nominal interest rate differential, 22
Nordern, W., 205
Note issue, 162

Oakshott, W., 247, 261
Obsolescence, 130
Ohlin, B., 156, 159, 160
Oil prices, increase in, 254
Optimal cash balances, 90
Optimum conditions of exchange, 198
Optimum savings rate, 72, 73, 74

Paish, F.A., 161
Pareto, V., 26, 93, 192, 193
Patinkin, D., 15
Pearsson, K., 261
Pennington, J.R., 16
Perfect competition, theory of, 240
Perfect foresight, 81–2, 84
Phillips, C.A., 17–18
Pigou, A.C., 12, 30, 156
  average and marginal cost, 147
  criticism,
    of Fisher, 18–19
    of General Theory, 6–7, 184, 185
    of Hayek's theory of trade cycle, 75

Pigou, A.C., (*continued*)
  demand for money, 3, 15, 20
  Industrial Fluctuations, 69, 168
  lectures, Keynes's General Theory, 168–9
  measurement of capital, 129, 130
  net social income, 130–1
  Socialism versus Capitalism, 136, 143
  socialist debate, 143
  The Economics of Welfare, 28, 130, 147
  The Theory of Unemployment, 168
  unemployment, 167–8
  Wage policy and unemployment, 69
  Wealth and Welfare, 23, 28, 58, 93, 143, 145, 167
Pigou, A.C. & Robertson, D.H., *Economic Essays and Addresses*, 23
Pigou effect, 168
Plant, A., 69
  Economics of Patents, 30
Poland, 149
Popper, K., 28, 180, 181, 182, 238, 239–40, 253, 261
  The Poverty of Historicism, 239
Portfolio theory, 2, 96
Postwar inflation and deflation analysis by Keynes, 19
Pound, floating (1931), 184
Price fixing arrangements, 229
Price level of investment goods, 59, 60
Price stability,
  criterion, 48–9
  Keynes, 20
Prices, signals for the future, 85
Production, optimal conditions, 198
Productive processes,
           interrelatedness, 125
Productivity,
  determinant of investment, 126
  and price level, 217–20
Protectionist policies, 29, 68
Public expenditure, 68–9
Purchasing power doctrine, 21

Quantity theory of money, 18–23

Ramsay, F.P., 179–80
Religion, economic and social development, 253, 255, 256
Rents, 23
Research, factors affecting, 30
Rhodan, R., 30, 39
Ricardo, D., 1, 21, 101, 190, 191
Ricardo effect, 115–22
  acceptance by Robertson, 119
  criticism by Hick, 119–20
  criticism by Kaldor, 117–19, 131
  testing, 121
Risk, 87, 90–1
Robbins, L.C., 17, 23, 25, 44, 68, 72, 153, 157
  Autobiography, 13, 70, 171
  Consumption and the Trade Cycle, 70–1
  criticism of government spending to remove unemployment, 69
  criticism of Keynes, 171
  definition of economics, 135
  distinction between positive and normative propositions, 25
  Enquiry into Higher Education, 33
  free trade, 12
  influence of Mayer, 38
  influence of Mises, 24
  lack of response to *General Theory*, 184, 185
  LSE,
    arrival at 85, 86
    professor 13, 24, 259
    research programme, 4
    seminars and lectures, 29–30, 31–4 Tables
    support for Hayek's theory of trade cycle, 75
  The Great Depression, 2, 67–8, 70, 171
  The Nature and Significance of Economic Science, 2, 24–9, 45, 96, 141
  rank ordering of ends and means, 26–7
  tribute from Hayek, 45
Robertson, D.H., 6, 7, 17, 30, 58, 100
  A Study in Industrial Fluctuations, 52, 58, 100, 169

Robertson, D.H., (*continued*)
  analysis of monetary factors, 58
  Banking Policy and the Price Level, 15, 19, 23, 30, 52, 58, 100, 169, 173, 212
  criticism,
    of Hayek, 75, 260
    of Keynes, 60, 169–70, 184, 212
  forced savings, 58, 170
  interest rate, 211, 212, 215, 217
  Lectures on Economic Principles, 100
  lectures on Principles of Currency, 16
  period analysis and taxonomy of savings and investment, 58
  productivity and the price level, 217–18
  real and monetary forces, 52
  Ricardo effect, 119
  Theories of banking policy, 53–5
  underconsumption, 71, 74
Robinson, J., 30, 160, 161, 167
  The Accumulation of Capital, 221
  The Economics of Imperfect Competition, 145, 147
Rousseau, J.-J., 8

Samuelson, P.A., 29, 158, 159, 194, 205, 218, 222, 223 Fig
  trade cycle fluctuations, 225–6
Savings,
  forced, 58, 170, 173
  and investment, 56–7, 58–9, 65–6, 212
  relation to distribution of income, 73–4
Scarcity,
  definition in relation to demand, 25
  organizing principle of economics, 25
Schlesinger, K., 6, 93, 96
Schorske, C., 41
Schumpeter, J.A., 5, 40, 209
  A History of Economic Analysis, 33, 35, 183
  holding money, 207
  Keynes's vision, 183–4, 185
Scitovsky, T., 28, 40
Secondary deflation, 171

Shackle, G.L.S., 7
  Austrian capital theory, 128–9
  comparison of *Treatise* and *Prices and Production*, 70
  Expectation, Investment and Income, 127, 210
  interest rate and investment decisions, 202–3
  Oxford Studies in the Price Mechanism, 201–2, 203
Shiftworking and overtime, 121–2
Shove, G., 13
Slump *see* Boom and slump
Smith, V.C., 161, 162–3
Social science, distinction from natural science, 181
Socialism,
  economics of, 6, 135–52
  Lange–Lerner solution to economic problems, 139–40, 151
  revival of criticism in 1970s and 1980s, 141
  see also collectivist economic planning
Socialist debate,
  Cambridge contribution, 143, 145
  LSE contribution, 135–43
Solow, R.M., 218, 221
Soviet Union, living standards, 148
Spann, O., *History of Economics*, 38–9
Spot markets, 195–6
Sraffa, P., 22, 93, 96, 129
  criticism of Hayek, 65–7, 75, 260
Stalin, J., 147–8
Stamp, J., 129
Static economies, 191
Stationary state, 90
Stock market crash 1987, 209
Stolper–Samuelson, tariffs, 158
Surrogate production function, 222, 223 Fig, 224–5
Swedish theory, 174
  see also individual economists

Tariffs, 157–9, 164
Tarshis, L., 167
Taussig, F.W., 160
Tavlas, A., 208
Taylor, A.A.G., 157
Taylor, F.M., 139, 157

Temporary equilibrium, 195, 197, 229
Testing theories, 180
Thatcher, M., 235, 246, 247
Thirlby, G.F., 205
Thomas, B. & Richards, H., 82, 83 Table
Thornton, H.,
  Monetary experience and the theory of money, 190
  Paper Credit, 176
Time, 7, 101–5
Tinbergen, J., 261
Tobin, J., 92, 218
Torrens, R., 16
Trade cycle and growth, 225–7
Trade unions, 251, 256
Transfer problem, 156–7
Tsiang, S.C., 7, 215–17, 232

Underconsumption, 70, 71–2, 74
Undergraduate courses, LSE compared with Cambridge, 13
Unemployment, 167–8
  criticism of government spending, 69
  Hayek, 247–52
  problems, research, 30
  rates and unemployment benefits, 250, 251 Fig
  real wages, 121, 122 Fig
  solution, reducing working hours, 24
  wages in 1980's, 69, 248, 249 Fig
Unspent margin, 51

Value judgements, 27

Viner, J., 30, 160
Vision, 183–4, 185
Von Neuman, J., 193

Wages,
  effect on aggregate demand, 168
  high, effects on economy, 194
  and interest, equilibrium between, 115
  rates, 23
  and unemployment, 69, 248, 249 Fig
Wallis, G., 13
Walras, 26, 139, 151, 193
Walrasian auctioneer, 2
Wealth, distribution, 20, 91–2
Webb, B., 11, 12–13
Webb, S., 11, 12–13
Weber, 26, 253
Welfare economics, 28, 30
Whale, P.B.,
  Joint Stock Banking in Germany, 44–5
  The working of the pre-war gold standard, 163–4
White, H.D., 160
Wicksell, K., 5, 48, 49, 80, 174, 190, 217, 218, 219
Wieser, F., 26, 38
Williams, J.H., 160
Wilson, T., 121–2
Window dressing, 17
Wiseman, J., 141, 205
Withers, H., 16
Wooton, B., 236
World economy, postwar, 253–4

Young, A., 1, 23